PERMANENT STATE OF EMERGENCY

PERMANENT STATE OF EMERGENCY

Unchecked Executive Power and the Demise of the Rule of Law

RYAN ALFORD

McGill-Queen's University Press
Montreal & Kingston • London • Chicago

ISBN 978-0-7735-4919-7 (cloth)
ISBN 978-0-7735-4920-3 (ePDF)
ISBN 978-0-7735-4921-0 (ePUB)

Legal deposit second quarter 2017
Bibliothèque nationale du Québec

Printed in Canada on acid-free paper that is 100% ancient forest
free (100% post-consumer recycled), processed chlorine free

This book has been published with the help of a grant from
Lakehead University.

McGill-Queen's University Press acknowledges the support of the
Canada Council for the Arts for our publishing program. We also
acknowledge the financial support of the Government of Canada
through the Canada Book Fund for our publishing activities.

Library and Archives Canada Cataloguing in Publication

Alford, Ryan, 1975–, author
Permanent state of emergency : unchecked executive power and
the demise of the rule of law / Ryan Alford.

Includes bibliographical references and index.
Issued in print and electronic formats.
ISBN 978-0-7735-4919-7 (cloth).
– ISBN 978-0-7735-4920-3 (ePDF).
– ISBN 978-0-7735-4921-0 (ePUB)

1. War and emergency powers – United States. 2. Executive
power – United States. 3. Rule of law – United States. I. Title.

KF5060.A44 2017   342.73'062   C2017-900035-7
                                             C2017-900036-5

For Chelsea Manning, Julian Assange, and Edward Snowden, without whose courage this book would not have been possible.

Contents

Preface

Two court cases compelled me to write this book. These lawsuits brack-eted the assassination of a US citizen on the orders of the president: the first attempted to block the drone strike, and the second attempted to hold the president accountable for the murder. Both failed.

Although my involvement in these suits was tangential, they affected me profoundly. The opinions that disposed of them shook me to my core: they asserted that because the citizen subjected to extrajudicial killing has been designated a foreign target, the courts had no power to second-guess the president. The executive had never argued the killing was an act of war or that the citizen was a traitor – or even that he had been accused of a crime. It merely asserted that its power to kill him was unreviewable. The court agreed. The warped vision of the US Constitution it presented is horrifying: it ignores not only the particular protections of the Bill of Rights but the purpose of a constitution.

Counsel for the victim's next of kin cited my research, which noted that the Constitution's Bill of Attainder Clause specifically barred extra-judicial death warrants. This provision obviously applied to the executive; the fact that it applied to the president was not even worth noting in 1787, as an absolute restriction on the executive had been established five hundred years previously by Magna Carta. After the lawsuits chal-lenging the assassination failed, it was clear that the executive branch had obtained an arbitrary power over life and death that even late medieval kings had not possessed; when it comes to decisions about whom to kill, the president is above the law.

After I published my observations on the case, a prominent American scholar of constitutional law criticized my purported fixation on the killing of citizens. I realized that I had been unclear about why the case was significant: I believed it demonstrated that the executive had crossed the ultimate threshold. If the president could order a citizen killed without due process because he alone decided it was necessary, it demonstrated a fundamental change in the nation's constitutional order and to the concept of rights.

The US Constitution was created to enshrine inalienable rights. Even before a Bill of Rights was created, the constitution stated without qualification that "no Bill of Attainder ... shall be passed." These constitutional rights are now contingent and precarious. The secret memorandum addressing the legality of the targeted killing program argues that even the right to life should be balanced against the executive's objectives. The decision to deploy this argument presents a pressing question: What sort of nation remains when its citizens' most fundamental constitutional rights are taken away?

This book answers that question, arguing that the numerous alterations to American constitutional order that have occurred since 9/11 have began a qualitative transformation of the American state. However, to do justice to this phenomenon, it must be presented within a broad historical context. My earlier work as a constitutional historian guides my argument in many ways. Most of my scholarship to date has focused on Anglo-American constitutional history from the sixteenth to the eighteenth centuries. For generations of scholars, this period was defined by the reaction against arbitrary executive power, which can also be described as the struggle for the rule of law.

The rule of law is a solution to a problem that plagued early modern monarchies: the consistent expansion of royal power during wars and emergencies. Monarchs admitted that their authority was limited, but also claimed they were entitled to interpret the scope of their own powers, frequently invoking an extraordinary prerogative to excuse arbitrary action, and citing divine right as a means of avoiding legal scrutiny and judicial enforcement.

The rule of law holds that not only were there inviolable legal rights the monarch was bound to respect, but rulers could be held accountable when these were violated. This concept is arguably the most important element of any constitutional order. It is the yardstick by which bodies such as the United Nations judge the progress made by developing nations and those emerging out of totalitarianism. However, to date no one has asked whether it could be used to evaluate the regression of a constitutional order.

Recent history demonstrates that one should not be sanguine about this possibility. While Francis Fukuyama argued after the fall of the Soviet Union that we have reached a sublime end of history in which liberal democracy has become the unrivalled paradigm of governance, this has become more difficult to sustain after the last fifteen years. Large and influential states have slid toward authoritarianism or worse, and frightened populations have endorsed xenophobia and extralegal repression.

America is not immune to these dynamics. During the Vietnam War, President Richard Nixon brought the country perilously close to what historian Arthur Schlesinger called an "imperial presidency." Nixon's theory of government can be best summarized by an infamous assertion that will forever be associated with his name: "When the president does it, that means it is not illegal." The similarity between this and King Louis XIV's assertion that "l'État, c'est moi" is not superficial; it defined Nixon's theory of the presidency as imperial and antithetical to the rule of law.

The Supreme Court and Congress restored the constitutional order, by ordering disclosure of Nixon's White House tapes, threatening his impeachment, and re-imposing legislative and judicial oversight after his resignation. Unfortunately, Nixon's view of executive power did not end with his ignominious departure. Those who attempted to shape it into law re-attained prominence. One of Nixon's accomplices became the US chief justice, while another became the vice-president. However it was not until the 9/11 attacks that William Rehnquist, Dick Cheney, and their allies regained the initiative.

This book describes the neo-conservative dismantling of the rule of law in the United States, replacing constitutional supremacy with unreviewable executive power, whenever the president invokes national security. America no longer complies with the minimum requirements of the rule of law, as the president can violate even the most fundamental human rights with impunity. Nixon only dreamed of this level of legal unaccountability, as the other branches of government that resisted him have since accepted a diminishment of their constitutional authority without much complaint.

The United States is now best described as an elective dictatorship, as the right to elect an unaccountable ruler does not diminish the fact that all of one's rights are held at the sovereign's pleasure. This shift from a Lockean to a Hobbesian theory of government can also be described as having created a very real threat of "turn-key totalitarianism," as there are no firewalls standing in the way of any president who would create an authoritarian state.

While no president to date has authorized drone strikes within the United States, the attorney general has asserted that the president has an unreviewable authority to do so. The same is true for indefinite arbitrary detention, in the form of Guantánamo Bay or in the "homeland." Should America elect a populist strongman, he could set these initiatives into motion with the stroke of a pen. This is why the rule of law matters, and why I use it as the metric to judge the United States.

This book does not have a monopoly on negative assessment of America's appalling human rights record during the "war on terror," nor on criticizing the effects this state of emergency has inflicted on the body politic. Many excellent books address the degeneration of the American constitutional order. In the interests of making my case to the reader, however, I have not engaged with their work in this text.

Foremost among the books that examine the structural transformation of the American constitutional order are Michael J. Glennon's *National Security and Double Government,* Bruce Ackerman's *Decline and Fall of the American Republic*, and Giorgio Agamben's *State of Exception. Permanent State of Emergency* differs from those titles insofar as it takes a more thoroughgoing normative approach to the developments Glennon describes, and because it is much less optimistic about the possibility of a return to constitutional governance than Ackerman's. Indeed, in describing the nation's exit from the rule of law paradigm, this book concludes that the regeneration that Ackerman promotes is now impossible. Finally, while this book agrees with Agamben about the centrality of emergency powers to the nature of the state, it operates from the position that the rule of law is a meaningful regulative ideal, and one that is worth fighting for.

Unlike a multitude of other books that focus solely on George W. Bush's administration, this volume concludes that there is now a bipartisan consensus on the desirability of an elective dictatorship over foreign affairs and national security. In this respect, it comes to similar conclusions to those found on this subject in Garry Wills's *Bomb Power: The Modern Presidency and the National Security State*, although the two books differ on the historical genesis of threats to the rule of law.

There are a number of books to which I owe a substantial debt of gratitude. These include Phillippe Sands's *The Torture Team*, which addressed the Bush administration officials responsible for the implementation of a torture program; and Andrew Rudalevige's *The New Imperial Presidency*, which drew the parallels between the Nixon and Bush administrations that became essential to this book's theoretical orientation. I also drew heavily on articles by legal scholars that are too numerous to mention, but special mention should be made of Jenny Martinez's work on extrajudicial detention, and Erwin Chemerinsky's and Stephen Vladeck's writings on the failures of the judiciary to intervene against assertions of executive supremacy.

This book would have been impossible without the unceasing efforts of journalists covering the war on terror and the many abuses of the legal and democratic processes, which, without their tireless efforts, would have blurred out of the historical record. Foremost among them are Glenn Greenwald, Barton Gellman, Charlie Savage, James Bamford, and Seymour Hersh, who have all written outstanding books that are essential reading for any scholar addressing the topics covered here.

I would also like to thank family and friends who provided editorial assistance on either this book or the dissertation that preceded it, in addition to my editors at McGill-Queen's University Press (Jacqueline Mason and Ryan Van Huijstee), my research assistant (Daniel Brockenshire), and my copy editor (Carol Harrison). My partner Cheryl Reid was an indispensable source of encouragement and inspiration while I wrote the book, in addition to providing her editorial assistance.

Before writing this book, I accepted a position at a Canadian law faculty, where I was exposed to the Canadian literature on these topics. Ken Roach and Craig Forcese have written tirelessly on parallel threats to the rule of law in Canada. Robert Diab's *The Harbinger Theory* chronicles the power of ideas in the battle for the rule of law, which I sincerely wish I had in my hands before starting this book.

I am indebted to the late Anthony Mathews, who demonstrated how the rule of law could be used to evaluate the degeneration of a legal system in a permanent state of emergency. Mathews broke with the consensus of South African legal scholars, most of whom argued that the apartheid regime had merely deformed its constitutional order, while retaining its essential features. He was one of the few scholars with the integrity to say otherwise.

My conclusions about the United States mirror Mathews's observations about South Africa during the apartheid era. A set of laws and a judiciary do not themselves guarantee the rule of law. I hope that other scholars will agree with me and act accordingly – a country that has exited from constitutional governance is no longer self-correcting. If the rule of law is to be restored in the United States, this will likely require significant efforts by the international community, including global civil society, as was the case in South Africa.

PERMANENT
STATE OF
EMERGENCY

Islands on which the rule of law prevailed were
left amid an ocean of lawlessness, reassuring
preserves in which traditional ideas of order
continued apparently undisputed, and this
made it harder to assess the legality or illegality
of the regime and decide whether to support
or oppose it.

– Joachim Fest

Introduction

The Road from 9/11

After the attacks of 11 September 2001, the United States launched several initiatives that were either at the outermost limit of what international human rights law allows, or beyond. They involved systematic violations of non-derogable rights. Four examples stand out. First, killing people considered terrorists with drone strikes, in areas that are not currently the site of armed conflict.[1] Second, continued indefinite detention of prisoners classified as "enemy combatants" at the Guantánamo Bay detention camp, over ten years after the 9/11 attacks.[2] Third, torture of those prisoners and detainees held elsewhere, some of whom were seized by the intelligence agencies far from combat zones.[3] Fourth, rules authorizing the military to hold suspects accused of providing material support for terrorism, so that they do not receive the protections of the criminal justice system.[4]

Special Rapporteur Philip Alston noted in his 2010 study on targeted killings that "the US adopted a secret policy of targeted killings soon after the attacks of 11 September 2001." This program sanctioned targeted killing in other nations, which were not in armed conflict.[5] Estimates of civilian casualties in Pakistan alone range to "many hundreds."[6] Alston noted that the justification for drone strikes in Pakistan, Yemen, and other countries "does not address some of the most central legal issues" they present, including "the scope of the armed conflicts in which the US asserts it is engaged, the criteria for individuals who may be targeted ...

and the existence of accountability mechanisms." After discussing international humanitarian law, Alston concluded that "these factors make it problematic for the US to show that ... it is in a transnational non-international armed conflict."[7] Therefore, these killings are unlawful.

Despite this criticism, the United States dramatically expanded this program in scale and in scope during Barack Obama's presidency. For the first time, American citizens are now subject to extrajudicial killing. "American[s] ... are placed on a kill or capture list by a secretive panel of senior government officials ... there is no public record of the operations or decisions of the panel, which is a subset of the White House's National Security Council ... Neither is there any law establishing its existence or setting out the rules by which it is supposed to operate."[8]

On the fifth anniversary of the Guantánamo Bay detention camp, Amnesty International described it as a human rights scandal.[9] "International law has been flouted from the outset. None of the detainees was granted prisoner of war status, nor brought before a competent tribunal to determine his or her status, as required by the Third Geneva Convention. None has been granted access to a court to challenge the lawfulness of his detention. The International Covenant on Civil and Political Rights (Article 9), to which the United States is a party, mandates this access."[10]

After seven years establishing the detainment camps, the US Supreme Court held in *Boumediene v. Bush* that detainees must have a "meaningful opportunity" to obtain writs of habeas corpus.[11] However, the court gave the executive "reasonable time" to begin combatant status review tribunals. It "waffled again on the ultimate standards, announcing that certain accommodations can be made to reduce the burden habeas corpus proceedings will place on the military."[12] The Supreme Court's 2012 decision not to overturn *Latif v. Obama*[13] reduced the chances of obtaining the writ to nearly nothing. In *Latif*, the DC Circuit held that "federal judges must 'presume' that government intelligence reports used to justify detention are reliable and accurate."[14]

There is ample evidence that Guantánamo detainees were tortured. There is also substantial documentation to prove that cabinet-level officials approved. "Based on this evidence, Human Rights Watch believes there is sufficient basis for the US government to order a broad criminal investigation into alleged crimes committed in connection with the torture and ill-treatment of detainees … Such an investigation would necessarily focus on alleged criminal conduct by the following four senior officials – former President George W. Bush, Vice President Dick Cheney, Defense Secretary Donald Rumsfeld, and CIA Director George Tenet."[15] In his autobiography, former president Bush admitted authorizing the waterboarding of detainees. Waterboarding "is a relatively recent name for a form of water torture that dates to at least the Spanish Inquisition."[16]

Despite this evidence, the Obama administration has refused to prosecute anyone for approving or carrying out this torture. It also failed to prosecute a former CIA official who spoke openly of destroying evidence of torture in violation of a court order.[17] The Supreme Court has refused to disturb a DC Circuit opinion that held that no US court has jurisdiction over claims of torture by the Guantánamo detainees.[18] Additionally, the Military Commissions Act of 2006 granted the torturers immunity.[19] Owing to the complete failure to create accountability for torture and ill-treatment of detainees, it continues. Prisoners at Camp Seven are held in conditions that do not comply with the minimum standards of Article 3 of the Geneva Conventions.[20] Evidence obtained using torture is considered competent by Combatant Status Review Tribunals. Intelligence files that are considered presumptive evidence of guilt contain evidence obtained by torture. A prisoner was "'leashed like a dog, sexually humiliated and forced to urinate upon himself' before implicating himself and other prisoners … those claims [implicating others] appear in the [other detainees'] files 'without any caveat.'"[21]

During the Bush administration, lawyers working for the executive branch made strong claims. They wrote memoranda claiming the president possesses a unilateral power to authorize the seizure and detention of US citizens accused of support for terrorism.[22] The military held and tortured José Padilla, an American, for four years.[23] During his detention, the Supreme Court evaded reviewing his case.[24] Congress approved of this conduct. It passed legislation in 2012 approving military detention of anyone accused of providing material support for terrorism. The legislation does expressly allow for military detention of citizens arrested within the nation's borders.[25] However, "an amendment that would have expressly barred citizens from long-term military detention was considered and rejected."[26]

The rights not to be killed without due process, not to be subjected to indefinite arbitrary detention, and not to be tortured are all peremptory norms.[27] Therefore, America's compliance with fundamental human rights law following the 9/11 attacks is, at the least, an open question. However, the absence of these rights does not provide a basis on its own for judging whether a nation now has a fundamentally different constitutional order. To assess the transformation of the US legal regime since the 9/11 attacks, it must be determined whether the rule of law allows for a binary categorization of nations, in a way that other norms related to human rights cannot. The conclusion that a nation does not comply with the rule of law differs from the observation that it does not comply with particular norms, leading to different implications about its status in international affairs.

The crucial political and legal developments in the United States following the 9/11 attacks created an unaccountable presidency that neither the nation's legislature nor its courts can restrain. This was due to the failure to resist problematic theories of the executive constitutional reserve powers in times of crisis. These theories became dominant within the executive branch after the 9/11 attacks and were implicitly ratified by Congress and the courts over the following decade.

To prove the importance of resisting these theories to the preservation of the rule of law in the United States, one must first detail their history. The Nixon administration nearly destroyed the rule of law by creating an unaccountable "imperial presidency." The 9/11 attacks allowed the Bush administration, which included Nixon-era officials, to redeploy theories of presidential power in a crisis. These officials argued that the 9/11 attacks and the passage of the Authorization for the Use of Military Force of 2001[28] activated a broad range of implicit presidential powers. These assertions of powers were invoked to authorize indefinite military detention,[29] warrantless wiretapping,[30] torture,[31] and targeted killing.[32]

These theories became legally effective largely because of the other government branches' inaction. Congress bolstered the executive by giving it statutory powers whenever the executive's assertions of reserve powers were untenable, passing legislation that implicitly recognized these theories and normalized problematic arguments about presidential authority. Congress comprehensively dismantled the clear limits on executive power, which had preserved the rule of law in the United States for almost thirty years. Congress also neutered the oversight structures and accountability-reinforcing mechanisms created in the wake of the Watergate crisis.

The judiciary abandoned its responsibility to hold the executive branch accountable. This book corrects the prevailing account of the judicial review of indefinite detention and torture at Guantánamo. It demonstrates that the courts deliberately adopted a ponderous pace, allowing the executive branch to evade review of its most egregious abuses. The courts also tacitly accepted the executive's theories of its reserve powers and developed doctrines that ensured these theories could not be challenged successfully in the courts.

The end result is an executive that now has the powers described by the Bush administration's lawyers. These powers allow the executive to violate non-derogable norms without fear of correction or redress. There is negligible disagreement on these issues between the Obama and Bush administrations: the book details the creation of this "bipartisan consensus" between the two American political parties on the unrestrained executive.[33] Finally, it reveals how the executive branch has been able to lay the foundation for the robust use of these powers in future crises. The theory that the executive can wage aggressive war on its own authority is now also uncontested. The executive can now create the conditions that allow it to extend its powers, seemingly without limit. This type of constitutional order does not comply with the minimum requirements of the rule of law state.

The Structure of the Argument

Chapter 1 discusses that while in some respects the concept of the rule of law is essentially contested, there is general agreement about what constitutes its essence. The history of the rule of law demonstrates that its historical core is the regulation of the activities of the executive by the other branches of government and the ability to hold it accountable to clear legal standards, particularly when its activities implicate citizens' non-derogable rights. It is possible to draw upon this consensus to create a global "yardstick" to judge whether any given nation is a rule of law state. Rather than engaging with the disputes over the outer limits of the rule of law that rage within the field of jurisprudence, the chapter outlines the rule of law's minimum requirements, by drawing on Brian Tamanaha's historical scholarship, Anthony Mathews's work on the degeneration of the rule of law in apartheid South Africa, and the consensus definition of the concept elaborated by the Congresses of the International Commission of Jurists.

Chapter 2 addresses whether the constitutional order of the United States that existed between the time of the Nixon administration and the 9/11 attacks was wholly consistent with the rule of law principles being used to judge its contemporary non-compliance. The chapter demonstrates that it was, as Congress and the courts rejected theories of unbridled presidential power in the wake of Watergate and the findings of the Church Commission.[34] In that era, these branches proved to be effective checks on the enlargement of executive power. The most notable demonstrations of that efficacity were the rulings in *United States v. Nixon*[35] and the passage of legislation that made the president accountable to Congress for his actions in national security matters, including the Hughes-Ryan Act and the War Powers Resolution of 1974.[36]

Establishing that the elements of the American constitutional order constraining the executive branch between 1974 and 2001 were largely congruous with the minimum requirements outlined in the commission's reports is essential for two reasons. First, it shows that the concept of the rule of law that is being used here is not an inappropriate measure; rather, when functional, the protections found in the constitutional provision for the separation of powers embody the criteria for the rule of law. Second, it demonstrates that the failure to abide by these domestic constitutional restraints constitutes a problematic abrogation of legal order; indeed, chapter 1 argues that the failure to meet these requirements constitutes a prima facie case that the state should not be considered to be governed by the rule of law.

Chapter 3 discusses the overbroad delegations of authority from the legislative branch to the executive, particularly the Authorization for the Use of Military Force of 2001.[37] It focuses on whether the executive is still responsible to the legislature after these cumulative delegations of broad powers. This chapter also addresses the executive's appropriation of legislative authority, which has not been checked by Congress. Special attention is paid to the doctrine and use of executive signing statements accompanying legislation. Significant attention is also devoted to the use of the Department of Justice's Office of Legal Counsel as binding interpretations of the law within the executive branch. Both of these sets of sources were used to justify such actions as the targeted killing of American citizens and to make claims that the executive branch possesses constitutional powers that cannot be overruled by legislation. The book answers the related question of whether the executive branch's ability to make proclamations with the force of law is subject to any checks and balances, as these are essential to the separation of powers and for the rule of law that they protect.

Chapter 4 looks at the judiciary's responses to the executive's assertions of its self-assumed powers to violate non-derogable rights. The key question to be answered is whether the courts have been willing, when able, to rebuke the executive branch's interpretation of its pre-eminence in matters of national security in principle, or whether they have restricted themselves to narrow holdings that address only the most problematic overreaching, or even to evasion of their responsibility to review allegations of violations of non-derogable rights. To that end, the book addresses the issue of whether the courts, and in particular the US Supreme Court, have acted to enforce the constitutional and statutory restrictions on executive authority. More particularly, this chapter will discuss the restrictions erected in the aftermath of the Watergate crisis, and the question of whether judgments that have been interpreted as rebukes to the executive have actually limited its freedom of action or created any accountability for the serious and systematic failure of the executive to observe the laws. The book will also examine other restrictions on executive authority imposed by the other branches of government that protect the rule of law, and the *jus cogens* norms that it is bound by these laws and restrictions to observe.

Key Supreme Court cases this chapter will discuss include *Hamdi v. Rumsfeld*,[38] *Rumsfeld v. Padilla*,[39] and *Boumediene v. Bush*.[40] Another important issue is whether the Supreme Court has proven itself unwilling to review opinions that have given judicial imprimatur to the executive branch's expansive interpretation of its power. Examples of these rulings include the decision in *Al-Aulaqi v. Obama* and the DC Circuit's decisions in the habeas corpus cases brought following *Boumediene*, particularly *Latif v. Obama*,[41] *Kiyemba v. Obama*,[42] and *Al-Zahrani v. Rodriguez*.[43]

Chapter 5 explains the inadequate responses from the other branches of government, demonstrating that both the judiciary and legislative branches have been compromised. This shows that effective oversight is no longer possible. Accordingly, this chapter concludes that the twenty-first-century crisis of the rule of law is not temporary, as was the case in the Nixon administration. As the two other branches cannot restrain the executive, even when it violates non-derogable rights, the United States is no longer a rule of law state. The first sections of this chapter explore the process by which the executive fostered a deferential judiciary. They detail the colonization of its highest branches with jurists who were closely connected and loyal to the executive. In particular, the executive has filled the benches of the nation's highest courts with former officials who possessed no public record of their extensive support for executive supremacy.

Chapter 6 focuses on Congress's failure to address the executive's assertions that it can violate non-derogable rights. This chapter discusses the judiciary's apparent inability to address claims that the executive branch has exceeded its powers or used them in a manner that implicates citizens' non-derogable rights. Particular attention is paid to jurisdiction-stripping statutes, such as the Detainee Treatment Act of 2005[44] and the Military Commissions Act of 2006.[45] These statutes purport to deprive the judiciary of the right to review certain classes of claims, including petitions for the writ of habeas corpus. The chapter also explains Congress's failures, which are rooted in changes to campaign financing and the implied power of the military-industrial complex to influence elections.

The conclusion recapitulates the chapters' findings, explaining their importance to the key conclusions related to the question of whether the United States should be considered a rule of law state. Throughout, the book treats the rule of law as a meaningful concept because of its connection to a particular historical context and the purpose that it was designed to serve; it is a legal framework designed to control systematic violations by the executive of the most fundamental human rights, which is worth defending. Conversely, the book shows that any nation that engages in sustained and unreviewable violations of non-derogable rights cannot be considered to be in compliance with the basic requirements of a rule of law state.

CHAPTER 1

The Minimum Requirements of the Rule of Law

Before addressing the nature of the American state in the twenty-first century, one must have an operational definition of the minimum norms of the rule of law state. That definition is a necessary precondition of any answer to the question of whether or not a country that engages in gross human rights abuses is being governed in accordance with the rule of law.

Rule of Law: A Concept Shaped by History

Brian Tamanaha described the rule of law as a constitutional concept that "congealed into existence in a slow, unplanned manner that commenced in the Middle Ages, with no single source or starting point."[1] It is a constitutive concept, one that has acquired its meaning through its historical development. Accordingly, an explanation of the history of the rule of law is central to its identification of a normative yardstick that measures a state's compliance.

An understanding of how this concept is rooted within constitutional history allows one to avoid certain theoretical problems that would otherwise make a functional definition of the normative core of the rule of law impossible. As Shklar noted, "contemporary theories [of the rule of law] fail because they have lost a sense of what the political objectives of the ideal of the rule of law originally were and have come up with no plausible restatement."[2]

The Medieval and Early Modern Pre-history of Rule of Law

Tamanaha developed his historically based definition of the rule of law by building on the works of legal historians. Central among these are the efforts of Kenneth Pennington[3] and Harold Berman.[4] These historians describe the tension in the Middle Ages between powerful monarchs and the legal theorists who sought to constrain their powers. There was a prolonged legal struggle between the monarchy and the nobility over the scope of royal authority.[5] The result of this process was a stable legal order in which "[t]he principle foundation upon which medieval political theory was built was the principle of the supremacy of law."[6] In England, the process that led to this state was the passage of Magna Carta as a statute.[7]

This legal order, which was characterized as a mixed monarchy or *dominium politicum et regale*, was destabilized during the early modern era. Monarchies became more powerful as commerce and roads made more centralized control possible. This development frequently led to the development of absolute monarchies, predicated on theories of royal supremacy.[8]

These theories had their adherents in England during the early modern era.[9] However, Parliament's defeat of the royalist cause during the English Civil War meant that they would never be put into practice. The Glorious Revolution established the constitutional order for the remainder of that era; the English constitution now firmly constrained the executive. In particular, after the reign of Queen Anne virtually all reserve powers could only be exercised on the advice of a government responsible to Parliament.[10]

The constitutional histories of the nineteenth century lauded Parliament's triumph over the executive. The works of the Whig historians praised the English constitution, and in particular its restraints on the executive. In particular, this was the theme of Lord Macaulay's *History of England from the Ascension of James II*.[11] Samuel Rawson Gardiner's work on the English Civil War also attests to the fact that this was the orthodox view of the English Constitution at that time.[12] This viewpoint was not merely dominant at the time, but unchallenged.[13] The essential feature of these histories was their glowing portrayal of the triumph over the executive.

In addition to Macaulay and Gardiner, the lawyer and historian Henry Hallam shaped the nineteenth-century view of the English constitution. His *Constitutional History of England* argued that the English subject's greatest liberty was not to be governed arbitrarily.[14] This volume was so influential that it was described in the early twentieth century as "one of the text-books of English politics, to which men of all parties appealed."[15]

Before the twentieth century, the rule of law had not been defined in theoretical terms; rather, it was seen as a desirable product of a process of historical development. Historians, jurists, and lawyers lauded Parliament's installation of a new dynast, who claimed he came to the throne in order to relieve the people of the oppression of an executive who "subjected them in all things ... to arbitrary government ... contrary to law ... and to that express provision that no man shall lose his life ... but by the law of the land."[16] They celebrated England's constitution as one that restrained the executive.

The first influential definitions of the rule of law were produced during this period. This concept in constitutional law was shaped by this history and the way in which this history was interpreted at that time. The next section discusses A.V. Dicey's formative definition, how it is linked with certain political objectives. These can be understood by reference to the constitutional history that he drew upon when creating it. After this discussion, it will be possible to identify the normative core of the rule of law.

The Modern Relevance of the Pre-history of the Rule of Law

Dicey defined the rule of law as follows:

> It means, in the first place, the absolute supremacy or predominance of regular law as opposed to the influence of arbitrary power, and excludes the existence of arbitrariness, of prerogative, or even of wide discretionary authority on the part of the government ... It means, again, equality before the law ... the "rule of law" in this sense excludes the idea of any exemption of officials or others from

the duty of obedience to the law which governs other citizens or from the jurisdiction of the ordinary tribunals ... The notion that ... affairs or disputes in which the government or its servants are concerned are beyond the sphere of the civil courts ... is utterly unknown to the law of England.[17]

The definition has three elements. The rule of law forbids the exercise of arbitrary power, subjects officials to the law, and bars the executive from setting up special courts when citizens bring claims against the executive. It is evident to anyone acquainted with the English legal history that this definition did not spring from Dicey's head fully formed; rather, it is a highly conventional Victorian interpretation of the limitations on power imposed by the English constitution, which was connected with an orthodox view of the nation's history, particularly the legal history of the seventeenth century.

Dicey was a serious student of legal history. Unlike those who criticized his definition of the rule of law under the banner of analytical jurisprudence, he believed that the essential features of law could be explained by reference to its historical development. "[T]he English Constitution is historical in being in a special sense the immediate result of conditions that govern English history."[18] In a footnote to this passage, Dicey laments what he sees as the failure of the English people to recognize the importance of "the English history of tradition & its influence." Accordingly, it is imperative to approach this definition with a sense of the meaning that its words acquire when seen in the light of the historical tradition upon which he drew heavily.[19]

His use of *arbitrary power* and *prerogative* indicate the importance of legal history to his constitutional theory. These terms have precise meanings in the context of seventeenth- and eighteenth-century constitutionalism.[20] They link Dicey to a constitutional tradition that is particularly concerned with control over the executive. This continuity is demonstrated by his particular attention to the executive's reserve powers, and its subjection to the law in the regular courts.

Dicey's definition of the rule of law is more than merely influential; it is foundational.[21] In discussing the modern history of this concept, H. Patrick Glenn notes that "the notion of the rule of law dates at least

from Dicey's adoption of it, arguing notably for submission of executive
authority to review by superior courts of general jurisdiction."[22] It is
scarcely an exaggeration that later definitions of the rule of law as a constitutional concept gloss on Dicey's, but this is not the case within the
field of jurisprudence. These legal philosophers' arguments against Dicey
will be discussed on page 23. Nevertheless, his influence and ongoing importance in global constitutional law warrant further discussion.

The Universal Declaration of Human Rights of 1948 states that "human
rights should be protected by the rule of law."[23] However, the Declaration does not define this concept, despite identifying it as necessary to the
preservation of human rights. There is no binding international definition of the rule of law, although some comments from the leaders of
the international community provide an indication of how the concept is
defined in practice. In 2004, Secretary-General Kofi Annan defined the
rule of law as:

> [A] principle of governance in which all persons, institutions and
> entities, public and private, including the State itself, are account-
> able to laws that are publicly promulgated, equally enforced and
> independently adjudicated, and which are consistent with inter-
> national human rights norms and standards. It requires, as well,
> measures to ensure adherence to the principles of supremacy of law,
> equality before the law, accountability to the law, fairness in the
> application of the law, separation of powers, participation in
> decision-making, legal certainty, avoidance of arbitrariness and
> procedural and legal transparency.[24]

This language was drawn from a report from the secretary-general to
the general assembly delivered in 1994, which also provides that nations
seeking to develop into rule of law states should possess "a strong constitution, which ... incorporates internationally recognized human rights
and freedoms."[25] Notice that this definition starts with the Diceyan definition, which is found in the first sentence. The second sentence contains
further requirements, many of which are the subject of debate between
legal philosophers. The introduction of these additional requirements
with the phrase "it requires, as well" indicates the relationship between

the requirements found before and after these words. Those which come after are intended to promote or to realize what is found before; namely, the submission of all authority to regular law.

The secretary-general's and the general assembly's formulations bear witness to Dicey's enduring influence and to how the glosses to Dicey in global constitutional law have added to his definition, rather than subtract from it. These examples also demonstrate that prevailing definitions have both a core and a periphery, where the peripheral rules serve to implement or protect the essential Diceyan elements. The only addition to the core found in these definitions is the caveat that this accountability shall be "consistent with international human rights norms and standards."

The prevailing conception of the rule of law promoted by international organizations contains more than just the features necessary for the neutral adjudication of disputes and for holding the state itself responsible for legal wrongs. It also refers to substantive provisions that define a set of wrongs that will be actionable, which are connected to the evolving definition of human rights. However, these standards add little to Dicey's definition. This is because the human rights standards that are applicable in every circumstance are minimal, universally recognized, and recognized by as non-derogable even in Dicey's era.

The Rights Protected by the Core of the Rule of Law

The pre-history of the rule of law involved struggles against an executive that claimed the power to kill, to torture, and to detain its subjects indefinitely. The first of these rights was established as non-derogable in England by clause 29 of the Magna Carta of 1297. Repeated confirmation of this statute which elevated it above any other, giving it constitutional status.[26] A century before Dicey, William Blackstone confirmed that it was central to the rule of law and non-derogable:

This natural life ... cannot legally be disposed of or destroyed by any individual ... merely upon their own authority ... [T]he constitution is an utter stranger to any arbitrary power of killing or

maiming the subject without the express warrant of law ... To be-
reave a man of life ... without accusation or trial, would be so
gross and notorious an act of despotism, as must at once convey
the alarm of tyranny throughout the whole kingdom.[27]

Torture on the order of the executive was banned in England shortly before the Civil War. This was accomplished by a statute now known as the
Act Abolishing the Star Chamber 1641, which was at the time formally
styled "an act for the regulating of the privy council, and for taking away
the court commonly called the star-chamber."[28] After Parliament eliminated the jurisdiction of the Privy Council in the form of the Council
Board, it was no longer possible for it to issue writs that authorized rack-
ing and other forms of torture.[29]

Prolonged arbitrary detention by the executive was eliminated by the
passage of the Habeas Corpus Act 1679, which closed several existing
loopholes in earlier legislation.[30] The act specified that a writ from the
executive could no longer be considered sufficient cause for detention. It
also prevented the executive from moving prisoners in order to avoid the
jurisdiction of the court to which a petition for the great writ was submitted.[31] While the right to the writ could be suspended, this could only
be done by Parliament and not the executive.

These rights were all firmly established within the English constitutional tradition by the time Dicey created the modern definition of the rule
of law. They were also featured heavily in the works of the Whig historians which Dicey drew upon when creating his definition. In setting up
the rule of law as the antithesis of "prerogative" and "arbitrary power,"
Dicey was operating within a tradition where these rights were unar-
guably non-derogable by the executive.

The international human rights standards that define the concept of
the rule of law within global constitutional law add very little to what was
present in Dicey's era. The rights established as non-derogable by the
International Covenant on Civil and Political Rights (ICCPR) were protected by law in England at the time Dicey formulated his definition.[32]

Both Dicey's definition and that of the United Nations implicitly recognize that the protection of these non-derogable rights is the essence of
the rule of law. In Dicey's case, this becomes clear when one considers the

constitutional tradition in which he participated, and its relationship to English legal history. In the case of the UN, one might note that General Comment 29 to the ICCPR states that article 4's provisions are "essential for the maintenance of the ... rule of law."[33]

Accordingly, it is possible to conclude that the protection of non-derogable rights from the executive, even during times of crisis, is the normative core of the rule of law. This was the problem that the rule of law was meant to address, and which it continues to address. Additions that expand its reach should not distract from this fact. However, controversies over the extension of the scope of the rule of law's protections have led to significant debate. This has led some scholars to question if the concept of the rule of law continues to have a stable meaning.

Philosophical Debates about the Rule of Law Confirm Its Core

Within legal philosophy, the key dispute in the mid-twentieth century about the meaning of the rule of law relates to the debate between positivists and natural law theorists.[34] At the most fundamental level, it is a dispute about whether there is a connection between law and morality.[35] This disagreement is important to the rule of law because this concept implies that there are more and less desirable legal regimes, and this may require moral in addition to legal judgment.[36]

The criticism of the concept of the rule of law in jurisprudence can be traced to the reception of Lon Fuller's assertion that positivist approaches in legal philosophy did not adequately account for all of the necessary features of a legal system.[37] Fuller contended that the rule of law, which he presents in the form of the principle of legality, was essential to any legal order worthy of the name.[38] The principle of legality requires that there be fixed laws, rather than merely someone who enforces his or her personal preferences.

Fuller's equation of the rule of law with the principle of legality accords with another influential twentieth-century definition of that concept. Friedrich Hayek stated that "stripped of all technicalities th[e] [rule of law] means that government in all its action is bound by rules fixed and announced beforehand – rules which make it possible to foresee with fair certainty how the authority will use its coercive powers in given circumstances."[39]

Positivist legal philosophers did not take issue with this type of description. Indeed, Jeremy Waldron notes that H.L.A. Hart did not disagree, despite the fact that Fuller's definition was prompted by Fuller's disagreement with Hart.[40] Waldron notes that in "a little known essay," Hart wrote the following:

> The requirements that the law ... should be general (should refer to classes of persons, things, and circumstances, not to individuals or to particular actions) ... should be publicly promulgated and easily accessible ... are usually referred to as the principles of legality. The principles which require courts, in applying general rules to particular cases, to be without ... bias ... are referred to as rules of natural justice. These two sets of principles define the concept of the rule of law.[41]

Waldron also points out that Hart took a similar position in his book *Law, Liberty, and Morality*.[42] When discussing the offence of conspiracy to corrupt public morals, Hart notes that "the particular value which they sacrificed was the principle of legality."[43]

Naturally, Hart and other positivist legal philosophers did not agree with all of Fuller's positions. The key disagreement was whether or not the principle of legality demands recourse to moral principles. This dispute, which is critically important in jurisprudence, is not important to an empirical evaluation of the US constitutional order. However, for this measurement against the rule of law to be meaningful, that concept must be internally consistent. At the conclusion of the Hart-Fuller debate, there was as yet no evidence that the concept itself was unstable. Instead, both parties agreed that it was essential to constitutional legitimacy. Additionally, there was a consensus about the contents of the rule of law; namely, rules of general application and neutral adjudication.

Unfortunately, fifty years after the Hart-Fuller debate, there is no such consensus about the meaning of the rule of law as a concept in jurisprudence. Waldron has noted that in that field of jurisprudence, the concept of the rule of law has been the subject of such intense disagreements that it should be considered an essentially contested concept. He meant that it was not merely a concept which is hotly debated, but rather one about which agreement is impossible.[44] Tamanaha has also noted that there is no agreement among its leading legal philosophers as to precisely what it means.[45] However, the terms of this debate confirm the existence of the normative core of the rule of law.

The late twentieth-century debate about this concept revolves around one question: whether a state can be characterized as being governed in accordance with the rule of law if it merely provides for neutral adjudication of disputes, without stipulating that citizens possess fundamental rights that the state is bound to respect. The substantive or "thick" theory of the rule of law asserts that the procedural or "thin" version of the concept is insufficient.[46] However, the advocates of thick theories of the rule of law do not dispute that the components of the thin theories are also necessary. While there is no agreement on the question of which rights the state must respect, there is no disagreement about the importance of the principle of legality.

Another source of dispute is whether the legislature of a sovereign state possesses the power to change the laws and to abrogate citizens' rights.[47] This can also take the form of an argument over whether a written constitution that prevents the legislature from passing statutes that would violate fundamental rights is a necessary element of the rule of law.[48] However, there is no disagreement on the need to restrain the executive from ignoring duly enacted law, in accordance with the non-arbitrariness principle. As Arthur Goodhart argued, "[W]hen we turn from the control of the legislative power by the rule of law to the control of executive power we are on less controversial ground because all jurists – certainly in Western countries – agree that this is an essential part of government under law."[49]

The terms of these debates in legal philosophy demonstrate the implicit consensus about its normative core. There has been no decisive break between the meaning of the concept of the rule of law in jurisprudence with that of the equivalent term in constitutional law. Dicey's definition was not destabilized in the late twentieth century. Instead, there are numerous arguments about whether the rule of law should guarantee further protections, or whether by definition it must protect certain rights. The extension of the rule of law to the protection of non-derogable rights is uncontroversial. This state of affairs exists because these are *jus cogens* norms that are common to humanity, which states have also bound themselves to observe in international instruments such as the ICCPR.

Rule of Law Applies to Matters Involving National Security

There is another debate on the meaning of rule of law outside of constitutional law. It is located primarily within political science, and relates to the boundaries of the rule of law. Certain political theorists, some working at the intersection between political science and law, have argued that the rule of law is of limited application to situations when the executive is responding to threats to national security.[50]

One critic of a rule of law that is limited to situations that do not involve national security has argued that:

> It was a commonplace of classical political theory that assertions of threats of this kind are endemic to constitutional states, since this is the manner in which the executive branch of government typically seeks to extend its powers. Consequently, constitutional theorists across millennia (many of whom were known to and respected by the Framers) have rejected the emergency-based rationale for the expansion of executive powers. Indeed ... the development of both the notion of constitutional government and the rule of law often stems from resistance to these claims on the part of consuls, emperors, and kings.[51]

Accordingly, these theorists' definition of the rule of law would not be consistent with the historical context of its emergence, and would destabilize its normative core. On a more pragmatic note, David Dyzenhaus has noted that "the very fact that the exception [an unconstitutional response to a threat to national security] is brought within the law makes it susceptible to the rule of law – it gives to judges, *minded to do so*, the opportunity to impose the values of the rule of law on the administration."[52]

The ICJ's "Yardstick"

"The demand that the executive be subject to the laws was the main postulate of the rule of law state."[53] This was the reason the International Commission of Jurists (ICJ) decided to focus on control over the executive when establishing the minimum standards of the rule of law.

The ICJ provided the relevant guidelines in the resolutions and reports from its congresses held in Athens (1955), in New Delhi (1959), in Lagos (1961), and in Rio de Janeiro (1962). Its conception of the necessary controls over the executive are adopted here for several reasons. First, its definition is the result of a consensus developed by jurists from many different nations. The ICJ surveyed more than 75,000 lawyers from twenty-five countries in preparation for the conferences that created its definition of the rule of law.[54] Second, this definition has proved influential, as the ICJ's reform efforts have initiated rule of law–related reform efforts by the legal profession around the world, attesting to its popularity.[55] While the ICJ's definition of the rule of law has been criticized by legal philosophers such as Joseph Raz,[56] these criticisms do not relate to the topic of the control of the executive.

The ICJ's Prohibition on the Executive Legislating

The Rio Report specifies that legislation delegating the authority to make rules to the executive must "carefully define the extent, [and] purpose of the intended rules," while standing committees of the legislature should scrutinize and report on the rules and their enforcement.[57] The Rio Congress proceedings indicate that the commissioners were concerned with "the possibility of encroachments by the executive" that "could arise for reasons of expediency, or from a desire for greater power."[58] Its approach to limitations on executive power was not merely a response to the possibility of an inadvertent delegation of overbroad discretion to the executive, but to the reality that any executive branch responds to powerful incentives any to enlarge its own authority in a manner that might upset the balance of powers inherent to any given constitutional order.

Judicial Review of Executive Action

The Rio Congress focused on challenges to the rule of law presented by executive branch abuses of state power. The report of the Committee on Control by the Courts and the Legislature over Executive Action noted that "the existence of effective safeguards against the possible abuse of power by the Executive is an all-important aspect of the Rule of Law." Accordingly, it mandated that an "inviolable right of access to the courts" must exist "whenever the rights, interests, or status of any person[s] are infringed or threatened by executive action."[59] It provides a more explicit formulation than what is found in the conclusions of the Lagos Congress, which set up only "minimum requirements" for judicial review of administrative or executive action; namely, adequate notice of pending action, full disclosure of the reasons for such action, and a "fair hearing" in which "the grounds given by the Executive for its action shall not be regarded as conclusive but shall be objectively considered by the court."[60]

The Rio Congress further specified that in addition to *ex ante* determinations of the legality of executive action, the judiciary should have ample powers for *ex post facto* review of that conduct, whenever this is challenged by a citizen who is affected by this action. Its report specified that courts should have broad powers when sitting in judgment on claims alleging executive abuses. Accordingly, the judiciary must not only be empowered to determine whether "the Executive acts within the powers conferred upon it by the Constitution and [whether] such laws are not unconstitutional," but also to examine whether the executive's discretion "has been exercised in a proper and reasonable way and in accordance with the principles of natural justice," and whether "the powers validly granted to the executive are not used for a collateral or improper purpose."[61] In order for the courts to be able to make this determination, the report mandates that "it should be for the Court to decide whether any claim not to disclose State documents is reasonable and justified."[62]

These criteria have sufficient substantive content to provide a clear yardstick against which the avenues of judicial review of executive action can be measured. However, one might criticize this mandate of judicial control over the executive for being too vague, not on the basis of the standard against which the executive will be judged, but rather on the question of whether it fails to define the type of executive action that should be considered reviewable. Speaking of the requirement for judicial review contained in the Rio Report, Anthony Mathews has noted that it "either claims too much for the rule of law by suggesting that legal remedies are (or should be) available for every prejudicial executive action; or it avoids the question of precisely when an actionable invasion of rights, interests, or status takes place."[63]

Accordingly, Mathews suggests that the rule of law requires only that there be "limited and specific requirements for the legal control of the executive"; namely, that the executive should be prevented by the judiciary from abrogating basic civil rights.[64] He outlined the minimal criteria, so that there can be no disagreement on the basis of these differing models of the rule of law. There can be no disagreement, even where more ample review of executive action might be thought by some jurists to be desirable, that if judicial review is a necessary component of the rule of law, that this should extend at the very least to claims that the executive has or will deprive a citizen of their non-derogable rights. However, the ICJ also noted that this important safeguard of citizens' rights can be easily circumvented if the judiciary itself can be controlled. This is because the right to bring these cases matters little if the judges are little more than creatures of the executive branch.

Accordingly, the Act of Athens states that judges must "resist any encroachments ... on their independence"[65] in order to enforce the provisions of the rule of law that depend upon their scrutiny of the executive. The New Delhi Report specifies the conditions under which judges must work in order for the judiciary to be considered independent. The preconditions for independence are that judges are appointed in accordance with a procedure that involves the judiciary, and receive adequate remuneration, which should be fixed and inalterable during a lifelong term of office.[66]

The Resolution of Rio noted that the ICJ needed to address "the independence of the judiciary ... and its freedom from control, direct or indirect, by the Executive."[67] The Rio Report concluded that the judiciary must also have adequate authority for judges to be considered independent. It states that the judiciary "must be given the jurisdiction to determine *in every case* upon application whether the circumstances have arisen or the conditions have been fulfilled, under which such power [delegated from the legislature to the executive] is to be or has been exercised."[68] This formulation implies that the courts must have the final word when determining their jurisdiction over the executive. In other words, they must have a Kompetenz-kompetenz power.[69]

This jurisdiction must extend to every possible claim of infringement of non-derogable human rights by the executive, and includes the power to determine whether evidence sought from the government by the plaintiff can be properly withheld in the interest of state security.[70] The jurists responsible for the Rio Report also reaffirmed that the review of executive action should not be reserved to special tribunals, but "entrusted to the ordinary or the administrative courts."[71]

It should be noted that these reports contain no exceptions in these requirements of an independent judiciary and legal profession for times of crisis or even for states of emergency. The Act of Athens further states that jurists should enforce the rule of law "without fear."[72] However, the greatest challenge to this requirement relates to the pressure put on the justice system during these periods, and accordingly the ICJ has discussed the challenges to the rule of law that relate to states of emergency in detail.

The ICJ on the Legislative Oversight during an Emergency

The last requirement is vital to ensuring the rule of law remains in place during any state of emergency. The Rio Report reiterates that in a constitutional state, the proclamation of such a crisis does not suspend all of the laws and abrogate every fundamental right; rather, the state of emergency exists within a legal framework.[73] The executive must act in accordance with legislation that remains in place during an emergency. The New Delhi Report also states that the legislature may not abrogate fundamental human rights.[74]

Separation of Powers as Implementation of the Rule of Law

Within domestic American legal discourse, the concept most often employed when discussing constitutional safeguards against abuses of authority and excessive accumulation of power in a manner that damages the integrity of the legal system is not the rule of law, but the separation of powers. This is largely the result of the time when the US Constitution was created. The phrase "rule of law" was popularized after 1787, whereas before that date, the concept was normally described by reference to the political structures advocated by proponents of limited monarchy. In Anglo-American jurisprudence, the terminology that described the sort of constitutional order that protected the supremacy of law over the rule of men was usually referred to as a "mixed" or "balanced" constitution.[75]

The genesis of this idea within the anglophone jurisprudential tradition lies in the response to monarchs who attempted to govern in a manner that was inconsistent with England's traditional mode of governance, which was not absolute monarchy, but rather *dominium politicum et regale*.[76] The monarch's key constitutional function was not to make law or to act as a judge, but rather to execute the laws. Unfortunately, under a mixed constitution, no clear barriers to the monarch's usurpation of these other functions of government existed.[77] The reaction to the early Stuarts' overreaching created the demand for a constitutional order that limit royal powers. "[After 1649] [t]he idea that the King should be limited to the exercise of the executive function was now well understood."[78]

"When the Restoration came in England it all but swamped the new doctrine [of separation of powers] by assimilating it ... to the complex theory of the balanced constitution; in the America of 1787 the doctrine of the theory of checks and balances was modified ... by the theory of checks and balances drawn from the older conception of English constitutional theory."[79] The American revolutionaries' approach, which was influenced strongly by Montesquieu and Blackstone, was to create a more rigid division of responsibilities between the branches.[80]

This theory of the separation of powers grants the legislature exclusive authority to make law and the executive only the power to enforce it, and to the judiciary it gives the ability to referee disputes and to determine whether the actions of the other branches of government comply with the Constitution's commands. This approach is outlined explicitly in the US Constitution. The exclusivity of Congress's law-making power is explained at the beginning of article I: "All legislative Powers herein granted shall be vested in a Congress of the United States."[81] To prevent the president from enlarging the scope of his own powers, article II makes it clear that the constitution invests him with "executive powers," which are specifically enumerated in section 4.[82] Article III vests the judicial power of the United States exclusively in the judiciary. It is granted in section 1 to the federal judiciary and section 2 specifies that "the judicial power [thus vested exclusively in the courts] shall extend to all cases in law and equity."[83]

The constitutional design's intent was to prevent one government branch from accumulating power, as contemporary writings by its key authors urging its ratification confirm; these tracts pay special attention to the problem of executive aggrandisement. James Madison, who is commonly called the "Father of the Constitution,"[84] justified the proposed constitution's separation of powers by reference to principles of fundamental justice:

> No man is allowed to be a judge in his own cause, because his interest would certainly bias his judgment, and, not improbably, corrupt his integrity. With equal, nay with greater reason, a body of men are unfit to be both judges and parties at the same time; yet what are many of the most important acts of legislation, but so many judicial determinations, not indeed concerning the rights of single persons, but concerning the rights of large bodies of citizens?[85]

On this same subject, in the "Federalist No. 47," he argued that "The accumulation of all powers, legislative, executive, and judiciary, in the same hands ... may justly be pronounced the very definition of tyranny." Quoting Montesquieu he put the question as follows: "'When the legislative and executive powers are united in the same person or body,' says he, 'there can be no liberty, because apprehensions may arise lest *the same* monarch or senate should *enact* tyrannical laws to *execute* them in a tyrannical manner.'" Further, in the same letter Madison argues, "[w]ere the power of judging joined with ... the executive power, *the judge* might behave with all the violence of *an oppressor*." Some of these reasons are more fully explained in other passages; but briefly stated as they are here, they sufficiently establish the meaning which has been put on this celebrated maxim of this celebrated author.[86]

Alexander Hamilton explained the importance of judicial review of the constitutionality of the laws in "Federalist No. 78." He argued that "where the will of the legislature, declared in its statutes, stands in opposition to that of the people, declared in the Constitution, the judges ought to be governed by the latter rather than the former. They ought to regulate their decisions by the fundamental laws, rather than by those which are not fundamental."[87] Accordingly, one can see in the US Constitution a clear commitment to the principles of the supremacy of law and to checks on the powers of the government in an organic law establishing the nation's constitutional order.

The executive's enlargement of powers in the twenty-first century, combined with the other branches' acceptance of that aggrandizement, subverts the US Constitution. The executive definitively rejected the core principles of the rule of law embedded within it, which are found in the principles of the separation of powers and judicial review of unconstitutional law-making. This separation of powers defines the principles of control over the executive specified in the ICJ's reports within the United States. Accordingly, the subversion of these principles, when it empowers the executive to violated non-derogable norms with impunity, is also the destruction of the rule of law in the United States.

CHAPTER 2

The Historical Development of the Rule of Law in the United States

The Resiliency of the Rule of Law from 1787 to 1940

Until the twentieth century, the rule of law was protected adequately by the separation of powers defined in the US Constitution.[1] In the nation's first 150 years, Congress and the courts checked presidential powers as the Framers intended.[2] Although ambitious presidents attempted to expand their powers during crises, they were repeatedly rebuffed, from the earliest days of the American republic.[3]

The Framers contemplated the possibility of these sorts of crises, and believed that the design of the Constitution was sufficiently robust to resist the dangers to the rule of law that would ensue. While they were concerned about the ability of the executive branch to enlarge its own powers and to become unaccountable,[4] the Federalists who exercised a decisive influence on the framing believed in a science of politics that would allow them to construct a system that could preserve a stable constitutional order.[5] They found another possibility more worrisome. Like many other political theorists before them, the Federalists were concerned with the impact of prolonged warfare on the balance of powers.[6] Hamilton noted that "[i]t is of the nature of war to increase the executive at the expense of legislative authority," as it necessitates "strengthening the executive arm of government, in doing which their constitutions would acquire a progressive direction toward monarchy."[7] This was an alarming prospect. It is clear that the isolationism and general disengagement from European controversies[8] during the republic's early years was driven by the fear that prolonged warfare would distort the separation of powers that ensured that their constitutional order was "a government of laws and not of men." As Hamilton argued, "Safety from external danger is the most powerful director of national conduct ... the continual effort and alarm attendant on a state of continual danger, will compel nations the most attached to liberty to resort for repose and security to the institutions which have a tendency to destroy their political and civil rights."[9]

Hamilton also noted that since warfare empowered the president and led to dangers to civil rights, there was a persuasive rationale for taking the powers of war and peace out of the hands of the executive, as these powers would subject it to excessive temptation. He argued that "[t]he history of human conduct does not warrant that exalted opinion of human virtue which would make it wise to commit interests of so delicate and momentous a kind ... to the sole disposal of ... a president."[10] Hamilton, in short, thought that since the executive branch could enlarge its powers during a prolonged war, the power to declare war must be jealously guarded by Congress. James Madison argued in 1793 that "war in fact is the true nurse of executive aggrandizement. In war, a physical force is to be created; and it is the executive will, which is to direct it ... Hence it has grown into an axiom that the executive is the department of power most distinguished by its propensity to war: hence it is the practice of all states ... to disarm this propensity of its influence."[11]

He also concluded that Congress should hold the exclusive power to declare war, since its powers would not be increased, but rather diminished by a prolonged state of conflict. Madison later intimated that a president might create a foreign crisis merely to increase his domestic powers, noting that "[p]erhaps it is a universal truth that the loss of liberty at home is to be charged to provisions against danger, real or pretended, from abroad."[12] The Framers' fears were not misguided: the contemporary relevance of executive unaccountability after the executive's creation or manipulation of crises as a threat to the rule of law deserves serious consideration.

Alexis de Tocqueville foresaw the possibility as well, predicting that "[i]f the existence of the American Union were perpetually threatened ... the executive would assume an increased importance."[13] He, like Madison, underlined the conflict of interest that would be created if the executive branch managed to obtain control over foreign affairs such that it could bring the nation to war by either overt or covert means. This problem was apparent to many political thinkers during the nineteenth century.

The prophecies about the dangerous temptation to create an empowered executive finally came to pass in the twentieth century. The executive branch used prolonged warfare and sustained alarms from abroad (real or imagined) to broaden its powers and curtail liberty, threatening the separation of powers and the rule of law. In 1941, America broke decisively from its isolation, and over the next thirty years of warfare the powers of the chief executive grew to the point that they could be described as those of an "imperial presidency."[14]

Rule of Law from Framing to 1860: Constitutional Supremacy

The first clear example of attempted executive aggrandizement is instructive. President Thomas Jefferson tried to become the ultimate arbiter of constitutional questions, in a bid to supplant the Supreme Court, which he derided once in office.[15] Attempting to pursue political ends in the courtroom, he sought to withhold documents from the defence during a politically motivated treason trial.[16] The Supreme Court rejected his arguments for an executive role in legislative and constitutional interpretation in *Marbury v. Madison*.[17] Chief Justice John Marshall did the same when disposing of Jefferson's claims of executive privilege against subpoenas, in *United States v. Burr*.[18] During the republic's early years, the judiciary quickly proved itself to be an effective check on the executive. Marshall established that the judiciary was a co-equal branch of government with a special responsibility to protect citizens' constitutional rights against invasion by the other branches of government.[19]

The Rule of Law in the Nineteenth Century: Tested, but Unyielding

During the next century, the Civil War would put separation of powers to the test, by offering compelling rationales to expand executive powers beyond the accountability to the law and the other branches of government. President Abraham Lincoln unilaterally suspended habeas corpus at the beginning of this conflict, but he acknowledged that his action was irregular and that it required Congress's sanction.[20] Furthermore, the executive's decision to try alleged conspirators before military tribunals while the civilian courts remained open was rebuked by the Supreme Court in *Ex Parte Milligan*.[21]

Accordingly, the four years of civil war did not result in substantial changes to the separation of powers. As had been the case with other crises, presidential assertions of emergency powers and allegations of superiority over the other branches of government were soon forgotten after the danger receded.[22] Lincoln had never argued that the Constitution gave him legal power to abrogate its protections or to ignore the laws. He had merely done what he thought was necessary and relied upon the legislature to see the wisdom in not punishing him for having done so, as it had the power under article I either to impeach him or to ignore his excesses.

After the Civil War, Congress re-established its power to punish executive encroachments of its authority to set government policy. President Andrew Johnson was impeached for attempting to undermine Congress's policies by dismissing officials in a manner that violated the Tenure of Office Act of 1867,[23] which it passed over Johnson's veto. This action demonstrated that the legislative branch was determined not to allow the executive to interpret legislation in a self-serving manner that enlarged the president's powers.[24] Johnson believed that the act was unconstitutional, and argued that because of that fact he still possessed the power to dismiss Secretary of War Edward Stanton, who was implementing Congress's Reconstruction policy of using the military to enforce its laws enfranchising African-Americans. The impeachment sidelined Johnson, destroying his credibility and his ability to influence policy. On this basis, one can conclude that the legislature proved itself an effective restraint on executive usurpation during the nineteenth century.

The Cold War Presidency and the Rule of Law

Between 1941 and 1971, a period in which the United States was continuously at war (hot and cold), the executive branch exceeded the limits of what the Constitution allowed. It did so by starting new wars on the president's own initiative, wiretapping political activists and preventing bills limiting the executive's powers from becoming laws. At the same time, the oversight and regulation of the other branches of government withered during this slow process of aggrandizement.[25] The presidential unaccountability that this created[26] was the genesis of the severe constitutional crisis that erupted during the Nixon administration. At that time, the executive used these broad powers in a manner that openly sidelined both the legislature and the courts, until these branches acted decisively to restore the separation of powers.

Until the twentieth century, the United States pursued an isolationist foreign policy.[27] Outside of crises like the Civil War, the executive branch was presented with few opportunities to expand its powers, much less expand them to the point that it could violate citizens' non-derogable rights without facing scrutiny and rebukes from Congress and the courts. The decision to commit American troops to battle in Europe in 1917 was controversial, and the one year of warfare did not yield any opportunities for the executive to gain or to use executive powers that might destabilize the rule of law.

In the early years of the Second World War, it appeared likely that the United States would remain neutral, thereby avoiding a political crisis.[28] The nation shifted suddenly into crisis governance after a devastating surprise attack. The attack on Pearl Harbor plunged the United States into a state of war that would transition repeatedly from hot to cold, but the nation remained in a constant state of emergency. This attack also initiated a shift away from the requirements of the rule of law, such that even the most fundamental rights of citizens – due process, freedom from prolonged arbitrary detention, and even to life itself – were abrogated by the executive without any resistance from other branches of government, and without any redress. This would remain the norm until this process reached its logical terminus during the Nixon administration.

Between 1941 and 1968, the executive branch acquired extensive powers that far exceeded what was granted by article II of the US Constitution.[29] This gradually made it unaccountable, defeating the purpose of the separation of powers that safeguards the rule of law and guarantees citizens' protections against violations of *jus cogens* norms by the executive branch. While these powers were initially used only infrequently, they created a precedent.[30]

The crisis period began with the attack on Pearl Harbor, an act so shocking to Americans that it allowed President Franklin Roosevelt to take unprecedented action in a political atmosphere that precluded any resistance or criticism.[31] The president was able to assume broad new powers, which were in the main not derived from Congress, but from Declarations of National Emergency that he issued.[32] These national emergency powers authorized the president to "seize property, organize and control the means of production, seize commodities, assign military forces abroad, institute martial law ... and, in a variety of ways, control the lives of United States citizens."[33] The Second World War allowed Roosevelt to assume supplementary authority that was not expressly delegated by Congress; he obtained powers which conflict with the requirements of the rule of law.

Roosevelt believed that he also possessed emergency powers owing to his status as the commander-in-chief in wartime, and because of his inherent duty to "take measures to avert a disaster which would interfere with the winning of the war."[34] The president elevated this duty above the laws. In one early example, he told Congress that if agricultural provisions of the Emergency Price Control Act were not repealed within three weeks, he would refuse to enforce the statute.[35] Congress capitulated to this unwarranted assertion of executive power. More regrettably, the Supreme Court did likewise when Roosevelt took actions that deprived American citizens of their right to be free from arbitrary detention and from death sentences imposed without due process. These actions illustrate the implications of the abrogation of the rule of law.[36]

On 19 May 1942, all American citizens of Japanese ancestry were ordered to leave their homes and relocate to internment camps, pursuant to the Civilian Restrictive Order. This order was authorized by Executive Order 9066, itself issued three months earlier by the president.[37] It should be noted that the Office of Naval Intelligence earlier found that there was no evidence that Japanese Americans were involved in any clandestine activity at that time. Despite the fact that this vitiated the rationale of internment, Solicitor General Charles Fahy withheld this evidence from the Supreme Court, in violation of his duty of absolute candour.[38] However, the Supreme Court appeared predisposed to rule in the government's favour during the internment cases that followed, especially after Congress acted quickly to rubber-stamp this "most shameful abuse of power."[39]

Certain justices believed that the internment was unconstitutional, as it was recognized some forty years later.[40] Despite that belief, they failed to follow Chief Justice Marshall's example in standing up to executive overreaching. Instead, they defended broad presidential powers in wartime even when they are unconstitutional on their face. Justice Robert H. Jackson (who later served as chief prosecutor at the Nuremburg trials) wrote in dissent that "defense measures will not, and often should not, be held within the limits that bind civil authority in peace," as "military decisions are not susceptible of intelligent judicial appraisal."[41]

To meet the basic requirements of the rule of law state, a nation must have a judiciary empowered to stand up to the executive when it violates citizens' non-derogable rights. However, a dangerous precedent was set during the Second World War, when both the executive and public opinion were aligned against the justices. If this same dynamic can be seen at work outside of a transient crisis, it calls into question whether the state is in compliance with the basic requirements of the rule of law state.

Another example of the court's abdication of responsibility during the intense political pressure created by the fear, anxiety, and hatred fomented when the United States was propelled into the Second World War is found in its *Ex Parte Quirin* opinion.[42] This opinion discussed the military trial of eight alleged German saboteurs, one of whom was an American citizen, captured shortly after arriving in the United States by submarine. Rather than trying these prisoners in the civilian courts, as *Ex Parte Milligan* requires, Roosevelt convened a secret military tribunal for an unconstitutional purpose. The tribunal process was designed to introduce otherwise inadmissible evidence, in order to secure a favourable verdict.[43]

The Supreme Court, when presented with a petition for a writ of certiorari after the denial of writs of habeas corpus, went to great lengths to accommodate Roosevelt, announcing the denial of relief almost immediately, even before agreeing on a rationale for the decision. After the court declined the petition, but before it publicly explained its reasoning in this momentous case, Jackson circulated a draft opinion.

This opinion influenced the development of the court's deferential approach in the cases challenging executive power that were to follow.[44] In it, Jackson argued that the treatment of prisoners of war was an issue related to foreign policy and national security with which the president was entrusted, and which the court was not competent to second-guess. This approach set a precedent for the court's later attempts to maintain its legitimacy when it chose not to decide cases involving invasions of citizens' non-derogable rights. The justices now possessed the raw material from which they could build a doctrine of deference to the executive in matters involving the military and national security. To do so, the court developed a tactic to be deployed when faced with controversial cases when there was no popular or political support for challenging the other branches of government: to use "procedural rules to avoid decisions of substance."[45]

In addition, despite the fact that the type of military tribunal at issue in *Quirin* was not provided for by statute, Jackson argued "the president had *inherent* authority to create military commissions ... a remarkable analysis [that] hints at an exclusive Commander-in-Chief power without any citation of authority."[46] The published decision also distinguished *Ex Parte Milligan* by stating that in the case at bar, the petitioners were "unlawful combatants,"[47] despite this having only been proven in a trial that lacked due process. It ruled in this manner despite this being the key fact that the petitioners contested in their request for the writ; they were motivated to seek an order transferring them to civilian court because it would allow them to prove otherwise. Again, this proved to be a dangerous precedent for cases in the future that make claims related to arbitrary and indefinite detention. It provided the basis for the executive to claim that the judiciary possessed no right to review its own determination of the facts that the petitioners claim were wrongly decided, even if the executive branch's procedure did not comply with the principles of natural justice.

If in wartime the executive possessed, after declaring a national emergency, the unreviewable authority to refuse to enforce statutes, to imprison thousands of American citizens, and to unilaterally designate citizens as enemy combatants who could be tried and executed without due process and without access to the civilian courts or writs of habeas corpus, it seems possible to conclude that the United States was not a rule of law state during the Second World War and its aftermath. Here, the executive violated citizens' non-derogable rights not to be subjected to prolonged arbitrary detention, to have access to the courts, and ultimately, not to be killed.

Despite these manifest failures to conform to the minimum standards of the rule of law, no one made the argument that the United States was, at that time, not a rule of law state. This omission can be attributed to two factors. First, criticism of the president and commander-in-chief during wartime was considered tantamount to sedition. Second, many hoped that this was merely the result of a transient crisis, such as that which led Lincoln to suspend habeas corpus.

Admittedly, there is a distinction between a state that is temporarily out of compliance with the requirements of the rule of law and one which is no longer a rule of law state. What must be addressed is the state of affairs that ensures when a state of emergency becomes effectively permanent. The first example that must be discussed is the Cold War.

From Hot War to Cold: New Challenges to the Rule of Law

In the wake of American triumph in the Second World War, the failures of the rule of law were quickly forgotten, as no one had any interest in calling attention to actions they thought were aberrations. Even the victims of Japanese internment were anxious to ignore and forget the injustices that they suffered. Congress briefly reasserted itself against the executive branch, which also was weakened considerably by the succession of Harry Truman. It should be noted that at this time, Vice-President Truman was elected only three months prior to Roosevelt's death. He lacked an independent power base in national politics. His approval rating fell to 33 per cent by September 1946.[48]

This formal return to the strictures of the rule of law, made possible by the American executive's weakness outside times of crisis, was very tenuous, as that year also heralded a new conflict – the Cold War. "The end of the Second World War brought the customary diminution of power ... But this time the diminution was brief. The Cold War, by generating a climate of sustained and indefinite crisis, aborted the customary reversion of power to the coordinate branches."[49] While the nature of this crisis was initially unclear, it was soon recognized as an existential threat to the United States. This emergency became the justification for ever-broader assertions of unreviewable executive powers, the termination of which waited for some resolution of what appeared to be an irresolute conflict between the "free" and communist spheres of influence.[50]

In 1947 the Central Intelligence Agency (CIA) was established. It soon became a key tool for the executive, allowing for great freedom of action without any accountability. This unaccountability involved a failure to provide for effective legislative oversight of incredible discretionary powers, including the ability to direct the CIA's private armies, to instigate new wars, and expand to those already in progress.[51]

The Berlin blockade quickly demonstrated that minor skirmishes between the two blocs could develop into serious crises. The Soviet Union's development of a nuclear arsenal in 1949 invited a level of destruction that was previously unimaginable. The invasion of South Korea by the North Korean army (equipped by the Soviet Union) led President Truman to declare a national emergency, because "world conquest by communist imperialism is the goal of the forces of aggression that have been loosed upon the world."[52] This state of emergency would remain in effect until 1978.[53] The declaration gave the executive specific extraordinary powers, but these were less significant to its political fortunes than the political climate the Cold War created. This new atmosphere allowed the executive branch to assume powers that dwarfed those emergency powers that were expressly delegated. "From the start, the Cold War fostered an overarching sense of crisis. By 1947, the concern of the nation was focused on the perceived threat posed by Soviet expansionism ... the first comprehensive analysis of the nation's position after World War II predicted an indefinite period of foreign relations crisis and recommended a massive military expansion ... [which] echoed throughout the Cold War."[54]

Truman set another important precedent that greatly expanded executive power when he committed American forces to battle without a declaration of war, or even implicit congressional approval.[55] Truman decided not to seek one, relying instead on a constitutional case that "was far from conclusive."[56] However, Congress failed to react, as "Korea be-guiled the American government first into an unprecedented claim for in-herent presidential power to go to war and then into an ill-advised resentment against those who dared bring up the constitutional issue."[57] The political atmosphere of the Cold War prevented Congress from chal-lenging this overreaching, which contradicted the Constitution's War Powers Clause.[58]

This set a precedent that continued throughout this prolonged crisis, which was used to justify actions such as the American invasion of the Dominican Republic in 1965.[59] Congress uncovered President Johnson's misleading comments about the circumstances of the invasion, but he was not held accountable.[60] The legislature failed to exercise oversight or hold the executive responsible. Congress felt that this would expose it to negative public opinion and the charge that it was "soft" on communism. Congress also feared that its defence of the principle of legislative over-sight and the constitutional limits of executive power would be charac-terized as nothing more than a cover story for purportedly unpatriotic and ideologically suspect motives.

Truman suffered one major setback. The Supreme Court ruled against him in *The Steel Seizure Case*.[61] The court held that the executive did not have the power to seize private property except when it was given that right explicitly by article II of the Constitution or by statute, although the fractured plurality makes it very difficult to determine the case's hold-ing and legal effect. The majority opinion restated the traditional rule that the president possessed no power to act except where authorized by the Constitution or Congress, but the concurring opinions made it clear that this holding did not have the support of a majority of the justices.

This lack of consensus illustrated a momentous shift in the court's theory of the Constitution,[62] which is explained by the political climate created by the Cold War. Edward Corwin applauded the concurring opinions, arguing that "Nature abhors a vacuum; so does an age of emergency."[63] He made it clear that he thought that the executive simply must have implied constitutional powers. This argument directly contra-dicts the Framers' views on the powers given the executive. It also ignores their well-founded fears of how such powers could be used to destabilize the separation of powers that is an essential element of the rule of law.

Nevertheless, these concurrences did set some limitations on executive power, as the Constitution would not bear the interpretation that the executive could act directly contrary to statute. The president still could not defy clear congressional orders, as Truman had when seizing the steel mills. However, this limitation was taken only to apply in domestic matters, where the court held the Commander-in-Chief Clause conferred no authority,[64] leaving the president largely unimpeded to regulate foreign affairs when Congress remained silent.[65] This reservation to domestic affairs can also be explained by the unwillingness of the other government branches to be seen as impediments in the struggle against communism during the Korean War. This perception would have impaired their popular legitimacy in this highly charged political atmosphere.

In foreign affairs, the president could rely not only on the power to mobilize and control the military but also on his ability to direct the CIA, which was used to overthrow foreign governments during the Cold War: Iran, Guatemala, Egypt, Chile, and Laos.[66] Executive orders

> had, in effect, amended the National Security and Central Intelligence Acts by a long series of Top Secret NSC directives, thereby creating a "secret charter" to which the Agency became far more responsive than to the statutes themselves. Though the CIA was persistently, ingeniously and sometimes irresponsibly engaged in undertakings that confronted the nation with the possibility of war [i.e., provoking the Cuban Missile Crisis], Congress had no effective means of control or of oversight or of even finding out what the Agency was up to.[67]

This failure of oversight is not in accordance with the minimum requirements of the rule of law. Here, the power to conduct covert operations was delegated to an agency that reported only to the chief executive. No limitation were set on those powers, even where it was apparent that misuse or even overuse of those powers could lead the nation into war – precisely the conflict of interest for the executive branch that the Framers feared.

It is possible to conclude that between 1950 and 1968, the executive branch was acting in ways that violated fundamental precepts of the rule of law. That said, there were still some checks on the executive branch during this period, such that it might be said that the nation had not diverged significantly from the rule of law. The president, at least in domestic matters, was still nominally responsible to the other branches of government, which consecutive presidents chose to evade rather than to openly defy.[68] Citizens subjected to serious abuses that implicated the rule of law, such as the threat of arbitrary detention, were able to challenge the executive successfully in the courts. Following *The Steel Seizure Case* and other key cases from this period, the courts continued to police the executive's actions when they acted in a way that directly contradicted the law of the land. Notably, in *Joint Anti-Fascist Review Committee v. McGrath*[69] the Supreme Court declared the unconstitutionality of the executive branch's blacklists barring alleged communists from government employment, and it banned them in *Peters v. Hobby*.[70]

Accordingly, Congress was inclined to give the executive freedom of action. It was concerned about being outflanked politically and vilified for impeding the intelligence agencies' and the military's ability to fight a cold war against a shadowy communist enemy that many American citizens believed was lurking in every corner, both at home and abroad. It could do so and retain some legitimacy and a justification for its efforts owing to its continued ability to pass domestic legislation that responded to the interest of its constituents and competing interest groups. However, the judiciary faced a more difficult dilemma.

The courts could not abdicate their responsibilities to monitor and control the executive's actions where they implicated the constitutional rights of citizens without a fatal loss of institutional legitimacy. The federal judiciary's key mandate since *Marbury v. Madison* has been the enforcement of constitutional limitations on the other branches of government. As such, its decisions can usually be described as accommodations of competing values. On one side, it wanted to allow the executive to have some freedom of action where this was universally popular, despite the fact that the disputed action was often unconstitutional and in conflict with core principles of the rule of law. On the other, it could not allow the executive complete freedom to ignore either congressional or constitutional commands without consigning itself to irrelevance.[71]

The Supreme Court protected the constitutional rights of alleged communists who were mistreated by the executive at the height of McCarthyism, which sent a strong message that the judiciary would continue to assert its relevance. During the Cold War, the federal judiciary remained an effective, albeit imperfect, forum for those challenging violations of their civil rights, at least whenever the executive's actions could not be ignored without putting the courts' institutional relevance into question. An accommodation was achieved: as long as the implications of the executive control over the intelligence agencies and the military were ignored by the other branches of government, it continued to comply with the commands of Congress and the courts. Accordingly, there was no assertion immediately following *The Steel Seizure Case* of a constitutional theory that would give the executive branch pre-eminent powers to act in the interest of national security.[72]

Covert evasion of the requirements of the rule of law, however, would not be sufficient for an administration that was determined to take radical action when opposed by the legislature and judiciary. The executive branch proved willing to take actions that would unilaterally expand its own power at the expense of the other branches which were charged with restraining it. It would then be impossible for the legislature and the judiciary to ignore this overreaching, without permanently conceding the role in overseeing and restraining the executive, as required by the rule of law. Nixon was confronted with a dilemma, to admit defeat or provoke what theretofore were quiescent branches of government. He chose to escalate the Vietnam War in the face of determined opposition from Congress and the populace.

The stage was set for a confrontation between the executive on one side and the legislature and the courts on the other. This was the decisive test of whether or not an executive empowered as it was in the course of the Cold War was consistent with the rule of law. Nixon attempted to use all of these powers to create an unaccountable executive, even when he took actions that enlarged his own powers unilaterally and asserted directly that the executive was above the law. If he were to have succeeded in this endeavour, it would have been evident not only that there was no rule of law in the United States during a crisis. It also would have been clear that this was a permanent state of affairs, with no apparent means of reversal. However, by this time the other branches were aware that they would lose all of their own constitutional powers if they did not restore the executive to a state of legal accountability. This, however, required a constitutional crisis over the executive's right to declare war, bar legislation even when passed over his veto, and derail investigations into many other abuses. It ended in Nixon's resignation. The consensus about enlarged presidential powers during the Cold War buckled under the strain of this conflict. Afterwards, the period of détente provided an opportunity to reimplement the separation of powers that undergirds the rule of law.

The Battle over an Unaccountable Presidency

It was under President Nixon that the American executive began to elaborate and act upon theories of its inherent powers, in a radical break with both the constitutional separation of powers and the rule of law that it protects. Nixon inherited the responsibility for the Vietnam War from his predecessors. President Johnson obtained some measure of congressional approval for committing American troops to battle, in the form of the Gulf of Tonkin Resolution.[73] Nixon was elected on a promise to end the war. It should be noted that his predecessor had initiated peace talks that might have succeeded, were they not sabotaged by Henry Kissinger, on Nixon's orders.[74] Once in office, Nixon decided to escalate the war. For this he was alone responsible, as Congress did not countenance any expansion. However, the war was deeply unpopular by the time Nixon assumed control; he could no longer rely on reflexive support for war-making predicated upon popular support for anti-communist measures. Nevertheless, Nixon was determined to escalate the conflict as part of a set of policies about which only he and his closest personal advisors were aware. His inability or unwillingness to create any support in Congress for his policies set the stage for significant conflict between the branches of government. The legislature and the judiciary were goaded by a more aggressive use of the executive powers his predecessors had accumulated during the Cold War. These powers were now being directed against the legislature and the judiciary, in a way that challenged their continued relevance.

In March 1969, Nixon ordered secret bombings of Cambodia. This involved assigning targets within Vietnamese air space as a cover story, and then issuing substitute orders to pilots specifying new locations in Cambodia after they launched their aircraft. "[F]alse reports on each mission were filed through regular channels," such that "'only a few United States officials were aware of the B-52 operations in Cambodia.'"[75] "The State Department, the Secretary of the Air Force, and the Air Force Chief of Staff were all kept ignorant of the bombing, as were the relevant congressional committees."[76] This was not legal, but there was no immediate fallout, as the secrecy of Operation Menu was maintained for almost another three years. The bombing led to the fall of the neutral Sihanouk regime and the North Vietnamese decision to support the Khmer Rouge. Nixon decided to follow up the bombing with a ground assault in April 1970, something which could not be kept secret.

Nixon announced the invasion to the American people on television, arguing that despite the fact there was congressional authorization, he possessed not only the right but a duty to launch this offensive into a neutral nation. He argued, "I shall meet my responsibility as Commander-in-Chief of our Armed Forces to take the action necessary to defend the security of our American men."[77] He argued that "[t]he legal justification ... is the right of the President of the United States under the Constitution to protect the lives of American men."[78] This theory of a constitutional reserve power to protect the nation vested in the executive implied that congressional authorization was wholly unnecessary. It was also a harbinger of assertions to come.

Nixon's invasion of Cambodia was prompted by the fact that its neutral government was allowing the North Vietnamese Army to use the South Vietnam border to transport arms and as a staging area for attacks. Nevertheless, it was uncertain whether he would get congressional support to widen the war in Indochina, so he put the legislature on the horns of a dilemma. Congress could either allow him to continue over its protests and risk irrelevance, or it could flout the danger of appearing unpatriotic at the very moment that American soldiers were in harm's way. The latter course of action risked their popularity, even though Nixon was responsible for the decision to place the troops in danger.

Congress perceived the second course of action to be excessively hazardous, but this moment still marked a turning point in its relations with the executive branch. As popular support for the war weakened, and the tendency to rally behind the president subsided, Congress boldly opposed executive usurpations of legislative power, because it learned that its inaction would pose a more serious risk. There was now a very real danger that it could be sidelined permanently.

Restraining Executive War-Making: The WPR

Nixon's unilateral escalation of the Vietnam War shocked both the legislature and the country. Senator Jacob Javits spoke for many legislators when he argued that "the President has apparently defined his authority as Commander in Chief in such a broad and comprehensive manner as to intrude upon, and even pre-empt, the powers reserved so explicitly to the Congress under the Constitution."[79] Student protests erupted nationwide, and transformed into a student strike after National Guardsmen and police officers shot and killed unarmed protesters at Kent State and Jackson State Universities.[80] The antiwar movement soon became a serious threat to the Nixon administration.

Congress reacted to the invasion of Cambodia by revoking the Gulf of Tonkin Resolution in January of 1971. When voting, members noted that this would "[deprive] the President of his legal authority to carry on the [Vietnam] war."[81] In response, Nixon turned to William Rehnquist, then the head of the Office of Legal Counsel of the Department of Justice, to justify his theory that the Commander-in-Chief Clause authorized him to continue the war, which was quickly forthcoming, despite the fact that Rehnquist's "case was persiflage"[82] (i.e., frivolous). (Perhaps not surprisingly, Rehnquist was later nominated by Nixon to be chief justice, setting a dangerous executive precedent of arranging for the appointment of reflexively pro-administration jurists to the body that scrutinized its theories of executive power.) Nixon would use the same logic for the initiation of a massive bombing campaign in another neutral country, Laos, which was done not only to impair the transit of Vietnamese forces but also to intervene in a domestic conflict by destroying the Pathet Lao.[83]

Nixon was at this point engaging in the second of the three categories of action outlined by Justice Jackson in *The Steel Seizure Cases*. This decision held that executive authority was strongest when it acted with explicit authorization, but that less deference was due when it intervened where the constitution and Congress were silent. Shortly, Nixon would venture into the third category, taking action that exercised powers allotted by the Constitution and which Congress expressly forbade. He did this despite Jackson's admonition that this could never be considered constitutional.[84] Nixon soon resolved to prevail over both Congress and the courts, and to destroy the separation of powers, replacing it with what Theodor Lowi called a "plebiscitary presidency"[85] that was accountable periodically to the electorate, which is incompatible with the rule of law.

Schlesinger and Lowi argued that Nixon intended to create an executive branch that was not accountable to any other part of government, not even theoretically, for violations of citizens' non-derogable rights, but which was only accountable at four-year intervals to the electorate. By the beginning of Nixon's second term, the executive was positioned to do so because it had seized or expanded upon its delegated powers, and because Nixon now refused to recognize any attempts to control his freedom of action or to remove or trim these grants of power. His officials flouted legislative and court oversight by refusing to provide candid testimony, and he later interfered with investigations into his conduct more directly. Nixon developed a theory that purportedly established that he need not comply with laws of which he did not approve. He developed another theory that allowed him to prevent bills that were against his interests from being passed into law. This is the point at which Congress was compelled to resort to sterner measures.

In 1972 Congress began to consider bills that would explicitly require the president to obtain its approval before committing troops to battle,[86] to explicitly forbid actions like Nixon's unilateral invasion of Cambodia. The War Powers Resolution of 1973 gave the executive a sixty-day deadline for obtaining legislative approval for military action.[87] It was "acclaimed as a triumph of congressional self-assertion," but Nixon indicated that he intended to ignore it, as he argued "any attempt to make such alterations [to his purportedly constitutional reserve powers] by legislation alone is clearly without force."[88] In the winter of 1973, the executive again ordered heavy bombing of Cambodia in support of the Lon Nol government, and not merely to protect American troops in Vietnam, relying this time exclusively on a theory of the executive's constitutional powers.[89] In response, Senator J. William Fulbright commented that he "retain[ed] total confidence in the ability of this administration to come up with some specious legal justification ... the Nixon administration has shown that it will not be gotten the better of by anything so trivial as a law."[90]

Nixon's failure to comply with a clear legislative command would await the reckoning of all his unconstitutional actions. However, he was not restrained by the Constitution itself, as it was apparent from its text that he could cite no basis to declare or expand wars, especially against Congress's explicit command. It was now obvious that the legislature needed two things. First, it required much more effective oversight, so that it could remain aware of how the executive was using its powers in an illicit manner even when the administration sought to disguise that fact. Second, it required enforcement mechanisms to call the executive to heel when it was caught abusing its powers. The problem was that the executive exercised delegated powers so great, Congress could not lawfully restrain it.

Congress's Response to Distortions of the Legislative Process

During Nixon's final years as president, Congress finally roused itself to deal with other assertions of unconstitutional executive powers. Two of the most problematic implicated Congress's control over legislation and spending; namely, impoundment and the pocket veto. The first of these challenged the legislature's competence to spend tax monies, a power explicitly committed to Congress by the Constitution's Taxing and Spending Clause.[91] The second challenged Congress's ability to pass any legislation at all, by ignoring the manner in which the Constitution's Presentment Clauses[92] indicated that the legislature could override the president's failure to sign a bill into law.

Nixon followed his predecessors in claiming a right not to spend money that Congress allocated for particular purposes, although he initially claimed that this was justified by the need to balance the federal budget. However, it was clear by 1972 that Nixon was using this process to derail policies that he did not like, even when these were outlined in duly enacted laws, and to assert legislative powers he did not possess in order to reward loyalists and punish his adversaries in Congress, who were increasingly bold in confronting him over his escalation of the conflicts in Indochina. In doing so, Nixon "breached the rule usually followed by his predecessors of avoiding a direct and open flouting of the will of Congress."[93]

"Here, as in other areas, Nixon raised the ante at the outset by defining his powers as inherent and nonnegotiable,"[94] relying on advice from the Office of Legal Counsel (OLC), which argued that "substantial latitude to refuse to spend" flowed from the "executive power vested in [Nixon] by the Constitution."[95] Deputy Attorney General Joseph T. Sneed grounded the president's power on a combination of constitutional and statutory language but left little doubt that in the department's opinion, the inherent powers were sufficient.

While the OLC generally supported the chief executive's positions owing to its status as part of an agency located under his direct control, the of politicization of this office accelerated during the Nixon administration. It argued that "[t]o legislate against impoundment even in the domestic area would deprive the President 'of a substantial portion of the "executive power" vested in him by the Constitution.'"[96] A federal court noted that "if the power sought here were found valid, no barrier would remain to the executive authorizations if he deemed them ... to be contrary to the needs of the nation."[97]

In addition to frustrating congressional policies by impounding duly authorized funds, Nixon attempted to derail the passage of whole acts of legislation when he could, by failing to return bills he refused to sign to Congress so they could attempt to override his veto. This was wholly unprecedented, and had the potential of not merely delaying the passage of the bills but denying Congress any power to legislate entirely.

Article I, section 7 of the Constitution states that the president may either sign a bill into law or return it unsigned to Congress within ten days whenever the legislature is in session. In 1938, the Supreme Court held in *Wright v. United States* that Congress could appoint representatives to accept bills when it was in session but temporarily adjourned.[98] In 1970, however, Nixon decided not to return a bill to Congress after it appointed a representative to receive it, in precisely the manner *Wright* approved.[99] Had he done so, his veto would have been overruled, as this bill was passed in the Senate with a vote of 64 to 1 and in the House of Representatives by 345 to 2, where only two-thirds majorities would be required to override his failure to sign the bill into law.[100] For the first time, but not the last, Nixon asserted that he possessed the power to prevent a unanimous Congress from passing legislation, despite the Constitution explicitly specifying that it possessed the power to override his objections.

This tactic and numerous other measures were elements of "the Nixon revolution [which] aimed at reducing the power of Congress at every point along the line and moving toward rule by presidential decree."[101] This was necessary, since no consensus supporting his policies existed in either Congress or the population as a whole. Indeed, from 1970 onwards his administration was under sustained pressure from continuous protests and other forms of popular resistance.[102] An impasse was on the horizon. The executive was committed to extraconstitutional extensions of its own power, which invaded the legislature's prerogatives. However, this was made possible owing to Congress's failures during the Cold War. Congress gave such broad discretion to the executive that it was unclear whether domestic law allowed the legislature and the courts to survey and regulate the president's activities when he claimed otherwise. However, the full range of the executive's secret and unreviewable powers was yet to come to light. After the full range of discretion and domestic power that flowed from the ability to control the intelligence agencies' clandestine activity became clear, there would be a new sense of urgency to efforts to re-implement the rule of law.

Nixon's Trump Card: Control over the Intelligence Agencies

In order to reinforce his power against his enemies, Nixon turned to the intelligence agencies, which during the Cold War became tools the president could use at his discretion and in secret. He used this power to overturn governments and assassinate unfriendly foreign leaders, while Congress remained blithely unaware. During the early phases of this conflict, many citizens were swept up due to over-inclusive definitions of "subversives" or "threats to national security," but under Nixon these agencies were used to specifically target people for whom he harboured personal animosity, often merely because they threatened his political agenda. These actions were illegal, but they could be undertaken owing to pervasive secrecy. This secrecy was made possible by the lack of congressional oversight.

The executive's unilateral control over the intelligence agencies made possible the most grievous abuses of the Nixon administration, but it also led to his downfall. There is evidence that Nixon made use of his personal control over the secret services from 1970 onwards. In 1970, he ordered the head of the CIA, Richard Helms, to organize a coup in Chile,[103] actions which Kissinger, the president's closest advisor, oversaw personally.[104] Nixon frequently confused constitutionally protected dissent with subversion, and radicalism with communism. The temptation to direct covert action against personal enemies became powerful as his struggle to impose his unilateral will intensified.[105] Nixon's first authorization for illegal wiretapping was a response to leaks about the secret bombing of Cambodia, as he feared, correctly, that this information threatened to reinvigorate the antiwar movement.[106] To justify this activity, his attorney general claimed that the chief executive possessed "inherent presidential power to tap without warrants in the interest of domestic security."[107] Again, the chief executive was relying on self-serving advice from an executive-branch official, although it could be argued that such a prominent figure would want to protect their good name and would thus be restrained from offering strained interpretations of the constitution.

By the time that Nixon sought to wiretap his personal opponents, the Supreme Court had already rejected Nixon's argument that the executive was the only branch competent to decide whether he was using his surveillance powers in the interest of national and domestic security. The likely reason was because the court recognized that the executive's theory of the interpretation of its own powers would reduce the judiciary to irrelevance. In the *Keith* case,[108] the court addressed this issue squarely after John Mitchell refused to disclose the source of electronic surveillance information. Mitchell argued that the applicability of an exception to the requirement for a warrant when "a clear and present danger to the structure or existence of the government"[109] was a question that only the president could decide.

The executive's allegation of an existential threat to the nation appeared quite questionable, however, as the defendants were members of a Detroit collective described as "radical counter-culturalists" who advocated "rock and roll, dope, sex in the streets and the abolishing [sic] of capitalism."[110] The judge at the trial court disagreed with Mitchell's conclusions about unreviewable executive discretion, noting that the lack of disclosure was a critical violation of the defendants' due-process rights, and ordered the information released.[111]

When the appeal reached the Supreme Court, Justice William O. Douglas outlined the stakes of this dispute about the executive's inherent powers, noting that "if the Warrant Clause [of the Fourth Amendment to the Constitution] was held inapplicable here, then the federal intelligence machine would literally enjoy unchecked discretion."[112] The court's unanimous decision was a stinging rebuke to Nixon's constitutional theory that he could interpret the scope of his own powers. The justices understood that this idea was an assault on the rule of law that threatened the court itself. Justice Lewis Powell's opinion held that executive discretion of this sort constituted "unchecked surveillance power," noting the implications of a lack of oversight. Nixon was "saying that the President, on his own motion, could declare – name your favorite poison – draft dodgers, Black Muslims, the Ku Klux Klan, or civil rights activists to be a clear and present danger to the structure or existence of government."[113] Unbeknownst to Justice Powell, this was far more than a *reductio ad absurdum*. The intelligence agencies were monitoring civil rights activists in this manner, as the subsequent revelation of the warrantless wiretapping of Martin Luther King, Jr, would later confirm.[114]

The decision was significant both because of the explicit nature of the president's claims and the fact that the judiciary presented a united front against executive overreaching. The Supreme Court's opinion was not merely a rejection of the executive's contention that it could judge whether its wiretapping fit into a statutory exception allowing it not to seek a warrant; rather, it took a more general view, in line with the requirements of the rule of law. It held that broad "presidential discretion

... is inconsistent with the [Constitution]. Neither the President nor the Attorney General can act as [a] neutral and detached magistrate" when it is in its interest to construe its own powers broadly.[115] The executive branch was stunned by the decision, as "When Keith came to the Court, President Richard Nixon had appointed four new Justices considered to be law-and-order conservatives sympathetic to the President's position on wiretapping. One of those new appointees, Lewis F. Powell Jr., had prior to his appointment penned a controversial op-ed article supporting wiretapping in national security cases a few months before Keith was decided."[116] Both the "public and the press saw this [as] stunning,"[117] but it was predictable from the point of view of functionalist institutional theory. Nixon's arguments directly challenged the court's core justification, its special competence to interpret and adjudicate constitutional disputes, implicitly threatening to reverse *Marbury v. Madison*. No jurist could accept this, not even one who was so inclined to law and order as Lewis Powell.

Nixon had no intention of complying with the court's holding in the *Keith* case. However, faced with the possibility that official records created by the intelligence agencies might be made available to those they prosecuted, Nixon was compelled to create his own secret unit within the White House, which would pursue his personal enemies without obeying even the minimal restrictions that bound the intelligence agencies. Members of this "Special Intelligence Unit," better known as the White House "Plumbers," were later caught breaking in to plant recording devices at the Democratic National Committee's headquarters in the Watergate Hotel, and within a week after their arrests Nixon "approved a plan to have the CIA obstruct the FBI investigation into the burglary."[118] Unfortunately for Nixon, this conversation was conducted within a room that automatically recorded all discussions.

Nixon attempted to withhold the incriminating tapes from the special prosecutor appointed to investigate Watergate, but the Supreme Court ruled against him in *United States v. Nixon*.[119] It is important to note that Nixon used these proceedings to articulate his theory of unchecked executive power, and that the court's rejection of this theory proved vital to the preservation of the rule of law in the United States. If the court had not done so, the executive would have retained the power to determine whether it was in compliance with the requirements of the Constitution. Within such a legal regime, the executive branch would be able to use this power to operate with impunity even when it violated non-derogable rights, as it would then be the judge of its own cause. This is precisely the opposite of what the rule of law requires.

In essence, the court ruled that the president should not be allowed to determine whether the documents are irrelevant or too sensitive to divulge; rather, the judiciary should have the last word when the president asserts a privilege.[120] This is an affirmation of one of the key principles of the separation of powers and the rule of law, that no one should be the judge of their own cause. This decision was a vital step toward the reestablishment of the rule of law in the United States after years of erosion during the Cold War. The Supreme Court again declared that it possessed the power to determine whether the executive was violating citizens' rights. However, the battle would not be won until the legislature followed suit, taking back the delegations of legislative power that far exceeded what the rule of law allows, and re-imposed oversight and legislative regulation of these powers.

Nixon's Resignation as Restoration of the Rule of Law

Congress's attempts to remove Nixon from office were not merely a response to his obstruction of the investigation of the Watergate. The Judicial Committee of the House of Representatives passed the Articles of Impeachment against Nixon for destroying the separation of powers that serves to protect the rule of law in the United States by constraining the executive. Article 2 alleged that he "repeatedly engaged in conduct violating the constitutional rights of citizens" by misusing the intelligence agencies to compile information intended to "prejudice the constitutional right of the accused to fair trial," and that "in disregard of the rule of law, he knowingly misused the executive power."[121] Article 3 states that "in refusing to produce these papers and things [viz., the tapes of incriminating conversations] ... [Nixon] interposed the powers of the Presidency against the lawful subpoenas of the House of Representatives."[122]

This indictment highlighted the fact that Nixon abused the extensive executive powers that it assumed to itself during the Cold War in a manner that impinged upon citizens' constitutional rights, and condemned him for having attempting to avoid the oversight of Congress and the courts when they investigated these abuses. Unfortunately, Nixon denied Congress the opportunity to prove these charges against him by resigning before he could be tried in the Senate. However, a meaningful opportunity to address these abuses presented itself after Nixon's resignation. Congress could take advantage and ensure that the powers that he abused would be permanently denied to the executive. It could also restore meaningful oversight over the executive in the manner that the rule of law requires. Congress did so, and this would constitute a large part of its legislative agenda over the next five years.

The success of this legislative agenda created a new framework for the rule of law. The legislative grants of discretion to the executive branch, particularly in the most dangerous areas, such as control over the military and the intelligence agencies, were now limited and oversight over these limitations was retained by Congress. The legislature and the judiciary also asserted explicitly that the executive would not have the final say over whether it was complying with these restrictions on its powers.

Reimplementation of the Rule of Law, 1974–80

The congressional resurgence that allowed for the reimplementation of the rule of law did not happen overnight. It took concerted action to close all of the loopholes in the broad grants of discretionary power that the executive exploited during the course of the Cold War. However, by the end of this process, both oversight and a means of holding the executive responsible were now guaranteed. This took place over the course of several stages of legislative and judicial action, beginning with the reclamation of the ability to declare war and the destruction of the executive's purported legislative powers.

Even before Nixon's fall, Congress wrested back formal control of war powers from the executive branch. Soon afterwards, Congress, "led by a bipartisan coalition in the Senate, forced Nixon to accept a legislatively imposed cut-off of funding for military activity in Indochina as of August 15, 1973."[123] Congress exercised its power of the purse to terminate

American involvement in Indochina, another bill prevented monies from being used for "reconstruction,"[124] in order to prevent back-channel military funding, and finally, the War Powers Resolution (WPR) served to prevent the creation of another military crisis that would empower the executive. By April 1973, support for further measures wresting control back from the executive branch was quite broad. As Representative Gillis Long stated:

> The President has overstepped the authority of his office in the actions he has taken. Congress will not stand by idly as the President reaches for more and more power … Our message to the President is that he is risking retaliation for his power grabs, that support for the counter-offensive is found in the whole range of congressional membership.[125]

The reckoning arrived later that month, but it did not end with Nixon's resignation. This merely cleared the field for the attempt to subject the executive branch to limitations. "Congress, having battled Nixon the president, was now ready to turn its attention to the institution of the presidency."[126] This was essential, as all of the levers of power that Nixon used to subvert the separation of powers, and thus, the rule of law, remained in place. It appeared to be a matter of time before another president would make the same use of them, thereby imperilling the rule of law and the relevance of the other branches of government. The next phase of the struggle focused on taking control of the legislative process, into which the presidency intruded during the Cold War. The Supreme Court aided Congress in this endeavour. The court consolidated all of the legal challenges to impoundment under the caption of *Train v. City of New York*.[127] The Supreme Court's unanimous ruling against the executive in that case was a "clear defeat for the administration," and other courts interpreted it as holding that "the executive [was] trespass[ing]" into law-making and this could not be permitted, as this would "make impossible the attainment of the legislative goals" set forth by Congress in its bills.[128]

The *Train* decision served to ratify Congress's passing of the Impoundment Control Act,[129] designed to protect the legislature as a "viable institution" in the face of concerted action aimed at creating a "presidential government."[130] The act, combined with the Congressional Budget Act of 1974,[131] put Congress firmly back in control over its spending powers, as the Constitution mandated.[132] Congress "recaptured from the executive its constitutional role in controlling the power of the purse,"[133] that power that allowed Congress to terminate the Vietnam War.

Addressing executive interference within the legislative process was only the beginning of Congress's efforts. Another battle in its campaign to restore the rule of law involved a struggle to impose statutory restrictions on the executive, which would underline the illegality of the type of violations for which Nixon was forced to resign. Alongside this struggle was another related effort to establish the oversight mechanisms that would serve to bring any such violations to its attention. "When the House Select Committee on Committees held its hearings on structural reform of the House of Representatives in 1973, no single weakness commanded more attention than 'the failure ... really to engage ... in anything like the beginning of an adequate oversight function.'"[134] To make it possible for the legislature to police the limits of executive discretion, however, it would first need to set clear limits on these delegated powers, as the rule of law requires.

This Congress accomplished through a series of laws limiting the executive passed between 1974 and 1980, which would then be enforced by a new committee structure. In implementing this reform agenda, Congress created bodies that were specifically charged with ensuring the executive branch did not overstep the boundaries of the powers delegated by the legislature.

Establishing Clear Statutory Limits on Executive Discretion

One of the ways in which the defective separation of powers did not meet the minimum obligations of the rule of law related to the broad grants of discretionary authority by the legislature to the executive during the Cold War. These grants were so broad that it was often impossible to determine if the executive was exceeding its powers, due either to the vagueness of the provisions or the utter failure to specify what the executive could not do in support of these very general directives. Congress brought the executive back into line by passing statutes that clearly specified what the executive could not do; in particular, explicitly barring violations of non-derogable norms, and by creating other laws that would make it impossible for the executive to hide any such abuses.

The Privacy Act of 1974[135] responded to such abuses as Nixon's scrutiny of his enemies' tax returns, which warranted a mention in the Articles of Impeachment, and created limitations on governmental use of private information provided to agencies for limited purposes. Citizens' right to control over these records was further underlined by the 1974 amendments to the Freedom of Information Act.[136] Now citizens could request the files compiled on them by government agencies, even intelligence agencies. It should be noted that the subsequent release of these files shocked many activists and politicians, and helped to build support for a sweeping reform of the intelligence agencies' oversight.

The Privacy Act also confirmed the principle of judicial oversight over executive decisions that affected citizens' rights, as "[j]udicial review of executive determinations that something needed to be kept secret was now authorized," over President Ford's veto of the legislation.[137] This legislation made it more difficult for the executive branch to operate in secret, something which it relied upon when using the intelligence agencies in ways that contradicted relevant statutory law, while avoiding any oversight from Congress. The increased likelihood of abuses being uncovered by individuals targeted by the executive, and the possibility of subsequent congressional investigations and censure, was a clear victory for the rule of law.

In response to Nixon's attempt to exploit statutory exceptions that referred to national emergencies, Congress sought to restrain all of the executive's emergency powers. The clear priority, however, was the emergency power that allowed for the violation of one of citizens' most important non-derogable rights: the right not to be subjected to prolonged arbitrary detention. The Internal Security Act of 1950,[138] which was passed at the beginning of the Cold War, allowed for executive detention of the type to which Japanese Americans were subjected during the Second World War. These provisions, which were also known as the Emergency Detention Act, were never invoked during the Cold War. However, some feared that Nixon might invoke its provisions as protests against the Vietnam War escalated.[139]

Congress was spurred to action by a grassroots movement fearful of Nixon's discretionary power under this statute, which included subjecting American citizens to indefinite detention without trial. These fears were later revealed to be warranted. In 1970, the director of the Federal Emergency Management Agency at the Army War College wrote a report calling for the detention of "up to 21 million 'American Negroes' in the event of a national black militant uprising."[140] Congress passed the Non-Detention Act of 1971,[141] which explicitly barred any and all executive authorization of internment.

The executive branch's powers under the state of emergency declared by Truman in 1950 to invoke discretionary powers were terminated by the National Emergencies Act of 1974.[142] This act also served to prevent any future emergency from becoming indefinite, by requiring the president to justify the declaration of any national emergency to Congress. The legislature asserted its power to override the executive's determination, thereby terminating the broad powers contained in 470 statutes that granted discretion to the executive in the event of a national emergency.[143] The president's ability to order sanctions against foreign nations on his own initiative, which was a simple matter during the pendency of Truman's Declaration of National Emergency, was also limited by the passage of the International Emergency Economic Powers Act of 1977,[144] which was "designed to constrain emergency economic powers over the regulations of international and domestic financial transactions and to limit the latter to periods of declared war."[145]

Presidents were able to use their power to restrain trade with nations they deemed to be enemies of the United States in a manner that took control of foreign policy entirely out of Congress's hands. This state of affairs did not conform to the rule of law, as it invaded the legislature's exclusive prerogative of law-making. Emergency powers also allowed the executive to breach minimal rule of law norms in more dramatic ways, such as when they were used by President Roosevelt to violate the nonderogable rights of Japanese Americans not to be subjected to prolonged arbitrary detention. Accordingly, it was essential that the emergency powers be reformed to conform to the ICJ's criteria.

The Church Committee's Call to Action

Between 1941 and 1973, the executive branch violated citizens' non-derogable rights, calling into serious question whether the United States was a rule of law state. However, these abuses did not come to light until after Watergate, as previously the executive possessed unquestioned and unreviewable control over the intelligence agencies.

When various committees investigated the secret activities of these agencies, the abuses that came to light quickly set off a movement to make the executive branch accountable for its covert affairs. The executive branch did not need to rely upon emergency powers when taking action that violated citizens' fundamental rights if they relied on the intelligence agencies.[146]

There was, however, impetus for intelligence reform in the period immediately following Nixon's resignation, as the Church Committee revealed that these agencies facilitated the White House Plumbers' illegal surveillance, which included providing false identities to the Watergate burglars, and the electronic equipment required for bugging and wiretapping.[147] This momentum would be accelerated significantly by other revelations of unlawful activity, which were repugnant to both the rule of law and popular opinion.

The Committee's Outline of Structural Problems and Solutions

Exposing the problems related to a broad grant of discretionary and un-reviewable authority over the intelligence agencies to the executive would not itself help to bring the United States back into line with the rule of law. In order to subject the executive branch to legislature's oversight and control, the earlier vague and overbroad delegations would need to be repealed. The Church Committee did much, however, to illustrate how vital this reform was to the rule of law.

By the time its final report was published, the committee rejected a theory of renegade intelligence agencies, faulting instead the "senior officials who were responsible for controlling intelligence agencies [who] generally failed to assure compliance with the law" after they "delegat[ed] broad authority" by invoking "national security" or "subversion."[148] Looking back after the committee's findings were supported by other subsequently declassified documents, scholars have concluded that "ultimate responsibility was fixed with presidents, attorneys-general, and other high executive branch officials."[149] In particular, Senator Walter Mondale identified the key problem that led to the abuses detailed in the report as "presidential unaccountability to the law" since "the grant of power to the CIA and these other agencies is, above all, a grant of power to the President."[150] The committee's report made it clear that in allowing unreviewable executive control over the intelligence agencies, the legislature enabled the executive's violation of one of the key norms of the rule of law state.

The Church Committee's ultimate aim was to "determine what secret governmental activities are necessary and how they best can be conducted under the rule of law."[151] In keeping with the American conceptualization of how the rule of law is best protected, the committee proposed legal restraints on the executive's discretion when directing the activities of the intelligence agencies, as "'power must be checked and balanced ... the preservation of liberty requires the restraint of laws, and not simply the intentions of men."[152] However, it remained to Congress as a whole to determine how best it might constrain the executive branch with legal restraints on its discretion and to impose oversight to ensure these limitations were observed. A statutory regime that served these ends would be developed during the four years following the issuance of the Church Committee Report.

The Church Committee understood that the rule of law required that the executive not be able to use the intelligence agencies in secret, as this led to violations of non-derogable rights. In articulating its message clearly, it helped to motivate the legislative reform that re-implemented the rule of law in the United States, a state of affairs that would last until the 9/11 attacks. After this crisis, the statutes passed in response to the Church Committee's report would be the first targets of an executive branch determined to re-establish its dominant position of unreviewable authority, with the secrecy and efficiency of the intelligence agencies used as a rationale for abandoning this statutory regime.

Reforming the CIA, the NSA, and the FBI

The Church Committee's report revealed that the executive's unilateral and unchecked control over the intelligence community allowed it to plan and execute operations that threatened the rule of law in secret. "Unsurprisingly, one of the Committee's main points was the need for clear laws to guide and limit the intelligence agencies. In 1976, the CIA, the NSA, and the FBI all lacked detailed statutory mandates ... the NSA was entirely a creature of executive branch regulations."[153] This meant that since Congress frequently issued to the executive a blank cheque, via a delegation of power merely to use these agencies in the interests of "national security," the executive could create regulations that empowered problematic conduct. When doing so, agency staff began to regard their violations of the law as unproblematic, owing to the fact that this behaviour was not challenged by Congress. However, this sort of challenge was impossible at the time, as the executive insisted that it had the right to withhold the evidence from the legislative committees that nominally possessed the responsibility of oversight. Accordingly, the first step toward crafting delegations of legislative authority for the operations of these agencies that conformed to the ICJ's criteria would be for Congress to create statutory charters outlining clearly what these agencies could and could not do.

One major reform of intelligence activity was the requirement that the NSA's wiretapping would now be comprehensively supervised by the judiciary. This mandate was created by the Foreign Intelligence Surveillance Act of 1978 (FISA).[154] This was in part a reaction to Nixon's argument that he possessed an inherent presidential power to conduct wiretapping in the interest of both national and domestic security, leading to similar abuses as his unwarranted scrutiny of private citizens' tax records. The scale of this abuse was revealed when intelligence records were released pursuant to Freedom of Information Act (FOIA) requests and the Church Committee's subpoenas. Congress's reaction was forceful. Representative William Cohen noted that "[w]hen the chief executive of this country starts to investigate private citizens who criticize his policies ... the rattle of the chains that would bind up our constitutional freedoms can be heard."[155]

Watergate's Wake

While the creation of this new oversight apparatus was a victory in the struggle for the rule of law, the possibility of legislative control did not guarantee that this would be effective. Senator Frank Church opined that while oversight, and, in principle, the power to enforce clear restrictions on the use of these delegated powers and to police any abuses now existed, "[p]olitical will can't be guaranteed. The most we could do was to recommend that permanent surveillance be established. We did that knowing that the Congress being a political animal will exercise its surveillance with whatever diligence the political climate of the time makes for."[156]

That said, in the political climate after Watergate, the political will to supervise and discipline the intelligence agencies was evident. "By the end of the decade [the 1970s] Congress had appeared to have made its point. There could be no more secret wars, no more secret covert operations, not even secret scandals ... the attitude of defiance toward the legislature's claims that characterized the later years of the Nixon administration was gone."[157] It remained to be seen how long this newly restored separation of powers allowing for oversight and control of the executive's use of the intelligence agencies in national security matters would last. At this point it remained unclear whether Congress could weather the storms of a new political climate, in which legislators' attempts to use these powers would be challenged. In particular, during the Reagan administration, exercising this oversight would require them to withstand challenges from a resurgent executive, buoyed by a high level of public support.

The effect of these new legislative oversight mechanisms can best be judged in light of the Iran-Contra scandal. During this time, the executive was prohibited from using the official channels within the intelligence services when it attempted to derail Congress's foreign policy agenda and ignore laws that were passed to prevent unilateral executive action. The legislative branch possessed the capacity to quickly uncover the extent of the wrongdoing, and to hold senior executive officials responsible, in the manner that the rule of law requires to maintain accountability. The executive was now subjected to oversight, which meets the criteria specified at the ICJ Rio and Lagos congresses. The mechanisms proved robust enough to function during a non-emergency period. One question re-mains: after comparing this control to the formal requirements of the ICJ, would they be sufficient during a prolonged crisis, such as that which was inaugurated by the 9/11 attacks?

At the end of this period of resurgence, scholars doubted whether this trend would continue. Writing in 1978, Harvey Zeidenstein argued, "Un-likely in the near term, but not in the more distant future, is the reasser-tion of presidential primacy ... The conditions for this scenario would include one or more of the following: the dimming of Vietnam and Wa-tergate in Congress's institutional memory ... and some severe crisis or emergency ... comparable to the Depression or World War II, in which Congress gave the President virtual carte blanche."[158] Zeidenstein was correct, but although there were many challenges to the framework that was created between 1973 and 1980 during the two decades that would follow (due to events such as the Iran-Contra crisis and the bombing of Serbia),[159] the new legal framework remained largely intact. While these decisions (along with others, such as Reagan's decision to approve covert operations to mine Nicaraguan harbours) were reprehensible, they did not involve assertions that the president had a constitutional power to ignore the laws. Rather, "it is George W. Bush's presidency that provides the clearest, because most openly claimed and aggressively argued, case of presidential unilateralism in the post-Watergate era."[160]

CHAPTER 3

Overbroad Authority Given to and Appropriated by the Executive after the 9/11 Attacks

The 9/11 Attacks as an Opportunity to Empower the Executive

The restoration of the rule of law after Congress and the courts erected clearer legal restrictions on the executive proved relatively stable from 1974 to 2001.[1] (The Iran-Contra affair is an exception that proves the rule, as it was uncovered by Congress and executive branch officials were sent to prison.) However, during this period, members of presidents Nixon's and Ford's senior staffs were unhappy with both the US failure to make aggressive use of its military and the reduced role of the executive during this period of relative peace.[2] This faction, commonly known as the "neo-conservatives,"[3] argued that reasserting constitutional order characterized by the separation of powers and the rule of law was unconstitutional, owing to the limits it placed upon the executive's ability to take action it deemed to be in the interest of national security. These theories are antithetical to the rule of law (especially when considered as an historically rooted response to the problem of arbitrary executive power to violate non-derogable rights). However, the opportunity to unshackle the president from legal restrictions was never as clear as it was in the days following massive terrorist attacks on American soil.

The 9/11 attacks set in motion a remarkably broad delegation from the legislature. This single piece of legislation alone put in question America's compliance with one of the core principles of the rule of law. The legislature's initial grant of authority to the executive was a text that was given a number of expansive glosses in what amounted to executive law-making, in the form of signing statements and the opinions of the Department of Justice's OLC. During this period, unrestrained and unsupervised executive law-making, which was specifically marked out by the ICJ as antithetical to the rule of law,[4] was used to justify radical departures from the most fundamental norms, both international and domestic.

Executive law-making and the assumption of unsupervised emergency powers were not merely aimed at securing freedom of action to violate the aforementioned *jus cogens* norms. Rather, the executive now aimed to succeed where Nixon failed, creating a state of affairs in which the executive would not be accountable to the other branches of government. America's constitutional order risked being abrogated in perpetuity if Congress and the courts did not reassert themselves vigorously.

Executive Resistance to the New Rule of Law

The American rule of law was restored by 1980, owing to the imposition of statutory restraints on the executive and permanent oversight to ensure that vague delegations of power were never again used to violate non-derogable rights, or as part of an attempt to create an unaccountable presidency. While the political climate created by the revelation of the "Watergate horrors" and the Church Committee's report on the gross abuses of the intelligence community created a near consensus that this was necessary, these changes were bitterly resisted by some executive branch officials.[5]

Foremost among those was Dick Cheney, who occupied a number of prominent positions inside the executive branch at key moments in its recent history. This is not only because of his central role in the presidential administration when it was first affected by the congressional resurgence, although this is significant. Cheney was Gerald Ford's chief of staff, "an extraordinarily powerful position"[6] within the executive branch. However, what is even more significant is the fact that while serving in that position, Cheney developed the strategy for the executive's eventual counteroffensive. As vice-president, he would also be the key to putting it into place, after the 9/11 attacks.[7]

Cheney consistently resisted the congressional resurgence and attempted to restore to the executive branch the powers it possessed during the Nixon administration. He was at the centre of a group of officials who would occupy critical positions in the executive branch after the 9/11 attacks, especially in the OLC. This group included Deputy Assistant Attorney General John Yoo and Assistant Attorney General Jay Bybee. Within the Department of Defense, this group included Donald Rumsfeld and Paul Wolfowitz. These men formulated and implemented theories of executive power that are incompatible with the rule of law.

Cheney became White House chief of staff directly following Nixon's resignation. Accordingly, he received "his chance to wield the powers of the presidency from high in the executive branch hierarchy just as those powers had come under fierce assault."[8] On Ford's behalf, Cheney opposed the Freedom of Information Act and the Church committee's attempts to obtain information on the executive's role in the CIA's assassination campaigns.[9] Following the Democrats' return to the White House in 1976, Cheney entered the legislature.

Despite the change of parties occupying the executive branch, Cheney's views on its supremacy remained constant. "Throughout its fights to expand presidential power at the expense of the legislative branch, the White House would find no greater ally than Representative Cheney."[10] He acted in this capacity most notably when the other branches of government, exercising an oversight and accountability-creating function essential to the rule of law, investigated and punished the executive for the Iran-Contra affair.

Cheney's Minority Report on Iran-Contra and Its Significance

The majority report of Congress's Iran-Contra Committee was clear on the wrongfulness of the executive's conduct. It noted, "The common ingredients of the Iran and Contra policy were secrecy, deception, and disdain for the law." The culpable officials "undermined a cardinal principle of the Constitution" and the "most significant check on Executive power."

Executive "officials viewed the law not as setting boundaries for their actions, but raising impediments to their goals. When the goals and the law collided, the law gave way."[11] Cheney, however, broke ranks with his own party leadership in disavowing the report and its conclusions.[12]

In doing so, Cheney revived theories about inherent presidential power that dated to the Nixon administration.[13] Like Nixon, Cheney argued that Congress and the courts simply possessed no authority to operate a check on the presidency when he purported to act in the interests of national security. It must be remembered that Nixon stated that "any action a President might authorize in the interests of national security would be lawful."[14] This position was unconstitutional, and it was fundamentally antithetical to the rule of law that it protects.[15] Ignoring this, Cheney argued that his position simply must be constitutional, as he held that the imperatives of national security required a concentration of power within the executive branch.[16]

Using this reasoning, Cheney condemned all the statutes that set limits on the executive branch's actions in the field of national security, particularly when this involved the intelligence agencies. He argued, "[T]he President has the authority, without statute, to [order covert operations] … Congress cannot … invade an inherently presidential power."[17] This meant that any statutes or court orders to the contrary could simply be ignored. The Iran-Contra Minority Report that Cheney commissioned made it clearer what these inherent powers entailed. According to the report "the Constitution allocated 'powers of deployment and use of force,' as well as 'negotiations, intelligence gathering, and other diplomatic communications,'" and accordingly, the "'president's inherent powers' … allowed the executive to act 'when Congress was silent and even, in some cases, where Congress had prohibited an action.'"[18]

This reasserted Nixon's view, which was contrary to the Supreme Court's decision in *The Steel Seizure Case*, the Articles of Impeachment, the Constitution itself, and by numerous statutes passed after Watergate.[19] Furthermore, if Nixon and Cheney were correct, then there would be no rule of law in the United States, at least according to the ICJ's definition; the executive would be able to make its own rules, which were given the force of law. The executive would also be able to ignore the other branches that were charged with supervising the constitutionality of the exercise of the rules and emergency powers that it invoked.[20] However, before the 9/11 attacks Cheney was in the minority, even within his own party. Indeed, the senior Republican senator on the Iran-Contra Committee described Cheney's report as "pathetic."[21]

Despite the unpopularity of his views, Cheney persisted in advocating them. He also made the claim that the WPR is unconstitutional, despite it merely reiterating in more flexible terms what is found in the Constitution's Declare War Clause.[22] Extending his view that the president possessed a "constitutionally protected power of withholding information from Congress,"[23] which would make the legislative oversight the rule of law requires impossible, he argued that the executive could launch covert operations and initiate military action without informing Congress, as only the president can decide "when it is safe to tell Congress about them."[24] "Cheney hence rejected any legislative limits on executive power in national security matters."[25] As Nixon's resignation under threat of impeachment made clear, the executive might apply the convenient label of "national security matters" to any program it might undertake, even if what was envisioned was a mass violation of citizens' non-derogable rights in support of a drive to elevate the executive above all legal limitations. This is simply a rejection of the rule of law. Consistent with these views, Secretary of Defense Cheney counselled President George H.W. Bush to ignore the constitutional requirements for the use of force that the WPR merely reiterated. He "urged Bush to launch the Gulf War without asking Congress for authorization."[26]

In Cheney's and Nixon's views of inherent presidential reserve powers, this was acceptable, but this does not answer the question of why this was desirable. Cheney's unpublished writings provide the key. In them, he argued that Congress does not like to authorize war, and accordingly the "War Powers Act tilt[s] the balance away from a patient, measured application of force either toward a quick strike or inaction."[27]

For this argument to be logically valid, one must make explicit the hidden premise; namely, that war (or, as Cheney euphemistically described it, the "measured application of force") is desirable. Once that is granted, the argument for expansive executive powers can be reformulated as a complete syllogism. The second premise is that the executive is more likely to use the power to declare war than the legislature. The conclusion is that the executive must have been given the power to commit the nation's troops to battle, despite the law to the contrary. However, the desirability of war is a minority view, but it was advocated by a number of former executive branch officials and foreign policy experts who returned to prominence shortly before the 9/11 attacks.

The Project for the New American Century and Its Blueprint for Executive Supremacy in Foreign Policy

To understand why Cheney believed that war was desirable, one must turn to the discourse of the neo-conservative policymakers with whom he is closely associated. Many other executive branch officials from the Nixon and Reagan years are on record supporting Cheney's view, as signatories of the report "Rebuilding America's Defenses: Strategies, Forces, and Resources for a New Century," commissioned by a think tank known as the Project for the New American Century (PNAC). The drafters and signatories included many who would return to power in the George W. Bush administration: Cheney, Donald Rumsfeld, deputy director of the Defense Department Paul Wolfowitz, chairman of the Defense Policy Board Advisory Committee Richard Perle, and under-secretary of state for arms control and international security affairs John Bolton, among many others.[28]

The report argued that war is desirable whenever America's pre-eminent position in global affairs is challenged, or merely when its interests are threatened. It must do so, the report argues, because this is the most effective means by which the United States can maintain its hegemony, which, its authors argued, was imperilled. Accordingly, PNAC's report contained "plans for an era of American global domination, for the emasculation of the UN, and an aggressive war against Iraq."[29] It noted that to achieve this goal, what was needed was principally "a foreign policy that boldly and purposefully promotes American principles abroad; and national leadership that accepts the United States' global responsibilities."[30] However, the authors mentioned the inertia that would make it difficult for Congress to authorize "simultaneous major theater wars";

progress toward that goal would be slow "absent some catastrophic and catalyzing event – like a new Pearl Harbor."[31]

When George W. Bush was elected, there was no sign of such an event on the horizon. The crisis precipitated by the arrival of such an event would be all the more useful an opportunity for the executive branch, or at the least for those officials who wanted to disregard the rule of law after it was re-established by the congressional resurgence. These officials wished to re-create a state of affairs in which the executive was unbounded by the laws and free of any oversight from the legislature.

Impetus for Executive Authority after 9/11

President Bush was elected in 2000 after a campaign in which he "spoke frequently of the diminution of presidential power," something which he pledged to oppose, saying, "I'm not going to let Congress erode the power of the executive branch. I have a duty to protect the executive branch from legislative encroachment."[32] Bush's press secretary clarified that this meant he "wanted to restore ... the executive authority that the President had been able to exercise."[33] However, the controversial circumstances of his victory[34] were such that he did not possess much political capital in the first phase of his presidency. In addition, Bush was confronted with the Democratic majority in the House of Representatives, and with a Democratic minority in the Senate that was large enough to prevent bills from passing, owing to the Senate's complex rules for invoking cloture.[35]

This stalemate ended abruptly on 11 September 2001. It is difficult to exaggerate the American public's immediate and overwhelming response to the events of that day. To say that the national psyche plunged into a profound state of shock would not be an overstatement. On 9/11:

Rumors flew as people stayed glued to their television sets and their cellphones, watching endless replays of the crumbling towers – of the desperate people on the upper floors leaping to their deaths ... speculation was reported [on television] as widely as fact. Were

there more targets? Was Washington burning? Media reports suggested car bombs at the State Department and fires on the Mall,
with tens of thousands dead in New York.[36]

One must remember that not only was the United States unaccus-
tomed to sizeable terrorist attacks, a substantial portion of its population believed that their nation was unassailable. For over two centuries,
its home continent was safe from attack from its enemies. Many of its
citizens attributed this to divine providence.[37] It seemed as if the majority of the populace was suffering from post-traumatic stress disorder for
months afterwards, existing in a state where even the briefest and most
oblique reminders of the events of 9/11 could bring back the terror they
experienced that day, such that "television producers rushed to digitally
remove the Twin Towers [of the World Trade Center] from segments shot
before 9/11 to be aired later. They feared the viewers would be trauma-
tized ... by the sight of the towers."[38] This state of anxiety was amplified
by what seemed to be a new phase of attacks using weapons of mass destruction. Panic ensued after weaponized anthrax was discovered in letters at various locations, along with the message "09-11-01 This is next
take penacilin [sic] now death to America death to Israel Allah is great."[39]

Predictably, a frightened and angry population rallied behind President
Bush. In his first speech after the attacks, he announced the inauguration
of what he described as an epic battle between the forces of good and
evil, which he was to lead: "I will not forget the wound to our country
and those who inflicted it. I will not yield, I will not rest, I will not relent in
waging this struggle for freedom and security for the American people."[40]

A week before the attacks, Bush's approval ratings were at approximately 50 per cent of the electorate. After the speech, they were at approximately 90 per cent. One of the most liberal American legislators
conceded that in the wake of this speech, the president possessed support
for almost "anything that he wants to do."[41]

The 9/11 attacks were precisely the catalyst that the PNAC report contemplated, allowing the two interconnected objectives detailed by Cheney
to be realized: stronger executive power and a new era of war. "The un-
folding crisis provided an opportunity to expand presidential power"[42]
and much like the attacks on Pearl Harbor, they cleared the way for in-

volvement in a war that had seemed unthinkable only days before. The PNAC report's authors and signatories quickly understood this opportunity. "[E]ven as the Pentagon building was still burning on the morning of September 11 … [Secretary of Defense] Donald Rumsfeld told his aide Stephen Cambone … 'Hard to get a good case. Need to move swiftly. Near term target needs – go massive – sweep it all up, things related and not.'"[43] These notes, released ten years later, after a FOIA request, appear to indicate that Rumsfeld was aware that the executive, if it moved swiftly to take advantage of the new political climate, would be able to strike targets, like Iraq, that were unrelated to the terrorist attacks.

This interpretation is confirmed by comments Richard Clarke, the national coordinator for counterterrorism, made about a meeting held on 12 September 2001: "At first I was incredulous that we were talking about something other than getting al Qaeda. Then I realized … that Rumsfeld and Wolfowitz were going to try to take advantage of this national tragedy to promote their agenda about Iraq."[44] This would be a difficult endeavour, as a drive for an aggressive war unrelated to the 9/11 attacks produced a significant antiwar movement, which threatened this agenda and the administration itself, just as the anti–Vietnam War movement threatened Nixon's. War could empower the executive but it also might bring about the end of an administration.[45]

Cheney, a keen student of executive power in American history, was determined not to repeat Nixon's mistakes. This would be vital, as the executive branch now led the nation toward what the neo-conservative executive branch officials understood to be an open-ended era of warfare, against not only those who sponsored terrorism but those who stood in the way of continued global hegemony. Nixon understood how war could empower the executive. During the Vietnam War, he almost succeeded in becoming permanently unaccountable to the law and to the other branches of government, in a manner that violated the fundamental norms of the rule of law. However, he did not use the tools of repression effectively against his opponents, and this led to his downfall.[46]

Nixon had deemed wiretapping, harassment, and the threat of widespread arbitrary detention necessary, but they created a backlash from the other branches of government. If these powers could instead be obtained from Congress, a key source of opposition could be pre-empted.

The key would be to obtain authorizations for the use of force and other measures that were much more explicit than the Gulf of Tonkin Resolution, a slender legislative reed upon which Nixon relied to his detriment.[47] The executive would seek that authorization on the day following the 9/11 attacks, in the form of what appeared merely to be an authorization for the use of military force, but which the executive would subsequently argue allowed for all the aforementioned Nixonian measures, which would have taken the United States outside of the rule of law if the other branches of government had not intervened.

The Authorization for Use of Military Force (2001)

The key piece of legislation delegating broad and vague powers to the executive branch was passed within days of the 9/11 attacks.[48] The legislative history of the Authorization for the Use of Military Force of 2001 (AUMF) reveals that the executive branch attempted to shape the discretion they were accorded such that it would effectively free it of any restrictions whatsoever. The AUMF, despite being narrower than initially envisioned when passed, was ultimately invoked in defence of purportedly implicit delegations of incredible power; however, in its original form presented to Congress on 12 September 2001, it is strikingly broad.[49]

"The language ... prepared by the White House ... would have given the President power to deter and pre-empt future acts of terrorism or aggression against the United States."[50] "It would have seemingly authorized the President, without durational limitation, and at his sole discretion, to take military action against any nation, terrorist group or individuals in the world, without having to seek further authority from Congress."[51] This formulation would have effectively handed the executive branch the power to declare war in perpetuity. The president would not have needed the approval of Congress to go to war in Iraq, or indeed to invade any other nation, if he indicated that he believed that it would "pre-empt aggression," whether this might come from the distant future or in forms of aggression that fall short of traditional *casus belli*.[52]

It should be noted that this would have constituted a delegation of power broad enough to allow the executive to wage aggressive war, something known since Nuremburg as the "supreme international crime."[53] It would also have allowed the executive to do so on its own initiative, in any situation where the executive saw fit to rely on its theory of pre-emptive self-defence, which was itself a gross distortion of fundamental norms of international law. President Bush also asserted that he possessed constitutional power to do that exactly that, even without congressional approval. This claim was later set forth in the National Security Strategy of the United States published on 17 September 2002:

> [T]he first duty of the United States Government remains what it always has been: to protect the American people and American interests. It is an enduring American principle that this duty obligates the government to anticipate and counter threats, using all elements of national power, before the threats can do grave damage … To forestall or prevent such hostile acts by our adversaries, the United States will, if necessary, act preemptively in exercising our inherent right of self-defense. The United States will not resort to force in all cases to preempt emerging threats.[54]

The executive did not succeed in its effort to convince Congress to rubber-stamp its theory of a constitutional reserve power that would allow the executive to commit the nation to "pre-emptive" warfare. This would make it necessary for the executive to attempt to create additional sources of authority that surpassed even the broad statutory delegation. Significantly, "Congress limited the scope of the President's authorization to use military force … to military actions against only those international terrorists and other parties directly involved in and aiding or materially supporting' the 9/11 attacks."[55] It also added that "[n]othing in this resolution supersedes any requirement of the War Powers Resolution."[56]

In this manner, Congress avoided a "wholesale, perpetual delegation of the war power."[57] However, even this limited delegation of power may not be compatible with the rule of law's requirement that such delegations of power must be carefully constrained and scrutinized after the fact. What was clear even as this bill was passed is that the executive sought complete freedom of action, by seeking to insert language that would prevent

Congress from questioning the way in which it exercised the unfettered discretion that it sought.

When the Senate was preparing to pass a bill that trimmed the authorization to those who instigated or supported the 9/11 attacks, the executive attempted to broaden its scope in another key fashion: it tried to obtain authority to use military force and authorize military detention inside the United States, in a manner that had been explicitly foreclosed by various statutes, some of which responded to Nixon's abuses, such as the Non-Detention Act (and others, such as the Posse Comitatus Act of 1878,[58] which were even more firmly rooted in American law).[59]

It is telling how the executive attempted to use the political environment created by the fresh crisis to achieve its objective, which purportedly created substantial time pressures. The Senate voted on the bill after only two of its members spoke on it.[60] With respect to the executive's drive to obtain authorization to employ the military within the United States, former Senate majority leader Thomas Daschle noted that

> [l]iterally minutes before the Senate cast its vote, the administration sought to add the words "in the United States and" after "appropriate force" [against those nations, organizations of persons he determines planned, authorized or committed or aided the terrorist attacks] in the agreed-upon text. This last-minute change would have given the President broad authority to exercise expansive powers not just overseas – where we all understood he wanted authority to act – but right here in the United States, potentially against American citizens.[61]

Congress rejected this and accordingly the AUMF does not supersede those earlier restrictions on the use of military force within the United States. However, this clear legislative history would not prevent the executive from arguing that it contained an implicit authorization for this action.

The AUMF was not the blank cheque for war the executive sought, which it would later claim could be found in other sources of law. It also did not free the executives from the constraints of the War Powers Resolution, the Non-Detention Act, and other explicit protections against the executive taking on powers that would give it unlimited discretion without any possibility of effective oversight or control by the other branches of government.[62] Nevertheless, the AUMF was a victory for an executive intent on obtaining significant freedom of action after the 9/11 attacks.

First, it should be noted that Congress authorized military force against non-state actors, something that was "unprecedented in American history, with the scope of its reach yet to be determined."[63] This allowed the executive to continue to use military force for a longer period; it also allowed the executive to create a political climate that was conducive to its attempts to expand its own powers at the expense of the rule of law. Second, Congress authorized the executive to take action against countries, organizations, and individuals that were yet to be determined.[64]

This second feature of the bill was problematic in itself, but the breadth of the discretion granted to the executive is even more notable. One must note that it was the executive alone who was given the authority to make this the central decision about military action. The AUMF explicitly states that "the President is authorized to use force against" those "he determines" to have been involved with the 9/11 attacks. While the members of Congress believed that they were authorizing a limited campaign against those who were responsible for one particular terrorist attack, and, possibly, Afghanistan as the nation that harboured them,[65] the bill's language made it possible for the executive to expand this into approval of a broader struggle, much as the Gulf of Tonkin Resolution empowered Nixon to escalate hostilities far beyond what was envisioned by the legislators who approved it. However, Bush now possessed significantly more legal authorization for his actions.[66]

For the AUMF to serve the purposes that the executive envisioned, as evidenced by the original draft presented to the legislature, the executive would need to find a way to ignore its explicit words. By the beginning of the Bush administration, a set of infrequently applied techniques now existed that would allow the executive to put the laws into force as the executive wished they read, rather than according to their actual text.[67] These were the signing statement and the OLC memorandum.

Executive Law-Making Construing the AUMF

Cheney, along with the other veteran executive branch officials who returned to the White House in the Bush administration, understood the levers of power that the executive could use against Congress, many of which emulated the Nixonian strategies that placed the United States outside of the boundaries of the rule of law.[68] As was the case with the Gulf of Tonkin Resolution,[69] the AUMF could be construed to imply authorization for many activities that it did not explicitly mention.[70] The executive's goal would be to direct its officials to interpret the document as the president and his close advisors indicated. As these officials took their orders from the president, this was a simple matter.[71] The difficulties would lie in making these implausible interpretations of this legislation appear authoritative, and where this was impossible, keeping these secret. There are two main methods by which the executive can frustrate or subvert Congress's legislative intention. The first is the signing statement, wherein the executive purports to reveal the true construction of a bill that Congress just passed. In these statements, the executive purportedly clarifies how the law it describes should be executed.[72]

The signing statement as a formal tool of statutory interpretation was developed in order that this process might appear to produce a document that had the status of law, as the executive purportedly fixes a single authoritative meaning to the supposedly ambiguous statute at one point in time, rather than as it sees fit on a case-by-case basis.[73] However, the signing statement can be more opaque than the law it purports to interpret. This allows the executive great discretion, such that it can be said that it used an illicit procedure to make law, in such a way that it regains unfettered freedom of action to act against the wishes of the other branches of government, thus destabilizing the rule of law.

The second method of executive law-making to expand upon the AUMF is the use of the memoranda of the Department of Justice's OLC. While these memoranda might embellish the interpretations the executive gave to legislation, the executive branch's internal memoranda were given the status of laws within the executive, despite this being extraconstitutional. This allowed the OLC to write memoranda that could go even further than signing statements in frustrating Congress's intent. Following

Cheney's logic, which vitiated that of Justice Jackson in *The Steel Seizure Case*, the executive encouraged the OLC to write memoranda that directly contradicted what the legislature ordered, thus allowing the president to do what Congress prohibited.

Both of these methods were used to construe the AUMF in a number of problematic ways, which contradict both the ICJ's limitation on executive law-making and the requirement that the executive be accountable to the other branches of government. If the legislature and the judiciary did not react adequately to these attempts by the executive to make laws that effectively gave it unfettered discretion, then the United States cannot be considered a rule of law state, as in that situation the executive would be able to commit violations of citizens' non-derogable rights with impunity.

The Development and Use of Presidential Signing Statements

Signing statements are letters written by the president that in certain cases are attached to bills when he elects to sign those bills into law. Until Ronald Reagan's presidency, these statements did not purport to have any legal significance; rather, they served only a rhetorical purpose. Only 75 statements were issued over the course of the two centuries that preceded his inauguration. After Reagan revitalized the practice, he, George H.W. Bush, and Bill Clinton together issued 247 signing statements. Assistant Attorney General Walter Dellinger noted that at this point, they were no longer being issued for a rhetorical purpose, but were used to order the executive branch in a contentious manner, either by shaping the interpretation of key terms in the law, or by asserting that the law should not be enforced owing to its purported unconstitutionality.[74] Both of these new uses are in conflict with the rule of law.[75] This became apparent when President Bush used them after the 9/11 attacks to define the scope of his powers under the AUMF to act in the interests of national security.

His using signing statements was notable in terms of both the purposes of these statements and their sheer volume. "Bush ... broke all records, using signing statements to challenge about 1,200 sections of bills over his eight years in office, about twice the number challenged by all previous presidents combined." This figure was eighty times more than the combined total of all the statements issued before the Reagan administration.[76] In addition, Bush claimed explicitly that "his constitutional power as head of the executive branch gives him the right" to do so.[77] Signing statements have a dual role. They allow the president to signal his intention that he will not execute the statute as written, and they also allow him to articulate a controversial theory of his powers under the Constitution. Both are problematic, both in theory and in practice. The precedent set by Bush was embraced by Obama, who has outpaced every president other than his predecessor,[78] and used them in a manner that is just as problematic.

The American president plays a limited role in the legislative process: to sign or veto bills, and to propose laws. Scholars point out that "the Framers took great pains to limit and qualify this power through the painstaking process of enactment, [which was] embodied in Article I, section 7, clause 2."[79] These "[e]xplicit and unambiguous provisions of the Constitution prescribe and define the respective functions of the Congress and of the Executive in the legislative process."[80] The Constitution also assigns him the duty to *faithfully* execute the laws.[81] The use of the signing statement as means of making law, in particular by nullifying legislation, is inconsistent with the separation of powers that is at the heart of both the Constitution and the rule of law's mandate. This practice grants to the executive a legislative power far in excess of what the Constitution granted; namely, the power to propose and veto bills.

The Signing Statement of the AUMF and Its Significance

Given that the AUMF gave the executive very broad powers to declare war and expand it, it may seem surprising that it was deemed necessary to widen the scope of this delegation by means of a signing statement. Despite this fact, the executive did issue a significant signing statement. To adequately understand the executive's drive to become paramount and unaccountable after 9/11, which centred on the tacit declaration of an open-ended era of war, one must first be clear on the importance of the statement appended to the AUMF.

As usual, the statement purports merely to explain the text of the legislation. In fact, it expanded the executive's freedom of action significantly. Whereas the AUMF itself gives the executive freedom to use the military without oversight, it at least attempted to define some limits to such uses of force, by specifying that the executive was authorized to target only the nations involved in the 9/11 attacks, or in sheltering the perpetrators. On the contrary, the signing statement claimed that the AUMF "recognizes the seriousness of the terrorist threat to our Nation" without noting that the statute was not a response to the threat of terrorism in general, but rather that it referred to the acts of one terrorist group in particular: al Qaeda. The signing statement goes on to state that the AUMF is a response to the nation's commitment not merely to "a direct, forceful, and comprehensive response to these terrorist attacks," but also to a military response to "the scourge of terrorism against the United States *and its interests*."[82]

The AUMF Signing Statement: Authority over the Residuum of al Qaeda The signing statement unshackles the legislative authorization for military force directed at al Qaeda from any restrictions, whether these relate to time or space. Insofar as any attack that influences the global markets has an impact on the United States, terrorism in any corner of the globe can then be said to threaten that nation's interests. Accordingly, the signing statement effectively transforms an authorization for attacks against a specific set of wrongdoers into a charter for unlimited war.

This interpretation did not end with the Bush administration. Indeed, there is ample evidence that the Obama administration has embraced this vision of a war on terror as articulated by Bush's signing statement, which was not repealed or otherwise disavowed. The best evidence of this proposition stems from the speech of Jeh Johnson, general counsel of the Department of Defense, at the Oxford Union on 30 November 2012. In this address, Johnson states that the war against al Qaeda "'and associated forces' is an unconventional conflict, against an unconventional enemy, and will not end in conventional terms." It should be noted that the term *associated forces* is not in the AUMF. Despite this absence, this term plays an increasingly important role in the executive's arguments that it is empowered to use military force worldwide on its own initiative.

Johnson goes on to rule out how the "war against terror" might end. He states, "I can offer no prediction about when this conflict will end, or whether we are, as Winston Churchill described it, near the 'beginning of the end.'" He then details what criteria the executive branch would use to decide whether it has destroyed the enemy, at which point a war would presumably be considered won. "[T]here will come a tipping point – a tipping point at which so many of the leaders and operatives of al Qaeda and its affiliates have been killed or captured, and the group is no longer able to attempt or launch a strategic attack against the United States."

The AUMF Signing Statement's Creation of al Qaeda Affiliates Johnson's criteria would seem to put some meaningful limit on the war on terror, even if it still lies entirely within the executive branch's discretion to determine whether this "tipping point" has been reached. However, close attention to this sentence reveals this to be an illusion. The key problem is the inclusion of the word *affiliates*. The executive, in both the Bush and Obama administrations, has affixed this label to groups that have no connection to those responsible for the 9/11 attacks. For instance, the terrorist group known as al-Shabaab was deemed by the executive to be an affiliate of al Qaeda, although the group is an indigenous offshoot of one of the factions in Somalia's civil war. It is difficult to take seriously the claim that this group presents a threat of a "strategic attack" to the United States, of the type contemplated by the AUMF.

Furthermore, al-Shabaab was only designated a terrorist group in 2008.[83] According to the intelligence agencies within the executive branch, it then merely "affiliated" with a set of individuals that had no direct connection to the 9/11 attacks. That latter group is known as Ansar al-Sharia/al Qaeda in the Arabian Peninsula, which comprises primarily Yemeni tribesmen. However, as al-Shabaab was a designated terrorist group, which already was being subjected to sustained drone strike campaigns before this purported affiliation with Ansar al-Sharia, this affiliation was used to justify the prior use of military force directed against it retroactively.

The executive's freedom of action in designating "affiliates" of new franchises of al Qaeda is facilitated by the fact that it is very difficult to determine whether reports that clandestine groups did in fact identify with al Qaeda are drawn from objective sources, or whether they simply represent the say-so of the intelligence agencies the executive controls.

Similar comments could be made about purported affiliates in locations such as Mali, Niger, and Nigeria. Experts in area studies have also questioned the executive's assertion that these groups should be considered affiliates of al Qaeda,[84] rather than merely threats to the United States' omnipresent regional interests.

Al Qaeda and its affiliates are like Theseus's ship: its parts are replaced repeatedly, but it sails on. The question of whether it should be considered to be the same organization is never asked, despite the very tenuous relationship between, for example, a Tuareg guerrilla movement challenging the government of Mali and the group of largely Saudi terrorists who executed the 9/11 attacks. By introducing the idea that the AUMF applies equally to the "affiliates," the signing statement made possible a series of low-intensity wars on multiple continents. Finally, the United States has broadened its reach even further by claiming that the AUMF's authorization also applies to "associated forces," which are not even affiliates of that group, but which have "entered the fight alongside al Qaeda and are co-belligerent with al Qaeda in hostilities against the U.S. or its coalition partners," a definition that now expands America's "interests" to encompass those of its allies.

This is a far cry from the relevant statutory text, which is the actual grant of discretionary authority. If the executive continues to be able to make this argument about "affiliates" and "associated forces," then there may never be an end to the general declaration of war against terror that the executive crafted out of the AUMF in its signing statement. One prominent legal scholar commenting on Johnson's speech noted that the "AUMF [as construed by the executive] identifies the affiliates of al-Qaida as the enemy, as well as al-Qaida itself ... As long as those affiliates remain in existence, the United States will be at war with them. And because 'al-Qaida' has become a kind of brand that any group can lay claim to, al-Qaida affiliates will be around as long as radical Islam is."[85] On this basis, the war on terror, itself an expansion of delegated powers that offended the rule of law, was thereby expanded into a war against an ideology, which can be defined ever more broadly by the executive.

It should also be noted that this interpretation does not only authorize limited attacks such as drone strikes against members of these groups. The AUMF's construal to allow military force to be used against these affiliates also purportedly allows for conventional wars to be waged against any nation that the executive concludes is sheltering a member of this proliferating and unlimited set of terrorist groups. For example, as of 2015 the executive uses this rationale to engage in combat operations in Yemen, despite the international community's consensus that the internal conflict in that country does not justify the use of military force.[86]

Before discussing the use of OLC memoranda that would construe the AUMF as allowing for the invasion of Iraq, torture, indefinite arbitrary detention, and extrajudicial killing, one final comment must be made about the AUMF text and the signing statement expounding upon it. Both of these documents appear to recognize inherent executive reserve powers under the Constitution, though these do not appear in the text.

The AUMF's final "whereas" clause states that "the President has authority under the Constitution to prevent acts of international terrorism." This is likely a reflection of the uncontroversial belief that the president has some limited reserve powers in an emergency to act when time is of the essence and Congress cannot react in a timely manner. The signing statement broadens this power. It states that "the authority of the President under the Constitution [is] to deter and prevent acts of terrorism against the United States," implying that the executive may act even when the threat is not immediate.

This second statement reiterates what Cheney and other officials in the Nixon and Ford administrations said about the WPR: that it was an "unconstitutional invasion" of executive prerogative. This should be considered a fringe theory (despite its popularity in some circles since Attorney General Edwin Meese adopted an extreme version of the Vesting Clause thesis), as it has no jurisprudential support and contradicts the text of the Constitution's Declare War Clause, and the explanation of its principal author, James Madison.[87] Congress recognized after the Vietnam War how executive discretion to start wars was entirely incompatible with the rule of law; executive declarations of war would once again destabilize the separation of powers.

The AUMF and its signing statement inaugurated a new crisis for the rule of law in the United States. The document has the characteristics of both the 1950 declaration of a national emergency and the Gulf of Tonkin Resolution. The former strengthened the executive immeasurably, while the latter gave the executive vague and unspecified powers to create wars and crises. The second set of powers allows the executive to create favourable conditions for adopting even broader authority, and to remove itself from other branches' control.

OLC Memoranda Construing the AUMF and Their Significance

The OLC "has been deemed 'the most important governmental office you've never heard of.'"[88] It functions like a private law firm, with the president as its only client. Accordingly, it often presents the president with aggressive interpretations of the law that suit his own purposes. Many signing statements, for example, followed after OLC memoranda stated that so-called intrusions into the exclusive domain of the executive branch were unconstitutional.[89] However, these memoranda can function as a sword as well as a shield.[90] They may advise the president that he need not heed the laws as they are written. This has been described as a "'Get Out of Jail Free Card' for the party seeking the opinion."[91] OLC memoranda can also specify the particular interpretation of the law that will govern, despite Congress's intentions to the contrary.

The possibility of executive law-making by the OLC is particularly problematic because this office is both unaccountable to Congress and a highly politicized body. The head of the agency and all four of his deputies are political appointees of the current president. The tenure of the attorneys who serve under these appointees is generally shorter than that of the president.[92] This politicization and the self-serving legal interpretations that it fosters are exacerbated by the fact that these opinions are confidential, protected by assertions of "deliberative prerogative" and attorney-client privilege, despite the fact that they may purport to make law, in addition to opining upon it.[93]

That said, it is best to begin a survey of the OLC memoranda with a description of how they can serve the president and his agents in a defensive capacity. As a former head of the OLC opined:

It is practically impossible to prosecute someone who relied in good faith on an OLC opinion, even if the opinion turns out to be wrong … OLC speaks for the Justice Department, and it is the

Justice Department that prosecutes violations of criminal law. If
the OLC interprets a law to allow a proposed action, then the Justice Department won't prosecute those who rely on the OLC ruling.
Even independent counsels would have trouble going after someone who reasonably relied on one ... It is one of the most momentous and dangerous powers of the government.[94]

OLC memoranda, purportedly interpreting the AUMF, were used to
authorize the violation and protect the violators of numerous non-
derogable rights. However, these memoranda were also used for a more
fundamental and troubling purpose: to prolong and expand the state of
emergency that allowed the executive to assume further powers. One particular claim of this nature found in the OLC memoranda was the argument that the AUMF allowed the executive to order the invasion of Iraq
without further authorization from Congress.[95] This was done to build
support for an aggressive war and with the additional aim of destabilizing the rule of law.

OLC Memoranda Authorizing an Invasion of Iraq

As was the case before the 1990–91 Gulf War, Dick Cheney resisted the
suggestion that the executive should obtain an authorization for the use
of military force from Congress. Bush administration officials were candid about their reasons for avoiding this, at least when speaking anony-
mously, saying: "We don't want to be in the legal position of asking
Congress to authorize the use of force when the President already has
that full authority."[96] The executive was able to take this position because of the memoranda of its own lawyers.

First, they argued that the AUMF "encompassed such action," and second, that the executive possessed reserve constitutional powers that
would allow it to do this on its own initiative, were this not the case.[97]
The first argument was quite problematic, as it rested on the administration's claims that Saddam Hussein's regime was sheltering members of al
Qaeda, which did not appear even minimally plausible, owing to the well-
documented animosity between the Baathist regime and Islamism.[98]

Despite this implausibility, the executive argued that Hussein was
sheltering "terrorists," and noted that the signing statement did not limit

the use of military force to only those individuals involved in planning and executing the 9/11 attacks. This was a rather poor justification, as it turned out that the "terrorists" to which the executive referred were members of Mujahedin-e Khalq, a group that focused its efforts exclusively on overthrowing the Islamist regime in Iran.[99] The executive settled upon the theory that Iraq was planning terrorist attacks against the United States, which the signing statement purportedly authorized the president to pre-empt, no matter where they might originate. It was argued that this attack might involve the nonexistent weapons of mass destruction, which formed the central premise of the executive's argument that it was empowered by international law to attack that nation. "Secretary of State Colin Powell even raised the alarming prospect that ... pilotless aircraft could sneak into the United States to carry out poisonous attacks on American cities."[100]

These claims also failed to meet the minimum requirements of plausibility, even in the overheated media environment that followed the 9/11 attacks. Descriptions of drones that could spread chemical or biological weapons were revealed to be references to a "primitive craft – its wings held together by tin foil and duct tape and two wooden propellers – [that] looked more like a high school science project than the 'smoking gun' that could spark a war."[101]

Since the executive could not convince the legislature that Iraq was connected with the 9/11 attacks or that it was planning terrorist attacks on the United States, it was forced to argue that it possessed inherent authority to launch an attack against that nation for an entirely different reason. They argued that Iraq had not divested itself of weapons of mass destruction as the UN ordered in 1991. However, the OLC argued that the executive possessed the inherent authority to enforce this command,[102] even after the UN failed to sanction an attack on that basis.

In essence, the executive resorted to the argument that it could launch an aggressive war on its own initiative. The alleged source of law for this proposition was an internal and secret OLC memorandum that argued for the existence of constitutional reserve powers that empowered the executive to act as he saw fit in the interests of national security.

OLC Memoranda Creating a Parallel Legal System Devoted to Violating Non-derogable
Rights and Prolonging the Emergency

Dicey noted when proposing his definition of the rule of law that one of
its key features is its guarantee of regular legal procedures for all those accused of crimes. This precludes the creation of special courts controlled
by the executive branch that deprive suspects of the basic protections of
due process. However, creating this system was a priority for the executive after the 9/11 attacks. Furthermore, these military tribunals were created though executive law-making, thereby violating two of the minimum
requirements of the rule of law. This was done as part of a plan to prolong
the state of war and political crisis that its architects hoped would allow
for a permanent return to the imperial presidency.

The creation of these special executive tribunals and the detention
regime established under their jurisdiction at Guantánamo Bay was undertaken with the goal of giving the executive freedom to ignore the most
basic safeguards preserved by the rule of law. Foremost among these are
the rights to be free from prolonged arbitrary detention and torture. It
created this regime to violate these non-derogable rights while immune
from all oversight and possible restraint. This is a situation that is not
merely a violation of the core norms of the rule of law – it is the creation
of a legal order that is its exact opposite.

In addition, the executive branch had an underlying goal for precisely these violations of non-derogable rights within the detention facilities that struck at the heart of the rule of law: it put these measures
into place with the goal of obtaining false confessions that would make
the case for further military campaigns, thereby prolonging the state of
emergency and allowing for additional consolidation of power within
the executive branch.

OLC Memoranda Establishing Special Tribunals The Bush administration has
consistently characterized the commissions that it erected after the 9/11
attacks as normal features of its military justice system, employing orthodox procedures to deal with individuals who traditionally would have
been subjected to military trials.[103] These assertions are false.

The United States has a system of law known as the Uniform Code of
Military Justice (UCMJ). This code was created by Congress, pursuant to

the authority granted by the Constitution's article I, § 8, in 1950. It is the latest iteration of Articles of War established by Congress that date back to a code enacted in 1806, which itself replaced regulations dating to the Revolutionary War.[104] In addition to providing regulations for the disciplining of members of the armed forces, the UCMJ also specifies that other classes of individuals may be subjected to its jurisdiction, such as prisoners of war, and details the legal basis for their trial and punishment as war criminals.[105]

Although Congress established the jurisdiction and procedures of the nation's military justice system, the executive, over the protests of many dissidents, including the military's own lawyers,[106] created a new set of procedures after the 9/11 attacks, which would redefine who could be detained and tried, and how they would be treated in custody. This effort began in October 2001, when lawyers from the White House Counsel's Office were charged with drafting an executive order that would set up the new military commissions.[107] Even before the OLC gave its imprimatur to the executive's plan, it was decided that the commissions would admit "any evidence 'of probative value'" (i.e., no matter how that was obtained, including by means of torture), and that the commission's judgments would be subject to "no review of any U.S., foreign, or international courts."[108]

After lawyers participating in a State Department initiative argued that this would require a specific authorization from Congress, the executive directed its lawyers to bypass the State Department and the National Security Council. Vice-President Cheney finalized the order setting up the tribunals over the US attorney general's vociferous objections.[109] "Cheney circumvented normal government processes" in doing so, preventing the relevant officials from making their views known, especially where they might have objected to his views about the proper scope of executive power.[110] Observers within the executive branch wondered how to finesse the question of presidential authority to order commissions that ignored both a statute and the Constitution. The answer was provided by the OLC, which wrote a secret memorandum to that end.

The memorandum's author, Patrick Philbin, had no experience in constitutional law. He had joined the OLC a month earlier with the understanding that he "would handle only questions of administrative law."[111] Nevertheless, Philbin was selected to write this vital memorandum, titled "Legality of the Use of Military Commissions to Try Terrorists."[112] In it, he argued that the AUMF and inherent constitutional reserve powers authorize the president to establish these tribunals. Notably, the only case that Philbin cites in the summary introducing his argument is *Ex Parte Quirin.*

This case involved a gross abuse of justice in which the president initiated an *ex parte* communication with the chief justice, indicating that he would never comply with any order to release the defendant, which ultimately ended with the court's decision to allow the executive to execute an American citizen despite the fact that the conviction depended upon hearsay. It did so in the absence of a judicial opinion justifying this order, as the justices who had agreed on the result could not agree upon a rationale until several months later.

The AUMF had not explicitly authorized the creation of military commissions. Furthermore, Congress had already expressly defined the jurisdiction and procedure of military tribunals in the UCMJ, in a manner that should have precluded the executive's plans. Accordingly, the argument of Philbin's secret memorandum was strained and circular. He argued that the UCMJ's text should not be construed as "restricting the use of military commissions" set up unilaterally by the executive, because if the statute was read that way, this would constitute "an infringement on core executive powers," thus begging the question of whether these powers existed. This memorandum also inaugurated the trend of using "contingent constitutional arguments [based on exceptionally aggressive interpretations of inherent executive powers] to preserve authorization for executive action even in the event that relevant statutes were found to prohibit it."[113] This argument flies in the face of *The Steel Seizure Case* and the minimum requirements of the rule of law, which make it clear that the legislature must have the power to prohibit executive rulemaking, especially when the executive branch seeks to ignore *jus cogens* norms.

On 13 November 2001, on the basis of the OLC memorandum, which followed the draft order given to Philbin by Cheney's counsel David Addington, Bush signed the "Military Order." While the ostensible rationale for the order was to provide for the trials of the terrorists who plotted the 9/11 attacks, it became apparent that the Military Order allowed for a wide range of activities, against a broad number of subjects. The first use to which it was put was to authorize military detention.

Memoranda Authorizing Indefinite Arbitrary Detention The Military Order "directed the Secretary of Defense to create military tribunals and to take into custody at once anyone the President names as subject to the Order."[114] The creation of the tribunals' jurisdiction thus justified the immediate detention of anyone whom the executive nominated. The order did not specify that only those suspected of a connection with the 9/11 attacks could be apprehended and detained; it merely required that the executive affirm that it had "reason to believe" that they are involved in some form of "international terrorism,"[115] echoing the signing statement's broadening of the AUMF from retribution against the 9/11 plotters to an unbounded global war on terror. Despite this, the executive promised Congress that the executive would imprison only "foreign enemy war criminals,"[116] a claim that was soon exposed to be false.

On the contrary, the executive repeatedly attempted to expand the tribunals' jurisdiction, such that it would have unlimited freedom of action to subject those it nominated to violations of their non-derogable rights. The executive attempted to ensure that it would be able to apprehend and indefinitely detain anyone, without restriction. This incarceration rises to the level of a violation of the non-derogable right not to be subjected to prolonged arbitrary detention. The executive refused to provide any timeline for adjudication of its claims, or even any due process at all, by blocking detainees' attempts to obtain judicial review of the executive's detention orders with petitions for writs of habeas corpus.

After the invasion of Afghanistan, the executive quickly obtained prisoners, some of whom were foreigners suspected of involvement with al Qaeda, at least by those who sold them for bounties to the CIA. The executive claimed that they could hold these prisoners as unlawful combatants without first allowing them to prove that this status was inapplicable as required by Protocol I to the Geneva Conventions.[117] It did so on the basis of OLC memoranda that interpreted international law in a manner that would allow for complete discretion on the part of the executive.

A draft OLC memorandum, from January 2002, written by John Yoo, flatly stated that the Third Geneva Convention's protections did not extend to members of al Qaeda. Yoo extended the category of those whom the executive could hold under the commissions' jurisdiction to include Taliban soldiers who fought openly and in an organized fashion. He claimed that because this government was not recognized as legitimate, it was not a continuing party to the Third Geneva Convention.[118] The finalized memorandum argued that despite the fact that the Taliban was the de facto government of Afghanistan, they were not entitled to the conventions' protections because it was a "failed state." It also argued that even if the Geneva Conventions did apply, the executive possessed the power to "determine that they [the detainees] all, as a class, could be said to fall outside of the definition of prisoners of war."[119]

The Obama administration has continued most of these policies. First, in May 2009, the president accepted several key premises of the detention regime; namely, that certain prisoners could be held indefinitely without trial, while others could be tried by military commissions.[120] Later that year, the administration then revived the then-dormant commissions by initiating new proceedings against five detainees.[121] The administration has continued to press the same tenuous arguments for executive supremacy in the litigation brought by detainees seeking writs of habeas corpus. In particular, the executive continues to appeal orders that detainees be released, including those who the executive admits are factually innocent. It argued in these appeals that federal district judges lack any power to order the release of detainees who have been properly granted the writ.[122]

President Obama, however, has managed to avoid significant criticism for perpetuating these policies, largely because many believe he made a good-faith effort to reverse the course set by the Bush administration. This is false, but it is an understandable error, given the many statements that the president has made about his desire to "close Guantánamo," something that was a key promise of his electoral campaign in 2008 and which he reiterated shortly after being admitted to office.[123] This misunderstanding stemmed from the supporters of the new president's optimism and willingness to read much more into his promises than what was intended.

When running for office, Obama promised only to "close Guantánamo"; after his election, he revealed that this was a promise to attempt to shutter one custodial facility. This statement did not imply that he would dismantle the military detention regime. That fact is made clear by the pertinent executive order, which explicitly charged various departments with identifying new sites at which the same prisoners would be held, on the same authority.[124] Anonymous leaks soon revealed that the executive was considering purchasing a disused prison in Illinois to this end.[125]

This plan to relocate Guantánamo quickly ran afoul of bipartisan Congressional opposition, because the proposal would require spending money within the United States, something which Congress can control easily through its power of the purse.[126] This opposition makes it possible for the executive to shift the blame for the failure to "close Guantánamo" to the legislature, as do laws that require executive certification when detainees are released to third countries.[127]

This disguises the fact that the executive possesses incontrovertible power to dismantle the entire detention regime by merely releasing every detainee. Under the National Defense Authorization Act of 2011, the president possesses the power to release any detainee, should he invoke "reasons of national security."[128] The executive could simply do this passively, by not opposing requests for the writ of habeas corpus. However, for undisclosed reasons, the Obama administration has fought hard in the courts to preserve this detention regime, which violates one non-derogable right directly while facilitating the violation of others. One should note that it has used this battle as an opportunity to reassert claims of executive supremacy that are inconsistent with the rule of law. For example, in 2011 the Obama administration issued an executive order re-authorizing indefinite detention, arguing implicitly that it possessed the power to do so independent of any delegation of legislative authority.[129]

None of the arguments in support of executive power to create and maintain a parallel regime of indefinite arbitrary detention were well-founded. The Inter-American Commission on Human Rights (IACHR) took issue with this analysis, and pointed to the incompatibility of the executive's position and the rule of law. The IACHR noted that these memoranda amounted to a carte blanche from the executive to itself:

> According to official statements from the United States government, its Executive Branch has most recently declined to extend

prisoner of war status under the Third Geneva Convention to the detainees, without submitting the issue for determinations by a competent tribunal or otherwise ascertaining the rights and protections to which the detainees are entitled under US domestic or international law. To the contrary, the information available suggests that the detainees remain entirely at the unfettered discretion of the United States Government.[130]

The IACHR correctly concluded that the executive was simply declaring that these detainees were subject to the jurisdiction of its commissions, which were entirely the creature of the executive branch. Not only did the executive set them up in a manner that ignored a statute that remained in force, but it did so via an order that "installs the executive branch as lawgiver as well as law-enforcer, and law-applier, asserting for the executive branch the prerogative to revise the jurisdictional design of the system as it goes along."[131] As the Supreme Court observed, the "blending of executive, legislative, and judicial powers in ... one branch of government is regarded as the very acme of absolutism."[132] It is also important to note that this is the exact opposite of what the rule of law requires.

The OLC created the legal rationale for a system of executive detention at Guantánamo Bay that resulted in some prisoners being held for over a decade without any semblance of legal process. Rendering this detention completely arbitrary required that it be insulated from any form of judicial review. This was a key objective for the executive when this system was being established. Even before the decision was made to transfer detainees to Guantánamo, Yoo and Philbin opined that anyone transferred there would have no access to habeas corpus.[133] These officials came to this conclusion even before the OLC had concluded that the executive possessed the legal power to commit detainees to that facility.

Indeed, the executive's decision to locate the detention facility at Guantánamo Bay was largely motivated by the belief that the federal courts would not entertain petitions from detainees held there. They decided to erect a "legal black hole"[134] where those who were detained on the say-so of the executive could be held for years without access to the courts. The executive contended that anyone could be held in such a facility, with one exception: US citizens, as this was explicitly forbidden by the Non-Detention Act of 1971. However, the OLC soon drafted new memoranda that again stated that executive was simply not bound by that law when it impeded its freedom to act in the interest of national security, and shortly thereafter even American citizens were subjected to prolonged arbitrary detention.

On 8 May 2002, US citizen José Padilla was arrested in Chicago pursuant to a material witness warrant issued by a federal court. The following month, President Bush issued an order directing Secretary of Defense Donald Rumsfeld to take custody of Padilla. This was purportedly authorized by OLC memoranda,[135] which referenced the executive's "inherent powers as Commander in Chief."[136] Similarly, the authority of the Domestic War Powers Memo and the Military Commissions Memo were invoked to authorize the transfer into military custody and detention of Ali Saleh Kahlah al-Marri, a Qatari national in the United States lawfully in possession of a student visa, which should have given him the legal protections due to a citizen, albeit temporarily.[137] A Senate Judiciary Committee Majority Staff Report described these two cases as follows:

> The *al-Marri* case, like the *Padilla* case, has the following features: the civilian arrest of a person lawfully in the United States; the order by the President that the person be turned over to military custody for potentially indefinite incarceration ... the denial to that individual of legal counsel and other essential aspects of due process to permit him to challenge the bases of his detention; the claim that the President enjoys such powers over the individual's right to liberty as Commander in Chief ... The implications of the President's view of his power are obvious and ominous: "This intolerable reading of the law would leave a President free to suspend the rights of anyone, including American citizens."[138]

It was unclear to many at the time why the executive branch was so committed to creating a legal black hole. They asked how the utility of the Guantánamo Bay camp could possibly outweigh the considerable loss of respect the United States suffered in the international community, when even the leading jurists of its staunchest allies lined up to condemn this practice?[139] The answer only became clear after leaks revealed more about the nature of the questioning of its prisoners, and after it was revealed that the OLC was arguing that detainees should not be formally charged or given Geneva Convention protections in order "to facilitate interrogations."[140] Various memoranda made it clear that the end not only justified the means, it was the reason these means were adopted. White House counsel Alberto Gonzales wrote that the "nature of the new war places a high premium on ... the ability to quickly obtain information from captured terrorists and their sponsors ... [this] new paradigm renders obsolete Geneva's strict limitations on questioning of enemy prisoners."[141] The executive was determined to free itself of even the most basic international norms, such that it possessed complete freedom of action to violate non-derogable rights in secret – breaking free of the rule of law.

OLC Memoranda Authorizing Torture Torture was not incidental to the prolonged involuntary detention at Guantánamo Bay. While there are many reports of atrocious conditions and of casual abuse by the facility's staff that would suffice to support findings of torture or degrading treatment, these pale in comparison to the techniques that were authorized at the highest level of the executive branch and then employed in order to obtain spurious information from the detainees.

Again, this behaviour was specifically prohibited by both domestic and binding international law. Even torture outside of the United States is specifically prohibited by federal law,[142] and the Convention against Torture[143] is both customary international law and an international instrument ratified by the United States. What this means is that even if the OLC's conclusion that the Geneva Conventions did not apply to the detainees, these instruments barred it. However, the OLC proved itself perpetually prepared to give the executive complete discretion to violate non-derogable human rights.

John Yoo drafted a memorandum (on behalf of Jay Bybee) which concluded that the state of war created by the AUMF relieved the executive of the burden to respect these prisoners' rights. Insofar as the president possessed the power to command the army on the battlefield, Yoo argued, he had unreviewable authority to direct how prisoners should be interrogated. Legislative and judicial "restrict[ions on] the President's plenary power over military operations, including the treatment of prisoners" would, according to Yoo, be "constitutionally dubious."[144]

The claim that inherent constitutional reserve powers allowed the executive to authorize torture was put more forcefully in another memorandum written by Yoo and signed by Bybee seven months later. In it, they claimed that "[a]ny effort to apply [laws against torture] in a manner that interferes with the President's direction of such a core war matter thus would be unconstitutional."[145] Here, the OLC claimed that any laws that Congress might pass to forbid torture would be ineffective. The executive simply could not be restrained by another branch of government when it decided to commit these violations of non-derogable rights. When it came to torture, the executive "was above the law."[146]

The OLC memorandum signed by Bybee explicitly authorizes torture. It also describes waterboarding in detail, as follows: "In this procedure, the individual is bound securely to an inclined bench, which is approximately four feet by seven feet. The individual's feet are generally elevated. A cloth is placed over the forehead and eyes. Water is then applied to the cloth in a controlled manner. As this is done, the cloth is lowered until it covers both the nose and mouth."[147] It should be noted that this is not "simulated drowning" but actual asphyxia, which quickly causes death if the torturer does not carefully monitor the victim's oxygen levels. It is a sign of these memoranda's paucity of analysis that they failed to note that waterboarding had been repeatedly recognized as torture in international law, particularly at the International Military Tribunal for the Far East, where American military judges presided,[148] and in American law:[149] "Historical analysis demonstrates that U.S. Courts have consistently held that artificial drowning interrogation is torture, which, by its nature, violates U.S. statutory prohibitions."[150]

Once approved, waterboarding was applied without any sense of proportion. While just one session of this form of torture can leave psychological scars that last for years, a CIA briefing document reveals that one detainee was waterboarded 183 times.[151] This detainee confessed during interrogation that he "was responsible for the 9/11 operation, from A to

Z," and that he was responsible for plotting the assassinations of Jimmy Carter and Pope John Paul II and the 1993 World Trade Center bombing. It is clear that at least some of these confessions were false, as it is was established beyond all reasonable doubt that this last crime was the work of others.[152] The detainee himself alleges that he revealed false information "to please his captors," including statements incriminating innocent parties. Even US authorities recognize this to be the case. "One CIA official cautioned that many of [his] claims during interrogation were 'white noise' designed to send the U.S. on wild goose chases or to get him through the day's interrogation session."[153] This, however, has not prevented the OLC from arguing that waterboarding this detainee produced results when justifying the use of torture. One unfounded claim referenced in subsequent memoranda was that the waterboarding of the detainee helped to foil a major plot to destroy Los Angeles' Library Tower.[154] This is an illogical assertion, as the plot was abandoned by the conspirators a year before this detainee was captured.[155]

There is no credible information that waterboarding yielded actionable intelligence,[156] which is not surprising, as the leading experts in interrogation have long derided the efficacy of torture.[157] It is difficult to explain the executive's single-minded focus on promoting this and other methods of torture, especially over the objections of its own military and experienced interrogators from the FBI, the International Committee of the Red Cross, the governments of certain key allies, and the united front of civil society.[158] The executive's motivation becomes clearer when one considers why torture has been used in the past: to break detainees' spirits and to extract false confessions. Indeed, waterboarding in particular was identified by Americans as a particularly useful technique for this purpose when it was used by its adversaries.[159]

A 2008 Senate Armed Service Committee report identified the particular false confession that the executive was pushing its torturers to obtain from detainees. The executive sought confessions that al Qaeda was sponsored by Iraq during Hussein's dictatorship.[160] The report details that Department of Defense "reverse engineered ... Cold War communist techniques [e.g., waterboarding] used to secure false confessions,"[161] as a response to pressure from senior executive officials. Major Paul Burney testified before the committee that "while we were there [at Guantánamo

Bay] a large part of the time we were focused on trying to establish a link between Al Qaeda and Iraq and we were not being successful in establishing a link between Al Qaeda and Iraq. The more frustrated people got in not being able to establish this link ... there was more and more pressure to resort to measures that might produce more immediate results."[162]

This pressure for torture aimed at producing false confession came from the highest reaches of the executive branch. The Armed Services Committee report details how Paul Wolfowitz called "to express concerns about insufficient intelligence production" at Guantánamo Bay; that it had not yielded a link to Iraq. Wolfowitz suggested that the interrogators use more brutal methods. Another intelligence official confirmed this account and specified why these interrogations were so persistent, and why "extreme methods were used ... for most of 2002 and into 2003, Cheney and Rumsfeld, especially, were also demanding proof of the links between al Qaida and Iraq."[163] Lawrence Wilkerson, former chief of staff to Secretary of State Powell, also asserted that Cheney personally ordered waterboarding of detainees shortly before the interrogators produced a breakthrough in obtaining the false confession that the executive was seeking in February 2002.[164]

In February 2002, the torture authorized by the OLC finally produced the desired results. Ibn al-Shaykh al-Libi was waterboarded regularly until he "confessed" that Iraq trained al Qaeda members to use chemical and biological weapons. Immediately afterwards, "[al-]Libi's statements became a key basis for the Bush-Cheney administration's claim, in Secretary of State Colin Powell's pre-war United Nations Security Council presentation," which stated that "Al Qaeda continues to have a deep interest in acquiring weapons of mass destruction ... I can trace the story of a senior terrorist operative [al-Libi] telling how Iraq provided training in these weapons to Al-Qaida. Fortunately, this operative is now detained, and he has told his story."[165]

Al-Libi soon recanted his statements, however, and the CIA admitted that he "had no knowledge of such training [in weapons of mass destruction by Iraqi agents] or weapons and fabricated the statements because he was terrified of further harsh treatment."[166] He then was seen as a potential embarrassment, and dealt with accordingly. Rather than being put on trial before a military commission, he was transferred to Libya in

2006, despite the fact that refoulement to that country violated the Convention against Torture's provisions barring the repatriation of those who would be subjected to further abuse.[167]

Human Rights Watch (HRW) rediscovered al-Libi in a Libyan prison in April 2009, after having lost track of him when the United States refused to disclose his whereabouts. Within a week of this visit, he was dead of what his captors described as a suicide. However, "Those with whom Human Rights Watch spoke who knew al-Libi said he was very religious and cited this as the main reason why they were surprised by – and disbelieved – the government's claim that he had committed suicide."[168] Photographs obtained by HRW show a sheet looped around his neck and attached to the wall, but his feet are "firmly on the ground" and his body was marked with "large" and "dark" bruises and long "scratches."[169]

His death occurred as a Senate report into torture was nearing completion, something which Powell's former deputy Wilkerson insinuated not to be coincidental. He described al-Libi's death by noting that "al-Libi just 'committed suicide' in Libya." At that time, several US lawyers working with tortured detainees were attempting to get the Libyan government to allow them to interview al-Libi.[170] Wilkerson's suspicions were shared by the HRW's Laura Pitter, who confirmed that al-Libi's testimony to the Senate committee might have had a very negative effect on the executive: "I would speculate that he was missing because he was such an embarrassment to the Bush administration. He was Exhibit A in the narrative that tortured confessions contributed to the massive intelligence failure that preceded the Iraq War."[171]

That narrative should also include that OLC memoranda that authorized the prolonged arbitrary detention and torture of these detainees freed the executive of all of the limitations of domestic and international legal obligations, and clarify that this was done with a purpose that challenged the rule of law's fundamental norms. The aim of the executive's violations of non-derogable rights was to make the case for an aggressive war, which would serve to prolong the wartime emergency. This would then allow the executive to further entrench its immunity from the law and freedom from the oversight and control of the other branches of government.

Additionally, as the authorization of the detention and torture of Padilla and al-Marri make clear, the OLC was determined to give the executive complete freedom of action to violate non-derogable norms not only outside of, but within the nation's borders. To do so, it needed to vitiate the Foreign Intelligence Surveillance Act.

Memoranda Authorizing Intelligence Agencies' Surveillance One of the most prominent statutes passed during the congressional resurgence against the executive lawlessness was the FISA. It specified that even if the executive believed it needed to conduct surveillance of citizens in the interests of national security, it needed to obtain warrants. The phrase "in the interests of national security" had served previously as a nebulous catch-all allowing for complete freedom of action, but after FISA the executive would need to obtain judicial warrants even when it invoked that rationale. Like many pieces of legislation that were passed in the wake of Watergate, FISA reiterated that the executive was subject to the Constitution's clear commands. In this case, the requirement that judicial officers specifically describe and delimit search parameters after probable cause is set out in the Fourth Amendment.

This limitation on executive power was seen as a crucial means of preventing the executive from obtaining sufficient leverage to make another push for supremacy and unaccountability. In 1976, Senator Church "warned that total tyranny would result if the agency were to turn its awesome technology against domestic communications."[172] Church was not referring to the FBI or the CIA, but the NSA, an agency devoted to using its massive computing resources to gather vast amounts of data, out of which it might winnow actionable intelligence. It became one of the key tools after the post-Watergate reforms, as "[t]he law has not kept up with communications technology and the technology of spying."[173] Few could have imagined at that time that the NSA would one day have the resources to record and review every telephone call between the United States and another country.

FISA's warrant requirement ostensibly prevented the NSA conducting a massive surveillance program involving all of the electronic communication within the United States, one which would dwarf Operation Minaret and the other unlawful programs exposed by the Church Commission. After the 9/11 attacks, the executive was unhappy with these restrictions. In October 2001, Cheney asked what sort of program would

be possible if the NSA were not constrained by the laws.[174] After learning about the NSA's capabilities, Cheney presented a draft authorization
for surveillance unconstrained by FISA to President Bush. The executive
"did not seek legislation. They would rely on the president's asserted
authority as commander in chief to defy explicit prohibitions of law."[175]
Only later, when the OLC was called upon to provide a minimally plausible justification, would it argue that this was also implicitly authorized
by the AUMF.

The argument that the hostilities authorized by the AUMF relieved the
executive of the burden of complying with FISA's warrant requirement
was implausible on its face. The statute itself expressly considered the possibility of a congressional declaration of war, and stated that this would
give the executive only a fifteen-day grace period before its provisions
would return into force. Other contemporaneous legislation, namely the
USA Patriot Act, as passed on 26 October 2001, altered the time period
during which the executive would need to present the warrant application to the judge, but left the requirement itself firmly intact.[176]

Once again, Yoo was asked to provide a legal opinion that would allow
the executive to claim that it was not violating the law when it chose to
ignore the commands of the legislature and the judiciary. By this time,
however, it was clear that the executive was deciding to disregard a statute
and the Constitution even before it asked for what purported to be a neutral evaluation and interpretation of the relevant legal framework.

Yoo and Robert Delahunty's memorandum concluded that the United
States was a battlefield after the 9/11 attacks, and the new program could
therefore be justified as the collection of "battlefield intelligence." In a
shocking lapse, the memorandum failed to mention FISA. They preferred
to address the Fourth Amendment rather than clarify the burden FISA
imposed on the executive, in a statute that was passed with the intention
of preventing exactly the sort of program that was currently being implemented.[177] This level of negligence was only possible because these
memoranda were classified, despite the fact that they were considered
binding law within the executive branch, and because they allowed for
the creation of a surveillance program of staggering size and scope.

The program, which was first titled "Total Information Awareness," quickly became a sprawling enterprise:

> The U.S. government was sweeping in emails, faxes and telephone calls made by its own citizens, in their own country. Transactional data, such as telephone logs and e-mail headers, were collected by the billions ... The program branched out from the NSA. Other government agencies, including the CIA, the FBI, and elements of the Defense Department, used information gleaned from the NSA to do additional surveillance. Vehicles could be tagged. Cell phones could be located, even when switched off. Cash machines, credit cards, bank transfers, changes of address, air and hotel and rental car reservations – all of these could help the government track not only the activities but the physical locations of its targets.[178]

All of this was illegal, and precisely what Congress banned explicitly in statutes after the scope of the executive's misuse of the intelligence services and the "White House horrors" were revealed by the Church Committee. The executive decided to overrule FISA, the *Keith* case, and the Fourth Amendment. It did so in secret and then obtained classified advice that could have only approved of such activity either due to manifest bias, ineptitude, or both. Most importantly, it concluded that the executive could take this action because of constitutional powers that it did not possess. Moreover, if it did in fact possess this ability to ignore the laws in the interest of national security, the rule of law that was reconstructed after Watergate would no longer exist.

Defending Inherent Executive Reserve Powers

The OLC memoranda written between 2001 and 2003 made two sets of arguments. First, that Congress implicitly authorized the violation of non-derogable rights and the abrogation of statutes and treaties when it passed the AUMF. Second, that the executive possessed inherent constitutional reserve powers that allowed it to ignore even the most explicit prohibitions of domestic and international law pertaining to *jus cogens* norms. The OLC's arguments about the AUMF are not plausible, given the legislative history of the statute that reveals its limited purpose, and which shows that Congress rejected the interpretation which the executive subsequently gave to the bill.

The consensus within the American legal profession was that these memoranda were not merely incorrect, but egregiously negligent. One memorandum in particular was the subject of a "near consensus that the legal analysis was bizarre."[179] For example, Dean Harold Koh of the Yale Law School described the memorandum authored by Yoo and signed by Bybee as "perhaps the most clearly erroneous legal opinion I have ever read."[180] Another highly qualified observer commented that this memo "has no foundation in prior OLC opinions, judicial decisions, or in any other source of law."[181]

The reasoning of all of the memoranda written by Yoo, Bybee, and Philbin was so problematic that after the change of administration in 2009, the Department of Justice's OLC withdrew at least some of these, along with another written by Steven G. Bradbury.[182] This effectively struck down the "law" that they established within the executive branch. The Department's Office of Professional Responsibility (OPR) then brought an investigation against officials involved in the production of these memoranda for ethical violations.

These senior career members of the OPR concluded that Yoo "knowingly failed to provide a thorough, objective, and candid interpretation of the law."[183] "Yoo placed his desire to accommodate the client [the head of the executive branch] above his obligation to provide thorough, objective, and candid legal advice, and that he therefore committed intentional professional misconduct."[184] The OPR also found that "Bybee knew or should have known that there was a substantial likelihood that the Bybee Memo did not present a thorough, objective and candid view of the law ... he acted in reckless disregard of his obligation to provide thorough, objective and candid legal advice."[185]

The investigation took over four years to complete, and the OPR only made its finding of professional misconduct after concluding that no reasonable doubts were possible as to Yoo and Bybee's culpability. However, in what was labelled an "unusual step," David Margolis, a power broker in the Department of Justice "who for decades has served as consigliore to top Justice officials" known for his "almost mythic powers of ... political foresight," overturned this decision.[186] Strangely, this official made the decision "to weigh Yoo's strongly held views of executive power as evidence against a misconduct finding."[187] Associate Deputy Attorney General David Margolis had been the subject of criticism in the past, after he had allegedly spared well-connected Department of Justice officials from ethics investigations, even when their behaviour arguably violated the rules of professional responsibility.[188]

Bybee and Yoo retired from government service and were spared any form of sanctions. Bybee went on to serve as a federal judge on the United States Court of Appeals for the Ninth Circuit, and Yoo became a professor of law at the University of California at Berkeley. As they now both serve in positions with lifetime tenure, "Judge Bybee and Professor Yoo ... are home free."[189]

In addition to absolving Yoo and Bybee, Margolis's memorandum had two other effects. First, it muddied the waters about whether it was proper to authorize techniques of interrogation that amounted to torture. One critic argued that "Margolis has codified the principle that we can make up new ethics standards depending on who the lawyers in question are and the exigency of the national security crisis, which isn't all that different from making up new interrogation standards depending on who the prisoner is, and the exigency of the national security situation."[190] Second, it left open the question of whether the executive has a constitutional reserve power that allows him to ignore the laws in a crisis. If this is true, then the United States cannot be considered a rule of law state.

Yoo testified before the OPR inquiry that the executive's power to ignore domestic and international law and to deprive individuals of their non-derogable rights was boundless. In one exchange, he was asked whether the executive could "order a village of civilians to be [exterminated]?" His response was "Sure."[191] As noted, Yoo was not punished for a view of executive powers that could not be more antithetical to the rule of law. He was exonerated because of his purportedly sincere beliefs in the executive's supremacy and unaccountability. Even after the change of administration, it was unclear whether this view of inherent constitutional reserve powers was current within the executive, even after it was used to justify the executive's purported power to wage aggressive war and to violate non-derogable rights.

As the executive's attitude regarding its accountability to the other branches remains at best ambivalent, the enduring compliance of the nation with the minimum requirements of the rule of law depends upon the reactions of the legislature and the judiciary. However, before turning to this issue, it is helpful to examine whether the framework for executive power that was erected by the executive after 9/11 can be reconciled with the basic elements of the rule of law, as outlined by the ICJ.

The 9/11 Crisis and the ICJ's Rule of Law

The aggrandizement of the executive branch following the 9/11 attacks jeopardizes America's standing as a nation governed in accordance with the principles of the rule of law. These delegations and assumptions of power by the executive offend against the four criteria identified by the ICJ as the minimum requirements of a state that operates within that paradigm.

Illicit Law-Making Granting Unbridled Emergency Powers

The OLC memoranda written from 2001 to 2003 were blatant and self-serving distortions of the existing law, including the AUMF, which created unreviewable emergency powers. The memoranda were so problematic because the executive branch insisted that it possessed the right to engage in clearly unlawful activities that violated non-derogable rights. However, after clarifying the executive's motivation for these activities, the most problematic challenge to the rule of law that these entail becomes apparent: that executive branch officials were determined to use information gleaned from a system that violated a number of *jus cogens* norms, constitutional provisions, and statutes, to extend the political crisis that made further illicit extensions of executive power possible.

The executive's underlying motivation for ignoring the law of war and setting up a parallel system of judicial black holes and ad hoc military tribunals was to allow for further military action against Congress's express wishes, which would allow the executive to prolong the crisis. This would allow the executive to extend its own powers at the expense of the other branches of government even further. To be precise, the goal of Guantánamo Bay and the regime of torture, which senior executive branch officials authorized, was designed to generate false confessions. It was hoped that these would implicate Iraq as an al Qaeda sponsor, leading to a much larger war, which would itself encourage further misuse of the intelligence agencies and the creation of a more elaborate system of scrutiny and repression within the United States.

In order to obtain these false confessions, many prisoners with no connection to al Qaeda or the Taliban were taken to foreign sites, denied the protections of the Geneva Conventions, denied access to lawyers and the courts, and subjected to torture. These violations of non-derogable rights were substantial, but the most lasting damage to the rule of law stemmed from the OLC memoranda's assertion that the executive could not be prevented from doing so by Congress or the courts. However, even more hazardous to the rule of law was the dynamic that the executive was attempting to put into place with these acts of executive law-making.

In essence, between 2001 and 2003, the executive was attempting to use illicit emergency powers to create a feedback loop between a state of war and the violation of non-derogable rights. The 9/11 attacks made it politically possible to set up the Guantánamo regime, which was explicitly designed to produce information that would extend the crisis into a near-permanent state of warfare in the Middle East. Warfare in Afghanistan gave way, after false confessions and other dubious intelligence reports, to war in Iraq, which might lead to the open military intervention into Syria and Iran that the PNAC's report advocated. These new wars, if the OLC memoranda written at that time are taken as any indication of the executive's plans, would likely have been followed by further violations of non-derogable rights.

These memoranda also show that the executive speculated that the political climate created by these larger wars would make it more difficult for the legislative and judicial branches to assert that the executive was assuming extraconstitutional emergency powers, or to stand up against a realignment started by a permanent crisis. This threatened to irrevocably destroy the separation of powers that protects the rule of law in the United States. Congress and the courts' political will during this crisis – its willingness to condemn the signing statement and OLC memoranda – would determine whether the rule of law would survive the first decade of the twenty-first century.

The Rule of Law in the Balance: The Importance of Congressional and Judicial Responses

After the 9/11 attacks, executive branch officials who opposed the imposition of the restrictions on the executive that the rule of law required during the Ford administration sought to restore the imperial presidency. These officials, who believed that the executive should have complete freedom of action in national security matters, seized the opportunity that the attacks presented to create an unaccountable presidency during the crisis that existed between 2001 and 2003. This was illustrated by the executive's decision to violate the non-derogable rights of terrorism suspects, by subjecting them to indefinite arbitrary detention and torture, while maintaining that these actions were unreviewable.

These abuses were not merely evidence of a failure to observe the basic norms of human rights, but of a breakdown of the rule of law. According to the ICJ, a nation is not a rule of law state if the executive is permitted to create the rules for its own conduct. This state of affairs is likely to become permanent if these rules are not subject to being scrutinized and overturned by the legislature or the judiciary.

No grant of rulemaking authority from the legislature may give the executive the final say over decisions that implicate fundamental rights, if the nation is to remain within the boundaries of the rule of law. Unfortunately, the AUMF did precisely this, by allowing the executive to determine which organizations and nations could be attacked and invaded in response to the 9/11 attacks. This delegation of authority was not in keeping with the ICJ's first criterion of the rule of law state.

The ICJ's second criterion is that the emergency powers of the executive must always be limited in scope and duration. This was not the case after the 9/11 attacks. Instead, the executive assumed, on its own initiative, vast emergency powers, bypassing the statutory scheme by which these are normally triggered, and ignoring the law-making process mandated by the separation of powers altogether. Instead, the executive branch wrote its own laws, creating its emergency powers by means of executive law-making, which the ICJ explicitly condemned as being incompatible with the rule of law.

For this crisis of the rule of law to be more than merely transient, the legislature and the judiciary must abdicate their responsibility to respond to executive overreaching. However, it should be noted that the executive attempted to use the overbroad delegation of power and the emergency powers it granted itself to make this more difficult. It is particularly unfortunate that the "intelligible principle" requirement of the non-delegation doctrine was "rendered virtually meaningless"[192] after Roosevelt's victory over the Supreme Court. If Chief Justice Marshall was right, and there are "important subjects which must be regulated by the legislature itself,"[193] surely he, along with his contemporaries among the Framers, would have included the right to declare war. As Marshall, Madison, and Hamilton recognized, giving the executive the power to declare war empowers it to destroy every other limit on its authority.

The post 9/11 constitutional crisis was made considerably more intractable by the fact that the executive was using these powers to create and prolong a political environment that would make it more difficult for Congress and the courts to respond. That said, it is clear that if these branches did not respond adequately to the executive's lawlessness, and in particular to its claim to be empowered by the Constitution to be immune and unaccountable to any restraint, then the United States would no longer be in conformity with the minimum requirements of the rule of law.

CHAPTER 4

The Response of the Judiciary to Executive Overreaching, 2003–12

The Importance of the Judiciary's Response

The federal judiciary is charged with ensuring that the executive does not violate constitutional rights. Its response to the lawsuits challenging these violations of non-derogable rights would be central either to terminating or prolonging this state of exception. One might reasonably expect that the judiciary would do what was required of it by both the US Constitution and the rule of law, but twentieth-century American history indicates that the courts may not protect constitutional rights, especially when doing so would be very unpopular. This is frequently the case during a serious crisis, when popular opinion falls solidly into place behind the executive.

The judiciary's response to the executive's reassertion of dominance after the 9/11 attacks entailed a consistent evasion of their constitutional responsibilities. Even after 2003, the higher levels of the American judiciary were satisfied with asserting their power to enforce the executive's constitutional limitations in purely rhetorical terms. Even after the executive proved it was committed to the on-going violation of non-derogable rights, the judiciary limited itself to chastising the executive, but producing decisions that only appeared to restrain the executive's freedom of action. The judiciary's inaction in the face of sustained violations of non-derogable rights by the executive calls into question whether the United States complies with the minimum requirements of any rule of law state.

Unless the courts adopt a different response to these issues, the only hope for the rule of law stems from the possibility that the legislature might act to re-impose restrictions on executive law-making and forbid the violation of non-derogable rights. Congress could empower the courts to enforce these limitations, in the manner that the rule of law requires.

Habeas Corpus

Long before court challenges to torture and illegal surveillance were brought, the executive's decision to openly defy worldwide opinion and create a parallel system of detention at Guantánamo Bay drew a strong reaction from the legal community, which fought a long campaign against indefinite arbitrary detention. Although the Supreme Court's decisions addressing prolonged arbitrary detention are frequently described as victory for the rule of law,[1] a close reading reveals that they allowed for the continuation and formalization of detention regimes, not only at Guantánamo Bay but also in Afghanistan.[2] The power to grant the writ of habeas corpus has become purely abstract after the DC Circuit held that lower courts have no ability to actually release detainees.[3] In addition, captives taken in other parts of the world who are removed to American detention centres in Afghanistan were barred by that court from even requesting a writ, even if this would only have symbolic force.[4]

The Supreme Court's Delayed and Inadequate Response

The first decision that was described as a rebuke to the administration was *Hamdi v. Rumsfeld*.[5] Yaser Hamdi was captured in Afghanistan and imprisoned at Guantánamo Bay, before being transferred to a military prison in the continental United States. His father filed a habeas petition on his behalf. In response, the government produced only a "vague and general declaration"[6] asserting that Hamdi was a Taliban militiaman. The trial court noted:

> While it is clear that the Executive is entitled to deference regarding military designations of individuals, it is equally clear that the

judiciary is entitled to a meaningful judicial review of these desig-
nations when they substantially infringe on the individual liberties,
guaranteed by the United States Constitution, of American Citizens.[7]

On appeal, the Fourth Circuit disagreed, in what was the first of many
cases wherein the lower courts would prove willing to defend constitutional rights while appellate courts would defer to the executive,[8] arguing that the "constitutional allocation of war powers affords the President
extraordinarily broad authority and compels courts to assume a deferential posture."[9] It was left to the Supreme Court to decide between these
two competing views about whether the judiciary should play any role in
policing the constitutional limits of executive power after it invokes a
theory of its war powers that is incompatible with the rule of law.

The court's fractured plurality opinion, in which Justice Sandra Day
O'Connor took the middle position, which was joined by Justices Anthony
Kennedy, Stephen Breyer, and William Rehnquist, while Justices Ruth Bader
Ginsburg and David Souter concurred in part and dissented in part, is most
often remembered for its assertion of the judiciary's responsibilities:

> [W]e necessarily reject the Government's assertion that the sepa-
> ration of powers principles mandate a heavily circumscribed role
> for the courts in such circumstances ... We have long since made
> it clear that a state of war is not a blank check for the President
> when it comes to the rights of the Nation's citizens. Whatever
> power the United States Constitution envisions for the Executive ...
> it most assuredly envisions a role for all three branches when indi-
> vidual liberties are at stake.[10]

However, this stirring defence of the court's role in protecting individual liberties seems rather less impressive when reviewed in the context
of the court's actual holding, which "nonetheless found that Hamdi's [in-
definite military] detention was in fact authorized."[11] The court found
that Congress implicitly authorized this detention when passing the AUMF,
though this statute does not appear to contemplate anything other than
military strikes themselves.[12] The court decided to allow the petitioner's

detention to continue, despite that the Constitution's Suspension Clause requires Congress to pass a statute explicitly authorizing military custody. It should also be noted that the AUMF ignores the Non-Detention Act, which the court failed to even mention. It also ignored that the civilian courts remained open, despite that its earlier opinions held that this fact precluded the use of military commissions.[13]

A second opinion in a case styled *Rasul v. Bush* was released the same day.[14] The primary issue in *Rasul* was whether a civilian court had jurisdiction to review a habeas petition filed by a Guantánamo detainee. The executive branch's decision to erect that detention camp was informed by John Yoo and the OLC's conclusion that the location was outside of the court's reach.[15] As Lord Steyn famously said, it was a "legal black hole."[16] The court's opinion differentiated this case from *Johnson v. Eisentrager*,[17] which held that American courts possessed no jurisdiction over the claims of German citizens captured by US forces in China and imprisoned in occupied Germany, after being found guilty of war crimes at a military commission convened in Nanking in 1946.[18]

The opinion noted that the petitioners in *Eisentrager* received some degree of due process at their trials, while the petitioners at bar faced indefinite detention without any possibility of proving their innocence.[19] Accordingly, the Court held that that "§ 2241 [the habeas corpus statute] confers on the District Court jurisdiction to hear petitioners' habeas corpus challenges to the legality of their detention at the Guantanamo Bay Naval Base."[20]

Commentators have described this holding as "an astonishing legal victory for the detainees."[21] However, it was merely a victory on paper. Not one detainee was released or even placed into confinement consistent with the Geneva Conventions as a result of this ruling or the opinions that followed. The purely preliminary nature of the relief granted by the court can be best illustrated by reproducing its statement about what it explicitly did not hold:

> Whether and what further proceedings may become necessary after respondents make their response to the merits of petitioners' claims are matters that we need not address now. What is presently at

stake is only whether the federal courts have jurisdiction to determine the legality of the Executive's potentially indefinite detention
of individuals who claim to be wholly innocent of wrongdoing.[22]

That said, access to habeas review seemed to provide the detainees
with a possible route to release. However, *Hamdi* and *Rasul* merely held
that the Guantánamo Bay petitioners must be given an opportunity to
assert that they were factually innocent, and that the executive was not
providing this due process. Nonetheless, it was "the language of the
Hamdi opinion [that is, its dicta, rather than the holding] that dominated
the media's attention,"[23] which reported that the court dealt a severe blow
to the administration's detention regime.[24]

These opinions' most stirring passages also distracted the press from
a third, rather dry and technical majority opinion released on the same
day, which failed to affirm the reasoning of multiple lower court opinions
that held squarely that the executive branch could not detain an American citizen arrested within the United States indefinitely and without
counsel. In José Padilla's case, the Second Circuit held that "when the executive acts, even in the conduct of war, in the face of apparent congressional disapproval, challenges to his authority must be examined and
resolved by the Article III courts."[25]

Despite the fact that "the Padilla case may have seemed the easier
one because it was not a battlefield capture and all the judges below
had found fault with the detention, the Supreme Court decided to avoid
the question."[26]

As Jenny Martinez wrote of the *Padilla* litigation as a whole, "The
courts' patience with the government's procedural games also left open
the possibility that other citizens might be similarly detained in the future
(particularly in the Fourth Circuit, where the decision finding some legal
authority for such detentions remains on the books as a precedent, albeit
a weakened one)."[27]

Another commentator noted that the Supreme Court's "odd decision
in the case can hardly be understood as anything other than an evasion."[28] The dissenting justices made it clear that this failure to address
Padilla's claims was an inexcusable failure to restore the rule of law:

At stake in this case is nothing less than the essence of a free society. Even more important than the method of selecting the people's rulers and their successors is the character of the constraints imposed on the Executive by the rule of law. Unconstrained executive detention for the purpose of investigating and preventing subversive activity is the hallmark of the Star Chamber. For if this nation is to remain true to the ideals symbolized by its flag, it must not wield the tools of tyrants.[29]

Another dissent to the companion case noted that "the very core of liberty secured by our Anglo-Saxon system of separated powers has been freedom from indefinite imprisonment at the will of the Executive."[30] The procedural evasion allowed the court not only to avoid whether the executive branch could imprison Americans indefinitely without trial, but whether it could do so despite the fact that Congress barred this practice. The Non-Detention Act of 1971 (NDA)[31] states that "[n]o citizen shall be imprisoned or otherwise detained by the United States except by Act of Congress," and while

the administration has argued that Section 4001(a) [of the NDA] "does not apply to the military's wartime detention of enemy combatants [and that the NDA] ... has no bearing on the military's authority to detain enemy combatants in wartime ... The legislative history does not support that interpretation, which would leave open some inherent presidential power to accomplish the same feat by military means."[32]

The Congressional Research Service's report on this statute concluded:

The political climate of the Non-Detention Act (fear and anxiety by U.S. citizens of arbitrary imprisonment and detention) combined with the legislative history provide persuasive evidence that the purpose of repealing the Emergency Detention Act and adding the Railsback Amendment was to strip from the executive branch – both its civilian and military components – of any claim of independent authority to round up, imprison, and detain disfavored individuals.[33]

Despite the presence of these pressing issues of paramount concern, owing to Padilla's alleged error in filing his petition in the wrong court, the majority forced Padilla to begin his quest for justice from the beginning, only to have his case made moot by his transfer to civilian custody after he again came before the Supreme Court.[34] The administration's attempts to avoid review of a crucial issue were so blatant that "Judge Luttig [of the Fourth Circuit] even stepped down from the bench, amid stories that the Bush Administration had lied about Padilla's involvement in terrorism and had therefore put him in the untenable position of upholding a controversial detention that had no basis in fact."[35] The Supreme Court facilitated this evasion by approving Padilla's transfer out of military custody.[36] The court could have written a judgment clarifying whether the president has the power to detain American citizens indefinitely. On that day it did not, and to date it has failed to do so.

The civil rights organizations that represented the detainees responded to this failure by filing challenges to the constitutionality of the purported congressional authorization of the executive's detention regime. The first of these cases to be decided was *Hamdan v. Rumsfeld,* which challenged the military commissions that were set up by the president in response to *Rasul.*[37] The *Hamdan* opinion ruled that these commissions did not meet the minimum standards specified by Congress's last word on how these must be conducted, found in the Uniform Code of Military Justice (UCMJ).[38] The court decided that either the UCMJ's incorporation of the Geneva Convention protections or Common Article 3 of the Geneva Conventions itself provided a set of minimum safeguards, which the president could not sidestep.

Despite having held that the tribunals were insufficient as they were then constituted, the plurality opinion left open two courses of action for the executive when defending indefinite military detention. First, the court seemed to indicate that in some circumstances the president could seek to demonstrate that there was a military necessity that allowed him to deviate from the UCMJ,[39] a line of reasoning that seems to implicitly approve of the executive branch's claims of inherent constitutional powers in wartime.[40] Second, the court's holding seemed to indicate that if Congress authorized new forms of tribunals, this would preclude further judicial scrutiny.

> The *Hamdan* decision also did not free any detainees. It restrained its relief to: requiring that the military commissions be put on hold while Congress took up the matter, [which] only served to delay Hamdan's trial while not substantially improving the procedures from his point of view … During this time, Hamdan was placed in solitary confinement. His lawyers argued that his mental state had deteriorated to the point that he could no longer assist in his own defense.[41]

This narrow holding necessitated only the modification of the executive's system of prolonged arbitrary detention, rather than its abolition. Regardless, the decision was once again described by the press as a "[broad] rejection of the Bush plan to try detainees."[42] This is not an accurate characterization, unless undue weight is placed upon the opinion's rhetorical effect. However, the practical impact of the court's deference to the executive would not become clear to legal observers until after a series of cases brought by detainees were decided during the following five years.

An effective challenge to a new set of tribunal procedures set up after *Hamdan* would take two more years to wend its way through the courts. In *Boumediene v. Bush*, the court finally asserted that no one could rubber-stamp the president's plans to deny detainees evidentiary hearings that would meet the requirements of Common Article 3 of the Geneva Conventions, unless Congress formally invoked the Suspension Clause to deny the detainees habeas corpus.[43] This decision can be seen as a dare to "Congress to suspend the right overtly."[44] The court again seems to implicitly assert that the rule of law only applies insofar as the other branches of government have not explicitly rejected it. This approach can hardly be considered a heroic defence of the principles of natural justice, which demand access to a neutral arbiter and the opportunity to present one's defence.[45]

At best, the *Boumediene* decision merely sketched out what manner and degree of access to the courts the detainees still possessed in the absence of formal suspension of habeas corpus. Kim Scheppele described the court's fundamentally deferential approach to the administration as follows:

> According to the Court ... "The Executive is entitled to a reasonable period of time to determine a detainee's status before a court entertains that detainee's habeas corpus petition." Then the Court waffled again on the ultimate standards, announcing that "certain accommodations can be made to reduce the burden habeas corpus proceedings will place on the military without impermissibly diluting the protections of the writ," without beginning to say what those accommodations could be. At the end of what appeared to be a bold judgment, the lip service to old deference emerged, tempered by the new deference that has come to be the signature of the post-9/11 jurisprudence.[46]

It is important to also remember that it took the court almost six years to reach this position, and during this period it rejected several opportunities to rule that indefinite executive detention was simply unacceptable, as the Suspension Clause was not invoked by Congress and the civilian courts remained open. In the end, the court contented itself with merely a pressure valve in the form of tightly restricted opportunities for the detainees to prove their innocence, without even requiring release in that event. This failure to re-establish the rule of law was masked by soaring rhetoric, which unfortunately was followed only by minor adjustments to an inadequate status quo.

Furthermore, the *Boumediene* decision again provided support for theories of the president's inherent powers in national security, and left open the door for the reassertion of extreme variations on that theme by the executive:

> [P]roper deference must be accorded to the political branches ... The law must accord the Executive substantial authority to apprehend and detain those who pose a real danger to our security ... Security depends upon a sophisticated intelligence apparatus and the

ability of our Armed forces to act and to interdict ... Our opinion does not undermine the Executive's powers as Commander-in-Chief ... it has been possible to leave the outer boundaries of war powers undefined.[47]

The Supreme Court's indifference to the outcome of the habeas petitions brought after *Boumediene* appears to provide ample support for the conclusion that the court was more concerned with preserving the appearance than the substance of the rule of law in these post-9/11 cases. After implicitly validating executive detention pending court review of claims of actual innocence and military tribunals, the court left it to the DC Circuit to determine the rules for the hearings in which detainees can prove their innocence.

The DC Circuit's Repudiation of Habeas Corpus Relief

The court's decision to shift the responsibility to supervise the implementation of its purported remedy for prolonged arbitrary detention was telling, since the DC Circuit is the most reflexively pro-government of the federal appeals courts. Its bench includes unitary executive theorists such as Laurence H. Silberman, John Yoo's mentor.[48] Since 2009 the "Supreme Court has apparently lost interest in the difficult and important issues raised by the indefinite detention of prisoners at Guantánamo Bay ... [as] the DC Circuit has ... effectively nullified the Court's decision in *Boumediene*."[49]

After *Boumediene* was decided, a group of Chinese Uighur detainees filed a petition for habeas corpus. They had been living peacefully in small villages when they were swept up by bounty hunters searching for foreigners who could be sold to the American authorities and sent to Guantánamo. The "government had admitted as early as 2003 that the imprisoned Uighurs were improperly detained and eligible for release."[50] However, after concluding that they could not be repatriated to either Afghanistan or China, the executive could not locate a country that would accept them. This presumed that the United States itself was an unsuitable destination, an argument that the executive never articulated.

The petition in *Kiyemba v. Obama* was filed after months of waiting turned into years. In response, the executive branch effectively conceded that it had no basis to detain these men other than unspecified reserve powers, which one judge summarized as follows:

> The Executive chose not to file returns to the petitions for writs of habeas corpus for a majority of the petitioners ... the Executive neither claimed petitioners were "enemy combatants" or otherwise dangerous, nor charged them with a crime, nor pointed to other statutory grounds for detention, nor presented reliable evidence that the posed a threat to U.S. interests. The Executive did not deny it detained the prisoners. The district court understood the Executive to argue instead that it had extra-statutory "wind-up" authority.[51]

Unfortunately for the petitioners, the majority opinion of the DC Circuit overturning the trial court's order to release these petitioners agreed with the executive, and also concluded that the trial court possessed no power to order the detainees' release,[52] or even to order the executive to bring its prisoners before the court.[53] There is no way to reconcile these conclusions with the right to habeas corpus and the rule of law. If the authority to issue the writ has any meaning, it allows a judge to order the executive to produce a prisoner, and if his detention cannot be justified, to order his release. However, in allowing this opinion to stand the Supreme Court has reduced the right to habeas trumpeted in *Boumediene* to a charade. Following *Kiyemba* even where the petitioners can prove their innocence, the executive can continue to detain them indefinitely.

Despite the fact that this opinion was affirmed by the barest of margins on *en banc* rehearing, which usually provokes the Supreme Court into accepting review, the Supreme Court denied certiorari. Instead, it issued a statement that admitted that it had no interest in resolving what it apparently considered an abstract question. This question was whether a federal district court had the power to order a petitioner's immediate release when "other remedies" were purportedly available.[54] It might be argued that with this statement, the court blots out its fine phrases about the rule of law from its earlier opinions. This argument can be supported by reference to later opinions, which ignore the rhetoric and exploit every possibility for judicial deference to the executive. The majority of these opinions have been authored by the DC Circuit.

The court has also allowed the DC Circuit to eviscerate its *Boumediene* holding in ways that are less dramatic than the decision in *Kiyemba*. Whenever the executive has been able to produce some form of evidence, however slight, that would seem to suggest some association between the petitioners and any involvement in hostilities in Afghanistan, the DC Circuit has insisted that this justifies their indefinite detention in Guantánamo Bay, even where the district court, which was the finder of fact on the petitions, came to the opposite conclusion. This has created precedents that require trial courts to deny petitions for habeas due to this flimsy evidence.

The most problematic of the opinions creating these skewed evidentiary standards was *Latif v. Obama*.[55] This opinion follows a series of petitions granted by trial courts because of the use of highly problematic witness testimony credited by these detainees' Combatant Status Review Tribunals (CSRTs). In *Ali Ahmed v. Obama*, the trial court granted a petition for the writ where "the credibility and reliability of the detainees being relied upon by the government has either been directly called into question by government personnel or has been characterized by government personnel as undermined," or "based upon multiple levels of hearsay," or "riddled … with equivocation and speculation."[56] It also noted that the prosecution relied on testimony by a witness about which there was "evidence that [he] underwent torture" at Bagram Air Base and the CIA's "Dark Prison," and that as a result he suffered from severe psychological problems, about which the executive apparently knew when it relied upon his testimony.[57]

After this decision was released, it became apparent that every detainee seeking review of their CSRT would be able to make a similar challenge.[58] At this point, the DC Circuit found another way to uphold these rulings, by requiring trial courts to place inordinate weight on the only other evidence routinely used by the military tribunals – confidential intelligence reports. *Latif* held that "federal district judges must 'presume' that government intelligence reports used to justify detention are reliable and accurate."[59] In essence, this allowed the executive to repackage critically flawed witness testimony as intelligence reports, despite that this attenuated the aforementioned hearsay problems even further.

The DC Circuit appears to have placed its faith in these intelligence reports owing to the fact that they might be considered the product of careful and systematic procedures employed by intelligence professionals. Since these reports and the policy manuals and memoranda that guided their creation were classified, it was unlikely that anyone outside of the intelligence community would ever be in a position to say otherwise. However, a fortuitous leak of this information by WikiLeaks, which is now allegedly the subject of a grand jury investigation due to this activity,[60] exposed the shoddiness of this intelligence. It also revealed why the DC Circuit's instruction that these reports were entitled to "a presumption of regularity" reduced the habeas process mandated by *Boumediene* to a travesty of justice.

As the *New York Times* reported after reviewing these leaked files, "the documents reveal that the analysts sometimes ignored serious flaws in the evidence," including "that the information came from other detainees whose mental illness made them unreliable ... Some assessments quote witnesses ... but omit the witnesses' record of falsification or misidentification," and fail to note that these statements "were later withdrawn, often attributed to abusive treatment or torture."[61] Evidence obtained under torture, which was previously used to justify further wars of aggression, was now being used to justify the detention of those who were tortured to produce it,[62] in order to keep the details of this "intelligence production" secret.

The leak also revealed that the guidelines given to the intelligence professionals preparing the reports were highly flawed, leading "analysts [to seize] upon the tiniest details as a possible litmus test for risk."[63] For example, the Joint Task Force Guantanamo (JTF-GTMO) Matrix of Threat Indicators for Enemy Combatants lists the following as one of the criteria by which one might conclude that a detainee is a high risk: he "[o]perated or [was] captured in an area dominated by al-Qaeda or Taliban forces ... including but not limited to ... Kabul ... Kandahar ... Konduz

... Mazar-e-Sharif."[64] This memorandum fails to note that these are four out of the five largest cities in Afghanistan.

These guidelines appear to provide a basis for considering almost anyone to be an enemy combatant. Applying them, one intelligence report "suggests a dire use for his pocket calculator, namely '[c]alculators can be used for indirect fire calculations such as those required for artillery fire.'"[65] The analyst fails to note any instances in which al Qaeda or the Taliban have employed artillery fire after the 2001 invasion.

While this is merely one example of this sort of paranoid reasoning to which a "presumption of regularity" deference is now owed following *Latif*, it appears that on the basis of the JTF-GTMO Matrix, more than fifty detainees have been assessed as some degree of threat on the basis of, in addition to other bizarre criteria, the possession of Casio F91W-1 or A-159W wristwatches. "JTF-GTMO identified the watch as 'the sign of al-Qaida,'"[66] as it was allegedly used by al Qaeda bomb-makers to build timers. The report fails to note that this model of watch has been a "'huge seller' all over the world" for over twenty years.[67] Detainee Usama Hassan Ahmend Abu Kabir told his tribunal that "I have a Casio watch due to the fact that they are inexpensive and last a long time. I like my watch because it is durable. It ... was waterproof."[68]

In addition to attributing peculiar significance to various quotidian items, the Threat Matrix displays further paranoia, by suggesting that innocent explanations were actually a potential sign of sophisticated counter-intelligence training. "A prisoner caught without travel documents? It might mean he had been trained to discard them to make identification harder, the guide explains. A detainee who claimed to be a simple farmer or a cook? ... Those were common Taliban and Qaeda cover stories, the analysts were told."[69] The Threat Matrix forecloses every innocent explanation if detainees refused to co-operate or to explain themselves, this was also evidence of their guilt, as this is noted to be an al Qaeda resistance technique.[70] The Threat Matrix is perverse, yet the intelligence reports created following its instructions were held to be so trustworthy that district courts must rely upon them.

The Supreme Court Fails to React to Denial of Habeas Corpus

In his dissent from the decision in *Latif,* Judge David S. Tatel noted that "it is hard to see what is left of the Supreme Court's command in *Boumediene.*"[71] However, the Obama administration directed the solicitor general to submit a brief opposing the petition for certiorari, and the Supreme Court duly declined review. As Hanna Madbak noted, "[T]he question the Supreme Court has refused to answer is whether a detainee truly has a 'meaningful opportunity' to challenge his detention if he cannot unseal evidence against him, or if a mathematical evaluation of the evidence allegedly lowers the government's burden of proof against him even below the low preponderance of the evidence standard."[72]

The decision to give the DC Circuit free rein to ignore *Boumediene* casts doubts on the Supreme Court's commitment to maintaining the rule of law. In declining review of *Kiyemba* and *Latif,* the court allows the limited remedy afforded by *Boumediene* to become doubly pointless. First, one cannot meaningfully challenge indefinite detention. Second, even if one could, the trial court cannot grant a petitioner's request for release. Once again, Guantánamo Bay can be described as a black hole, from which not even an innocent detainee can escape.

Erwin Chemerinsky, who argued the first petition for habeas corpus of the detainees held in military custody, noted that at that time he:

> [C]ould not have possibly imagined that more than ten years later ... the government would still be holding these individuals as prisoners. When the Supreme Court finally ruled in *Rasul v. Bush* and *Boumediene v. Bush* that Guantánamo detainees had a right to seek habeas corpus relief in federal courts, I never could have imagined that this would be a pyrrhic victory and the Court would allow the D.C. Circuit to nullify the availability of habeas corpus.[73]

Chemerinsky should not be accused of naïveté, as the amount of cynicism appropriate to the court's jurisprudence can only be discerned in retrospect. The timid and halting approach to the problem, and the abandonment of the issue (once it faded from public view), is not the result of an attempt to do justice, but rather to convince the public that justice was being done and that the rule of law was being upheld. The slow timetable itself operated as a pressure valve, periodically dissipating liberal concern for the erosion of the separation of powers. The court's stirring rhetoric concealed fundamental concessions to executive power, but it nevertheless convinced many that it was protecting non-derogable rights against executive overreach. This was largely a spectacle for the benefit of the legal profession and others concerned with human rights and the rule of law.

The court, while preserving the appearance of habeas corpus to save its own blushes, has implicitly affirmed the executive's right to indefinitely detain suspects in military custody even without Congress's approval in certain situations, and has also affirmed the existence of other unenumerated presidential "war powers." Some might argue that this does not deserve serious concern, relying on the assumption that the Obama administration is winding down the military detention regime at Guantánamo. This supposition initially appears to be correct, given the fact that no one has been transferred to that facility since 2008 despite leaving this possibility open.[74] However, it ignores the replacement built by the executive, and the many other places where detainees were held in secret. This includes CIA-run detention facilities known as the "black sites," which were first acknowledged only five years after the 9/11 attacks.[75]

The DC Circuit Preserves a Judicial Black Hole

The first replacement for the Guantánamo Bay detention camp is located in Afghanistan. It is located within the Parwan Detention Facility (Parwan), which is found next to Bagram Airfield. This larger facility is also known as the Bagram Theater Internment Facility. As of 2014, it held nearly three times as many detainees as Guantánamo did at its peak.[76] Some of these detainees are not Afghan citizens, or even foreign fighters captured in Afghanistan. They are prisoners who were transferred there, rather than to Guantánamo, after the courts allowed petitioners held at the Cuban base to have access to counsel and the right to file petitions for habeas corpus.[77]

Insofar as some foreigners held at Parwan alleged that their transfer to that facility was an attempt to evade the judiciary scrutiny, and as they alleged they were held there for over six years, it was not surprising that trial courts would be receptive to their claims. In *Al-Maqaleh v. Gates*,[78] a trial court addressed the claims of non-Afghan detainees at Parwan apprehended in Dubai and Thailand, among other places. As in *Boumediene*, the trial court found that attempts to strip the judiciary of its jurisdiction to receive these petitions were unconstitutional,[79] and that "detainees who are not Afghan citizens, who were not captured in Afghanistan and who have been held for an unreasonable amount of time ... without adequate process" were entitled to the writ.[80]

Unfortunately for the petitioners – and for the rule of law in the United States – the DC Circuit again disagreed.[81] It ruled that the executive did not have as much control over Parwan as it did over Guantánamo, such that it could distinguish the holding of *Boumediene*, which was that federal courts possessed that jurisdiction.[82] The court alluded to "differences" between these facilities,[83] such as the fact that the United States needed to co-operate with the Afghan government to run the facility, to justify this conclusion. This is poor legal reasoning. It also ignores the reality of the relationship between America and its client state, which is run by a regime that exists at America's pleasure. The DC Circuit also failed to note that the Afghan government opposes the detention of foreigners at Parwan, of which there were at least fifty in 2014,[84] although the executive refuses to confirm a figure or release details of where and how they were captured, but this is irrelevant in practice, because the tools of the American executive are in no way answerable to President Hamid Karzai. As Stephen Vladeck noted when describing how the DC Circuit misconstrued *Boumediene*:

> Even if [the court's] logic follows (and I don't think it does), it's beside the point ... To the extent that the United States is simply *not* "answerable" to the government of Afghanistan for the detentions of non-Afghans at Bagram (and the related extent to which the government of Afghanistan has no incentive to play such a role for non-Afghans captured outside of Afghanistan), the second *Boumediene* factor should militate in *favor* of habeas, not against it.[85]

Not only is the detention regime at Parwan contrary to Afghan law,[86] but the United States also resisted Afghan demands to transfer the facility to its authority.[87] The nominal Afghan commander of the facility had no control over who entered or left, and he was not allowed to attend any meetings outside of the presence of his "advisors."[88] This appears to demonstrate both that the executive is not answerable to the nation's "ally," and that the DC Circuit's ruling distorted not only the law, but the facts. The argument that the Afghan government has any control over these prisoners' confinement is not supported by any evidence.

The dismissal of the petitions for habeas corpus that were pending at the time of the DC Circuit's decision in *Al-Maqaleh* represents "the end of the line for the possibility of habeas jurisdiction" over black sites.[89] The executive can now abduct someone at any point on the globe, transfer them to the black jail in Parwan, and subject them to indefinite arbitrary detention, upon nomination by the executive. The detainees have no access to any court, something which the DC Circuit approved. However, the creation of another judicial black hole is only the beginning of what it will tolerate. These detainees can also be tortured, as the DC Circuit will not adjudicate claims that follow the executive's revival of this practice in Afghanistan. As was the case with prolonged arbitrary detention, torture was formalized and legalized, not least because of the DC Circuit's willingness to ignore violations of non-derogable rights: another demonstration that the United States is no longer in minimal compliance with the requirements of a rule of law state.

Torture

Lawsuits alleging torture in military custody followed on the heels of the challenges to prolonged arbitrary detention. This was a predictable sequence, as information about torture at Guantánamo Bay was not made public until revealed in the petitions for habeas corpus. Even as the executive made a public spectacle of the detention, it kept horrific details of this detention regime top secret.[90] However, after their release, many Guantánamo detainees brought suits alleging their jailers tortured them.

These suits also named the senior officials who developed and authorized these procedures, who also hoped to obtain false confessions implicating Iraq in terrorist plots. These lawsuits have all been dismissed, although many obtained initial success in trial courts. However, as the appeals of these cases were not followed closely in the media, the judiciary was free to elaborate new doctrines mandating deference to the executive. These doctrines allowed these courts, particularly the DC Circuit, to avoid decisions on the merits in lawsuits alleging torture. It then did so, even when there was no doubt of the relevant facts.

The first set of these cases will demonstrate that the appeals courts were willing to extend "qualified immunity" to those involved in gross abuses of non-derogable rights, as long as these officials purportedly lacked a subjective belief that they were breaking the law. This implicitly affirmed the OLC memoranda authorizing this conduct, since the courts were willing to accept that a rational lawyer could have created such poor legal arguments in good faith, and accepted that this was enough to give them immunity.

Discussing the torture cases, Stephen Vladeck argued that they demonstrate the "existence of a new national security canon – a body of jurisprudence in which distinct (and sometimes poorly articulated) national security concerns have prompted courts to disfavour relief, even when ... relief should otherwise have been available ... [given] the heads-we-win, tails-you-lose quality to this body of decision-making, it is difficult to rebut the conclusion that, at least at the circuit level, more is going on than just faithful application of existing precedent."[91] One of the clearest examples of the appellate courts' decision to create new doctrine to protect the executive from responsibility for torture is found in the opinion that disposed of the lawsuit brought by José Padilla against John Yoo. This case did not allow the judiciary to use the standard doctrinal arsenal of judicial evasion, since Padilla was a US citizen, located in the United States, and suing in his own name for conduct that occurred within that nation. However, the Ninth Circuit was more than willing to both misstate the facts and bend the law in support of a conclusion that absolved Yoo of any wrongdoing.

First, it should be noted that its opinion quibbled with the conclusion of the trial court, whose factual determinations are ordinarily accorded great deference on appeal – namely, that Padilla was tortured. The Ninth Circuit said that Padilla's allegations that his guards subjected him to severe mental and physical harm were "conclusory," but they did not remand for further fact-finding, since it also determined that even if his mistreatment amounted to torture, the fact "that such treatment was torture was not clearly established in 2001–2003."[92] Second, the court upheld Yoo's assertion that Padilla was not entitled to the Constitution's protections, because the executive's decision to authorize his military detention and torture was not "beyond debate."

The court accepted Yoo's argument that, owing to a doctrine known as "qualified immunity," he was liable for what it characterized a simple misreading of the law in the performance of his duties. This ignores the fact that Yoo was not merely mistaken, or even negligent. The OPR concluded that Yoo repeatedly ignored directly applicable law that made it clear he was authorizing illegal acts. It also bears mentioning that the Ninth Circuit was implicitly sitting in judgment not merely on Yoo, but his unindicted conspirator Jay Bybee. Bybee was the signatory of Yoo's OLC memoranda, who was likewise investigated by the OPR. Between the writing of Yoo's memorandum for Bybee and the filing of Padilla's lawsuit, Bybee was appointed to be the life-long colleague of the judges who decided on the merits of the claims being made against Yoo, and implicitly, Bybee.

The only way to reach this particular result was for the court to quietly put a thumb on the scales of justice, but other appellate courts openly advocated this approach. In a related appeal before Fourth Circuit, which addressed the conduct that occurred within its jurisdiction, the court opined that when assessing arguments such as those made by Padilla against Yoo, the courts should hesitate in construing facts against the government, since "the Constitution delegates authority over military affairs to Congress and to the President as Commander in Chief. It contemplates no comparable role for the judiciary."[93]

This statement renounces the responsibility of the judiciary to adjudicate constitutional claims against the executive, combined with acquiescence to the executive's erroneous theory of the scope of its powers to command the military. It makes the judicial oversight that the rule of law requires impossible. As one academic commentator noted, "If this [invocation of the interests of national security by the executive] is a 'special factor' counseling hesitation against inferring a ... remedy, one is hard-pressed to imagine any challenge to the conduct of national security policy, whether here or overseas, that could survive such a test."[94]

The suits brought by Guantánamo detainees alleging torture and other abuses were procedurally more complex than Padilla's, since they involved non-citizens and took place outside of the United States. This did not bode well for their success. However, the Supreme Court decided in *Boumediene* that despite these jurisdictional complications, petitions for habeas corpus could be brought to the US District Court for the District of Columbia.

It seemed likely that trial courts in the District of Columbia would conclude that they had jurisdiction to hear the detainees' tort claims. Unfortunately, while this prediction proved correct, it failed to account for the willingness of the DC Circuit to distort the holdings of the Supreme Court and to create new doctrines of executive deference to shut this down, something which the Supreme Court failed to rebuke, even as the DC Circuit dismantled its earlier jurisprudence, in the same manner as in the appeals of the denials of habeas petitions.

Apart from jurisdiction, the most significant procedural hurdle for the detainees bringing these claims was the sovereign immunity of the federal government, since under American law, the government may only be sued when it has expressly permitted plaintiffs to bring against it claims of that nature. Shafiq Rasul and three other British detainees who brought claims alleging "specific methods and acts of physical and psychological torture" would find that the clearest path to relief was afforded by the Religious Freedom Restoration Act (RFRA).[95] This is because that statute authorizes suits against the federal government. The trial court concluded that the government should be held responsible since "[f]lushing the Koran down the toilet and forcing Muslims to shave their beards falls comfortably within the conduct prohibited from government action" by RFRA.[96]

This much seemed clear, and it would be difficult to argue that even the most intellectually challenged executive branch officials would have recognized that this was prohibited conduct, which would appear to foreclose a qualified immunity defence. However, the DC Circuit held that the officials at Guantánamo, despite being aware that this conduct would violate the law if committed in the United States, may have reasonably believe that they could not be punished for breaking the law outside of the nation's borders.[97] Namely, it held they could have reasonably believed that the OLC was correct and that the detention camps were located within a "judicial black hole." Thus, even though the Supreme Court concluded that this was not the case during the applicable period, Guantánamo was retroactively deemed a zone of immunity because of executive officials' purportedly sincere belief that it was outside the law.

One year later, the DC Circuit proved ready to attack the Supreme Court's ruling in *Boumediene* more directly. The vehicle for the development of new doctrine that favoured the executive was the case of *Al-Zahrani v. Rodriguez*,[98] a case brought by the representatives of the estates of two detainees who died at Guantánamo Bay on 10 June 2006, in suspicious circumstances. These representatives alleged that although the executive labelled these deaths suicides, their relatives were killed during interrogations at a secret facility known as Camp Seven, the existence of which the executive formally denies. An investigation by reporters "raises serious questions ... and suggests the U.S. government is covering up details of what precisely happened ... before the deaths."[99] An academic report refuted the official narrative, concluding that "there is no explanation for how three bodies could have hung in cells for at least two hours while the cells were under constant supervision, both by video cameras and guards continually walking the corridors guarding only 28 detainees."[100]

The representatives' allegations were further supported by testimony from four American soldiers, and by the fact that marks were found on the victims' bodies that are consistent with torture. In addition, a Swiss pathologist noted that one of the victims' neck injuries were "not those he would normally associate with hanging."[101] Despite the seriousness of these claims and the presence of ample evidentiary support, the lawsuit was dismissed, and the DC Circuit used the appellate proceedings as an opportunity to make sure that no tort claims brought by former detainees, even if they involved shocking allegations of torture or unlawful killing, could ever be heard in any American court.

In *Boumediene*, the Supreme Court rejected the proposition that the detainees could be removed by statute from the jurisdiction of the federal courts. It held that section 7 of the Military Commissions Act could not prevent the detainees from filing lawsuits. In *Al-Zahrani*, the DC Circuit held that the holding of *Boumediene* applied only to petitions for habeas corpus, despite the fact that the Supreme Court struck down the entire section that had purportedly stripped the courts of jurisdiction, and despite the fact that this case held that "the United States, by virtue of its complete jurisdiction and control over the base, maintains de facto sovereignty."[102] There is no logic to the argument that the detainees should possess the constitutional right to habeas corpus but no other rights, except an argument premised upon belief that detainees should be deprived of as many rights as possible, and that the ends justify the means when doing so.

In misconstruing *Boumediene* and other precedents from the Supreme Court, which did not appear to foreclose damages claims owing to the executive's violation of constitutional rights where there was no alternate remedy or forum available,[103] the DC Circuit set up in its place a rule of remarkable breadth. The new rule is that a detainee cannot bring to an American court any action premised on "foreign" conduct, other than a request for a writ, a meaningless remedy after the DC Circuit's earlier rulings. Citing its opinion in *Kiyemba*, which held that innocent prisoners who were granted the writ possessed no right to be actually released, the court noted "not every right yields a remedy, even when the right is constitutional."[104] Here, the right at issue was perhaps the most fundamental of all: the right to life. There could be no clearer example of the courts abdicating their responsibilities. The doctrine which this opinion announced is incompatible with the rule of law.

Owing to the holding in *Al-Zahrani*, it is now simply impossible to bring a claim against the executive if the torture occurred outside the United States, even if it was in an area exclusively controlled by the agents of the executive – that is, Guantánamo, Afghanistan, ships on the high seas, or merely some foreign country that allows its prisons to be used as "black sites," and which permits the executive's agents to operate freely. For instance, this holding foreclosed actions brought by those abducted and subjected to "extraordinary" rendition, such as Khaled el-Masri,[105] a German national taken, beaten, and sodomised[106] by the CIA in Macedonia, and tortured in Afghanistan, merely because his name was similar to that of a terrorism suspect. He would only obtain relief at the European Court of Human Rights for the relatively minor conduct of the Macedonian authorities that allowed the CIA to kidnap him,[107] while the executive branch's conduct cannot be punished in any court. On the same basis, the DC Circuit has also dispensed with the claims of detainees held by the American military in Iraq and Afghanistan, "which are generally even more appalling than those that allegedly occurred at Guantanamo."[108]

The judiciary's unwillingness to end the regime of prolonged involuntary detention, and the torture which inevitably accompanies it, ignores the breakdown of the rule of law that it represents. Executive dominance above the laws has not only been tolerated, it was subsequently ratified in court opinions. While the executive sought to keep its internal legal advice secret, perhaps for fear of being rebuked by the courts, these opinions proved that these anxieties were groundless.

Consequently, a legal regime absolving the violation of non-derogable rights has been formalized by the courts. This has various effects. First, it ties the hands of judges in trial courts, many of whom now openly express dismay that they have been rendered powerless to offer relief to those who are suffering, or who have suffered, grievous harms. Second, it provides a green light for the executive to continue subjecting those it nominates to violations of their non-derogable rights.

The Response to the Appellate Courts' Green Light to Torture

Numerous violations of non-derogable rights have continued unabated after the transition to the Obama administration. The same *jus cogens* norms are being violated, and that this is being done for the same reasons, which serve to further undermine the rule of law. Consideration of the executive's ongoing attempts to hold prisoners who have been proven innocent sheds some light on why it is committed to perpetuating this regime of prolonged arbitrary detention and torture.

Certain difficult questions must first be addressed. Namely, why has the Obama administration fought so hard to keep detainees at Guantánamo Bay when the president campaigned on a promise to close it? Why does the executive continue to detain prisoners at Camp Platinum, where according to the chief military defense counsel of the Office of Military Commissions, prisoners are still held in conditions that do not comply with the minimum standards of Article 3 of the Geneva Conventions,[109] and where they can be tortured with impunity following *Al-Zahrani*? Finally, why did the Obama administration argue in 2012 that these detainees should no longer have access to lawyers?[110] Why did it build the Parwan Detention Facility? Even without answers, these questions themselves make it evident that the executive tried to return the detention system to one that no light can ever penetrate so that it can continue to torture detainees.

The Bush administration's impetus for the creation of this system was the extraction of false confessions. It is impossible to discern any other reason why the Obama administration has sought to return its detention and interrogation regime to the level of secrecy that the 2001–2003 OLC memoranda contemplated. That said, there are also indications that detainees are still being held and tortured at Guantánamo and various black sites, most notably at Parwan and other facilities operated by the Joint Special Operations Command in Afghanistan. This should be considered when discussing the executive's attempts to eliminate these detainees' access to lawyers and to grant immunity to torturers. At Parwan, detainees were held without any access to lawyers, since the DC Circuit affirmed that they have no right to petition for habeas corpus, and they can be tortured and even killed with impunity, since it also affirmed that they do not have rights that can be enforced in American courts.

There is substantial evidence that the executive subjected detainees at Parwan to conditions and interrogation methods that rise to the level of torture. For example, there are multiple reports confirming the torture of detainees at the "black jail," the facility at Parwan operated by the Defense Intelligence Agency's Defense Counterintelligence Field Activity. It is also staffed with personnel from the highly secretive Joint Special Operations Command.[111] The Open Society Institute has documented its conditions, and noted that they do not comply with the basic guarantees of the Third Geneva Convention. Its report also noted that representatives from the International Committee of the Red Cross have been barred from the facility and others that have been designated as Special Operations camps.[112]

Congress obtained a significant amount of positive publicity in 2005, when it restricted the military to the techniques of interrogation outlined in the *Army Field Manual*. This legislation was "sold to the public as a return to civilized norms,"[113] but few noted that this action left the executive free to rewrite the manual, something which it did shortly afterwards.[114] When President Obama, in a much-heralded executive order[115] restricted the CIA to the techniques outlined in the rewritten manual, few noted Amnesty International's conclusions that it now contained an appendix, which allowed techniques that "do not comply with the international law regulations prohibiting torture."[116] Furthermore, the manual continues to rely on a categorization of certain prisoners as "unlawful enemy combatants" whom the executive deems unilaterally not to be entitled to the protections of the Third Geneva Convention, a procedure which itself does not comply with the Geneva Conventions.

It should also be noted that Executive Order 13491, which purportedly prevented the CIA from torturing detainees, also contained an opt-out procedure wherein a "Special Task Force" could propose "additional or different guidance [than the *Army Field Manual*] for other agencies,"[117] such as the Defense Intelligence Agency (DIA), whose procedures would remain classified and would not receive much attention, despite the fact that it is the agency conducting interrogations at the black jail at Parwan Detention Facility and other Special Operations camps. "Although the CIA's interrogation program was investigated ... the Defense Department's parallel activities have been given little scrutiny."[118] Naturally, when this "different guidance" was adopted, it was classified above "Top Secret." Accordingly, it is unclear what methods the Defense Department has approved for DIA interrogations,[119] although one can infer from the fact that certain techniques amounting to torture have been declassified, these methods must be considerably less acceptable, although it is impossible to determine at this time whether particular techniques such as waterboarding have been re-authorized.

The executive has reaffirmed a detention regime involving black sites, secrecy, and torture even at a time when interrogators and intelligence officials continue to reiterate that this paradigm does not produce useful intelligence,[120] something which was evident not long after the 9/11 attacks. There is no explanation proffered for this, although it suggests that this administration has done so for the same reasons as its predecessor: to produce false confessions. It should also be noted that during the Obama administration, director of national intelligence Admiral Dennis Blair continued to credit "enhanced interrogation" with obtaining "high-value information" from detainees.[121] He made this case after it was already clear that this "information" was only considered "high value" at the time because it was helping the executive make the case for a war of aggression against Iraq. It remains unclear why the executive would want to leave a system in place that is perfectly designed to produce falsehoods that suit its interrogators.

Targeted Killing

While court challenges to the executive's violation of non-derogable rights began with challenges to prolonged arbitrary detention and only later addressed torture, this can easily be explained. The torture of detainees was a tightly controlled and highly secretive program designed to produce dubious evidence that would later be labelled "intelligence" that conveniently supported the executive's arguments for aggressive war. However, the targeted killing program was even more secretive, as it involved acts of war itself, within both Pakistan and Yemen. The Bush administration inaugurated a program that authorized drone strikes against suspected terrorists. Although the targeted killing program does not comply with basic norms of international humanitarian law, the Obama administration oversaw a tenfold increase in drone strikes.[122] This program did not lead to much litigation, however, as the cases presented serious jurisdiction problems, and they would also challenge the use of military force, something which creates the danger of flouting public opinion.

That said, a test case presented itself when the executive, which traditionally kept these programs secret, openly announced its intention to subject an American citizen to a drone strike. On 6 April 2010, the *New York Times* reported that after a discussion within the National

Security Council, President Obama authorized the extrajudicial killing of Anwar Al-Awlaki.[123] His father, Nasser al-Aulaqi, then asked a federal trial court to enjoin the killing.[124] The *Al-Aulaqi* lawsuit was filed on 30 August 2010.[125]

Nasser al-Aulaqi sought a declaratory judgment stating that the targeted killing program, insofar as it targeted US citizens who did not present concrete, specific, and imminent threats to life or physical safety, was unconstitutional.[126] He also sought an order requiring the executive to disclose the criteria used to identify its targets.[127] The executive filed a motion to dismiss, arguing that the plaintiff lacked standing to file a claim and that adjudicating the claims would require the court to decide non-justiciable political questions.[128] The motion was granted.[129] However, the court's decision that Nasser al-Aulaqi did not have standing to bring the suit as his son's representative was paradoxical.

The court concluded that such a suit must be brought personally, since "Al-Awlaki can access the U.S. judicial system by presenting himself in a peaceful manner," a leap of logic that depends on the premise that "[a]ll U.S. citizens may avail themselves of the U.S. judicial system if they present themselves peacefully."[130] First, it should be noted this presumes that those administering the targeted killing program will act in accordance with the Constitution, even after the executive has already concluded that its guarantees do not apply to the targeted person. Second, the court opined that Al-Awlaki could turn himself in merely because of its allegation that there is "there is nothing preventing him from peacefully presenting himself at the U.S. Embassy in Yemen."[131] Since the executive was actively trying to kill him this assertion is highly questionable.

The court also dismissed the suit for presenting a non-justiciable political question. The court rested its reasoning chiefly on the precedent provided by *El-Shifa v. United States*.[132] In it, the "DC Circuit examined whether the political question doctrine barred judicial resolution of claims ... seeking to recover damages after their plant was destroyed by an American cruise missile. President Clinton had ordered the missile strike."[133] The court reasoned: "[T]he plaintiff asks this court to do exactly what the D.C. Circuit forbade in *El-Shifa* – assess the merits of the President's (alleged) decision to launch an attack on a foreign target. Although the 'foreign target' happens to be a U.S. citizen, the same reasons that counseled against judicial resolution of the plaintiffs' claims in *El Shifa* apply with equal force here."[134]

Although the court decided that it would not address Al-Awlaki's claim that he should not be killed without due process, it opined further:

> [I]t does not appear that any court has ever – on political question doctrine grounds – refused to hear a U.S. citizen's claim that his personal constitutional rights have been violated as a result of U.S. government action taken abroad. Nevertheless, there is inadequate reason to conclude that Anwar Al-Awlaki's citizenship – standing alone – renders the political question doctrine inapplicable to plaintiff's claims.[135]

Owing to this conclusion and the court's concern that the relief sought "would be vastly more intrusive upon the powers of the Executive" than those typically sought by a petitioner seeking habeas corpus, and because "the questions posed in this case require expertise beyond the capacity of the judiciary and [since there is a purported need for] *unquestioning adherence to a political decision by the executive*,"[136] the court held that the claims were non-justiciable. This was presented as a felicitous result that avoided demonstrating "a lack of respect due to coordinate branches of government," and creating "the potentiality of embarrassment of multifarious pronunciations by various departments on one question."[137]

In summary, the court decided not to examine the merits of a suit brought on behalf of a US citizen who claimed he was the subject of an executive death warrant issued without due process on two grounds. First, because of speculation and adverse inferences the court concluded that the plaintiff had no standing to bring the suit. It did so despite the fact that this prudential consideration has routinely been waived when "human lives are at stake." American courts have often expressed disdain for the argument that such a case should turn on "fine points of procedure or a party's technical standing to bring a claim" in that circumstance.[138] However in this case a judicially crafted limitation was used to trump constitutional claims of the highest importance.

Second, and more importantly, the case was dismissed because the court did not believe that the judiciary possessed the power to determine the constitutionality of a decision by the president to issue an executive death warrant. Instead, it held that such a decision is best left to the executive branch itself, to which an almost obsequious level of deference is apparently due, even from the courts that were set up to enforce the limitations of the constitution against the executive. Again, this abject abandonment of the judiciary's most fundamental responsibility simply cannot be reconciled with the rule of law.

Secrecy of Executive Action

The secrecy of the executive's efforts involving the systematic violation of non-derogable rights was an integral feature of these programs and essential to defeating court challenges, as appellate courts pronounced themselves helpless to proceed in the face of stonewalling by the executive. Certain sections of the federal judiciary were quick to erect further barriers to court challenges by affirming the right to keep evidence of fundamental rights violations out of the hands of those who would seek to hold the executive accountable. The judicially created doctrines invoked by the courts when dismissing lawsuits challenging prolonged arbitrary detention, torture, and extrajudicial executions, which include the doctrine of qualified immunity and so-called special factors, jurisdictional bars, heightened standing requirements, and the political question doctrine, have all been highly effective means of denying relief to plaintiffs who alleged violations of *jus cogens* norms. Another contributing factor has been the withholding of government records that should have been provided to those bringing the lawsuits pursuant to FOIA requests, or in response to discovery requests made in the course of this litigation.

Given the fact that these lawsuits are now consigned to failure by the judicially created doctrines that facilitate the evasion of any review on the merits of claims against the executive, one might argue that restrictions on public records are superfluous, and thus do not affect the assessment of whether or not the United States is in compliance with the norms of the rule of law. However, this would fail to account for the additional political benefit of keeping certain activities secret.

If the executive branch carries out programs that, if disclosed, would shock the public, maintaining secrecy is integral to preventing the sort of political backlash that occurred after the revelations of the Church Committee, which helped to restore the rule of law. As the final hope for the restoration of the rule of law in the United States is the prospect of legislative action spurred on by public outrage, the executive's attempts to keep its most dubious programs secret is pertinent.

The most problematic covert action undertaken after the 9/11 attacks was the targeted killing program. Journalists attempted to bring it to light by litigating the government's failure to provide information about the killing of an American citizen: Anwar Al-Awlaki. The proceedings illustrate how judicially created rules have created a system where it is possible for the executive to keep almost anything secret, even programs that violate the fundamental rights of its citizens.

Before discussing how appellate court decisions have made obtaining such information virtually impossible, it should be noted that the executive branch provided the lead to the judiciary. Despite campaign promises to restore transparency, the Obama administration has done the opposite. One example of this is an executive order allowing retroactive classification of a document. This means that someone may file a valid request for a government record, but before it is released, the executive can decide that it should have been considered classified and therefore exempt from FOIA, even if those who created the document saw no need to consider it confidential, if "the original classification authority [in its sole discretion] determines that the unauthorized disclosure of the information reasonably could be expected to result in damage to the national security."[139]

The effects of this regime become apparent when one considers *New York Times v. Department of Justice*,[140] which sought information "about the legal basis ... for authorizing the targeted killing of Anwar Al-Awlaki."[141] In particular, the suit sought to compel disclosure of an OLC memorandum written in 2010 and signed by David Barron, which "concluded that Mr. Awlaki could be legally killed."[142] The quality of the legal reasoning of this memorandum appears highly questionable, since leaks have confirmed that it failed to even mention a key provision of the Constitution that specifically prohibits extrajudicial execution.[143]

This perception of flawed legal reasoning is not helped by the statements of the US attorney general who defended the program by stating that the due process mandated by the Constitution "is not necessarily judicial process," even when the right being taken away is not Social Security Disability Insurance payments before a judicial hearing,[144] but when a citizen is being deprived of his life after a process[145] conducted by counterterrorism officials.[146] Other officials from the Department of Justice also asserted on the executive's behalf that no court possessed any jurisdiction to question whether this deprivation of life was a violation of a citizen's constitutional rights.[147] Given these assertions, disclosure of the legal justification in the OLC memorandum for this program is of paramount importance to the rule of law.

The executive responded to the suit by moving to dismiss it, refusing to confirm or deny the existence of the OLC memorandum because "this would cause harm" by revealing "information about the interests, priorities and capabilities of the subject agencies."[148] This is a strange assertion, since the requested document would presumably contain only a legal argument, since that is what it purports to be. In its response to this motion, the New York Times clarified that it "seeks only legal analysis, not the details of any operation, past or future, which can properly be subject to redaction, if necessary."[149] In addition, it noted that the government provided no explanation why "legal analysis is properly characterized as a national security secret."[150]

Despite the cogency of the plaintiffs' arguments, the court dismissed the case, but in doing so exposed the way in which earlier appellate court rulings made it impossible for the plaintiffs to prevail under any circumstances, regardless of the importance of the information they sought to the rule of law. Perhaps owing to this distressing conclusion, the trial court's opinion lapsed into the first person:

I find myself stuck in a paradoxical situation in which I cannot solve a problem because of contradictory constraints and rules – a veritable Catch-22. I can find no way around the thicket of laws and precedents that effectively allow the Executive Branch of our

Government to proclaim as perfectly lawful certain actions that seem on their face incompatible with our Constitution and laws, while keeping the reasons for their conclusion a secret.[151]

The court noted that because the government chose to label the requested documents as classified, a request to the judiciary was fruitless. "It lies beyond the power of this Court to determine if a document has been improperly classified."[152] The trial court cannot order the disclosure of "final policies that have been adopted by the Executive to target individuals and to decide whether or not they can lawfully be killed by Executive fiat."[153]

What is most notable is that the trial court found that it was compelled to reach this conclusion by the "thicket of laws and precedents" despite the fact that it appears to have concluded in dicta that the targeted killings were extrajudicial assassinations punishable under domestic law. The court came to this conclusion after pointing out that the statute forbidding "[f]oreign murder of United States nationals ... contains no exception for the President ... or anyone acting at his direction ... Presidential authorization does not and cannot legitimize covert action that violates the constitution and laws of this nation."[154]

The court also noted that the "literal language of the Fifth Amendment, the Treason Clause, and the cited statutes notwithstanding, the Administration ... has gone so far as to mount an extensive public relations campaign in order to convince the public that its conclusions [about its authority to order extra-judicial executions] are correct."[155] The court implicitly argued that though the executive authorized covert operations that unlawfully killed citizens and argued at length that it has the power to do so, the court cannot order the executive to release its own rationale, or even compel them to admit formally and on the record that it engaged in these operations.

Unfortunately, it is impossible for the victims of state-sanctioned murder and other violations of non-derogable rights to bring successful court challenges without these classified documents. As the trial court noted, "the Alice-in-Wonderland nature of this pronouncement is not lost on me."[156] Presumably, the nature of this crisis of the rule of law is such that when the executive construes a law, it "means precisely what [it] choose[s] it to mean – neither more nor less," as "the question is which is to be master – that's all."[157] The trial court might as well have observed that its opinion was the death knell of the rule of law. Despite the executive's admission of its murderous actions, no court can order the executive to release the documents that might make it possible for the court to hold it accountable for that crime.

Unlawful Surveillance

In addition to keeping information about the executive out of the hands of those who sought to challenge its violation of citizens' non-derogable rights, the higher courts systematically empowered the right of the executive branch to gather information about the citizenry. It also used this power against its critics, and in particular against those who challenged its policies, in an echo of Nixon's abuses. The executive argued that it could ignore the laws and constitutional provisions restricting warrantless surveillance, owing either to the AUMF or its purported reserve powers, triggered by what it characterized as a state of war. Again, while it is difficult to understand how the authorization to deploy troops in battle implies clearance to eavesdrop on conversations, the OLC was prepared to provide the necessary legal justification. Problematic legal reasoning was simply beside the point, because the relevant memorandum was kept secret, even from the agencies that conducted the surveillance: "In late 2003, the NSA's General Counsel and the Inspector General sought access to Mr. Yoo's memoranda ... Mr. [David] Addington angrily rebuffed them."[158]

This tight secrecy was motivated by the audacity and scale of the "President's Surveillance Program" (PSP) which dwarfed the Cold War NSA programs. This program was gargantuan. It involved diverting every single personal communication transmitted across the telecommunications companies' trunk lines. The NSA simply inserted a shunt that relayed all of this communications traffic from these hubs to their headquarters, where all of these messages could be parsed.[159] This rendered unnecessary the earlier methods of obtaining this type of data, which often involved knowingly providing false information in warrant applications.[160]

While the executive insisted that it was merely conducting surveillance on al Qaeda terrorists, such that the President's Surveillance Program and other operations might appear to be implied by the AUMF, this mandate was quickly extended. Attorney General Alberto Gonzales later revealed that the NSA was "not just targeting terrorists but anyone deemed 'affiliated' or 'working in support' of terrorists." One prominent law professor noted that "this definition casts so wide a net that no one can feel certain of escaping its grasp."[161] These anxieties appeared warranted given a widely publicized statement of the chief executive. As he said before a joint session of both legislative bodies, "Either you are with us, or you are with the terrorists."[162]

After the 9/11 attacks, peace activists were perceived as not being "with us," and this led to abuses that continued long after 2001, especially after the executive put into place its strategy of extending the crisis period by launching new wars. In 2005, a leak revealed that the Counterintelligence Field Agency (CIFA) database contained extensive records of spying on the political activity of antiwar groups opposed to the Iraq War. In it, innocuous activities, such as a meeting at a Quaker meeting house, were described as a "threats."[163] The range of targets for this surveillance was also extended to include academics, as "military personnel also attended academic conferences and tracked participants' private statements."[164] The military intelligence agencies were not alone. "CIFA was far from unique. The FBI, returning to its old habits, was also spying on antiwar activists ... the FBI's Pittsburgh office kept the interfaith Thomas Merton Center under surveillance" for at least three years.[165]

What is particularly problematic about this surveillance is what was fed into vast databases and cross-linked, in a manner that the architects of Operation CHAOS could only have dreamed about. "One of the CIFA-funded database ... dubbed 'Person Search,' is designed 'to provide comprehensive information about people of interest.'" Presumably, this linked to the President's Surveillance Program and other databases, and could provide information about those whom any particular activist called or emailed and field reports from undercover agents, and other files, at the click of a mouse. The Total Information Awareness database was the result of "a huge data mining scheme ... [that] track[ed] Americans' credit-card transactions, website visits, travel records, bank transactions, and [linked to] other database files at the Pentagon."[166]

The use of these technologies and methods of surveillance against antiwar activists makes it "disturbingly clear that the mistakes of the past [and in particular, the Nixon administration] are being repeated once more. Rather than focusing on the nation's enemies, intelligence services are trained on American dissenters from the government's policies."[167]

That said, any keen student of Nixon's presidency, including the many located in the executive branch after the 9/11 attacks, would have remembered that his efforts to control the antiwar movement were not incidental to his agenda. Rather, the Church Committee and other investigations revealed that escalating the Indochina War was an integral part of his attempt to free the executive from all legal restraint and oversight. Destroying the movement that stood in the way of an expanded war and concomitant crisis was essential to Nixon at that time. It is entirely possible that Cheney and others saw the movement against the Iraq War in the same manner, given the similarities in their goals. Cast in this light, the assumption that the Bush administration sought to use the intelligence agencies in the same manner as Nixon and for the same ends does not appear unwarranted, and this was confirmed by subsequent revelations about these programs.

These efforts to implement surveillance and control would present as serious a challenge to the rule of law as the "White House horrors" that brought about Nixon's resignation. However, in the absence of a thorough congressional investigation, opponents of the executive who were subjected to unlawful surveillance and other abuses can only turn to the courts.

The first serious challenge to warrantless surveillance of peace activists, scholars, and others engaging in constitutionally protected political activity was brought on 17 January 2006.[168] The suit alleged that the "NSA engaged in wholesale data-mining of domestic and international communications" in violation of FISA, and that some of the plaintiffs would have been targeted for surveillance merely because of the topics they researched on the Internet.[169] The plaintiffs included the American Civil Liberties Union, owing to its work in connection with the United

Nations Working Group on Arbitrary Detention, which involved the investigation of "special interest" detainees who were "rendered ... to detention and interrogation facilities operated by the CIA outside U.S. sovereign territory," including Khaled el-Masri.[170]

The executive's eavesdropping on these privileged attorney-client communications made this legal representation more difficult. Journalists and scholars also alleged that their work investigating law-breaking by the intelligence community, including the NSA, in the case of the author James Bamford, was now more difficult, as their sources believed they were being subjected to warrantless surveillance.[171] Owing to these effects on constitutionally protected speech, these plaintiffs alleged violations of their free speech and associational rights, along with violations of the Fourth Amendment, and noted that this surveillance "violates the principle of separation of powers because it was authorized ... in excess of his Executive authority under ... the United States Constitution and contrary to limits imposed by Congress."[172]

The trial court's ruling in this case was a stirring rebuke to an over-reaching executive. Despite the fact that the NSA withheld numerous documents on the assertion of "state secrets privilege," the court held that this information was not required in order for the plaintiffs to establish their standing, and to make the prima facie case of a constitutional violation that would justify an injunction.[173] On the question of standing, the absence of which was invoked by appeals courts when dismissing claims after the 9/11 attacks, on the basis that plaintiffs cannot prove they were targeted by the executive without access to secret documents that cannot be released, the court reasoned as follows:

[I]f the court were to deny standing based on the unsubstantiated minor distinctions drawn by Defendants, the President's actions in warrantless wiretapping, in contravention of FISA, Title III, and the First and Fourth Amendments, would be immunized from judicial scrutiny. It was never the intent of the Framers to give the President such unfettered control, particularly where his actions blatantly disregard the parameters enumerated in the Bill of Rights. The three separate branches of government were developed as a check and balance for one another.[174]

Citing the *Keith* case, the trial court noted that these plaintiffs now complained about the sort of activity that had brought down the Nixon administration. Furthermore, it noted that Congress had prohibited these practices by FISA, which did not acknowledge any constitutional reserve powers in the executive. It also observed that the Fourth Amendment was itself a response to this sort of executive overreaching, in the form of the general search warrants executed in the American colonies. Quoting the *Steel Seizure Case*, the court reasoned:

> [E]mergency powers are consistent with free government only when their control is lodged elsewhere than in the Executive who exercises them. That is the safeguard that would be nullified by our adoption of the "inherent powers" formula. Nothing in my experience convinces me that such risks are warranted by any real necessity, although such powers would, of course, be an executive convenience … With all its defects, delays and inconveniences, men have discovered no technique for long preserving free government except that the Executive be under the law, and that the law be made by parliamentary deliberations.[175]

The trial court concluded that the PSP was contrary to statute and unconstitutional. In doing so, it refuted the notion that the executive possessed emergency powers that would allow it to ignore duly enacted laws "[T]he Office of the Chief Executive has itself been created, with its powers, by the Constitution. There are no hereditary Kings in America and no powers not created by the Constitution. So all 'inherent powers' must derive from that Constitution," which grants the executive no emergency powers.[176] It also concluded that the AUMF could not be construed to support this activity, as this would amount to a general statute implicitly overruling another, FISA, which was more specific.

Unfortunately for the plaintiffs, this ruling was never put into effect. It was stayed immediately and subsequently vacated by the Sixth Circuit.[177] The court held that plaintiffs lacked standing to bring any of their claims, since they could not demonstrate that they were subjected to warrantless surveillance. "[B]ecause of the State Secrets Doctrine [the plaintiffs] cannot … produce any evidence that any of their own communications

have ever been intercepted by the NSA, under the TSP, or without warrants."[178] The court did not appear to appreciate the irony of allowing a
defendant to frustrate plaintiffs' constitutional claims by refusing to turn
over the documents they need to prove those claims.

Rather than decrying a Catch-22, in the same manner as the trial court
in *New York Times v. Department of Justice*, the Sixth Circuit created
one. The pattern that emerges from the court challenges after the 9/11 attacks is clear. Plaintiffs are barred by a "thicket of precedents" that block
their path to a review on the merits the appellate court opinions disposing of these claims persist and proliferate, creating precedents that doom
future lawsuits challenging violations of constitutional rights.

For instance, a subsequent suit challenging warrantless surveillance
filed in the Southern District of New York, *Amnesty International v.
McConnell*, was dismissed owing to the plaintiffs' purported failure to
demonstrate their standing to sue, in which the decision of the Sixth Circuit in *ACLU v. NSA* was cited multiple times.[179] This is another example
of a case in which a clear failure of the executive to comply with its obligations during the discovery process was exacerbated by the circuit
courts' willingness to create precedents that deprive the trial courts of
any ability to challenge disingenuous assertions of "state secrets privilege," in the same manner that they were stripped of the ability to
challenge the retroactive classification of documents as "secret" after
they become the subject of FOIA requests, as seen in *New York Times v.
Department of Justice*.

There are other pertinent examples of this process. During the discovery process, the plaintiffs in *Amnesty International* requested a legal
opinion purportedly justifying the FBI's participation in warrantless
wiretapping programs. A document that appears to be a legal memorandum from the FBI's general counsel was disclosed. However, despite
the fact that it was initially marked "Precedence: Routine" and "All information contained herein is unclassified exc[ept] where shown otherwise," four months after it was written, shortly before it was turned over
to the plaintiffs, it was reclassified as "Secret." As a result, the legal analysis was redacted from the version given to the plaintiffs.[180] It is unclear
how a legal analysis could be a state secret, but this was the rationale for
the redaction.

This principle is now not only accepted by the courts but embodied by some of them. One example is found in the decision of the Foreign Intelligence Surveillance Court of Review (FISCR), a special court set up to hear appeals of rulings disposing of the challenges of telecommunications providers and other data carriers to the orders of the executive to turn over their customers' private information.

In 2007, an unnamed telecommunications company refused to carry out the executive's demands that it turn over records without being served with warrants.[181] This was a perilous course of action. Former CEO of Qwest Communications Joseph Nacchio argued that Qwest was punished for refusing to comply with such an order by losing out on government contracts worth hundreds of millions of dollars. (He was also subsequently prosecuted on an unrelated charge of insider trading.)[182] The Foreign Intelligence Surveillance Court dismissed these objections, as did FISCR on review.[183]

These decisions are made in secret. The public is never even informed that challenges to requests for warrantless surveillance have ever been made. However, in a "rare public ruling," FISCR decided to affirm the constitutionality of the program. It did so in an opinion that was itself redacted. Not only are the executive's justifications for violations of fundamental rights now being withheld from the public, but a court of law now does the same. It is unclear how this could be reconciled with the rule of law. These secret opinions demonstrate that certain courts have become ever more compliant to the executive's demands. In particular, these courts have been amenable to arguments about the need for secrecy that make judicial review of violations of non-derogable rights impossible.

Judicial Tolerance of Unilateral War-Making

One of the key reasons for the executive's violation of non-derogable rights was to generate "intelligence" that would purportedly justify aggressive war. As during the Nixon administration, a vicious circle was a dangerous possibility. Violations of *jus cogens* norms could be used to launch wars, which would then justify more violations of non-derogable rights. The courts' response to the executive branch's destruction of the rule of law after the 9/11 attacks would need to address the executive's claim that it possessed the unilateral right to declare and wage aggressive wars. Just as Nixon's claims to this power needed to be rebuffed in order to restore the rule of law after the invasion of Cambodia, the courts would need to respond to similar claims made after the 9/11 attacks in order to terminate the crisis created by this new state of emergency. Unfortunately, this was not the case.

The final critical post-9/11 failure of the higher courts to support the rule of law as re-implemented in the congressional resurgence of 1974–1980 is the consistent refusal to give any effect to the War Powers Resolution. The WPR reasserted "the Constitution's broad textual commitment to Congress's key role in the war-making system."[184] Section 1542 requires that the executive notify the legislature whenever troops are committed to hostilities. Despite arguments from the executive's own lawyers and academics who propagate anachronistic arguments about scope of the Constitution's Declare War Clause,[185] "its constitutionality is not seriously in question."[186]

After this notification, if Congress does not pass a resolution approving the extension of hostilities within ninety days, the executive must withdraw them. While the executive branch argues that this provision is an "unconstitutional abridgement on the President's unitary power as Commander-in-Chief,"[187] during the congressional resurgence even the OLC accepted that it was constitutional.[188] If the president authorizes the military's use of force, even in a rescue mission, he must comply with the WPR. When Congress remained jealous of its constitutional prerogatives, the executive did what the statute required. For example, in 1975, President Ford's conduct during the crisis precipitated by the capture of the SS *Mayaguez* conformed scrupulously to the WPR's requirements.[189]

That said, when the executive has failed to comply with the WPR, the courts have consistently refused to enforce it. This is best illustrated by outcome of the lawsuit challenging President Obama's unilateral decision to intervene during the Libyan civil war, by attacking the government and armed forces of Libya. It should be noted that the Security Council Resolution does not itself provide the requisite authorization under US domestic law,[190] and Congress did not authorize the intervention within sixty days of its initiation as the WPR required.

Kucinich v. Obama[191] was filed after "Speaker [of the House of Representatives John] Boehner sent a letter to President Obama informing him that the ninety-day period under the War Powers Resolution would pass on June 17th and that the President ha[d] failed to comply with the statute."[192] Despite the executive's failure to comply with both the WPR and the Constitution, the court dismissed the suit. It did so without reaching its merits, relying instead on two judicially created doctrines. These are the doctrines related to standing and the political question doctrine, which were invoked to dismiss the claims of citizens subjected to targeted killing.

As the suit was brought by ten members of Congress who voted for the law that the executive ignored, someone unfamiliar with the myopic view of standing adopted in the United States might expect that they would receive their day in court. However, in what appears to be an attempt to evade responsibility for addressing such injuries, the DC Circuit has developed a restrictive view of legislator standing. This doctrine holds that the judiciary should not address the executive's violation of a statute if the issue is still susceptible to "political resolution."[193]

This doctrine ignores the fact that the WPR represents the already-existing political resolution of the crisis of the rule of law created by Nixon's arguments that he could declare war on his own initiative. If the executive is willing to ignore a constitutionally valid law, it is unclear why Congress's power to pass another law should be seen as a potential solution to the problem. Once the executive contends that it has the power to ignore the laws in the interests of national security in general (i.e., the OLC opines that any attempt by Congress to restrain the executive's power to declare war to protect the nation would be unconstitutional), what would a statute that explicitly rejects that view accomplish? As Judge Brett Kavanaugh stated in his partial concurrence in *El-Shifa v. United States*:

> There is good reason the political question doctrine does not apply in cases alleging statutory violations. If a court refused to give effect to a statute that regulated Executive conduct, it necessarily

would be holding that Congress is unable to constrain Executive conduct in the challenged sphere of action. As a result, the court would be ruling (at least implicitly) that the statute intrudes impermissibly on the Executive's prerogatives under article II of the Constitution. In other words, the court would be establishing that the asserted Executive power is exclusive and preclusive, meaning that Congress cannot regulate or limit that power by creating a cause of action or otherwise.[194]

A judicial decision applying the political question doctrine to claims under the WPR would endorse the OLC argument about the executive's unreviewable powers to act in the interests of national security. As such, the only option that might remain for Congress would be to impeach the president. The courts' restrictive view of legislator standing – which serves the same function as the application of the political question doctrine to claims under the WPR – puts the legislature on the horns of a dilemma. Congress can either do nothing and tolerate the erosion of the rule of law, or act and risk a constitutional crisis, as the courts stand idly by, in sharp contrast to their conduct during the Watergate crisis.

The court adjudicating *Kucinich v. Obama* did not address the political question doctrine, "as the Court has concluded that the plaintiffs lack standing to bring the claims alleged in their complaint, it need not proceed to the related issue of whether the plaintiffs' claims present non-justiciable political questions."[195] It is clear, however, that the precedents of the Supreme Court and the DC Circuit would otherwise have compelled the trial court to find that the issue presented was non-justiciable on that ground. At the outset of the Cold War, the Supreme Court held that "[c]ertainly it is not the function of the Judiciary to entertain private litigation – even by a citizen – which challenges the legality … of the Commander-in-Chief in sending our armed forces abroad or to any particular region."[196] Despite intervening legislation, the higher courts have cleaved to this position across five decades. The precedents are so well-settled that the trial court in *Kucinich* openly expressed frustration, in another unusual lapse from decorum, with the legislators' attempt to litigate the issue of whether the executive was complying with the WPR:

[T]he Court finds it frustrating to expend time and effort adjudicating the relitigation of settled questions of law. The Court is simply expressing its dismay that the plaintiffs are seemingly using the limited resources of this Court to achieve what appear to be purely political ends, when it should be clear to them that this Court is powerless to depart from clearly established precedent of the Supreme Court and the District of Columbia Circuit.[197]

As early in the Cold War as 1950, the Supreme Court believed that it was self-evident why the judiciary should not scrutinize the executive's decision to commit troops to hostilities, a proposition with which many surely agreed owing to the prevailing political climate. That said, the Supreme Court has not explicitly reaffirmed this conclusion after Congress acted to define the precise scope of the legality of any deployment of the military, via the WPR. It need not do so, however, as long as the DC Circuit is willing to release the executive from its statutory responsibilities. It has done so,[198] and the trial courts whose opinion it binds have been forced to follow this holding repeatedly.[199]

These judicially created doctrines that allow for these rulings are simply the courts' attempt to shirk their responsibility to intervene when the executive ignores a statute, which is a basic requirement of the rule of law. This dynamic is especially troubling when the executive ignores the law in order to prolong a crisis that will likely empower it to behave lawlessly.

The Strategic Denial of Certiorari

The question that remains to be answered after detailing the judiciary's inadequate response to the destruction of the rule of law in the ten years after the 9/11 attacks is how the Supreme Court has managed to preserve its credibility, even as the courts have utterly failed to re-implement the rule of law by holding the executive accountable for its violations of nonderogable rights. It should again be noted here that after deciding *Boumediene v. Bush*, the Supreme Court has not arrested the development of judicially created doctrines that prevent trial courts from reaching the merits of lawsuits alleging violations of non-derogable rights. On 11 June 2012 it disposed of seven cases with one-line orders denying review. In these cases, the DC Circuit held that petitioners had no right to habeas corpus on the basis of a presumption of regularity that must be extended to patently unreliable intelligence reports.[200] Earlier, the court declined review of *Kiyemba v. Obama*, in which the DC Circuit held that the district courts possessed no power to order the executive to release a detainee who was granted the writ, or even to order the executive to produce the detainee before the court.[201]

On the same day, the Supreme Court declined review of *Lebron v. Rumsfeld*, which held that José Padilla could not bring a lawsuit against those who ordered him to be tortured, as they were allegedly entitled to qualified immunity in the course of their official duties, which purportedly included authorizing violations of non-derogable rights.[202] The rights of former Guantánamo detainees to bring these suits was foreclosed by the decision in *Rasul v. Myers*, which held that federal courts had no jurisdiction of these claims. This holding ignored the Supreme Court's decision in *Boumediene*. Despite the openly disdainful tone of this opinion, the Supreme Court declined the petitioners' request for review.[203]

These decisions led to serious consequences. Adnan Latif was a Yemeni detainee who argued persuasively that he was visiting Afghanistan in order to obtain free medical treatment from Islamic charities. He alleged that his neurological issues, for which he sought help in Afghanistan, were aggravated by the detention regime, but despite the fact that "he had been cleared for transfer [i.e., acquitted of wrongdoing] ... he could see no end to his confinement, and he killed himself."[204] Further suicides would not be surprising, as

> a lawyer who has represented a number of Guantanamo prisoners, said the sense of despair among prisoners overall seems to have worsened since the Supreme Court announced in June that it would not review the way courts were handling the men's individual challenges to their confinement. "There are a lot of guys who are having a really hard time ... Many of them have lost any hope that they are ever going to be released regardless of their status."[205]

Lawsuits challenging the targeted killing of citizens have yet to reach the Supreme Court, or even the DC Circuit, although its invocation of political question doctrine, which purportedly prevents a citizen from challenging the "targeting decisions" of the executive branch, was recently allowed to stand in *El Shifa v. United States*.[206] The same is true for lawsuits challenging the violation of the WPR.[207]

The Supreme Court did agree to address the doctrines that purportedly justify the executive's failure to respond to requests filed under the FOIA and the retroactive classification and redaction of documents sought in discovery during litigation challenging warrantless surveillance.[208] However, it decided to do so only after the executive requested this, after it lost an appeal in the Second Circuit that overturned the decision of the district court in *Amnesty International v. McConnell*.[209] The Second Circuit ruled that the plaintiffs had standing to sue despite the executive's refusal to turn over documents that would have proved that the plaintiffs were being subjected to warrantless surveillance.[210] The Supreme Court's decision was to overturn the Second Circuit, adopting the executive's argument with practically no reservations. It is instructive to consider that when it was asked to review the Sixth Circuit's decision that disposed of the plaintiff's claims owing to alleged lack of standing and the executive's invocation of the state secrets privilege,[211] the Supreme Court declined to issue a writ of certiorari.[212]

Conclusion: The Judiciary's Comprehensive Failure

In order to exist within the confines of a rule of law state, the executive must not be able to define the scope of its own powers, whether in an emergency or otherwise. Its activities must be confined to legal limits, delimited and policed by the legislature and the courts. This was the common vision of the Framers of the US Constitution, which undergirds its doctrine of the separation of powers, and which guarantees the rule of law (as it is defined by the common consensus of legal scholars, and set forth by the ICJ's Rio and Lagos Congresses). However, while the separation of powers can survive transient crises unscathed, the executive is empowered significantly in periods of prolonged war.

The second half of the twentieth century saw the United States slipping outside of the rule of law paradigm. If Nixon had successfully implemented his agenda, it is likely that the executive would have become permanently unaccountable for its violations of *jus cogens* norms, for aggressive wars, and possibly even for creating a system of mass prolonged arbitrary detention. However, Congress and the courts prevented this by resisting his agenda and commencing procedures to impeach Nixon, ending the Indochina Wars, and by passing legislation that formally ended the emergency powers and tightly circumscribed its control of the intelligence community.

The rule of law as re-established in the congressional resurgence of 1974–1980 did not survive the 9/11 attacks intact. The executive was again given wide-ranging emergency powers, which it used to violate non-derogable norms. It then sought to expand its own powers by claiming a non-existent constitutional right to overrule the other branches of government when purportedly acting in the interests of national security. The end result was a set of secret laws that authorized executive branch officials to subject people to illegal surveillance, prolonged involuntary detention, and torture, and to launch wars of aggression without any legislative involvement.

After the immediate crisis passed, the question that presented itself was whether this would be a transient crisis of the rule of law, like that created by the Civil War, or a permanent state of emergency, like that which followed the Second World War, and threatened to create a boundless executive branch that violated non-derogable rights as a matter of course, with no accountability. The answer would await the responses of the judiciary and the legislature to executive illegality. Would these branches of government reassert themselves, as they had during the Nixon administration, or would the absence of a response further empower the executive?

The first set of challenges to the new executive resurgence was brought in the courts. The third criterion of a rule of law state is that the judiciary must be able to hold the executive accountable when they violate fundamental rights. This is no longer even possible in the United States. Owing to new precedents and doctrines (in particular, the political question doctrine, the state secrets privilege, and restrictive approaches to standing and jurisdiction that prevent courts from addressing abuse that occurred overseas) the federal courts cannot exercise any oversight or restrain the executive's most serious violations of non-derogable rights.

The executive is free to arbitrarily detain, torture, kill, engage in limitless warrantless surveillance, and retroactively classify and withhold information relating to all of these activities. No court at present can even reach a consideration of the merits of lawsuits challenging this conduct, to the frustration of many trial courts that have been presented with clear evidence of violations of these *jus cogens* norms. These often present compelling cases that the executive has violated their non-derogable rights, which could easily be proven conclusively, if only the records detailing the executive's unconstitutional conduct were not withheld by the executive.

It is as yet unclear why the federal appellate courts would develop doctrines that prevent the judiciary from policing the boundaries of the rule of law. The key to this explanation will be the close connections between these two branches of government, as illustrated by the appointments process, which allows the executive to choose those who will sit in judgment over its attempts to subvert the laws.

CHAPTER 5

Judicial Selection and Executive Branch Dominance

The Importance of Control over the Judiciary

The rule of law in the United States is now severely imperilled because of the judiciary's failure to enforce non-derogable rights when they are violated by the executive. The judiciary tolerates the system of prolonged arbitrary detention, torture, extrajudicial killing, and unconstitutional surveillance set up after the 9/11 attacks. The procedural evasions certain appellate courts employed in cases brought by those challenging these wrongs show that it is now impossible to obtain recourse against the executive.

This violates the minimum requirement for a rule of law state: that the executive be legally accountable when it violates basic *jus cogens* norms.[1] However, these cases also appear to raise the issue of whether the United States may no longer be in conformity with the underlying criterion: that the judiciary is not merely able but willing to protect non-derogable rights. It is important to understand both the formal process for the appointment of judges that the constitution specifies, and those possibilities for distortion that were exploited by the executive.

The Advice and Consent Clause and Judicial Appointments

The Advice and Consent Clause of the US Constitution[2] outlines the processes by which Supreme Court justices (and, by implication, judges who adjudicate federal constitutional rights) are appointed: "[The president]

... shall nominate, and by and with the Advice and Consent of the Senate, shall appoint ... Judges." This formulation was the result of a compromise between a faction among the Framers who wanted to strengthen the federal government, the executive branch in particular (the Federalists), and those who were afraid that this might devolve into an autocratic government (the Anti-Federalists).[3]

In particular, the Anti-Federalists were concerned that granting the executive the exclusive right to appoint judges would destabilize the rule of law put into place by the separation of powers enshrined in the Constitution. For instance, John Rutledge "claimed that if a single person held that power to appoint judges, '[t]he people will think that we are leaning too much toward Monarchy.'"[4] However, advocates of stronger executive powers were unwilling to grant this power to the legislature, or even to the smaller of its two chambers (Alexander Hamilton had proposed giving this power to the Senate),[5] for fear that Congress would appoint candidates that leaned too far toward what the Federalists considered to be populism.[6] As Marcotte concludes on the subject of the Advice and Consent Clause:

> The final language of the Constitution represents a compromise – one that permitted a great deal of discretion on the part of the Executive in making the selection of judges ..., while still allowing the Senate to maintain a substantive role in the selection and con firmation process.[7]

This compromise created precisely the sort of shared responsibility in the judicial appointments process that the ICJ reasoned was necessary for the protection of the judiciary's independence – and therefore for the preservation of the rule of law. The ICJ noted in the Lagos Report that there "are also potential dangers in the exclusive appointment by the Legislative, Executive, or Judiciary," and instead advised that the selection mechanism include "representatives of two or more of these bodies."[8]

That said, during the framing and ratification of the Constitution, substantial doubts were raised about whether the legislature would be able to play a meaningful role in practice, or whether the executive would quickly monopolize all power over judicial appointments. Edmund

Randolph (who later became the first US attorney general) "stated ... that the President's involvement in judicial nominations was one of the reasons he refused to sign the Constitution."[9] Luther Martin (a prominent Anti-Federalist) likewise refused to sign owing to "concern that without substantial involvement by the Senate in the appointments process, the President could have 'an army of civil officers as well as Military.'"[10] George Mason, the leader of this faction, spoke for all his colleagues when he claimed that "[n]otwithstanding the form of the proposition [for a division of responsibility found in the Advice and Consent Clause] the appointment was substantially vested in the [executive] alone."[11]

There is substantial evidence, however, that the Framers intended the wording of the Clause to represent a real compromise, which preserved a substantive role for the Senate in the judicial appointments process.[12] This, however, did not prevent the Federalists from arguing to the contrary during the ratification debates, in an attempt to shape the meaning of the document and the relative powers of the executive and the legislative branches as a result. In particular, Hamilton argued in the Federalist No. 66 "that Senate rejection of the President's nominee would not be a regular occurrence,"[13] thereby attempting to shape the boundaries of acceptable conduct for the legislature when presented with candidates for the bench.

It was evident as early as 1787 that the integrity of the judicial selection process, while formally meeting the minimum requirements of the rule of law, would depend upon the vigilance and energy of the Senate, which would be faced with an executive branch that might attempt to reduce it to a rubber stamp. However, the early years of the American republic are replete with examples of the Senate asserting itself to make its role in this process meaningful, and not merely formal.

Senatorial Vigilance over Early Judicial Appointments

After the ratification of the Constitution, the Senate soon indicated its unwillingness to accept a passive role in the judicial appointments process, as the Federalists had hoped. Even the first president – George Washington – was subjected to a check on his power to nominate Supreme Court justices. John Rutledge's nomination to replace the first US chief justice was blocked by the Senate in 1795 (on a vote of 14–10; most opposition stemmed from senators who were loosely associated with the nascent Federalist Party) though he was eminently qualified for the position: Rutledge had been a Framer of the Constitution, the governor of South Carolina, a legislator in the Continental Congress, and chief judge of South Carolina's Court of Chancery and Court of Common Pleas at different times, in addition to having served as an associate justice of the US Supreme Court.[14]

The senators' issue with Rutledge's nomination is that he had not supported the Jay Treaty, which resolved those issues between the United States and the United Kingdom that remained after the signing of the Treaty of Paris, which had ended the Revolutionary War.[15] The Jay Treaty was strongly supported by the Federalists, who controlled the Senate; Washington, who attempted to remain above the fray as a non-partisan chief executive, acquiesced on the advice of the secretary of state, Alexander Hamilton.[16] However, the treaty was bitterly opposed by Thomas Jefferson and James Madison, who supported an alliance with revolutionary France instead. Rutledge agreed with Jefferson and Madison, and openly opposed ratification of the treaty by the Senate.[17]

It was clear by 1795 that in the next presidential election (the following year) the faction headed by Madison and Jefferson (later to become the core of the Democratic-Republican party) would attempt to gain control over the executive branch. Their aim was to alter the course of American foreign policy that had been charted by the Senate (and Hamilton, who became the head of the rival Federalist Party).[18]

This was the first of many such conflicts.[19] However, the Senate had sent a message in denying Rutledge the chief justice's seat: that it could and would fail to confirm candidates selected by the executive, and that it would not restrict its scrutiny to the nominees' formal qualifications. Instead, the legislature set the first mark in what would become a pattern of opposition, which was seen during this early phase of the American republic; for example, in the Senate's failure to confirm Alexander Wolcott and John J. Crittendon, who were seen as being too closely aligned to the Democratic-Republican and National Republican parties, respectively.[20]

The Senate's behaviour remained consistent during the next era of American politics, Jacksonian democracy: "[b]etween the Jackson and

Lincoln Presidencies, no fewer than 10 out of 18 Supreme Court nominees failed to win confirmation."[21] It should be noted that this was not merely a function of the emergence of the Second Party System; instead, it reflected a longstanding belief that jurists should not have close connections to the executive or the legislature. However, this intolerance of stacking the bench came to an end during the twentieth century. The Senate's resiliency in the face of the executive's attempts to produce a Supreme Court that was attuned to its priorities would not survive the emergency caused by the Second World War, which extended seamlessly into the Cold War.[22]

Executive-Judicial Relations in the Early Twentieth Century

Franklin Roosevelt, who would raise the executive branch to new heights of power by assuming broad emergency powers during the Second World War (and by intimidating both the legislature and the judiciary into tolerating this by means of appeals to the populace),[23] had already demonstrated an imperious attitude toward the judiciary two years before it began. After the Supreme Court struck down some of the Depression-relief legislation that had formed part of Roosevelt's New Deal, the executive formulated the infamous court-packing plan.[24] It proposed that the executive should be given the power to appoint a new justice to the Supreme Court for each of their number who exceeded the age of seventy years and six months. This would give Roosevelt an essential – and unprecedented – opportunity to reshape the composition of the court.

Roosevelt was open about this motive, despite his associates relying on some dubious pretexts (such as the purported inability of the justices to keep up with their caseload). In a speech to the American people, he frankly admitted that the court-packing plan was an attempt to overturn rulings with which he did not agree, and to erect a Supreme Court that agreed with his own jurisprudential philosophy. In his words, the bill he proposed would "restore the court to its rightful and historic place in our system of constitutional government and ... have it resume its high task of building anew on the Constitution 'a system of living law.' The court itself can best undo what the court has done."[25]

Before the long emergency of the mid-twentieth century, however, the Senate demonstrated that it could prevent the executive from imposing its will on the courts. The Judiciary Committee's response to the bill was scathing:

> The bill is an invasion of judicial power such as has never before been attempted in this country ... It is essential to the continuance of our constitutional democracy that the judiciary be completely independent of both the executive and legislative branches of the government ... It is a measure which should be so emphatically rejected that its parallel will never again be presented to the free representatives of the free people of America.[26]

Owing in part to this vigorous legislative response, the executive's attempts in 1937 to destroy the independence of the judiciary were rebuffed, but Roosevelt used the emergency created by the bombing of Pearl Harbor in 1941 to intervene into the courts' affairs in the most egregious ways, beginning with his intimidation of the Supreme Court in *Ex Parte Quirin*.[27] Between 1941 and 1968 the executive branch was able to expand its powers owing to popular support for the argument that the president should be pre-eminent during dangerous times.

The expansion of the executive's powers during the Cold War prepared the ground for Nixon's attempt to create an imperial presidency.[28] However, in doing so, Nixon destroyed the basis for the harmony between the branches of government. One leading indicator of the tensions that would erupt into the congressional resurgence was the renewed dispute over judicial selection.[29] While the Senate had approved all of the executive's nominees from Roosevelt's time until 1968 (owing largely to the executive's selection of distinguished jurists, rather than party loyalists)[30] this peaceful period would end shortly before the beginning of the Nixon administration, as the executive attempted to shore up the personal loyalty of the judiciary. This threatened the rule of law in the same manner as Roosevelt's court-packing plan, and the Senate's response would again prove crucial to the preservation of judicial independence.

Judicial Selection and the Rule of Law, 1968–74

Until the growth of presidential power, the executive's level of self-interest in senatorial confirmation of its candidates was comparatively low: "the federal judiciary was not seen as an obstacle to administration policies, and there was no overriding imperative to change the direction of judicial decision-making."[31] However, this consensus ended when the Vietnam War (after the executive forced it upon both the legislature and the populace) was prolonged and intensified, and it became highly unpopular with the American people.[32]

The importance of executive influence over the judiciary became clear when it began to act outside of the scope of its constitutional powers; it now faced the prospect of being challenged in the courts by Congress or the citizenry. As the struggles over the Vietnam War intensified, and the antiwar movement grew,[33] President Lyndon B. Johnson paid closer attention to the appointment of those judges who might someday sit in judgment of his policies. As Goodman relates: "As the Vietnam War came to dominate Johnson's presidency and opposition to Johnson became increasingly vocal, Johnson wanted to make sure that those he appointed [to the bench] were his supporters. As he put it in a note ... concerning [a] nomination ... 'Will he be an all out J-man?' ... These appointments clearly point up Johnson's personal agenda concerns."[34]

When considering Supreme Court appointments, Johnson increasingly turned to individuals whom he knew he could trust, owing to long-standing personal connections.[35] To many, it looked as if he was determined to appoint hangers-on who could best be described as "cron[ies]";[36] this led to the first backlash against a judicial nomination since before the Second World War. Abe Fortas, who was at the time serving as an associate justice of the Supreme Court, was nominated by Johnson in 1968 to be chief justice.

Johnson's private comments about the nomination seem to suggest a clear link in his own mind between a possibility of increasing opposition to his national security policies and the need for support within the judiciary: "When Johnson told Fortas to come to the White House for the announcement of his nomination [as associate justice], LBJ said 'I've just sent 50,000 men to Vietnam and I'm sending you to the Supreme

Court.'"[37] Arthur Goldberg had resigned from the court precisely because of his disagreement with Johnson's approach to Vietnam,[38] and
Johnson knew that challenges to his controversial foreign policy (which
was open to doubts about its constitutionality (in particular, the propri-
ety of executive action purportedly authorized by the Gulf of Tonkin
Resolution) might be decided by the Supreme Court. Fortas served Johnson well, but in ways that were very troubling to Congress, and not
without reason: "Fortas continued to advise and do favors for President
Johnson after he took his seat ... Fortas' relationship with the President
bore on the constitutional question of proper separation of powers between the executive and judicial branches of the federal government. He
was accused of being a judicial vehicle for presidential wrath against
politicians who opposed LBJ's policies."[39]

The Senate was dismayed at the president appointing his close political ally to the leadership of the Supreme Court, as this was seen as a threat
to the rule of law.[40] Accordingly, Fortas's nomination for the position as
chief justice was rejected.[41] During the Nixon administration, Fortas was
forced to resign from the court after he was implicated in an influence-
peddling scandal.[42]

Richard Nixon was elected president mere months after the Senate's
rejection of Fortas, but he had not learned the lesson about the resurgence of substantive consideration of judicial nominees that it represented. From the outset, Nixon signalled his intention to remake the court
in his own image,[43] much as Roosevelt had attempted. However, Nixon
had far less political capital than F.D.R. and he would spend what little
he had during his escalation of the Vietnam War[44] and his attempts to
forestall resistance by establishing executive supremacy. The judicial selection process would become another battleground between the executive and the legislature in the struggle against Nixon's attempts to do
away with the rule of law.[45]

In the course of his 1968 election campaign, Nixon inveighed against
the Supreme Court, pronouncing it guilty of activism and committing
himself to a program of imposing a new judicial philosophy upon it, via
the appointment of "strict constructionists."[46] This was a new euphe-
mism for jurists who would show deference to the executive branch, purportedly because the Constitution required it.

The Senate expressed its disapproval with Nixon's attempt to stock the bench with jurists who agreed with his views by rejecting two of his Supreme Court nominees in succession.[47] Clement Haynsworth and G. Howard Carswell were both well-qualified nominees, then serving as federal appellate judges of the Fourth and Fifth Circuits, respectively. However, the Senate was determined to protect judicial independence, which was threatened by Nixon's drive to appoint justices who agreed with his views on the Constitution. His administration was twice subjected to the "debacle of Senate rejection."[48] As Goldman notes, "These events placed the selection process of Supreme Court justices – and Supreme Court policymaking – on the front burner of American politics."[49]

After this loss of face, Nixon nominated a highly esteemed judge, Harry Blackmun, who was affirmed unanimously.[50] However, Nixon had apparently not learned his lesson. In 1971, he was admonished for creating a short list of candidates (to replace Justice Hugo Black) that did not include noted jurists,[51] but was populated with those whom he trusted personally, or those whom his aides had decided to be politically reliable.[52] After the media and the American Bar Association spoke out against these nominees,[53] he relented and nominated Lewis Powell, a well-respected Wall Street lawyer, who was approved by the Senate after a vote of 89–1.[54]

The Enduring Significance of Rehnquist's Nomination

Nixon's final Supreme Court nomination deserves to be discussed in detail. The selection of William Rehnquist was not merely a tactical victory in the executive's struggle for immunity from judicial enforcement of the laws, but the development of a new paradigm for placing justices loyal to the executive branch onto the Supreme Court.

Rehnquist, who had served the same role for Nixon as John Yoo would for George W. Bush, would have increasing ideological influence within the judiciary over time; for example,[55] Rehnquist was the key pro-executive force on the Supreme Court during the early Guantánamo cases. Furthermore, his successful nomination did not merely provide one additional vote in favour of raising the executive above the laws, but it also provided a road map for future administrations' attempts to place trusted and compliant jurists onto the nation's highest court.

Rehnquist's nomination benefited from being conducted in the shadow of Lewis Powell's, which had resolved the impasse between the Senate and the executive created by Nixon's prior refusal to nominate well-qualified candidates to replace Justice Hugo Black. Rehnquist's resumé also differentiated him from those substandard nominees: it included a master's degree in government from Harvard University and his position as Stanford Law School's class valedictorian.[56] Upon graduation, he served as (Supreme Court) Justice Henry Jackson's law clerk, going on to success in private practice before returning to government service within the Department of Justice's OLC during the Nixon administration.[57]

While initially his confirmation had seemed assured, Rehnquist's nomination was stalled by the discovery of memoranda he had written for Justice Jackson, which were part of an archive that had been made public after Jackson's death. These had been written when the case of *Brown v. Board of Education*[58] was pending before the court. *Brown* is now remembered as the "case of the century," in which the Supreme Court finally repudiated racial segregation, holding that separate facilities for African-Americans could never be equal (and overturning *Plessey v. Ferguson*,[59] a case from 1898 that had said that barring blacks from whites-only facilities was constitutional).

Fifteen years after *Brown*, the record of Rehnquist's unabashed defence of segregation appeared shocking. He wrote, "I think *Plessey v. Ferguson* was right and should be reaffirmed. To the argument that a majority may not deprive a minority of its constitutional right, the answer must be made that while this is sound in theory, in the long run it is the majority who will determine what the constitutional rights of the minority are."[60]

The explanation that Rehnquist provided to the Senate for this memorandum was bizarre: he said that Jackson had been considering upholding *Plessey*. As he wanted to be prepared for counterarguments in the justice's conference after the oral arguments in *Brown*, Jackson had asked Rehnquist to prepare a list of possible objections.

This story is implausible. Jackson supported desegregation, and the idea that he wanted Rehnquist to ghost-write a set of objections for him in the first person in a memorandum signed by Rehnquist is absurd. A much simpler explanation is that a law clerk was providing his own view of the case to a justice, something which they do frequently. However, as the only person who could directly contradict his explanation was deceased, the senators apparently did not feel that they had the evidence necessary to accuse the president's nominee of perjuring himself. (Jackson's secretary subsequently claimed that Rehnquist had been guilty of "a smear of a great man ... Justice Jackson did not ask law clerks to express his views. He expressed his own and they expressed theirs. That is what happened in this instance."[61]) If this was Rehnquist's personal opinion it would correspond with many other statements in contemporary memoranda, such as that written for the case of *Terry v. Adams*,[62] which were written in his own voice and to express his own views: "I take a dim view of this pathological search for discrimination and as a result I now have something of a mental block against the case."[63]

Unfortunately, without time to scrutinize these memoranda or find witnesses to contradict Rehnquist, the Senate could not expose his lies. (The Senate was also woefully uninformed about many other troubling issues, including Rehnquist's anti-Semitism[64] and his addiction to Placidyl[65] – a powerful and "frequently abused" narcotic known on the street as "Jelly-Beans"[66] – although this was known to the executive at the time of his nomination.)[67] More importantly for Nixon, without access to confidential material, the senators were unable to discover that Rehnquist had also been quite willing to distort the law and the facts in the service of the executive during his nomination hearings.

At the time of his nomination, Rehnquist was serving as the assistant attorney general in charge of the OLC. Unfortunately, the Senate had no access to the memoranda he had written in that capacity for Nixon, as the executive jealously guards OLC memoranda from the legislature, relying on various doctrines of privilege to do so.[68] Had these documents been available to the senators, they would have discovered that Rehnquist had been the architect of many of the constitutional theories that were entirely incompatible with the rule of law, including that of implicit and unchecked constitutional reserve powers.[69]

As Schlesinger noted, "[f]or a systematic constitutional defense of his action in [invading neutral] Cambodia, Nixon relied on ... Rehnquist."[70] (The conclusion that the executive possessed an inherent constitutional reserve power under the Commander-in-Chief Clause was, in Schlesinger's words, "persiflage,"[71] but it had been so useful to the executive that it later served as the key model for arguments of this type made in the OLC after the 9/11 attacks.) Rehnquist had also defended the right of the executive to conduct warrantless wiretapping.[72]

While at the OLC, Rehnquist was the architect of a theory of executive power that is at odds with both the Constitution and the rule of law. The Senate could not know that, as his advice to the executive remained shrouded. Despite having offered advice that was as skewed and selective as that which led to John Yoo's censure in 2010,[73] after perjuring himself to remove the taint of his support for racial segregation Rehnquist was confirmed by the Senate, having received cross-party support: voting in favour were thirty-eight Republicans and thirty Democrats.

The Supreme Court and Nixon's Resignation

The full importance of these nomination battles (and the absence of one over Justice Rehnquist) in Nixon's first term only become apparent after the fact. During his re-election campaign, Nixon began to resort to blatant illegality within the United States, without recourse even to the lie that this involved matters of national security (the CIA refused to cover for the burglary at the Democratic National Committee headquarters, as any allegation that this involved matters of national security would have been manifestly implausible).[74]

It was during Nixon's second term that his earlier failure to undermine the judicial independence of the Supreme Court began to take on a greater importance, owing to the surge of cases challenging expansive theories of executive power. By that time, the court had already disabused Nixon of the idea that his theory of inherent constitutional reserve powers would pass muster (in the *Keith* case[75]) and it became apparent that the court would side with Congress when adjudicating claims of unconstitutional executive overreaching.[76]

By late 1973, the exposure of Nixon's law-breaking cried out for a reckoning. At that point, it had already been revealed that the Watergate break-in was part of Nixon's re-election committee's general pattern of misconduct (that included theft, wiretapping, and other "dirty tricks");[77]

additionally, it had become clear that a cover-up of these activities –
which included suborning perjury and obstruction of justice – had been
coordinated at the highest levels of the administration.[78] The investigation
into this illegality, conducted by a special counsel who operated as a prosecutor for the Senate Watergate Committee,[79] achieved a breakthrough
when it was learned that a special taping system in the Oval Office likely
had recorded evidence of Nixon directing this criminal conspiracy.[80]

The committee issued subpoenas for the Watergate tapes, but the executive refused to comply.[81] At this point, the executive took a momentous step in an attempt to actively impede the investigation as well, by
ordering the termination of Archibald Cox, the committee's special counsel, who was under the formal control of the executive.[82] However, since
the relevant statute allowed his termination only in the event of gross
misconduct, Attorney General Elliot Richardson (a well-respected political figure who had been appointed by Nixon after his two previous attorneys general had resigned after proffering perjured testimony) refused
to do so. In response, Nixon ordered Richardson to resign, and then ordered the acting attorney general (Deputy Attorney General William
Ruckleshaus, another distinguished official) to terminate Cox. Ruckleshaus refused, and was likewise asked to resign. Solicitor General Robert
Bork (who was now the acting head of the Department of Justice) complied. Immediately after doing so, he met with Nixon, who then promised
to nominate him for the next Supreme Court vacancy.[83]

Bork would not benefit from this promise; the Senate redoubled its
efforts and received vital support from the judiciary. It obtained affirma-
tions of the subpoena for the Watergate tapes from the appellate courts,
as the judiciary consistently rejected the executive's claims of privilege.
The ultimate test of the judiciary's resolve during this crisis was *United
States v. Nixon*, wherein the executive asked the court to confirm that he
had inherent constitutional reserve powers that would elevate him above
the other branches of government, effectively destroying the rule of law.
The court did not; rather, it held that there was not "an absolute, unqualified Presidential privilege of immunity from judicial process under
all circumstances."[84] The decision was supported by eight of the nine justices: conflict-of-interest rules required that Rehnquist abstain, as he had
in the *Keith* case.[85] Nixon resigned fifteen days later.

For the executive branch, Watergate's lessons could not be clearer. Nixon had failed in his attempt to appoint justices that owed him personal loyalty (with the exception of Rehnquist, whose nomination had been too little, too late); the independent jurists he had been forced to nominate because of the Senate's concern for the separation of powers had not only thwarted his agenda, but had helped to drive him from office. Nixon had been able to rely on the support of officials whom he had installed without significant oversight – such as Bork – even if this required corrupt bargains and illicit rewards. Conversely, jurists and lawyers who had been appointed after significant scrutiny by the Senate had later proven independent, by protecting the separation of powers and the rule of law. Nixon's successors would take note.

The Senate would also remember, and in the wake of the congressional resurgence the battle between the legislature and an executive determined to regain its former powers would be decided by the branch with the greatest endurance. However, as Senator Frank Church noted after Watergate,[86] it would be difficult for the legislature to maintain the will to prevent the executive from reasserting itself. It had numerous other matters to which it had to attend, but there was no greater prize for the executive than the legal impunity that Nixon had come very close to achieving.

Reagan's Threat to the Court's Independence

During the congressional resurgence of 1974 to 1980, the executive had no opportunities to place jurists who agreed with its views on inherent reserve powers possessed by the executive onto the nation's highest court. The year after Nixon's resignation, President Ford was increasingly constrained by the Senate; choosing to forestall conflict, he nominated John Paul Stevens, who would later serve to counterbalance Rehnquist on the Supreme Court.[87]

In 1981, Ronald Reagan's election renewed the executive's drive to expand its own powers (and consequently, the incentive to influence those branches of government that might oppose this agenda); it would also provide an opportunity to appoint justices who would defer to broad and

even unconstitutional assertions of executive powers. Reagan was determined to impose his agenda, and he brought back into the executive
branch many Nixon officials who embraced Nixon's (and Rehnquist's)
theory of implicit and unchecked reserve powers (who would again return
to prominence during the Bush administration): among others, Richard
Perle became the assistant secretary of defense, Paul Wolfowitz was named
director of policy planning at the Department of State, and Donald Rumsfeld became the executive's special envoy to the Middle East.[88] (It was
shortly after this appointment that he famously met and shook hands
with Saddam Hussein, in a clear show of support for the Iraqi dictator at
a time when he was enduring significant criticism for using chemical
weapons.) As the Iran-Contra affair demonstrated, the executive branch
was willing to engage in illegal activity and to defy explicit congressional
disapproval to pursue its foreign policy objectives.

Watergate (and in particular, *United States v. Nixon*) illustrated how
important it was for the executive to have support within the judiciary,
lest the judges ally themselves with the legislature to rebuke or remove
the executive when it tried to expand its own powers and violated non-
derogable rights.[89] Justice Rehnquist's dissenting opinions demonstrated
how different it might have been if Nixon had been able to appoint more
jurists to the Supreme Court who shared his views; while he was too late
to have been of any assistance to Nixon, he was a great help to Reagan.
Consequently, Rehnquist's nomination served as an ideal type for the justices that the executive would seek to appoint to the Supreme Court.

Rehnquist proved to be a highly controversial jurist, but a key ally of
the executive. Scholars alleged that the identities of the parties influenced
his decisions more than the relevant precedents – so much so that the cor-
relations between these variables could be statistically proven.[90] While a
correlation cannot definitively prove a bias, its statistical significance,
when combined with the fact that his opinions diverged widely from the
other justices, appeared to support the conclusion that his jurisprudence
was ends-oriented.[91] The most predictable relationship was when one of
the parties was the executive: the first and most basic proposition that
guided Rehnquist's votes in cases where the government was a party was
that "[c]onflicts between an individual and the government should, whenever possible, be resolved against the individual."[92] It became clear over

time that Rehnquist would support the executive branch reflexively. While this was relatively unimportant when he was a "Lone Ranger"[93] issuing dissenting opinions that no other justice would join, it demonstrated to the executive what the law of the land might look like, should four more jurists like Rehnquist be appointed to the Supreme Court.

As recounted by Bob Woodward and Scott Armstrong in their groundbreaking work on the Supreme Court (which was one of the first books to ignore the many taboos about reporting on the court's inner workings), this approach to judicial decision-making caused a great deal of friction with his fellow justices.[94] They noted his "willingness to cut corners to reach a ... result" and did not fail to note the many statements in his opinions that "glossed over inconsistencies of logic or fact."[95] Furthermore, frequently no other justice agreed with his reasoning: during his term as an associate justice he was known as "the Great Dissenter," because he wrote an unprecedented fifty-four solitary dissenting opinions.[96] Rehnquist's supporters contend that his differences with the rest of the Burger court were principled; the result of his adherence to the ideology of federalism and judicial restraint. However, this does not account for the support from the executive even when his failings were purely personal, or when they involved outright attempts at deception.

Despite this criticism, the executive continued to see great potential in Rehnquist, and it chose to elevate him to chief justice in 1986.[97] This was not long after Rehnquist's personal problems had spiralled out of control. Shortly after Ronald Reagan's election, Rehnquist's drug addiction became so problematic that he began to noticeably slur his words when speaking from the bench. By that point, his dependency was so great that it could not be addressed in a rehabilitation centre. It required confinement in a detoxification facility. Unfortunately, Rehnquist's addiction was so powerful that he attempted to escape that facility, in his pyjamas. (He attributed this to hallucinations of a "CIA plot against him.")[98]

This breakdown was known to the executive, as was the fact that he had perjured himself in the hearings before his confirmation as an associate justice. However, by then he had provided the executive a tantalizing vision of a Supreme Court populated by justices who were reflexively deferential. More importantly, those confirmation hearings had provided a template for what might be accomplished, a model whose validity was confirmed the next year – by a positive outcome when it was followed, and also by a negative result when it was ignored – after Antonin Scalia and Robert Bork were nominated. This portended greater support from the executive for both Rehnquist and those jurists who it thought might emulate him.

The executive was presented with an opportunity to supply Rehnquist with reinforcements in 1987, after Warren Burger and Lewis Powell retired. First, Reagan nominated Antonin Scalia. Scalia had served in the executive in a number of agencies and commissions, before agreeing to join the OLC under Rehnquist. (His nomination was derailed by Nixon's resignation, but he was renominated and served there during the Ford administration, under Chief of Staff Dick Cheney.) At the OLC, Scalia had attempted to insulate the executive from judicial and congressional oversight (as proposed by the Church Committee) of its control over the intelligence agencies.[99] Despite what appears in retrospect to be clear indications of a strong inclination to be deferential to the executive branch, he was confirmed by the Senate unanimously. This was because the Senate had no way of knowing his true views or learning about his controversial support for the extreme theories of executive power that hearkened back to the Nixon administration.[100] Shortly thereafter, the executive nominated Robert Bork.[101]

The difference between these two nominations could not have been clearer. Bork immediately faced a barrage of criticism from the Senate and many other quarters. It was manifestly clear that Bork would support the executive reflexively: he had proven that during the "Saturday Night Massacre" when he fired special counsel Archibald Cox on Nixon's orders, after Elliot Richardson and William Ruckleshaus has resigned rather than undermine the rule of law.

Furthermore, Bork had, in publicly available writings, "expounded broadly about his well-established ... legal philosophy,"[102] which included an indictment of the Supreme Court for interfering with the executive, when he believed it had no business doing so.[103] His critics claimed that this "reverence for executive authority, as much as his dismissal of Mr. Cox ... makes him unsuitable for the Supreme Court."[104] Conversely, since all of Scalia's work for the administration was protected by veils of secrecy and privilege, his views could not be used against him: had the

Senate known at that time how Scalia had opined while at the OLC that Nixon had personal ownership of White House recordings and paper and that President Ford should veto the FOIA,[105] they might have concluded that he shared Bork's views on executive power, but they did not have this access and so could not object.

Thus the path that an executive bent on expanding its own powers should take when attempting to shape the court's bench became clear: it needed to nominate candidates, like Rehnquist and Scalia, who had earned their stripes as advocates for strong executive power (and inherent constitutional provisions empowering the president to protect the nation) while working within the executive branch, especially in positions such as the OLC where their work would be well-known (and continually available to) the executive, but opaque to observers outside that branch of government. Conversely, those candidates who had left a "paper trail" advocating these views in public should be eschewed. Furthermore, the successful nomination paid substantial dividends: Scalia's nomination to the court reinvigorated the chief justice; later "much of Rehnquist's increased influence derived from the ... nature of several justices who joined the court following his confirmation," after he "formed a voting block with Justice Scalia."[106]

On the court, Scalia proved remarkably frank about the close connections between the executive and the members of the judiciary, as is best demonstrated by his opinion on the motion for recusal filed in *Cheney v. United States District Court*.[107] This case, reminiscent of *United States v. Nixon* (but on a smaller scale and with less at stake) involved then vice-president Cheney's failure to comply with one of those statutes from the time of the congressional resurgence, with which he disagreed: the Federal Advisory Committees Act,[108] which required advisory committees set up by the executive to make their records available to the public. After the District Court for the District of Columbia ordered disclosure, Cheney appealed this decision to the DC Circuit, where he lost, and then to the Supreme Court, where one of his long-time friends would sit in judgment.

The plaintiffs moved that Scalia recuse himself from the case, noting that it would be clearly improper for him to adjudicate a matter in which his friend "had a personal and political stake in the outcome."[109] The plaintiffs pointed in particular to the fact that Scalia had recently "travelled as an official guest of Vice President Dick Cheney on a small government jet" en route to a shared vacation, something that leading legal ethicists argued constituted "accepting a gift of some value from a litigant in a case before him."[110] While the plaintiffs did not mention it in their motion, it was also widely known that "Cheney and Scalia had been friends since the Ford years."[111]

Scalia was under no obligation to respond, but he took the opportunity to make his views clear by publishing an opinion on the motion (against the advice of his fellow justices)[112] that defended the principle of close connections between the executive and the judiciary, perhaps to make it clear that his support could be counted upon in matters of greater importance – those that might be closer to *United States v. Nixon* not only in form but also in significance. Deploying skills honed at the OLC, Scalia cited lamentable examples of poor conduct on the part of executive and the judiciary as precedent that should be followed, in effect turning the exceptions into the rule.[113]

Scalia noted that Justice Jackson, whom he describes as "one of the most distinguished" members of the court, "saw nothing wrong with maintaining a close personal relationship and engaging in quite frequent socializing with the President [Franklin Roosevelt] whose administration's acts came before him regularly."[114] Scalia then noted that Jackson and Roosevelt spent a weekend together (including a shared ride to and from its location) while the momentous case of *Wickard v. Filburn*[115] was pending; Jackson later wrote the court's opinion in that case, which approved a dramatic extension of federal powers that was controversial – even within the Supreme Court itself – over sixty years later.[116] Scalia's argument rests squarely upon the implicit claim that past bad behaviour, even if it is aberrational and unethical, excuses present-day misconduct.

Had Scalia cited Jackson's role in pushing through a draft opinion in *Ex Parte Quirin* instead, his conclusion that these extensive social contacts were harmless and permissible might have appeared far more sinister: one must remember that Jackson argued – after Roosevelt told the court that he would subject the petitioners to extrajudicial execution even were the writ of habeas corpus to be granted – that the executive had inherent executive powers in wartime to subject even US citizens to trials before military commissions, despite there being a Supreme Court opinion that held precisely the opposite.[117] (The OLC later argued that opinions that had created broad executive powers owing to pressure put on the judiciary during serious crises were good precedent, no matter how aberrant or poorly reasoned. For example, by using logic identical to that found in Scalia's response to the recusal motion, the OLC used *Ex Parte Quirin* as their key precedent for the actions taken by the executive after the 9/11 attacks).[118]

Additionally, Scalia's attempt to minimize his contacts with Cheney was quite disingenuous, given the much more troubling truth about his longstanding connections with Cheney, extending back to the Ford administration, when they had co-operated closely on a number of vital projects.[119] It is impossible to demonstrate a clear link between personal connections and any particular line of judicial reasoning. However, the popular interpretation of the outcome of this case was that Scalia "voted for Cheney's side"[120] when the case was decided (although the Supreme Court managed to divert away public attention by leaving the nominal final result to the DC Circuit, albeit with instructions that determined in advance that it would rule for Cheney). That said, it is more telling that "Scalia started referring to the Cheney controversy as his proudest moment as a justice."

Scalia's views on executive power were aligned with Justice Rehnquist's; like the chief justice, he would need to bide his time before these opinions might become influential. This was because Reagan's attempt to remake the court stalled, as he had only one more opportunity to appoint a justice after Scalia. Additionally, his half-hearted attempt to create an imperial presidency foundered in the Iran-Contra scandal.[121]

The key test of judicial independence (and the rule of law upon which it depends) would occur after the 9/11 attacks. One of the key determinants in the outcome of this struggle was the number of strongly pro-executive justices on the Supreme Court, and this in turn would depend on whether the executive – now determined to enlarge its own powers in a crisis – had learned the lessons of the Rehnquist and Scalia nominations, and could find jurists who had served faithfully within executive agencies, where even outlandish views could curry favour while avoiding scrutiny.

President Bush's Incentives for Deference

Even before 9/11, the importance of a supportive Supreme Court had been eminently clear to the Bush administration. In fact, it had become evident even before President George W. Bush took office, as the court had secured his installation – after he had failed to secure a majority of either the country's popular or electoral votes.[122] Instead, he obtained his position after the court overturned a decision of the Supreme Court of Florida and permitted Florida's secretary of state (who reported to Governor Jeb Bush, George W. Bush's older brother) to certify a result that did not take into account any of the ongoing recounts of disputed ballots.[123]

The Stakes of Control over the Judiciary Clarified: Bush v. Gore

The votes that mattered were those of the Supreme Court's justices. It is often reported that the tally in *Bush v. Gore* was 7–2 in favour of Bush, but this is incorrect.[124] The court had split 5–4 on the key issue: whether or not the counting of the Florida ballots would be allowed to continue.[125] In the majority, Rehnquist was joined by Scalia, Justice Clarence Thomas (whose correlation with Scalia's opinions was more close than any other pairing in the Supreme Court's history,[126] and who as of 2013 had sat on the bench for over seven years without asking a single question during oral arguments),[127] Justice O'Connor (who did not recuse herself, despite the fact that she had publicly lamented on election day that she would not be able to retire for another four years after it appeared that Al Gore had won;[128] she retired during Bush's first term of office, allowing him to appoint her successor),[129] and Justice Kennedy, a Reagan nominee notable for being a "swing voter" who frequently joins the prevailing side in order to secure the power to write the majority opinion.[130]

From the moment the court had decided to accept the appeal from the Supreme Court of Florida's decision, the result, the tally, and the identities of who would be in the majority were never in doubt. This is because when accepting the case, the court also voted to stay the lower court's ruling, in a vote of 5–4 (with the justices aligning themselves in exact same manner as they would when deciding the merits).[131] The dissent to that order noted that in granting the stay, the majority had already concluded that the petitioner (Bush) was likely to prevail on the merits; this is why the court had refused to issue such stays in the past.[132]

Furthermore, when writing for the majority (in a concurrence written to the order, which did not explain why it had been granted), Scalia chose to indicate that five justices intended to rule for Bush on the merits, saying, "It suffices to say that the issuance of the stay suggests that a majority of the Court, while not deciding the issues presented, believe that petitioners have a substantial probability of success."[133] He further tipped his hand by stating that a failure to stay the Florida ruling would cause irreparable harm to Bush "by casting a cloud upon what he claims to be the legitimacy of his election,"[134] thereby assuming that he would ultimately win the election, since a loser would not suffer any such harm to the legitimacy of his office, since he would never possess it.

The stay was unusual for a number of reasons. First, "[i]n normal circumstances – in all other circumstances – the Court would never have considered something so vague as the casting of clouds to constitute genuine legal harm, much less one that required the extraordinary step of issuing a stay."[135] Additionally, as the dissenters noted:

[T]he majority today departs from three venerable rules of judicial restraint that have guided the Court throughout its history. On questions of state law, we have consistently respected the opinions of the highest courts of the States. On questions whose resolution is committed at least in large measure to another branch of the Federal Government, we have construed our own jurisdiction narrowly and exercised it cautiously. On federal constitutional questions that were not fairly presented to the court whose judgment is being reviewed, we have prudently declined to express an opinion. The majority has acted unwisely.[136]

This language, which might appear provocative, was actually restrained, as it does not mention that it was the justices in the majority who had traditionally championed those principles (note that the second of these encompasses deference to the executive). None of this mattered now that control over the executive branch was on the line. "Scalia was looking at the election entirely through Bush's eyes; by his own words, the justice was clearly more concerned about producing a clean victory for the Republican."[137]

The opinion on the merits that followed three days later (after a charade of briefing and oral argument) was no better. It is rightfully regarded as one of the worst in the court's three-century history, not merely because of the faulty conclusion that it reaches, but because of its incoherency and remarkably poor reasoning.[138] Even the majority that wrote it disavowed it as precedent, holding that "[o]ur consideration is limited to the present circumstances."[139]

Justice Stevens wrote a dissent, which was joined by Justices Breyer, Souter, and Ginsburg. Along with Souter, Stevens had been appointed by a Republican president (in his case, Ford, at the height of the congressional resurgence). He deconstructed the majority's arguments, but also devoted some attention to the damage that it had done to the judiciary itself:

> The [opinion] by the majority of this Court can only lend credence to the most cynical appraisal of the work of judges throughout the land. It is confidence in the men and women who administer the judicial system that is the true backbone of the rule of law ... the identity of the loser [of the election] is perfectly clear. It is the Nation's confidence in the judge as an impartial guardian of the rule of law.[140]

The response to *Bush v. Gore* of Justice Souter, the only other nominee of a Republican president who had joined in the dissent, also provides key evidence of the incredible damage it had created to a political system predicated on a separation of powers and respect for the law. As Toobin describes it, Souter was "shattered" by the opinion, because "he came from a tradition where the independence of the judiciary was the foundation of the rule of law. And Souter believed that *Bush v. Gore* mocked that tradition. His colleagues' [in the majority] actions were so transparently, so crudely partisan that Souter thought he might not be able to serve with them anymore."[141]

By the end of *Bush v. Gore*, the American public had learned a hard lesson about the importance of judicial independence to the rule of law. After Gore and the Democrats accepted Bush's election (for fear of destabilizing the political structure should they challenge its legitimacy), it appeared that in the event of any court challenge to the presidential election, there were virtually no restraints on the Supreme Court's ability to decide that election. The question that remains is this: what lesson had George W. Bush learned after he was appointed to the presidency by the court? Also, it must considered whether he kept what he had learned in mind when selecting jurists to serve in the judiciary.

The Roberts and Alito Nominations

The *Bush v. Gore* decision raised the Supreme Court's public profile more than any other judicial opinion in its history.[142] Unfortunately for the court, it diminished its image proportionally. As Toobin noted, "In 1974, the justices had risen to the occasion when, in *United States v. Nixon*, they ordered the President to comply ... with the rule of law. Here in a moment of probably even greater significance, the Court as an institution ... failed."[143] This failure could not have been more public or more glaring, and as Justice Stevens predicted, the court suffered a powerful blow to its prestige, which depends on its credibility and impartiality.

It was evident at the time that a majority of its justices had decided that the damage created by this self-inflicted wound was less important than installing a president whose views about the scope and uses of executive power mirrored their own. The prime movers were those justices who had elaborated a broad theory of presidential powers in general while producing classified memoranda inside the executive branch, and developing theories of inherent reserve powers while working at the OLC in particular: Chief Justice Rehnquist and Justice Scalia.

In any event, by 2001 the executive's dependence on a compliant Supreme Court could not have been clearer, owing to the two cases that bracketed the re-emergence of the rule of law in the United States. These cases are *Unites States v. Nixon* and *Bush v. Gore*.[144] The first case revealed the power of an independent judiciary to help bring down the executive, while the second illustrated how certain justices, who were rewarded for promoting the powers of the executive with every significant promotion of their career, would take action to put an executive in place who would increasingly depend upon them for legal cover, owing to its drive to dismantle the rule of law.

These developments were foreshadowed by the appointment of several of the senior foreign policy advisors who had served in similar capacities during the last phase of executive resistance to the rule of law. Many of the officials who would serve at the centre of the Bush administration had chafed under the enforcement of the rule of law during the Nixon, Ford, and Reagan administrations. In addition to Rumsfeld and Cheney, these included Elliott Abrams, who served successively as National Security Council senior director for democracy, human rights, and international operations; National Security Council senior director for Near East and North African affairs; and deputy national security advisor for global democracy strategy. Abrams had earlier been found guilty of withholding information from Congress.[145] Another of these officials was John Poindexter, who oversaw the surveillance projects known as Total Information Awareness and the creation of various intelligence databases. He was appointed to that position despite having been convicted after the Iran-Contra crisis on five counts of making false statements to Congress.[146]

Those justices who were so inclined might expect further favour if they sanctioned the executive's policies and thus prevented the deposition of the administration they had installed. This dynamic was not new. Chief Justice Rehnquist had been elevated to that position after embarrassing himself with poorly reasoned and ends-oriented opinions that established him as "an outspoken proponent of executive power versus the other branches of government."[147] This occurred notwithstanding the executive's passive awareness of his drug problem and the fact that he had possibly perjured himself during the hearings that preceded his appointment as an associate justice.

The relationship between the executive and those justices who had always depended upon it for advancement was now symbiotic, and precisely the opposite of the separation of powers upon which the rule of law in the United States depends. The executive's incentives to reinforce this dynamic by appointing justices who would conform to this pattern were underscored by the *Bush v. Gore* decision.

Even before his election, Bush had made his views on the relationship between the executive and the judiciary clear:

> [Bush] invariably relied on the same catchphrases when describing his favored judicial philosophy ... when Bush said that judges were "legislating from the bench," he meant overturning laws on individual-rights grounds ... The President – and especially Vice-President Cheney – also felt strongly that judges should not interfere with what they felt were the prerogatives of the executive branch in the conduct of foreign policy or military affairs.[148]

This echoed Nixon's comments during his election campaign. Furthermore, "No issue mattered more to Cheney than preserving the power of the President ... The Vice-President believed that since the Nixon years the executive branch had steadily ceded authority to Congress, the courts, and even to international institutions, and he made it his mission to arrest that decline."[149]

Their subordinates in the executive branch understood what this meant. "Bush's staff had thought through precisely what stamp they wanted to place on the federal judiciary – and a network of Scalia and Thomas acolytes was precisely what they had in mind."[150]

Chief Justice Rehnquist's resignation presented the Bush administration with its first opportunity to install a Supreme Court jurist who would be deferential to the executive. The nominee that the subordinate officials brought to his attention was John Roberts. Few accounts of Roberts's selection by the executive focus on two key factors, those which had also allowed Rehnquist and Scalia to pass through the confirmation process unscathed. First, he had worked for the executive in various capacities that did not create a record of his views on executive power. Second, he made it clear to the executive that he did indeed support its view that it possessed inherent constitutional reserve powers that place it above the law.[151]

A year after graduating from law school, Roberts became a law clerk to Justice Rehnquist. This is evidence that he already agreed that the judiciary should show deference to the executive, as this was a hallmark of Rehnquist's jurisprudence, and justices carefully select their law clerks on the basis of ideological compatibility.[152] However, we have no record of the memoranda he wrote in that capacity, since Rehnquist was still alive when he was nominated and thus they remained confidential.[153]

Immediately after clerking, Roberts joined the executive branch, taking a position reserved for those who were being groomed for greater things. He was appointed special assistant to the US attorney general, having been recommended by Justice Rehnquist, according to the attorney general's chief of staff, and Roberts's immediate superior at the time, Kenneth Starr.[154] This was a highly political position. His most notable act in that capacity was writing a memorandum arguing that it was possible to eliminate some of the Supreme Court's constitutional jurisdiction; that is, whether the "power to emasculate the Court" existed.[155] The extreme nature of this advice is demonstrated by the fact that it contradicted the Reagan administration's OLC's position and that it was ignored by Attorney General William French Smith, despite the fact that he admitted to possessing "revolutionary zeal" at that time.[156] In 1982, Roberts began serving as assistant White House counsel. This is perhaps the only position where loyalty to the executive is prized more highly than at the OLC, since this office is not part of the Department of Justice, and as such has no theoretical obligation to do justice, but to serve the chief executive as faithfully as possible. No record of his privileged advice to the executive has been made public.

"With perfect timing, Roberts left the Reagan White House shortly before the administration nearly imploded during the Iran-Contra scandal."[157] However, he returned shortly thereafter as principal deputy to Starr, who is best remembered as Bill Clinton's investigator and the primary force behind his impeachment. According to Starr, Roberts was "my very closest [sic], most trusted adviser."[158] Again, Roberts's internal legal memoranda at the Solicitor General's Office are not public records. Owing to this, and to his failed nomination to the DC Circuit in 1992, he avoided "amass[ing] an extensive paper trail of controversial decisions."[159]

Roberts was eventually confirmed to a seat on the DC Circuit's bench on 8 May 2003. By the time that he was nominated to replace Chief Justice Rehnquist, Roberts had authored only forty-nine opinions. Few of these were controversial, as they generated only three dissents.[160] However, one amounted to a clear signal to the executive that Roberts shared its views on inherent reserve powers to ignore existing laws. This case, *Hamdan v. Rumsfeld*,[161] involved a challenge to features of the military tribunals at Guantánamo Bay, which were erected in response to the Supreme Court's opinion in *Hamdi v. Rumsfeld*.[162] In the opinion deciding that case, a bare majority on the Supreme Court had insisted that the detainees receive some form of due process. In *Hamdan*, the petitioner argued that even these new procedures did not comply with the minimum requirements of the Geneva Conventions.[163] This was indisputable, but Roberts ruled that "the Geneva Conventions cannot be judicially enforced."[164] This holding was later reversed by the Supreme Court, but Roberts "had proved himself worthy" to Cheney nonetheless.[165]

Shortly after his nomination, Roberts was confirmed by the Senate without difficulty, on a vote of 13–5 within the Senate Judiciary Committee and 78–22 on the floor.[166] Toobin concluded that "[h]is obvious intelligence [and] abundant qualifications ... would have made sustained opposition difficult."[167] This conclusion is correct, but it rests upon two unstated premises. First, that the Senate should accept that Roberts's executive branch service constituted abundant qualification, as he had barely two years' service as a judge at the time of his nomination to the nation's highest court.

Second, it ignores that "sustained opposition" might well have been possible if all of his memoranda written while he served the executive were made public. The Democrat's ranking member on the Senate Judiciary Committee requested these but was rejected on privacy grounds; the senator described this issue as a "red herring."[168] Despite that objection, the committee allowed the confirmation to proceed without receiving the memoranda. This rewarded obstructionism and the winning strategy of grooming compliant justices within the OLC, the White House counsel and Solicitor General's Office, and other positions where their legal advice would remain confidential and subject to claims of privilege.

The confirmation of the next justice would provide further proof that this was the optimal strategy for undermining the independence of the judiciary. Samuel Alito was another lawyer who had prospered due to his allegiance to the executive. By following the path blazed by Rehnquist,

Scalia, and Roberts, he quickly reached the heights of the American judiciary. After one year as a law clerk, he joined the Solicitor General's Office, like Roberts. This was directly after the "Reagan revolution," a time when ideological correctness was at a premium. It was there that he "quickly established himself as an enthusiastic supporter of the Reagan administration."[169] In 1985 he joined the OLC, during the tenure of Attorney General Edwin Meese, one of Reagan's closest and most ideological advisors. Meese was implicated during Alito's term of service in the Iran-Contra scandal.[170] Alito was then appointed to be the chief federal prosecutor for New Jersey, and three years later, given a lifetime appointment to the Third Circuit, at the age of forty.[171]

The existence of a fast track to the judiciary for executive branch officials who agreed that it could expand its powers at will was exposed during Alito's Supreme Court confirmation hearings. When he filed an application for a position within the OLC, he attached a personal statement. As it was written before he joined the executive branch, it was not protected from discovery by attorney-client privilege. The executive branch lawyers who vetted his candidacy for the Supreme Court had not, however, found this at the National Archives. Instead, it was found by journalists after Bush announced Alito's nomination.[172]

In this personal statement, Alito pledged fealty to every ideological premise of the Reagan administration, and insisted that these represent his own core values. "I am and always have been ... an adherent to the same philosophical views that I believe are central to this Administration."[173] This quickly became an issue during the confirmation hearings, as it made clear that Alito was being disingenuous when he claimed that he could address the issue of abortion with an open mind. While he had insisted that he would approach any case that challenged *Roe v. Wade*[174] with an open mind, he had said in his 1985 statement that, in addition to sharing all of the administration's views, "I am particularly proud of my contributions in recent cases in which the government has argued ... that the Constitution does not protect a right to an abortion."[175] When asked directly by Senator Charles Schumer whether that was still his view, he refused to answer. Toobin described his performance in these hearings by noting that "Alito was a dreadful witness on his own behalf – charmless, evasive and unpersuasive."[176]

The significance of abortion in contemporary American politics is impossible to overestimate. It was this discrepancy that defined his confirmation hearings. Indeed, the personal statement is now labelled the "personal statement on abortion" when it is no such thing.[177] Unfortunately, this distracted the senators' attention from other assertions in the personal statement that lead one to believe that Alito was nominated for a seat on the nation's highest court precisely because he did not believe in the importance of an independent judiciary. He wrote as follows:

In the field of law, I disagree strongly with the usurpation by the judiciary of decisionmaking [sic] authority ... The Administration has already made major strides toward reversing this trend through its judicial appointments, litigation, and public debate, and it is my hope that even greater advances can be made during the second term, especially under Attorney-General Meese's leadership at the Department of Justice.[178]

From this statement alone, one may reasonably conclude that Alito was allying himself with the views of Nixon, Rehnquist, Cheney, and Roberts about the limited powers of the judiciary. As they did, Alito states that he believes that one of the key ways to impose this view is through the appointment of judges who will not challenge the executive's "decisionmaking authority." This plausible interpretation becomes more troubling when one considers that Alito's comments appear to indicate his awareness that he was interviewing for a position that would groom him for a judicial appointment.

Alito goes on in his personal statement to say, "I believe very strongly in the supremacy of the elected branches of government."[179] This is a problematic opinion for a future Supreme Court justice to espouse, as that court is charged by the Constitution to exercise oversight over the elected branches, and to correct them when they overstep their bounds. Alito, when confronted with this at his confirmation hearings, said only that this was "a very inapt phrase," although it has a clear meaning within the context of Nixon and Rehnquist's influential views on executive supremacy.[180]

Despite his evasive testimony, the executive's failure to release all of the memoranda he had written, and the clear signals he had given to the executive of his view on its powers relative to those of the judiciary, the Senate did not reject Alito's candidacy. While on paper it appears that the vote confirming him was significantly closer than Chief Justice Roberts's, this is misleading. While the final floor vote was 58–42 in favour of confirmation, this result was guaranteed when the discussion on his candidacy was closed.[181] The vote that actually counted was that which ended the debate, which occurred after a motion for cloture. The margin here was 72–25,[182] very close to Roberts's totals.

The difference between the tallies on the two votes during Alito's confirmation reveals that the Senate's scrutiny of the executive's nominees had become dysfunctional and insufficiently protective of an independent judiciary and the rule of law. A number of senators voted against confirming Alito on the final vote, but voted in favour of closing the debate, something which they knew would ensure his confirmation. By doing so, they would be able to tell their constituents that they had opposed the nomination, despite the purely symbolic nature of this action. In essence, these members winked at the executive, showing deference but reserving the right to assert that they had not done so, at least to those who do not understand the significance of cloture votes.

Among those who split their votes cynically against a filibuster but later nominally opposed Alito's confirmation were many powerful Democrats, such as Daniel Inouye, who would later become the Senate's president *pro tempore*,[183] and Joseph Lieberman, future chair of the Senate Committee on Homeland Security and Governmental Affairs.[184] In addition, the attempt to prevent cloture was effectively sabotaged by that party's leader, Harry Reid, who had stated publicly that "everyone knew" he would be unable to gather enough votes to prevent the termination of the debate. Joe Biden, the future vice-president, ultimately voted against cloture even though he had spoken out publicly against an attempt to prevent a vote.[185] In any event, the effort to avoid cloture was effete, as Senator John Kerry, the future secretary of state, had initiated the campaign while at a skiing resort in Switzerland, something which did not pass unnoticed.[186] One might plausibly characterize this attempt to block Alito's confirmation as nothing more than political theatre, which diminished the Senate.

Kagan Nomination Confirms the Pattern Crosses Political Lines

The patterns of executive expansion and its claims of supremacy have not been affected by the transition between the Bush and Obama administrations in any fundamental way. This is also true with respect to the tactics of judicial nomination designed to protect the executive's power, which allowed it to create the parallel detention regime, apply torture, restrict access to the courts, and permit extrajudicial killing. The key proof for this continuity in the drive for an executive branch which is above the law stems from the choice of Elena Kagan for a seat on the Supreme Court.

In choosing to focus on Kagan's nomination and confirmation, one must justify the choice not to discuss Sonia Sotomayor's confirmation in detail. Sotomayor's nomination can be seen as a departure from the general pattern established by Nixon's and Reagan's nominations of Rehnquist and Scalia, as adopted and refined by Bush, as evidenced by the confirmations of Roberts and Alito, just as the nomination of Sandra Day O'Connor can be seen as aberrational in the context of the "Reagan revolution." At that time there was an overriding pressure upon the executive, which caused it to momentarily disregard the incentive to create a deferential Supreme Court. In both cases, this pressure came from identity politics.[187]

At the time of Reagan's election, there had never been a woman on the Supreme Court's bench. Owing to the success of the feminist movement over the past two decades, the male domination of the nation's highest court could not continue without exacting upon the executive a great political price.[188] Because of the dearth of Republican-affiliated women with experience at the highest level of the legal profession and with excellent academic credentials, the executive's choice of Sandra Day O'Connor[189] was tightly constrained.

Similarly, when Obama was elected, the Supreme Court had never had a justice of Hispanic origin. Since this demographic group constituted a major voting block that was central to his prospects for re-election, Obama needed to nominate a Hispanic justice, preferably a woman, owing to concerns about gender equity on a still male-dominated court. Sonia Sotomayor was the obvious choice. She had effectively been a justice-in-waiting, and undoubtedly would have secured a nomination much earlier had Al Gore's election not been subverted in 2000. Sotomayor was simply the candidate Obama was constrained to nominate, as she was the only candidate who had both the right demographic profile and the judicial and academic credentials, standing head and shoulders above other potential candidates.[190]

Conversely, after the retirement of Justice Stevens, who was the most consistently independent justice during the Bush administration, and the least deferential to the executive at that time,[191] the president had a relatively free choice, such that an observer might easily gauge his priorities by reference to the nominee's characteristics. This would provide a leading indication of whether judicial independence or deference to the executive would be prized during the new administration, and if the latter, whether the executive would resort to the same techniques that were employed by the Reagan and Bush administrations. The adoption of these techniques would demonstrate that the Obama administration was likewise committed to the erosion of judicial independence and of the rule of law itself, especially if it chose to nominate an executive-branch insider whose record could be obscured with claims of privilege or confidentiality.

At the time of her nomination, Elena Kagan had no judicial experience. Justice Sotomayor was the author of 380 judicial opinions, from which one could glean her approach to the issues and to the separation of powers.[192] Kagan had no public record, as she had pursued a career within the executive branch.

After clerking, Kagan served two short periods in large-firm legal practice and academia, a well-travelled road toward a legal position of significance in government. Kagan then began her service within the executive branch as assistant White House counsel. Her legal advice to the executive in this position apparently demonstrated sufficient political acumen, as she was soon appointed deputy assistant to the president for domestic policy and deputy director of the Domestic Policy Council.[193]

As was the case with the other justices who served as executive-branch lawyers before their appointment to the bench, Kagan left government with the change of administration, which highlights the political nature of her work within that department. Her departure underscores this point because lawyers who work in more neutral capacities within the executive branch (i.e., at the Department of Justice) do not typically resign when the opposing party's candidate is elected to the presidency.[194] Kagan returned to academia, becoming dean of the Harvard Law School after four years on its faculty. During that time, she published very little, something observers concluded was a calculated attempt not to generate a paper trail that would impair her nomination to the nation's highest court. By this point, as in Roberts's case, the executive's ambition to place her in this position was made clear by a failed nomination to the DC Circuit.[195] In 2009, Kagan was appointed solicitor general, the person responsible for arguing the executive's position before the Supreme Court. At the time of her nomination, she had never argued before any court.[196] She was nominated to replace Justice Stevens a year later.

At the time of her nomination, commentators noted that the lack of any evidence of her views on certain key legal issues, including the independence of the judiciary, the separation of powers, and inherent reserve powers purportedly possessed by the executive, was viewed positively by the administration.[197] This dearth of information was attributable to the fact that "her academic career is surprisingly and disturbingly devoid of writings or speeches on most key legal and Constitutional controversies, and ... she has spent the last year as Obama's Solicitor General."[198]

Nevertheless, there were indications within this scant record that Kagan consistently supported the expansion of executive power. In 2001, a law review article she published addressed the "proper limits of executive authority, and the view she advocated was clearly one that advocated far more executive power than had been previously accepted."[199] Neal Katyal noted that there was an essential continuity between the views she expressed in this paper and those advocated at that time within the Bush administration's OLC, although her "claims of executive power are not limited to the current administration ... Anticipating the claims of the current [Bush] administration, Kagan argued that ... the President has the ability to effect comprehensive, coherent change."[200] William West, in commenting on Kagan's article, noted that "[s]he is certainly a fan of presidential power."[201]

This conclusion is firmly reinforced by the statements Kagan made to the Senate during her confirmation hearings for the solicitor general's position. At that time:

[S]he agreed wholeheartedly with ... the rightness of the core Bush/ Cheney Terrorism template: namely, that the entire world is a battlefield, that war is the proper legal framework for analyzing all matters relating to Terrorism, and the Government can therefore indefinitely detain anyone captured on that battlefield (i.e., anywhere in the world without geographical limits) who is accused (but not proven) to be an enemy combatant.[202]

This agreement was particularly evident after "[t]here was no daylight between Ms. Kagan ... and [Senator] Lindsey Graham ... as he led her through a six-minute colloquy about the president's broad authority to detain enemy combatants."[203] For this reason, when the executive's potential nominees for Stevens's replacement were evaluated, the *New York Times* opined that Kagan "supported assertions of executive power."[204]

It is likely that it was her endorsement of the new detention paradigm, which entails an approach to executive power that is not compatible with the rule of law, that accounts for the ringing endorsement she secured from some of the lawyers who demolished the separation of powers for the Bush administration, such as M. Edward Whelan III, who was the first head of the OLC during the Bush administration. Whelan argued that "on issues of executive power and national security, Kagan is far from the Left," and he also approved of her display of "genuine admiration and appreciation for Justice Scalia."[205]

The Court's New Balance of Power on Rule of Law Issues

Owing to Kagan's academic credentials, her largely confidential record of service to the executive branch, and her support for its claims of power, she was confirmed without significant debate. As she replaced Justice Stevens, who defended an independent judiciary's role in enforcing the rule of law's minimum limitations on executive power,[206] her appointment had the capacity to fundamentally alter the balance of powers between the executive and the other branches of government.

In 2012, the court declined to exercise certiorari over seven habeas corpus petitions in a single day,[207] reaffirming a detention and torture regime antithetical to the rule of law. This decision can be explained by the fact that the court was dominated by justices with longstanding connections to the executive: Chief Justice John Roberts, senior associate justice Antonin Scalia, and Clarence Thomas (who happened to be another former Reagan administration official). Thomas rarely cast a vote that diverged from Scalia's.[208] These three strong supporters of executive deference were soon joined by Samuel Alito and, during the Obama administration, Elena Kagan. Justices with a history of close connections with the executive now comprised a majority on the court.[209] After Justice Scalia's death, it became clear that his replacement would not be confirmed until the 2016 election, but it is already evident that the next justice will join this block, as the Republican candidate promised to nominate a jurist "in the mold of Scalia," while Merrick Garland (the Democratic judicial nominee-in-waiting) has precisely the pedigree identified above, having served in a politically sensitive position in the Department of Justice before joining the DC Circuit, where he voted against recognizing the Guántanamo detainees' right to habeas corpus, such that his nomination was praised by Jeffrey Rosen as "a victory for judicial restraint."

On the Supreme Court, the majority rules, as Justice Brennan made clear: At some point early in their clerkships, Brennan asked his clerks to name the most important rule in constitutional law. Typically they offered *Marbury v. Madison* or *Brown v. Board of Education* as their answers. Brennan would reject each answer, in the end providing his own by holding up his hand with the fingers wide apart. This, he would say, is the most important rule in constitutional law. Some clerks understood Brennan to mean that it takes five votes to do anything, others that with five votes you can do anything.[210]

It remains to be seen how five justices might use this power to aid the executive branch. However, it should be noted that owing to the advent of the executive's successful strategy of appointing justices who proved themselves while serving within the executive branch, the court is left with a minority of only three independently minded justices who are likely to stand up for the rule of law. These justices – Ginsburg, Breyer, and Sotomayor – are a minority of three. That number is significant. While justices can exercise substantial power by forcing the majority to state its views clearly on the record, a minority of three is too small for this purpose, as it takes four justices to accept a petition for appellate review.[211]

This dysfunctional pattern of judicial selection is spreading to the influential circuits that rest directly beneath the Supreme Court in the hierarchy of the American federal judiciary, something which allows the pro-executive majority of justices to silently uphold executive power, by merely declining review. The circuit court with the greatest amount of oversight over the executive is the DC Circuit.[212] This makes it the intermediate appeals court that the executive has the greatest incentive to control. The same dysfunctional strategies of judicial selection have been employed to shape the DC Circuit's bench so that it is much more amenable to the claims of power made by the executive, destabilizing the separation of powers and the rule of law.

Executive Branch Control of the DC Circuit

"The DC Circuit has long been thought of as the second most powerful court in the land and a good breeding ground for the Supreme Court."[213] The first of these premises gives the executive an incentive to control it. The second premise, the prospect of promotion, provides the means to accomplish that end. This court's importance stems from the fact that it supervises a solitary district court that has jurisdiction over the governmental agencies and officials located in the nation's capital. Accordingly, "there is a built-in temptation to benefit the agency that can benefit the presiding judge's career."[214] Of the justices now on the Supreme Court, three served previously on the DC Circuit, where they did the yeoman service that proved them loyal. (A fourth – Kagan – had been nominated for such a position.)

The court's power to derail the executive's agenda became clear in the 1970s, as it began to exercise a larger administrative jurisdiction, owing to the Watergate crisis. At the height of the investigation into the Nixon administration's misconduct, the court exercised its infrequently used power to undertake *en banc* review of more than ten cases involving criminal charges against executive branch officials or their agents.[215] Executive control over the DC Circuit is, for these reasons, perhaps even more desirable than control over the Supreme Court, since it passes unnoticed. Preventing challenges to the enlargement of its own powers from reaching the Supreme Court allows the executive to avoid scrutiny and prevents that court from being placed under the pressure that this entails. The court's failure to review the DC Circuit's judgments, even when they approve of executive prerogatives that destabilize the rule of law, are rarely noticed.[216]

Denial of review garners little notice because of the nature of the Supreme Court's docket. It is commonly thought that the court is overburdened. Between 1970 and 1997, roughly 4,000 petitions for certiorari were filed at the court each year.[217] Throughout this period, the court granted "slightly less than four percent" of these requests.[218] There was a decline, however, in the rate of certiorari granted for cases from the DC Circuit during this period, something which Christopher Banks has argued is correlated with the increasing ideological convergence between the two courts.[219] This dynamic becomes increasingly apparent over time. By 2009, only slightly more than 1 per cent of petitions for review of DC Circuit decisions were granted.[220] Banks notes that "[t]his data is persuasive evidence that the United States Supreme Court has let the D.C. Circuit define the scope of legal policy in administrative law ... after 1970."[221]

This data also presents some evidence that the DC Circuit's decisions to affirm broad executive powers are part of a concerted attempt to take pressure off the Supreme Court, and that this is possible due to a majority of judges on both these courts' benches that support the executive, since "the Court uses its discretion to deny certiorari more and grant it less, especially if both courts are ideologically compatible in membership."[222] More evidence can be adduced in favour of this hypothesis if it can be shown that the executive attempted to create the necessary ideological compatibility by nominating judges to the DC Circuit who are amenable to its assertions of broad and troubling powers, in the same manner as it did with respect to the Supreme Court.

There is ample evidence that the executive attempted to gain control of the DC Circuit by appointing judges friendly to its aims in the period following the congressional resurgence and the concomitant re-imposition of the rule of law. After Reagan's election, it appeared that he "was going to have a number of opportunities to change the D.C. Circuit's membership ... [and] viewpoints on topics like litigant access to courts [and] separation of powers."[223] Reagan's first nominee was Robert Bork, one of Nixon's key allies during the Watergate crisis. Bork continued to serve on the DC Circuit after he failed to secure confirmation to the Supreme Court. He was followed onto the court by Antonin Scalia and Kenneth Starr.

Starr's appointment was followed by the confirmation of Laurence Silberman, who served as acting attorney general during the Watergate crisis, having recently been promoted from the position of deputy attorney general, where he was charged with overseeing the OLC during the dying days of the Nixon administration. He later served as ambassador to Yugoslavia, which was a key Cold War battleground. At the time of his appointment to the bench he was a member of the General Advisory Committee on Arms Control and Disarmament and the Department of Defense Policy Board.[224]

Reagan's next nominee was James L. Buckley, then serving in his administration as undersecretary of state for security assistance.[225] Buckley was previously the president of Radio Free Europe and Radio Liberty, broadcasters of American propaganda into Eastern Europe and the Soviet Union, and closely associated with the intelligence services.[226] In essence, Silberman and Buckley were executive branch insiders with links to the intelligence community.

The rejection of Robert Bork's nomination to the Supreme Court brought more scrutiny to the appointment of radical proponents of imperial presidency to the DC Circuit. However, the aforementioned judges formed a distinct and powerful block on the court, which, like the corresponding faction on the Supreme Court, would be strengthened considerably after the 9/11 attacks by the nominees chosen by George W. Bush: Janice Rogers Brown and Brett Kavanaugh.[227] When the detention-and-torture regime was coming under sustained pressure in the lower courts, this block could control the DC Circuit. The four Reagan nominees, joined by another three confirmed during the Bush administration, constituted more than half of the judges to whom these critical appeals might be assigned.

As a result of this ideological alignment, the Supreme Court could rely upon the DC Circuit to dispose of cases brought by those challenging the executive's policies that undermine the rule of law. The last piece of proof for the argument that this was a concerted strategy comes from the Supreme Court's decision to channel most of these cases to the DC Circuit exclusively, in "one of the most important decisions made by the United States Supreme Court in the terrorism-detention litigation in the past decade," which occurred in an "all-but-unnoticed 'GVR' order"[228] in *Bush v. Gherebi*.[229]

With this order, the Supreme Court forced all executive detainees to bring suit under the watchful eyes of the DC Circuit, despite there being no compelling reason why that should be the case, other than the implicit trust that these cases would be decided in a manner that relieved the Supreme Court of responsibility and scrutiny.[230] This order served to derail extant challenges in the forums that were the most attentive to claims that the rule of law was being undermined by the executive, such as the Second Circuit.[231]

This exclusive jurisdiction, now being exercised not only over claims brought by Guantánamo prisoners but those alleging wrongful conduct from Afghanistan to Germany, has been used to dispose of claims against the executive with increasing regularity. The DC Circuit has eviscerated the holdings of the much-vaunted Supreme Court opinions that subjected the executive to minimal legal restraints. The foremost among these cases was *Boumediene v. Bush*,[232] which granted petitioners the right to habeas corpus. Since *Boumediene* was decided four years after *Gherebi*, the court knew at the time that the case was decided that the DC Circuit would be the court deciding on the proper scope of its holding in practice. Unfortunately, but predictably, the DC Circuit subsequently eviscerated *Boumediene*. By the time of *Kiyemba*, it was clear that the "constant ... is the [DC] court of appeals' refusal to apply, or even acknowledge [*Boumediene*]."[233]

After the court declined certiorari to *Kiyemba* and the seven other post-*Boumediene* cases that it disposed of in a single day of one-line orders, it is impossible not to conclude that delegating the responsibility to the DC Circuit was part of a calculated strategy of reducing the Supreme

Court's earlier jurisprudence to a mere rhetorical shell. This active or passive collusion between the two courts allowed the minimal legal restraints on the executive branch erected in the line of cases leading to *Boumediene* to be dismantled. This was done without significant public attention, which reduces the probability of the popular outrage that mobilized resistance to the executive during the Nixon administration. In addition, this minimized the risk of harm to the Supreme Court's prestige, which was painstakingly rebuilt in the years following *Bush v. Gore*. This encouraged the public to continue to believe in the power of an independent judiciary, which the separation of powers requires and the rule of law in the United States depends on, but which is not actually present. This plan would have been impossible to implement, however, without the pro-executive majorities on both of these courts, which itself required the subversion of the judicial selection system.

The previous chapter detailed a troubling pattern of deference by the nation's two most important courts: the Supreme Court and the DC Circuit. As Stephen Vladeck persuasively argued that the creation of this new "national security canon" cannot be attributed to normal processes of doctrinal development, the hypothesis explored in this chapter is that this new judicial deference might be explained as a by-product of a breakdown of the mechanisms of judicial selection.

It can be argued that executive branch has effectively colonized the Supreme Court. Not only are there no longer enough justices committed to judicial independence and the rule of law to overturn a decision that favours the executive, they are not enough to even accept such a case. This fact is of particular importance owing to the colonization of the DC Circuit, to which the Supreme Court has directed the cases that challenge the executive's new regime of prolonged involuntary detention, torture, and extrajudicial execution. A DC Circuit ruling is effectively the final word on challenges to the executive's violation of non-derogable rights, as there are not enough votes for certiorari to the Supreme Court. This process protects the image of an independent judiciary while denying any publicity to lawsuits challenging the executive.

On this basis it is possible to conclude that there has been a comprehensive failure of the rule of law in the United States. The executive has determined the scope of its own powers, divorced from legislative oversight. It then assumed emergency powers to violate non-derogable rights, which cannot be challenged in the courts, owing to the existence of new rules that make the Constitution's guarantees meaningless, and higher courts that are entirely unwilling to hold the executive legally accountable, as the rule of law requires.

It remains only to determine whether this crisis is likely to be permanent, and to address the objections of those scholars who believe that there are other mechanisms that might hold the executive accountable: the possibility of a legislative resurgence and the likelihood that executive overreaching might again provoke impeachment.

CHAPTER 6

Congress's Failure to Exercise Oversight

As the executive branch is not subject to any legal control, it can no longer be said that the United States is being governed in accordance with the fundamental norms of the rule of law, as defined by the ICJ. Furthermore, it is by now clear that this situation cannot be rectified by the courts themselves. Jurists in the lower courts who have attempted to impose legal sanctions upon the executive have been reversed by the appeals courts that are now firmly controlled by the executive branch.

The question that remains is whether these abuses, which mirror in many ways the situation during the Nixon administration, might be curtailed in the near future by a congressional resurgence, in a manner similar to that which re-installed the rule of law in the United States in the years immediately following the Watergate investigations and Nixon's resignation.

Congress's Response to Arbitrary Detention

The Guantánamo Bay detention camp was not established by legislation, but by orders to the military issued by Secretary of Defense Donald Rumsfeld. Plans for the repurposing of facilities, which were built in the 1990s to house HIV-positive Haitian refugees, and its staffing were put into motion on 21 December 2001.[1] On 27 December the Pentagon announced that prisoners of war accused of terrorism would be brought there.[2] Congress's response to this information was remarkably muted.[3] The Congressional Record reveals that the first legislative discussion of detention camps, which occurred over a month later, after the traditional Christmas break, came when Senator Ben Nelson announced a bipartisan fact-finding trip. The trip appeared to be a public relations exercise, as Nelson decided in advance to absolve the executive, saying, "I can't imagine … that the United States is giving anything other than humane treatment … It is certainly going to be the case [sic] of humane treatment."[4]

Although the executive decided to revive a facility that was unconstitutional when it housed refugees[5] without consulting Congress, there were no immediate complaints about the executive's initiative. This was despite the fact that it did so when the legislature, which was not in session, could not respond. Furthermore, since the facilities were insufficient, executive branch officials submitted a funding request on 1 February 2002 to Congress, which was duly authorized.[6] In the ensuing ten years, the legislature never refused to provide funds necessary to run and expand the detention camp, without which the facility could not operate.[7] This was the first evidence of a general pattern that would emerge, in which the legislative branch would consistently enable the executive's indefinite arbitrary detention of suspects.

Congress later made its support for the parallel detention regime eminently clear after the Supreme Court issued its first opinions challenging the executive's theories about its rights to establish and run this facility and to set up military tribunals without any legislative authorization or oversight. In 2006, the court held in the case of *Hamdi v. Rumsfeld*[8] that the detainees were entitled to the common protections of Article 3 of the Third Geneva Convention, and further, that CSRTs established to determine whether the detainees were "enemy combatants" were not constitutional. This opinion stated that these tribunals were not consistent with existing legislation on military tribunals, in the form of the UCMJ. In essence, the Supreme Court rejected the OLC's theory that the executive possessed an inherent constitutional power – one derived from its all-encompassing ability to trump any law in the interest of national security – to erect new military courts that lack the guarantees of due process the Constitution requires, and which fail to meet the requirements of natural justice.[9]

Congress responded to the court's erection of this minor obstacle by passing the Military Commissions Act of 2006. This statute provided explicit legislative authorization for the executive's existing practices at Guantánamo, nullifying the *Hamdan* and *Hamdi* opinions. By that time, the United States was no longer in the state of panic induced by the 9/11 attacks, and numerous criticisms of Guantánamo were lodged by foreign nations, non-governmental organizations, and the Inter-American Court of Human Rights by 2006.[10] Congress's response to these objections was to explicitly authorize the "judicial black hole." Foremost among the objections to Guantánamo was the claim that rather than housing "the worst of the worst" terrorists,[11] or fanatics bent on suicide attacks who "would chew through hydraulics lines" of the aircraft transporting them,[12] many of the detainees were factually innocent and were being denied natural justice to cloak that fact.[13]

Congress Regularizes the Judicial Black Hole: The 2006 MCA

The Military Commissions Act of 2006 (MCA) accomplished five things. First, in response to Supreme Court's determination that the detainees were owed the protection of Article 3 of the Geneva Conventions,[14] it created by statute the category of "unlawful enemy combatants," to replace the label of "enemy combatants" that was invented by the OLC in a memorandum which concluded[15] that the detainees possessed no rights under the laws of war. Second, it authorized the military commissions that the court held in *Hamdi* could not be established without legislative authorization. Third, in establishing these commissions, it regularized indefinite detention by creating a jurisdiction to which the prisoners could now purportedly be lawfully subjected. Fourth, it stripped detainees of the ability to petition for the writ of habeas corpus. Fifth, it endorsed the executive's earlier enlargement of its own powers, in direct response to the Supreme Court's decision that this was unconstitutional and a grave violation of the separation of powers that undergirds the American rule of law.

In creating the status of "unlawful enemy combatant," Congress chose to deliberately ignore the Geneva Conventions, which extend their protections to members of militias and volunteer corps.[16] While the MCA appears to recognize this fact, it simply designates by fiat all members of

the Taliban and "associated forces" as unlawful combatants, for reasons
that are not explained. Those bearing arms for the de facto and effective
Afghan government at the time of the 2002 invasion, even when bearing
arms openly and as part of a responsible command structure, are defined
as "unlawful enemy combatants," merely because the legislation says so.
In drafting this statute, Congress endorsed the executive's view that the
members of the Taliban and associated forces, by resisting the American
invasion, were terrorists.[17]

This decision provided the legal authorization for Combatant Status
Review Tribunals. (One commission relied on evidence obtained by torture when ruling that that Omar Khadr, who at the time of the alleged
offence was fifteen years old, was guilty of murder in violation of the laws
of war and of material support of terrorism – because his torturer testified that Khadr admitted that he had thrown a grenade at an armed American soldier.)[18] This legislation made it clear that it was the executive that
was to have the exclusive power to submit someone to the jurisdiction of
these tribunals. Any decision of the secretary of defense to bring someone to Guantánamo for that purpose was now considered "dispositive"
of the issue.[19]

Both the Geneva Conventions and the Supreme Court's *Hamdi* opinion make it clear that trials held to determine that status of prisoners
must comply with the rules of natural justice.[20] The MCA, in establishing
the procedures for the military trials or CSRTs, fell short of that mark. It
prevented any lawyer without a security clearance from representing detainees,[21] which allowed the executive branch to bar any attorney by
denying him or her that clearance, as this decision is now unreviewable
in the courts.[22] The MCA prevented defence attorneys from invoking the
Geneva Conventions at the CSRTs.[23] It stripped away the procedural protections of the UCMJ, including the right to a speedy trial and not to in-
criminate oneself.[24] Congress also mandated that alleged confessions
obtained using torture were to be admissible in the CSRTs.

In abrogating the detainees' right of appeal, it insulated these tribunals from any challenge before an objective and neutral magistrate.
Now, not only was the executive branch the prosecutor, judge, and ex-
ecutioner, as the MCA explicitly authorized the imposition of the death
penalty,[25] it was now also unaccountable. This was accomplished via the

jurisdiction-stripping provisions, which state that "[n]o court, justice, or judge shall have jurisdiction to hear or consider an application for a writ of habeas corpus filed by or on behalf of an alien detained by the United States who has been determined by the United States [viz. the executive] to have been properly detained as an enemy combatant or is awaiting such determination."[26]

These provisions stood for something more significant than simple evasion of judicial scrutiny. They were also a legislative endorsement of the OLC's earlier position that only the executive should be able to determine whether someone was properly subject to its jurisdiction, which the executive itself both created and defined.

Shortly before the creation of this Star Chamber, then White House counsel Alberto Gonzales said that certain protections provided by the Geneva Conventions were "quaint," and thus the executive could ignore them.[27] In passing the MCA Congress affirmed that "the President has the authority for the United States to interpret the meaning and application of the Geneva Conventions."[28] This provided authority for the executive's claim that no other branch of government could judge whether its decision that article 3 simply did not apply was in error.

Furthermore, the same section of the MCA stated that these powers granted to the executive were not, in fact, a delegation of power from the legislature, as this might support an argument that Congress could revoke them. Instead, the legislation specified that these powers were "[a]s provided by the Constitution."[29] This provision was entirely in line with Yoo's 2002 memoranda. Here, Congress was not merely over-delegating; rather, it was disclaiming any responsibility for making sure that the executive faithfully executed the law. The Geneva Conventions, as treaties ratified by the Senate, constitute the "supreme law of the land,"[30] on the same level as federal statutes and the Constitution itself.[31] Congress now apparently agreed with the OLC that it was the executive branch which was empowered to provide binding interpretations of the laws, not the courts, and that its supremacy was derived from the Constitution.

It can hardly be said that in 2006 Congress was in a state of panic of the sort that reigned three days after the 9/11 attacks when it passed the AUMF. Further evidence that the MCA represented a measured legislative response to the *Hamdi* and *Hamdan* decisions can be found in the record of the debate over the bill. Several amendments that would have provided some degree of legislative oversight of the executive were considered and rejected. Senator Robert Byrd proposed an amendment in the Senate that would have introduced a sunset clause into the legislation, such that the executive's powers to subject those it designated to the jurisdiction of military commissions would have ended in 2011. The amendment was rejected.[32] In addition, Senator Edward Kennedy offered Amendment 5088 to the Senate Bill,[33] which would have specifically banned waterboarding. The executive remained determined to use statements obtained in this manner as evidence against detainees in the CSRTs. Kennedy's amendment also failed.[34]

The passage of the MCA cannot be attributed to the fact that the party in control of the executive branch possessed majorities in the legislature. During the 109th Congress, the Republican majority in the Senate was only 55–45.[35] Sixty votes are required to pass legislation in the Senate owing to its cloture rules. Passage of the MCA could only be assured if five Democrats were prepared to vote in favour. In the end, eleven Democrats crossed the floor. While the party leadership in the Senate cast their personal votes against the bill, a number of the party's power brokers ensured its passage. Among them were former vice-presidential candidate Joseph Lieberman, Senator Frank Lautenberg, and William Nelson, all of whom consistently supported illicit extensions of executive power. The Democrats failed to whip the vote, rendering their own votes against its passage largely symbolic. There were enough votes to prevent cloture, but no filibuster was attempted.[36] This mirrors the voting patterns established by the Supreme Court confirmation battles.

Keeping the Legal Black Holes Dark: The 2009 MCA

The bipartisan nature of legislative support for executive dominance during the war on terror is best demonstrated by the passage of the Military Commissions Act of 2009. Like its predecessor, the 2009 MCA was a response to a Supreme Court case that jeopardized the CSRTs, owing to the fact that the opinion pointed out that its procedures did not comply with the requirements of natural justice.

In *Boumediene v. Bush*,[37] the court held that the MCA's jurisdiction-stripping provisions were unconstitutional. It rhetorically rebuked Congress's capitulation to the executive branch, pointing out that the 2006 MCA gave the executive the ability to determine the scope of its own powers in a manner inconsistent with the rule of law. As the court noted, "to hold that the political branches may switch the constitution on or off at will would lead to a regime in which they, not this court, 'say what the law is.'"[38]

In *Boumediene*, the court recognized that the MCA had made the judiciary appear irrelevant, and it acted to forestall any loss in perceived power or esteem. This decision also derailed the CSRTs: the court held that these tribunals did not grant the detainees an adequate opportunity to prove that they were not enemy combatants. However, as was the case in 2006 following *Hamdi*, Congress enabled the executive by providing explicit legislative authorization for these drumhead proceedings,[39] granting the executive the power that it had unlawfully assumed.

This was not how the 2009 MCA was initially perceived.[40] At the beginning of the Obama administration, the executive possessed a substantial amount of goodwill, and accordingly the press and the public focused on the fact that the act allowed detainees more procedural rights in the CSRTs than before.[41] However, these observers failed to note that these were not concessions to the detainees; rather, they were features mandated by the Court's decision in *Boumediene*. As the Obama administration sought to continue the Guantánamo show trials, it needed to make these changes in order to protect the executive from effective challenges in the courts.[42] Congress's reflexive deference to the executive was supported by both parties, as they demonstrated their uncritical support by approving additional grants of unreviewable discretionary authority after the executive was stalled momentarily by the judiciary.

When the 2009 MCA was proposed, the Democrats controlled the executive branch and possessed majorities in both branches of the legislature. The bill introduced in the House of Representatives was sponsored by Isaac Skelton, the Democratic chairman of the House Armed Services Committee. The Senate version was sponsored by Democratic power broker Joe Lieberman. However, the Democratic control of the Senate was not absolute. Together with the two independents who voted with their party, they could only count on fifty-nine votes, one short of the super-majority necessary for cloture. However, in a turn of events that mirrored the voting on the 2006 MCA, a number of Republican senators voted for the bill. Mitch McConnell and John Kyl, the Republican Senate leader-ship, chose not to whip in the vote, although they cast personal and largely symbolic votes against it.[43] The roles of the party leaders in the kabuki theatre of symbolic opposition to a chief executive from the other party were the reverse of those they played in 2006.

What is most important to note is that because Robert Byrd did not vote against it, the final tally on the 2009 MCA was only sixty-five votes in favour. This is significant, because if the president chooses to veto a bill, a supermajority of sixty-six votes is required to override that decision. However, President Obama signed the legislation, making possible the renewal of commissions (and a renewed purpose for Guantánamo). Among the first proceedings brought at Guantánamo after this statute's passage was the final disposition of Omar Khadr's case. Khadr, labelled an enemy combatant, would have been more accurately described as a child soldier. Although an earlier set of charges against Khadr had been dismissed, new charges before the commission were made possible by the 2009 MCA.[44] Another case brought under the new rules was that of Ibrahim al-Qosi, who was later convicted of material support for terror-ism for having served as a cook at a training camp in Afghanistan.[45]

Torture Absolved: The Detainee Treatment Act

Top-level officials of the Bush administration considered torture to be critical to the task of generating a *casus belli* for the invasion of Iraq. The continued use of torture in these camps was of vital importance to an ex-ecutive bent on further expansion of the war on terror. However, threats to this process began to emerge as the details of waterboarding and other forms of torture were disseminated.

Fortunately for the executive, Congress was again willing to declare legal many gross abuses of *jus cogens* norms.[46] The Senate rejected amendments to the MCA that would have explicitly forbidden water-boarding. This tacit approval for torture was first seen in the Detainee Treatment Act of 2005 (DTA).[47]

As had been the case with the MCA, the DTA was characterized by many as a legislative response to executive abuses, one that would purportedly put a stop to unacceptable practices.[48] However, it is better understood as Congress's response to the exposure of executive wrongdoing, and not to the violations themselves. The legislation was so effective in heading off these challenges that Amnesty International argued that the amendment's loopholes made it clear that torture had become official US policy.[49]

The backlash against torture began with the Abu Ghraib prisoner abuse scandal,[50] which revealed numerous photographs of American jailors chaining hooded detainees in "stress positions," threatening them with dogs, and engaging in sexually charged humiliation. While the Bush administration blamed "bad apples" in the military, the Taguba report[51] revealed that jailors were frequently asked to "soften up" detainees for "enhanced interrogation," which used methods approved for Guantánamo by officials the highest levels of the executive branch.[52] The Abu Graib scandal revealed that the parallel detention regime and its endemic torture had metastasized worldwide.[53]

The photographic evidence of the torture and murder of detainees at Abu Ghraib sounded a chord that moved the public.[54] Congress would need to provide assurances that this was all in the past in order for the "enhanced interrogation" of detainees to continue in the future. Congress publicized the DTA's provisions requiring all interrogations would now need to be in accord with the provisions of the relevant *Army Field Manual*, which purportedly did not authorize degrading or inhumane treatment.[55] What passed largely unnoticed is that this again turned over to the executive the rights to define what did and did not constitute torture, since the executive alone has the power to determine what is included in its own internal regulations.[56] Congress gave the executive the power to reauthorize "enhanced" interrogation by merely amending the *Army Field Manual*. It did so with Appendix M, which now sanctioned torture under Congress's official imprimatur.[57]

Congress could have invoked and re-affirmed the legislation that the executive consistently violated; namely, the provisions of the United States Code, which prohibit "torture committed by public officials under color of law against persons within the public official's custody or control ... [and which] applies ... to acts of torture committed outside the United States."[58] Alternatively, it could have reiterated the fact that the Convention against Torture and Other Cruel, Inhuman or Degrading Treatment or Punishment is the supreme law of the land, since it was implemented by federal enabling legislation.[59] By referring only to the *Army Field Manual*, the legislation failed to close the door on "cruel and inhuman treatment" outside of military custody.[60]

The DTA granted immunity to the torturers, allowing them to claim that waterboarding and other forms of torture "were officially authorized and determined to be lawful at the time they were conducted."[61] Again, Congress acceded to the OLC's argument that the law on this point had been ill-defined, despite the fact that the John Yoo's reasoning had amounted to professional misconduct. In addition, the DTA, as modified by the Graham-Levin Amendment,[62] specified explicitly that statements that were obtained by torture were to be admitted as evidence in the CSRTs. Respectively, the MCA, the Graham-Levin Amendment, and the DTA offered the executive immunity for earlier torture, the ability to introduce statements it obtained using torture to justify further detention of its victims, and the power to continue to abuse detainees by modifying the legal definition of torture.

That said, the executive found even the suggestion that it might require a delegation of authority from Congress to accomplish these goals to be unacceptable. The Bush administration attached a signing statement to the DTA, which stated that "[t]he executive branch shall construe ... the Act, relating to detainees, in a manner consistent with the constitutional authority of the President to supervise the unitary executive branch and as Commander in Chief and consistent with the constitutional limitations on the judicial power."[63]

This statement reasserted fringe theories of executive power found in Yoo's OLC memoranda; that the commander-in-chief possessed inherent constitutional powers over detainees, an assertion that the Supreme Court had rejected in *Hamdi*.[64] The executive stated its intention to ignore duly enacted legislation; namely, the portions of the DTA that outlawed certain techniques of torture, because it thought that the sections barring waterboarding were unacceptable.[65] Despite this, Congress ignored the signing statement.

In this way, DTA served the same purpose for Congress as the *Boumediene* decision had served the Supreme Court: it allowed a branch of government that was under popular pressure to express its displeasure with obvious violations of *jus cogens* norms, without actually constraining the executive.

The DTA also foreshadowed the nullification of the *Boumediene* opinion, as it contained a provision directing appeals from the CSRTs to the DC Circuit.[66] Congress believed that the DC Circuit was more likely to be hostile to the detainees' claims than any other court. This can be deduced from the fact that this provision was placed within a bill that otherwise deprives every other court from hearing petitions for habeas corpus. There is only one plausible explanation for channelling all direct appeals from the CSRTs to that court: the legislators thought that it could be counted upon to dispose of them. Simply put, the DTA was designed to keep a judicial black hole – a facility designed to hide torture and to produce false confessions – in continued operation. In order to do so, Congress affirmed the executive's argument that no other branch of government possessed any power to challenge its actions.

Congress's Consent to Executive War-Making

By isolating, and then torturing, detainees, the executive could obtain statements that purportedly incriminated other states as sponsors of terrorism; the destruction of the rule of law in the United States has proceeded with a goal in mind: to preserve unilateral American hegemony around the globe, even when American popular opinion and legal norms would not allow for the military actions that make this possible. This process reinforces the power of the executive branch and stimulates a vicious circle of aggression.

Congress's inadequate response to the arguments that the executive possessed unilateral power to engage in aggressive war-marking in 2002–2003 were as momentous as its satisfactory response when Nixon expanded the Vietnam War dramatically without congressional sanction,[67] since executive war-making is incompatible with the rule of law. (It also runs contrary to the Constitution, as the Declare War and the Letter of Marque and Reprisal Clauses grant this authority exclusively to Congress.[68]) After 9/11, the executive seized this power, citing fringe theories of executive sovereignty over matters of national security.[69] This is fatal to the rule of law, because it allows the executive to create the circumstances in which it can expand its own powers without any fear of being checked by the other branches of government.

Congress's inadequate response to the executive's drive for war in various theatres in the decade following the 9/11 attacks was central to the destruction of the rule of law in the United States. The three key examples are the attacks against Iraq, Libya, and Syria.

Congress Deceived? The Executive and the Iraq AUMF

A year and a day after the 9/11 attacks, President Bush spoke at the United Nations, requesting a resolution that would authorize the use of military force, purportedly to enforce earlier resolutions related to weapons of mass destruction.[70] While the United States would never obtain this final explicit authorization from the UN, it was the basis for the executive's request for military authorization from Congress, which was assured that a firm basis for the attack under international law would soon be forthcoming.[71]

It soon became evident that the Bush administration would not allow the weapons inspectors to complete their mission in Iraq, a prerequisite of a Security Council resolution under Chapter VII. At this point, less than a third of Americans supported the executive's new policy of immediate attacks, favouring instead the completion of the inspection process and a diplomatic solution.[72]

When the United States moved to a war footing, the largest coordinated protests in world history were staged on 15 February 2003.[73]

Approximately 400,000 people took to the streets in New York City, while hundreds of demonstrations took place simultaneously across the country.[74] This was done in the face of obstruction and illicit surveillance by the intelligence community and the deployment of far more aggressive forms of policing than seen previously, including the "kettling" and mass arrests of peaceful protesters.[75]

Doubts about the *casus belli* were widespread, and reached almost to the top echelons of American society. Criticism came from various quarters, including the higher ranks of the military: *Time* magazine noted that almost one in three senior officers "question[ed] the wisdom of a pre-emptive war with Iraq."[76] Congressional approval was of crucial importance to the executive, as it would be able to point to this authorization for the invasion when the case for war fell apart, after it became evident that Iraq no longer possessed a weapons of mass destruction program.[77] The executive knew that its rationale for war was problematic. This was the reason that their intelligence community needed to work so diligently to camouflage faulty sources and conclusions through their allies' agencies, in particular the United Kingdom's Secret Intelligence Service, Germany's Federal Intelligence Service, and SISME – Italian military intelligence, now known as AISE.

In the case of the story of Iraq's supposed attempts to buy yellowcake uranium from Niger, this was laundered through Italian military intelligence.[78] The unfounded allegations of mobile chemical weapons laboratories were made by the informant dubbed "Curveball." He was later revealed to be "the brother of a top aide of Ahmad Chalabi, the pro-western Iraqi former exile with links to the Pentagon."[79] His statements were bolstered by citing the documents of the German intelligence service in which they were found, but the executive did not reveal that those intelligence reports did not evaluate his claims positively.[80]

These claims became the basis for the "sixteen words" used by President Bush to goad Congress and the American public to war in his State of the Union Address of January 2003: "The British government has learned that Saddam Hussein recently sought significant quantities of uranium from Africa." They were also the basis for Colin Powell's infamous PowerPoint presentation to the United Nations Security Council.[81] The secretary of state was so concerned about the veracity of the yellowcake allegations that he refused to cite them in that speech.[82] His suspicions were well grounded, as the State Department's Bureau of Intelligence and Research revealed eleven days before the State of the Union address that these allegations were based on forgeries.[83] Before his speech, Powell expressed doubts about the mobile weapons laboratories. He continued to do so until he was personally presented with the assurances of the director of the CIA.[84] Congress accepted these assurances uncritically and without independent investigation.[85]

A bill was put before in the House of Representatives on 2 October 2002. Its text was composed entirely within the executive branch, and it was introduced at the administration's request by Speaker of the House John Dennis Hastert.[86] The leading co-sponsor of the bill was the head of the Democratic Party in that chamber, House minority leader Richard Gephardt.[87] The Senate's identical version of the bill was introduced at the executive's request by Democratic Senate minority leader Tom Daschle and co-sponsored by Republican Senate majority leader Trent Lott.[88]

The pattern that would emerge whenever the executive sought approval for military action was established with the Iraq AUMF. The executive branch and the leaders of both parties in the legislature formed a united front against any possible ideological opposition. This included disagreement from both legislators on the fringes of the two parties (i.e., Representatives Dennis Kucinich and Ron Paul, Senators Russ Feingold and Lincoln Chaffee) and from the public. The bill passed through both chambers in just over one week.[89] Numerous amendments that would have limited the grant of unlimited discretion over whether to actually launch the attack were rejected, even as the executive equivocated over whether it might proceed in the event that it could not secure the passage of a Security Council resolution under Chapter VII.[90] These included the Spratt and Levin Amendments, which would have required such a resolution from the Security Council,[91] and the Byrd Amendment, which would have specified that the legislature was not agreeing that the executive possessed unspecified inherent constitutional powers to go beyond the text of the Iraq AUMF.[92] The Byrd Amendment would also have placed a time limit on the use of the authority granted by that statute.[93]

When Bush began the war, the Iraq AUMF was passed; thus, he could assert that he was in full compliance with the WPR and the constitutional requirement of congressional approval for military action.[94] The executive, however, maintained that it possessed an independent constitutional power to go to war against Iraq; the OLC's opinions made it clear that the executive did not seek the Iraq AUMF owing to matters of principle.

Congress failed to understand the executive's true motivation.[95] The executive did not want to be forced to take full responsibility for the Iraq War, in the event that it would become deeply unpopular.[96] In securing a statutory basis for its actions, it would also insulate itself from the legislators' criticism.[97] Congress struck a bad bargain with the executive. In exchange for the appearance of continued relevance in foreign affairs, they accepted shared responsibility for aggressive war-making.[98]

Congress and the 2011 Intervention into the Libyan Civil War

In February 2011, protests against Colonel Moammar Gadhafi erupted in Libya. Over the coming months, the movement against his government became an open revolt. There was only a brief lag between the eruption of this civil war and calls by Western leaders for a no-fly zone over the country.[99] Shortly thereafter, the United Nations Security Council approved a resolution to that end on 17 March 2011.[100] Within days, the member states of the North Atlantic Treaty Organization (NATO) were conducting air strikes that were not aimed at keeping the Libyan Air Force from bombing civilian targets. Libyan ground forces, especially armoured forces that the insurgents could not successfully defeat, were targeted.[101] The aim of the intervention was regime change. NATO achieved its ultimate goal when a convoy transporting Gadhafi was attacked by an American drone and French fighter jets. Gadhafi was then killed by insurgents while fleeing these air strikes.[102]

While these military actions were authorized by the Security Council, this does not relieve the executive having to comply with its own laws. Both the US Constitution and its statutory law require the executive to obtain authorization for the use of military force from Congress.[103] The executive, while now headed by a Democratic president, revived a theory of inherent constitutional authority developed within the OLC to evade the requirements of the rule of law. It now claimed the power to wage war, which is the most problematic instance of the executive expanding the boundaries of its own powers that can be imagined. Congress's reaction to these claims fits with the emerging pattern: when the executive circumvents statutory restrictions on its power, including those explicitly re-imposed in the congressional resurgence after Watergate, Congress simply turns a blind eye, or protests in the mildest possible terms.[104]

As the Libyan intervention approached the ninety-day limit imposed by the War Powers Resolution of 1973,[105] there were rumblings in Congress about the need for a resolution authorizing military force, although these were curiously muted. The Republican Speaker of the House John Boehner asked the executive to "explain the legal grounds for failing to seek Congressional authorization in the 90 days since Mr. Obama informed Congress of the start of the mission in Libya";[106] that is, rather than challenging the illegality of the executive's actions, he merely extended an invitation to the executive to produce legal arguments that would allow Congress to continue to ignore unilateral executive war-making.

The Obama administration responded, producing an explanation that was as puzzling and poorly reasoned as any of the OLC opinions written by John Yoo and his colleagues. Its rationale depended upon a strange distinction between involvement in hostilities and an allegedly different use of armed force, which it labelled "kinetic operations." In doing so, the executive pressed the unitary executive theory even further than the Bush administration. When the OLC refused to sign off on this theory, President Obama departed from the "traditional legal process the executive branch has developed to sustain the rule of law for over 75 years."[107] The press reported on this as follows:

> [Attorney General Eric] Holder – concluded that sustained U.S. support for the NATO campaign against Libya ... including drone strikes – amounted to "hostilities" [that triggered the need for a congressional resolution pursuant to the WPR] ... Rather than permit OLC to vet the issue, the White House adopted an unusual and far more informal procedure ... Obama ... concluded that he did not need congressional approval ... [by] reject[ing] the views of Holder and OLC's acting chief, Caroline D. Krass, he also overruled Jeh C. Johnson, the Defense Department's chief legal counsel.[108]

Here, the executive openly solicited a more pliant opinion within that would support its preferred interpretation of a statute, in the process overruling both the attorney general and the head of the office that is charged with producing objective interpretations of the law to guide the executive branch. This tactic could only succeed if Congress was willing to turn a blind eye. Despite one member of the House Judiciary Committee labelling the president's interpretation "ridiculous,"[109] no formal protests were made by Congress.

Congressional leaders successfully coordinated their efforts with those of the executive branch to avoid exercising oversight over the illicit use of war powers. Here, these powers were exercised quite openly to precipitate the overthrow of a foreign regime in favour of one more friendly to American interests. This was done in the manner that evades the requirements of the WPR, the Constitution, and the rule of law.[110] As for the members of the legislature who were less pliant or eager for regime change than Boehner and John McCain, they were caught between their own leadership, the executive, and the executive's allies in the judiciary. They could not get a bill through Congress's committee structure without the support of the party leaders,[111] and the party leaders were warned in no uncertain terms that if this happened, the results for Congress, would be dire: the executive would publicly humiliate the legislators by simply ignoring them, confirming their irrelevance.[112] Secretary of State Hillary Clinton told Congress in a classified briefing that "the White House would forge ahead with military action in Libya even if Congress passed a resolution constraining the mission."[113] Thanks to the executive's domination of certain key courts, no legislator wishing to bring a judicial challenge to this collusion would be able to do so. Any lawsuit challenging the executive would run up against the DC Circuit's decision in *Campbell v. Clinton*,[114] penned by Judge Silberman, which held that legislators have no standing to bring a claim that the executive is in violation of the WPR. This decision is effectively the final word on the issue, as any such challenge would need to be brought within the jurisdiction of the DC Circuit.

Congress and the Syrian Civil War

The Syrian civil war began with protests in March 2011, which were inspired by similar uprisings elsewhere in the Middle East known collectively as the "Arab Spring."[115] The governing regime's use of the military to suppress protests sparked an armed rebellion shortly afterwards. It appeared very likely from the outset of these protests that the United States would promote regime change, as this was its declared policy. This was the case since at least 2002, when then under-secretary of state for arms control and international security affairs John Bolton added Syria to the Bush administration's "Axis of Evil" owing to the conclusion it was a "state [sponsor] of terrorism that [is] pursuing ... weapons of mass destruction."[116] Syria was one of the few nations in the region that opposed the American war of aggression against Iraq, souring Syrian–US relations that until then were improving, to the point where a presidential summit in Geneva was possible. Indeed, Bill Clinton met with Bashar-al-Assad.[117] However, the Obama administration continued the Bush administration's policies toward Syria. Additionally, in 2010 it contended publicly that Syria was providing missiles to the Hezbollah for use against Israel.[118] In addition, the release of the State Department's classified diplomatic cables by WikiLeaks revealed that the United States "secretly financed Syrian political opposition groups and related projects" from at least April of 2009.[119]

In the summer of 2012, the head of the CIA and the secretary of state first proposed that the United States provide arms to and train the rebel forces.[120] It should be noted that during the previous three years, it did so indirectly, by "quietly encourag[ing] Saudi Arabia, Qatar and Turkey to ship weapons into the country."[121] In addition, "U.S. special operations troops have been secretly training Syrian rebels with anti-tank and anti-aircraft weapons since late [2012]."[122] The executive decided to move forward openly with these plans in June 2013.[123] Plans were being made at the highest levels of the executive branch for a bombing campaign and the enforcement of a no-fly zone over Syria.[124] However, it did not openly advocate going to war until two months later, purportedly in response to the use of chemical weapons in Ghouta on 21 August 2013.[125]

The United States seized upon this incident as a *casus belli* for aggressive war-making. In attempting to make its case, the executive used the same playbook as it did in 2002. This was contemptuous of Congress, as that body had recently learned that it had been deceived with almost identical claims before accepting shared responsibility for an aggressive war against Iraq.

After learning that Iraq did not possess weapons of mass destruction, the Senate concluded that the intelligence presented to them to justify that assertion was, at the very least, deeply flawed. The Senate convened the Senate Iraq Intelligence Committee (SIIC) to investigate the executive's representations about the Iraqi weapons programs and the way in which these were generated.[126] The investigation proceeded in two phases, which revealed systematic manipulation of the legislators by the executive, something made possible by its control over the intelligence community and an absence of any effective congressional oversight.[127]

The first line of inquiry for the SIIC was the executive's determined attempts to link Saddam Hussein to the 9/11 attacks. This "had been a strongly implied accusation made obliquely against Iraq in Administration statements since 2001."[128] These statements were a key pillar of the executive's case for war, along with allegations related to weapons of mass destruction. However, the Iraq AUMF itself, which was written by the executive, stated that Iraq was "continu[ing] to aid and harbor other international terrorist organizations."[129]

When pressed, the executive would admit that the intelligence that supported this assertion was limited to proof that Hussein aided organizations such as the People's Mujahedeen of Iran, which committed acts of terrorism within the Islamic Republic, which the United States subsequently protected after the invasion of Iraq for possible future use against Iran.[130] However, the executive continued to promote theories about Iraqi support for al Qaeda, even after these were discredited by the intelligence community.[131] While Cheney continued making these claims, Bush made ambiguous statements about Iraqi support of terrorism. The public took this to mean anti-American terrorism, owing to the vice-president's unsupported allegations. The SIIC refuted these claims in its Phase I report, concluding that "there was no evidence to support Iraqi complicity or assistance" in the 9/11 attacks.[132]

The siic also addressed the intelligence related to wmd, the second and apparently more substantive leg supporting the case for war. It concluded that not only was there no evidence that Iraq possessed these weapons, but that the executive consistently distorted intelligence reports to justify its agenda. The first of these conclusions was outlined in the Phase I report, which concluded that the secretary of state's case for war was based on "information provided or cleared by the Central Intelligence Agency (cia) for inclusion in Secretary Powell's speech [that] was overstated, misleading, or incorrect."[133]

Evidence that the executive pressured the intelligence analysts to alter their findings – the corollary of the directives to the torturers at Guantánamo to produce false confessions about Iraqi involvement – would remain hidden until the publication of the Phase II report. This was the siic's key failure. Senators John Rockefeller, Richard Durbin, and Carl Levin made clear that the committee had been forced by the executive to delay its consideration of "how intelligence on Iraq was used or misused by Administration officials in public statements and reports."[134] Accordingly, "the Committee's phase one report fail[ed] to fully explain the environment of intense pressure in which Intelligence Community officials were asked to render judgments on matters relating to Iraq when policy officials had already forcefully stated their own conclusions in public."[135]

The public release of the Phase II reports was delayed until July 2008. During the three-year interval, President Bush was re-elected and served almost all of his allotted final term. The report had been held back until it could have no real effect on the executive, since when it was finally released the legislature possessed no clear incentive to hold it accountable, given the fact that the Bush administration was then four months away from its natural end.

This lengthy postponement was unfortunate, since it revealed many facts that called for more than a stern rebuke. First, it concluded that the executive "repeatedly presented intelligence as fact when in reality it was unsubstantiated, contradicted, or even non-existent. As a result, the American people were led to believe that the threat from Iraq was much greater than actually existed."[136] This was only possible because the executive created what amounted to a new intelligence agency, one that was designed to promote conclusions that more seasoned analysts had rejected. After learning of the false assertions generated by the Department of Defense's Office of Special Plans and the termination of internal inquiries into its activities[137] the SIIC concluded that the executive crossed the line between "relying on incorrect intelligence and deliberately painting a picture to the American people that you know is not fully accurate," and in this manner knowingly "led the nation into war under false pretences."[138]

Certain delays in the release of this revelatory report are indefensible. While the Republican members of the SIIC were able to use procedural tactics to slow the committee's work before 2006, the midterm elections yielded a Democratic majority in the Senate,[139] which should have allowed Senator Rockefeller to proceed swiftly toward its completion and release to the public. One possible factor is that the Democrats wanted to reduce any possible pressure for impeachment,[140] which was the only remaining method for legislative control of a runaway executive that openly disdains the requirements of the rule of law, in the same manner as the Nixon administration. However, before addressing this issue, one should first consider a more pressing question: has Congress internalized the conclusions of the SIIC report, such that it might resist future temptations to give the executive unfettered discretion to wage war? The test that reveals whether it learned the lessons of Iraq would come in the form of the Obama administration's drive for aggression against Syria in 2013.

Congress apparently learned nothing from the committee's reports, as the executive's virtually identical tactics achieved a similar result. The executive made unsubstantiated public statements about WMDs that were contradicted by the nuanced intelligence reports, and in order to bypass these, the executive again relied on the "stovepiping" of intelligence. This involved the creation of special intelligence analysis units controlled at the highest level of the executive branch, which appropriated and interpreted raw field reports without allowing analysts from the relevant agencies that nominally report to Congress to scrutinize or interpret this data. As in 2002, this frequently involved the laundering of this stovepiped information through foreign intelligence agencies, which produced data that could be cited by the executive to Congress, but which the executive would argue could not be revealed.

The executive expected that, as in 2002, the credibility of its senior officials presenting intelligence reports would allow it to assemble an international coalition that would give the intervention the appearance of legitimacy, or even the sanction of international law if the Security Council could not approve a resolution,[141] because its processes were "broken" by states that did not agree with the executive's proposals.[142] As President Obama said in late August 2013, "If the U.S. goes in and attacks another country without a U.N. mandate and without clear evidence that can be presented, then there are questions in terms of whether international law supports it. Do we have the coalition to make it work? And, you know, those are considerations that we have to take into account."[143]

Unfortunately for the executive, its plans for an international coalition were dashed when the first and most important partner for such an endeavour was relegated to the sidelines by decisive legislative action. The United Kingdom, the United States' partner in the "special relationship," decided against joining the proposed military campaign. This was "disastrous" to the executive's initiative, as its "plans for air strikes against Syria were thrown into disarray" by the vote.[144] In part this response can be attributed to doubts about the *casus belli*. As Peter Flatters noted, "With the Prime Minister claiming that intelligence findings were compelling enough to warrant action, the remarkable thing was Parliament's response – namely that it did not believe him, or rather that it insisted on seeing the evidence for itself."[145]

It was not surprising that the members of Parliament took this position after reviewing the intelligence findings. What was released to them was a three-page memorandum from the Joint Intelligence Committee, which focused on the conclusion that chemical weapons were used in Ghouta. On the crucial issue of who used them, it said "there is no credible intelligence or other evidence to substantiate the claims or the possession of CW by the opposition."[146] MI6's argument can be paraphrased as a syllogism: all chemical weapons in Syria belong to Assad, chemical weapons were used, and therefore Assad used chemical weapons. Unfortunately, there appeared to be credible evidence that the opposition possessed these weapons; namely, the statements of Carla Del Ponte, a member of the International Commission of Inquiry on the Syrian Arab

Republic appointed by the UN high commissioner for human rights. Speaking on the commission's behalf months before the Ghouta attacks, she noted that "according to what we have established so far, it is at the moment opponents of the regime who are using sarin gas."[147]

Whether or not Del Ponte was correct is beside the point. What is crucial to note is that the British intelligence community completely failed to address her statement, which if true would have invalidated the central premise of its argument for war. It appears that Parliament was entitled to reject such an argument. It remained to be seen, however, whether Congress would simply give the executive the benefit of the doubt, and abdicate its responsibility to oversee and scrutinize the conclusions of the intelligence agencies.

Congress was only presented with this opportunity because of Parliament's rebuke to the British executive. Initially it appeared that the executive branch in Washington was prepared to begin the bombing campaign without seeking a congressional resolution. However, after the British declined to join a coalition, it appeared that the US executive would have borne all of the responsibility for the intervention, both in the eyes of the world and in the eyes of Americans. As in the case of the Iraq War, the proposed aggression was deeply unpopular both at home and abroad. At the end of August 2013, only 29 per cent of those polled favoured "the U.S. conducting military airstrikes against Syria in response to reports that the Syrian government used chemical weapons," and only 21 per cent favoured "the United States and its allies supplying weapons to the Syrian rebels."[148]

On 31 August 2013 the executive presented a draft of a bill to Congress entitled the Authorization for Use of United States Armed Forces.[149] It was a considerably broader authorization than the Iraq AUMF. A better comparison is the Gulf of Tonkin Resolution.[150] It did not limit the use of force to Syria, but rather "within, to or from Syria," and appears to propose the creation of a worldwide mandate to prevent the "use or proliferation" of "chemical or other weapons of mass destruction" so as to "protect the United States and its allies and partners against the threat posed by such weapons."[151] The bill was "nothing less than an open-ended endorsement of military intervention in the Middle East and beyond."[152]

In support of the bill, the executive sent Secretary of State John Kerry to the Senate. Kerry played a role similar to the one played by Secretary Powell ten years earlier. He presented assertions about WMDs as fact, cited foreign intelligence reports that could not be divulged, and made assertions that were not in line with the available American intelligence reports – precisely what the SIIC found so objectionable about manipulation of intelligence before the Iraq War.[153] Kerry made bold assertions about the high level of certainty that the Assad regime was responsible, relying on communications intercepts by German, French, and Israeli intelligence that he would not disclose.[154] Assertions about British confirmation of technical intelligence on the sarin gas would follow several days later.[155]

Kerry also hedged his answer when he was asked about whether the executive envisioned American ground troops deploying to Syria. He denied that there were any plans to do so, although he noted that it might be necessary in the event that the United States needed to "secure" the chemical weapons possessed by the Assad regime.[156] This was presented as though it were a mere detail, although released intelligence reports reveal that Syria had approximately 1,000 tonnes of chemical agents, which according to one study would require 75,000 soldiers to assume custody.[157] The high probability that "boots on the ground" would ultimately be required is made clear when one observes that Kerry misrepresented the consensus within the intelligence community on an issue of vital importance.[158] When asked about the presence of Salafist or al Qaeda– affiliated militants in the ranks of the Syrian opposition forces, Kerry minimized their importance in a manner that is belied by intelligence reports, which contradict both his figures and the reality of the situation. At that time, the mujahedeen of the al-Nusra Front, allegedly affiliated with al Qaeda in Iraq and Ayman al-Zawahiri, were the most effective and influential force in Syrian resistance.[159]

The Senate leadership's response demonstrated that its members learned little if anything from the SIIC's reports, as they took an immediately favourable attitude toward both Secretary Kerry's presentation and the executive's draft bill.[160] The Republican leadership gave it "*carte blanche.*"[161] The Senate amended the bill to explicitly authorize the executive to pursue regime change: "the policy of the United States ... [is]

to change the momentum on the battlefield in Syria."[162] As in 2002, the leadership of both parties in both chambers of Congress rallied behind the executive, with Republican senators John McCain and Eric Cantor taking the lead in the Senate and the Democratic leadership, particularly Nancy Pelosi, whipping in the votes in the House. This demonstrates that the legislative branch remains incapable of the intelligence oversight necessary to effectively control the executive branch that the rule of law requires.

Unfortunately for the executive, the process of securing formal congressional sanction for an aggressive war against Syria was derailed when the Russian government seized upon a statement by Secretary of State Kerry and made a well-publicized proposal to supervise the destruction of Syria's chemical weapons.[163]

Congress's Failure to Consider Impeachment

The ultimate method of legislative control over the executive is impeachment, which allows Congress to remove executive branch officials from office.[164] The provisions for impeachment might allow for the punishment of an executive that has attempted to become immune from legislative oversight, and this process could also inaugurate the reinstallation of the rule of law.

While still formally in existence, impeachment is by now a moribund method of legislative control, as the events of the last ten years demonstrate that it has fallen into desuetude. The leadership of both parties in the legislature have consistently blocked attempts to invoke this possibility. Given the failure of Congress to seriously consider impeaching President Bush, even after the exposure of serious misconduct, it is possible to tentatively conclude that no assertion of executive supremacy over the laws would provoke this response from the legislature as it currently constituted.

President Nixon was also the subject of these proceedings, although he resigned shortly before a scheduled vote on the Articles of Impeachment, after he was told by his advisors that it was certain that he would be convicted in the Senate.[165] He was to be charged with "violating the constitutional rights of citizens," "endeavouring to misuse the Central Intelligence Agency," and committing other abuses "in a manner ... subversive of constitutional government."[166] This assertion of legislative superiority over the executive set the stage for the congressional resurgence that reconstructed the rule of law in the United States for the twentieth century.

If Congress wanted to pursue the same course of action following the revelations that the executive branch engaged in similar misconduct during the twenty-first century, it has missed its chance. Efforts to impeach President Bush were impeded significantly by the indefensible delays in producing the SIIC's Phase II report investigating the manipulation of intelligence by the executive to justify an attack on Iraq. However, by 2005, certain legislators in the House believed that the parallel British investigation of the "Downing Street Memo"[167] provided a basis for charging the executive with impeachable misconduct. The memorandum of a British Cabinet meeting's minutes noted that "Bush wanted to remove Saddam, through military action, justified by the conjunction of terrorism and WMD. But the intelligence and facts were being fixed around the policy."[168]

On this basis, Representative John Conyers secured thirty-eight co-sponsors for a resolution calling for an investigation of whether impeachment was appropriate.[169] Further efforts followed in early 2006, but these were shut down by Speaker of the House Nancy Pelosi, who indicated that "impeachment was off the table";[170] that is, not approved for the legislative agenda set by the Democratic majority in Congress.[171] Democrat leaders decided that whatever sort of evidence it might unearth was beside the point.

After SIIC's Phase II report was finally issued, Representative Dennis Kucinich and Robert Wexler introduced a draft bill containing articles of impeachment against President Bush. The charges included "interfering with and obstructing Congress's lawful functions of overseeing foreign affairs and declaring war ... [by] allowing, authorizing and sanctioning the manipulation of intelligence analysis by those under his direction and control"; "declar[ing] the right to detain U.S. citizens indefinitely, without charge and without providing them access to counsel or the courts"; "authoriz[ing] ... as official policy ... [w]ater-boarding, beatings, faked executions" and other forms of torture; "establish[ing] a body of secret laws through the issuance of legal opinions"; "authorizing warrantless electronic surveillance of American citizens"; and with having "used signing statements to claim the right to violate acts of Congress even as he signs them into law ... [and having] proceeded to violate the laws the statements claimed the right to violate."[172]

All of these charges were undeniable. However, Speaker Pelosi referred the bill to the Judiciary Committee, from which it never emerged.[173]

The reasons why these bills failed can be found in Conyers's introduction to the House Judiciary's exhaustive survey of executive overreaching, "Reining In the Imperial Presidency: Lessons and Recommendations Relating to the Presidency of George W. Bush."[174] He wrote, "The simple fact is, despite the efforts of impeachment advocates, the support and votes have not been there, and cannot be expected to materialize ... The resolution I offered three years ago simply to investigate whether an impeachment was warranted garnered only 38 cosponsors in the House, and the Democratic leader in the Senate [Harry Reid] labelled it 'ridiculous.'"[175]

The impeachment resolutions introduced by Conyers and Kucinich were blocked by the leaders in each legislative chamber of the party nominally opposed to the one occupying the executive. Their motivations are worth exploring.

Explaining Congress's Tolerance and Inaction

To explain Congress's failure to check the executive, one must analyze the incentives and pressures on its members. This investigation begins with the question of whether the failure to exercise oversight and control has any consequences for these individuals. Scholars have concluded that it does not: "As long as members of Congress can rest secure in their re-election prospects even as popular confidence in Congress as an institution plummets, the impetus ... will be lacking. Until voters begin to value effective oversight as much as academics ... electoral incentives may continue to trump institutional incentives to protect Congress' power from a wayward executive branch."[176]

In the three years since this prediction was made in 2010, popular confidence in the legislative branch fell to its lowest level on record. As of 13 June 2013, only 10 per cent of Americans said that they possessed "a great deal" or "quite a lot" of confidence in Congress. (Not coincidentally, the highest rating for the legislature came directly after the Watergate hearings and President Nixon's resignation.)[177] However, the likelihood of incumbents being re-elected to either chamber remains both constant and exceptionally high. In 2012, the percentage chance of re-election was at or above 90 per cent for these legislators. This figure is roughly consistent with the average since the year 2000.[178]

Legislators' failure to conduct meaningful oversight of the executive did not affect their ability to remain in office. However, the question of what is required to thrive and succeed in the legislature, including obtaining positions of leadership within a party, provides insight into the issue of whether there are powerful disincentives to confronting the executive.

This cycle of negative reinforcement developed after the congressional resurgence. The correct place to inquire into the reassertion of executive power is the Carter administration.[179] The tumultuous disruption of the party system after Watergate allowed Georgia governor Jimmy Carter, an outsider candidate deeply and morally committed to international peace, to prevail over the preferred Democratic establishment nominee, Henry "Scoop" Jackson,[180] a war hawk and fervent anti-communist.[181] (Jackson later became a key influence on the neo-conservatives, especially Paul Wolfowitz and Richard Perle. Wolfowitz and Perle were both on Jackson's staff in the early 1970s, and Perle served in this capacity for eleven years.)[182] Jackson had also supported Nixon despite the revelations about his abuses of executive power, and in the wake of the resignation provoked by legislative investigations and the Supreme Courts' decision in *United States v. Nixon* Jackson nevertheless called Nixon "the first American President toppled by a mob."[183]

Carter's efforts to bring about peace with the Soviet Union were opposed within Congress and the Democratic Party, which sheds light on the incentive structures that emerged during the period. These rewards and punishments continue to influence legislators' inclinations to support the executive branch whenever its foreign policy agenda leads inexorably to war. Congress failed to support President Carter's efforts to reform the CIA and to achieve a comprehensive disarmament agreement with the Soviet Union, and subjected his efforts to promote peace to blistering criticism. This was followed by the unprecedented decision by his fellow Democrats to attempt to strip a sitting chief executive of his status as the party's nominee in the upcoming presidential election. Congress's hostility to Carter can be attributed to its renewed support for aggressive war, which in turn can only be explained by the connections between legislators and what President Eisenhower labelled the "military-industrial complex."

Carter was elected in 1976 despite a "Stop Carter" alliance involving almost all of the most powerful legislators and party bosses of the Democratic Party, including the Chicago mayor and Democrat kingmaker Richard J. Daley.[184] Opposition to Carter was motivated largely by his desire for peace; remedial action followed almost immediately. Nine days after his election, politicians and public intellectuals formed an alliance known as the Committee on the Present Danger (CPD), a "who's who of the Democratic establishment." It was supported by the leaders of America's trade union federation, and leading industrialists such as Richard Mellon Scaife, a billionaire who had given Nixon an illegal million-dollar campaign contribution.[185] The CPD announced a "declaration of war against Carter's hopes for arms control and improved relations with the Soviet Union," which they repeatedly compared to Neville Chamberlain's policy of appeasement.[186]

The CPD's central claim was that the Soviet Union was committed to obtaining military supremacy over the United States and defeating it. As in the case of the preparation for the Iraq War and the interventions into the Libyan and Syrian civil war, the CIA became a battleground in which competing assessments and interpretations of foreign states' intentions would stand or fall as justifications for aggressive American foreign policy. Congress and the executive were again on the opposite sides of this battle, but on the sides opposite to the positions they would assume in later policy disputes over aggressive war.

Carter refused to allow George H.W. Bush to continue in office as the director of the CIA, despite Bush's appeals to remain.[187] Instead, he nominated Theodore Sorenson, who was "the most important aide the President [Kennedy] had ever hired."[188] Sorenson, like Kennedy, was a proponent of international peace and effective arms control, and was an opponent of the Vietnam War. He was one of the few public figures to commend Daniel Ellsberg for revealing the executive branch's lies about the Vietnam War by leaking the Pentagon Papers, in actions that anticipated those of Chelsea (formerly Bradley) Manning, Edward Snowden, and other whistle-blowers.[189]

The CPD and its legislative allies would keep Sorenson from being confirmed to lead the CIA precisely because he was an opponent of falsified intelligence, and possibly because he would have been a powerful ally for Carter, who "had been elected with a mandate and an ambition to open up the government" in response to this sort of manipulation.[190] Sorenson was exceptionally attuned to the pressures on the executive to accede to suggestions for aggressive action, having served under Kennedy during the Cuban Missile Crisis and the demands for rapid escalation of American involvement in Vietnam after the assassination of Ngo Dinh Diem.[191] He would not have provided support for bellicose foreign policy.

On 13 January 1977, the Senate Intelligence Committee examined affidavits from Sorenson in which he asserted that the release of the Pentagon Papers presented no threat to national security, and that the classification system for intelligence-related documents was "grotesquely overblown."[192] The Senate responded with outrage at this defence of someone who was by now tarred as a traitor. Sorenson's fate was sealed when Senate majority leader Mike Mansfield, who was a member of Carter's own party, said at a press conference that he would not endorse Sorenson, without even bothering to inform the president in advance.[193] This was virtually unprecedented: "To gauge the full measure of the victory – and of Carter's stunning defeat – parliamentarians delve into the archives and report that … the last time a Senate of the President's own party had done such as thing was 1925 … and the lesson is: How feeble is a President with no party to support him."[194]

After Sorenson's nomination failed, Carter nominated Admiral Stansfield Turner, who proved to be a "fish out of water – actually as unfamiliar with the inner workings of the agency as George H.W. Bush had pretended to be" who was "unprepared for the ruthless internal politics of the CIA."[195]

Less than a year before Carter took office, Bush had appointed a special group of analysts who would produce politicized and faulty raw intelligence at the CIA director's bequest. Their conclusions were not subjected to the normal vetting process, in order "to get around the analysts who did not sufficiently hype the Soviet threat," and who "had accurately determined that the USSR was already in decline."[196] This group, known as "Team B," included Wolfowitz and Paul Nitze, who also served as founding members of the CPD.[197] The stage was set for the debate over competing estimations of Soviet military spending and military preparedness, which would itself determine the probability of success for Carter's arms control agenda.

With Bush's former deputy, E. Henry Knoche, in effective control of the CIA, the professional analysts who supported arms control with accurate assessments of Soviet military technology and strategic aims never stood a chance. The CIA soon "shifted 180 degrees" and produced an estimate that constituted "a high barrier for the Carter Administration to overcome in its pursuit of arms control," as it turned the Committee for the "Present Danger['s] alarms into the new official orthodoxy,"[198] something made easier by the support of the labour movement. During this period, the American Federation of Labor and Congress of Industrial Organizations (AFL-CIO), "in partnership with right-wing lobbyists for U.S. nuclear supremacy," produced a film "depicting the folly of détente and the menace of arms control."[199] The intelligence community, the think-tanks allied to it, and the labour movement were all in favour of an aggressive foreign policy and concomitant levels of military spending, and thus solidly against Carter.

Carter's attempt to formalize the Vladivostok Arms Control Accords was subject to constant obstruction in Congress by the Democratic Senate majority leader, who even attempted to prevent the president from lobbying the members of his own party with seats in that chamber.[200] In a bid to block a second strategic arms limitation treaty, Congress repeatedly forced Carter to ask the Soviets for further concessions, with which they thought no adversary could agree. However, the USSR was under severe economic pressure, as the CIA had concluded prior to Team B's formation. Accordingly Leonid Brezhnev agreed to each proposal in turn.[201]

Despite the fact that the treaty was never formally ratified by the Senate, the Soviet Union complied with its provisions for the next seven years.[202] It became evident that the Soviet Union was not nearly as belligerent as the proponents of increased military spending would have the American public believe, but the CPD succeeded in scuttling any policy initiatives that would expose the possibility of effective peace-making.

Carter describes congressional obstruction of his efforts to promote peace (by demilitarizing the Panama Canal Zone) in his memoirs: "Antagonistic House committees held public hearings even before the negotiations were completed. That summer, a stream of witnesses and some of the committee members had paraded before the television cameras their arguments that the treaty was illegal, unpatriotic, a cowardly yielding to blackmail, a boon for communism and a threat to our nation's security."[203]

These battles made it clear that legislative support for the executive after 1976 did not hinge so much on the party affiliation of the legislator and the president or even on the legislator's view of the relative constitutional powers of these branches of government. Carter was "surprised that ... [Senator] John Stennis would try to weaken his presidency by providing a forum for a few retired military officers to declaim against Soviet threats to the Caribbean, when this self-same Stennis was so strong a champion of a 'strong presidency' that he was prepared to lie through his teeth to conceal Nixon's impeachable offenses from the Senate."[204]

Smearing Carter as ineffectual and weak on matters of defence and national security was largely responsible for his defeat at the hands of Ronald Reagan in the 1980 presidential election, facilitated by the Democratic Party's remarkable betrayal of Carter by allowing candidates to challenge him in the party's primaries before the presidential election.[205] Reagan managed to project the opposite image, and was prepared to antagonize the Soviet Union to that end.[206]

The question that remains is why these legislators would act in such a manner. Why would they respond so favourably to the attempts of an assortment of public intellectuals, generals, trade unionists, and industrialists dedicated to increasing military spending and confronting America's purported enemies?

The answer lies in the label for this confluence of interest groups, one that President Eisenhower first used in his farewell speech to the American people, on the conclusion of his second term as president in 1961. The term was *military-industrial complex*, although earlier drafts of this speech used the clearer but less rhythmic phrase *war-based industrial complex*.[207] In this speech, Eisenhower, a former supreme commander of Allied Forces in Europe and architect of the D-Day landings, warned the nation:

> This conjunction of an immense military establishment and a large arms industry is new in the American experience. The total influence – economic, political, even spiritual – is felt in ... every office of the federal government ... we must not fail to comprehend its grave implications. Our toil, resources and livelihood are all involved; so is the very structure of our society. In the councils of government, we must guard against the acquisition of unwarranted influence, whether sought or unsought, by the military-industrial complex. The potential for the disastrous rise of misplaced power exists, and will persist. We must never let the weight of this combination endanger our liberties or democratic processes. We should take nothing for granted.[208]

By the end of the Cold War, the arms industry encompassed a much larger portion of the American economy and organized labour than it did in 1961. It remains one of the most profitable sectors,[209] and the captains of industry associated with it are among the nation's most wealthy. In addition, the use of American military power props up many other industries, such as the oil industry and others that rely on favourable access to raw materials and foreign markets.[210] It supports the American economy as a whole, insofar as the status of the US dollar as the world's key reserve currency allows the United States to continue to subsidize its economy even as its public debt reaches unprecedented levels.[211]

The power of the military-industrial complex to lobby Congress successfully increased steadily after Watergate. In 1971, Congress passed legislation allowing for corporate campaign contributions,[212] which were outlawed in 1907,[213] although it continued to forbid any corporation that had existing contracts with the government from doing so or forming a political action committee to that end. This measure barred defence contractors from influencing legislators in one highly effective manner. However, amendments passed in 1974 to the Federal Election Campaign Act of 1971 removed this limitation, and opened the floodgates allowing the defence industry's influence to inundate the political terrain. Further amendments followed in 1977, in response to the Supreme Court's decision *Buckley v. Valeo*,[214] which struck down many of the remaining limits on campaign contributions as violations of the Constitution's guarantee of free speech.[215]

This made it possible for corporations and labour unions to use unlimited amounts of "soft" money.[216] The effect on American politics was predictable, and has continued and accelerated over the course of the following three decades.[217] The net effect of this development is that success in American politics is now inextricably linked with fundraising, which not only secures re-election but also power and influence within parties, as the ability to direct the way in which campaign funds are spent is of vital importance to these organizations.[218]

By the beginning of the twenty-first century there was a very close nexus between support for war and success in American politics. This explains how after the congressional resurgence, the legislature can swing between opposition to the aberrational executive branches directed by administrations who supported initiatives for peace and support for those who agitate for war, even at the expense of congressional credibility. American legislators, owing to the nature of the campaign financing system, have not managed to serve as a check on the executive when it exercises its powers, including those it has appropriated to itself in contravention of the Constitution, in order to violate non-derogable rights so that it might produce justifications for aggressive war.

The executive's ability to launch wars on its own initiative not only is a repudiation of the rule of law, but makes possible a dynamic in which the executive becomes entrenched against attempts to reinstall the constitutional order, and which catalyzes violations of non-derogable rights that protect this position. The incentives that prevent the legislature from controlling executive war-making are highly important to the rule of law. This highlights the importance of whether it is possible for the legislature to interrupt a self-reinforcing cycle of aggressive war and an unchecked executive's violations of non-derogable rights. If the answer is no, it is difficult to imagine how the crisis of the rule of law in the United States can be described as anything other than a permanent state of emergency, with no prospects for a return to constitutional governance in the immediate future.

It fails to re-impose the rule of law for the same reasons that it preempted peaceful overtures to the Soviet Union. The military-industrial complex is simply too profitable, and it has become a simple matter to influence the legislators with these profits. The US military budget has remained constant at approximately $700 billion a year over the past decade,[219] most of which is distributed to American defence contractors.[220] This is more than the total of all discretionary federal spending.[221] Whistle-blower Edward Snowden revealed that intelligence agencies have a secret "black budget" of approximately $50 billion which is doled out to a large lobby of contractors who support covert activities. The majority of expenditures are made in the form of payments to private sector contractors. This is a figure "larger than the sums received by the Department of the Interior, the Department of Commerce and NASA this year combined."[222]

The military-industrial and intelligence complex is able to exert considerable influence over legislators by means of campaign spending that has also expanded exponentially over the past decade. The Supreme Court's decision in *Citizens United v. Federal Election Commission*[223] allowed for so much corporate spending that the head of the Office for Democratic Institutions and Human Rights of the Organization for Security and Co-operation in Europe opined that this judgment might create an electoral system that violates the ODIHR's two core requirements of "giving voters a genuine choice and giving candidates a fair chance," insofar as this ruling "threatens to further marginalize candidates without strong financial backing or extensive personal resources, thereby in effect narrowing the political arena."[224]

This prediction was accurate, as major defence contractors took advantage of the new rules to that end. For example, Koch Industries distributed up to $250 million during the 2012 election cycle, by making full use of tax-exempt vehicles, most of which were prohibited before the

Buckley decision.[225] The same dynamic is now presumptively at play with respect to garnering support for the intelligence activity that leads to war. It was recently revealed that the "lawmakers who upheld NSA phone spying received double the defense industry cash."[226]

The Ongoing Absence of Legislative Oversight

Recent events demonstrate that congressional oversight has become even less effective, as the legislature now assists the executive to keep abuses of its discretionary authority from the public. Congress's response to the 2013 disclosure of the NSA mass surveillance is a telling example. After the executive's statutory powers were expanded repeatedly by the Patriot Act[227] and various amendments to FISA, Snowden revealed that this agency routinely and indiscriminately collected telephone calls, emails, and information shared via social media from more than 1 billion people, including American citizens.[228] In addition to unveiling a vast illegal and unconstitutional domestic spying program, Snowden revealed that director of national intelligence James Clapper – America's most senior intelligence official – lied under oath when testifying about this surveillance before a congressional oversight committee. When asked by a Senator if "the NSA collect[s] any type of data at all on millions or hundreds of millions of Americans," Clapper replied, "No."[229] However, after Snowden's revelations, Clapper apologized and admitted his answer was "clearly erroneous."[230]

A small number of legislators called for Clapper to be prosecuted for perjury or obstruction of justice, as was recently the case with the baseball player Roger Clemens, who lied to Congress about using performance-enhancing drugs, and earlier for Reagan administration officials Oliver North and John Poindexter (although their convictions were overturned on appeal by Judges Silberman and David Sentelle of the DC Circuit). These legislators also called for the release of secret OLC memoranda that authorized this type of surveillance, which undoubtedly provided explicit authorization for ignoring both statutory law and the Constitution and establishing beyond doubt that Clapper knew he was not telling the truth before Congress.[231]

These proposals came to nothing. President Obama responded to Snowden's revelations by claiming falsely that "there is no spying on Americans."[232] He then headed off calls for a congressional investigation by announcing an internal executive branch review of whether laws were broken, ostensibly to be overseen by Clapper. Congress accepted this executive-branch review of its own conduct, taking the opposite course to the one it had adopted after Watergate when it rejected the executive's Rockefeller Commission. Obama successfully pre-empted calls for a congressional investigation like the Church Committee, demonstrating that there is little to no prospect of Congress reinstalling the oversight essential to the rule of law as it did from 1974 to 1980.

After Snowden's revelations, Congress was far more concerned with the purported illegality of making the executive's illegal conduct public than with the wrongdoing that was revealed.[233] This is lamentable, as Snowden revealed that it was not only Clapper who lied to Congress but also multiple "senior administration officials."[234] "Beyond its criminality, lying to Congress destroys the pretence of oversight. Obviously, members of Congress cannot exercise any actual oversight over programs which are being concealed by deceitful national security officials."[235] However, instead of focusing on this serious challenge to the rule of law, senior legislators fixated on the whistle-blower, who performed a public service in bringing this mendacity and illegal conduct to their attention. Chair of the Senate Select Committee on Intelligence Dianne Feinstein called Snowden a traitor,[236] and approved of the executive branch's remarkable act of international provocation: its interfering with the flight path of a foreign head of state in an attempt to arrest Snowden.[237] Feinstein did so while ignoring that the executive was acting in a way that rendered her committee's oversight nominal.[238]

Divergent and disproportionate responses to executive wrongdoing and those who reveal it are common in twenty-first-century America. John Kiriakou, a former CIA case officer and senior investigator for the Senate Foreign Relations Committee, was sent to prison for revealing details about the waterboarding of detainees to a journalist.[239] Private Manning was subjected to conditions the United Nations Special Rapporteur for Torture concluded amounted to cruel and inhuman treatment,[240] before being convicted and sentenced to thirty-five years in prison for presenting evidence about the intentional killing of unarmed Iraqi civilians and Reuters journalists by an American helicopter gunship.[241] Julian Assange, who helped Manning to publicize the video, was indicted in secret by an American grand jury.[242] Congress's single-minded attention to punishing those who reveal executive branch wrongdoing demonstrates that the legislative branch will not play the same role that it did after Watergate at any time in the near future.

Congress's attitude toward whistle-blowers allows the executive to interfere with the reporters who have brought abuses to the public's attention. Journalist Glenn Greenwald's courier was held at Heathrow Airport for nine hours pursuant to legislation pertaining to terrorism suspects, during which time he was questioned about Snowden and Greenwald's activities, allegedly at the request of American authorities. All of the files on this story were seized.[243] Speaking about the executive branches of the United States and the United Kingdom, the *Guardian*'s editor-in-chief noted that "[t]he governments are conflating journalism with terrorism and using national security to engage in mass surveillance. The implications just in terms of how journalism is practiced are enormous."[244] The rule of law itself is affected by this criticism of reporting, as legislative oversight now relies entirely on these exposés of executive wrongdoing, since thanks to these leaks we know that intelligence officials lie to Congress. If there are no whistle-blowers, the executive will not only be able to violate non-derogable rights with impunity, but be able to do so in secret.

Greenwald did the legislature a great service, by demonstrating how Congress has been "blocked" from receiving "the most basic information" about the activities of the intelligence community. The executive has denied it this information about the violation of non-derogable rights. It does so while executive branch officials perjure themselves about these activities before the legislature and prosecute those who attempts to reveal that fact. Congress's indifference to this blatant manipulation reveals that it has no intention of performing the oversight and control functions over the executive that the rule of law requires.

The Executive Can No Longer Be Checked

The answer to whether Congress has restrained the executive in the decade following the 9/11 attacks is no. This continued throughout both the Bush and the Obama administrations. Congress was not merely negligent in failing to conduct oversight and to restrain the executive when it violated non-derogable rights. It actively enabled the executive by enacting legislation that broadened its discretionary authority when these administrations' aggressive agendas were challenged, whether by the courts or by the public at large.

Congress has not simply broadened the scope of these grants of discretionary authority that do not accord with the rule of law, the legislature also accepted continued assertions by the executive that it was not subject to oversight by the other branches of government whenever it argued that it was acting to defend the nation from vague and ambiguous threats. Congress not only authorized continued indefinite arbitrary detention and passed legislation with loopholes allowing for continued torture, it accepted without comment the executive's statements that it could not be bound by this legislation.

Congress also allowed the executive to set a precedent that it did not need legislative approval for the extended use of force overseas and that it could ignore the War Powers Resolution of 1973. Like the Supreme Court, Congress has abdicated all responsibility for overseeing and restraining the executive's powers. Instead, the executive has been permitted to continue to violate a range of *jus cogens* norms as part of its agenda to justify acts of international aggression.

Owing to the release of substantial amounts of evidence that the executive manufactured the case for war with Iraq, Congress was forced to investigate this wrongdoing. It duly reported on this impeachable misconduct. However, the report's release was delayed so as to have no impact, and party leaders made it eminently clear that they would block any attempt to hold the executive accountable. Now that the executive claims the power to subject the nation's citizens to indefinite arbitrary detention and extrajudicial execution, there appears to be no line that the executive can cross that will induce Congress to reintroduce the legislative oversight that the rule of law requires.

This inaction can be explained by exploring Congress's contrary reaction when the executive attempted to achieve durable peace. This leads to an examination of campaign financing by the military-industrial complex, a coalition of interest groups bound together by their desire to profit from continued American aggression. The coalition exercises its control over the legislators' prospects of continued success, achieving this power through the deregulation of the campaign financing system.

For these reasons, one can conclude that the twenty-first-century crisis of the rule of law, characterized by an executive committed to expanding the boundaries of its own power to the point where it can violate non-derogable norms with impunity, is no longer temporary or anomalous. Neither the courts nor Congress are willing to re-impose the limitations that characterize this form of constitutional order. There is at present virtually no possibility of another congressional resurgence, as the legislative branch appears entirely beholden to those interest groups that support the executive supremacy that makes American aggression possible, even when it is consistently unpopular with the electorate.

Conclusion

It is appropriate to consider whether the United States, which is seen as the leading champion for human rights and democracy around the world, is no longer a rule of law state. Despite its self-image, over the past decade leading human rights organizations have accused the United States of systematic violations of *jus cogens* norms. These began with the creation of the Guantánamo Bay detention camp, which was constructed to house prisoners who are subject to what has repeatedly been determined to be indefinite and arbitrary detention.

These detainees, including those held without records as "ghost detainees" at secret prisons known as "black sites," have been subjected to what the executive would later admit was torture, inasmuch as it involved such actions as waterboarding some detainees hundreds of times. In doing so, the executive made use of a technique that was defined as torture several decades earlier. The executive branch relies increasingly on a practice known as targeted killing, in which persons suspected of involvement in terrorism are subject to extrajudicial execution. Numerous international observers, including the relevant Special Rapporteur, concluded that this could not be justified under international humanitarian law, as it took place outside of war zones. Furthermore, this practice violates certain basic guarantees of the US Constitution, especially when applied to American citizens. Most fundamentally, if the executive can commit violations of non-derogable rights with impunity, the state cannot be characterized as being in compliance with the minimum demands of the rule of law, since the rule of law emerged to supplant precisely that state of affairs.

The Cold War made it possible for the executive to extend its powers beyond all constitutional limits, although mass violations of non-derogable norms did not occur. However, this level of restraint was in doubt when the Cold War approached its apex. During the early 1970s, President Nixon's failure to win the Vietnam War brought America to the brink of a popular uprising against him. This led to a major constitutional crisis known as Watergate, when it became public knowledge that Nixon used the executive powers enlarged by the Cold War to conduct illicit domestic surveillance on a large scale. It also became known that he considered sweeping measures, including indefinite arbitrary detention, in response to the crisis, which was made particularly acute by exposure of his aggressive and unilateral war-making against Cambodia. Owing to Nixon's unpopularity with the people, the prospect of rebellion, and the fact that the other branches of government were very close to being rendered irrelevant during his drive for an "imperial presidency," the judiciary and the legislature took steps to remove him from office. The Supreme Court ordered the executive to turn over the Watergate tapes to the legislative committee investigating his misconduct. That committee then voted in favour of the Articles of Impeachment that forced his resignation.

Public exposure of Nixon's attempt to effectively create a presidential dictatorship led Congress and the courts to re-implement the rule of law by creating and enforcing new statutes. These statutes explicitly repudiated Nixon's theory of executive supremacy, which he pithily expressed as "if the President does it, then it is not illegal," and the theory of constitutional reserve powers that undergirded it, which were originally formulated by Nixon's chief legal counsel, William Rehnquist. Foremost among these post-Watergate legal developments that re-established the rule of law were the enactment of the Non-Detention Act, the Foreign Intelligence Surveillance Act, and the WPR, along with the creation of legislative oversight committees charged with ensuring that the executive did not violate citizens' non-derogable rights, or expand its own powers so that it might again do so in secret.

This new balance of governmental powers that protected the rule of law from the executive was in actuality the paradigm that existed before the Second World War. The separation of powers, buttressed by the statutes passed during the congressional resurgence, protected the rule of law until the 9/11 attacks.

After 9/11, a new quasi-legal framework for executive control over intelligence and foreign policy developed within the OLC. Dusting off theories of implicit constitutional reserve powers that lay dormant since Rehnquist's tenure, a cadre of neo-conservative officials, many of whom were Nixon-administration veterans, instructed compliant executive branch lawyers, most notably John Yoo, to write legally binding memoranda. These secret memoranda purportedly explained how the executive could make unilateral decisions to detain, torture, and kill alleged wrongdoers and to launch aggressive wars, all without congressional authorization. They also argued that the courts could not review the executive's actions; these arguments were insulated from court review by their classification as state secrets.

In addition to detailing the OLC memoranda setting up a theory of presidential primacy, another form of executive law-making was used to bypass the statutes that would otherwise restrain the executive; that is, signing statements. Rather than secretly overruling the Constitution and US laws, as did the OLC memoranda, the signing statements openly declared that the executive was unwilling to abide by duly enacted laws, including those which limited its ability to violate non-derogable norms.

While the Obama administration repealed some memoranda written by Yoo and others, it adopted this theory of executive supremacy. In addition to continuing to issue signing statements, the new executive also adopted identical reasoning to what Yoo drew up in his memorandum on the unilateral use of force. President Obama argued on this basis that he possessed the inherent constitutional authority to unilaterally initiate hostilities against Libya, and the administration later argued that he was not bound by the WPR. His secretary of state threatened to ignore any legislative action that would seek to restrain his war-making. One speech by the general counsel of the Department of Defense demonstrated the Obama administration's commitment to executive supremacy: it indicated that the executive had unilaterally expanded the definition of those subject to Congress's authorization for the use of force.

The Obama administration also dramatically expanded the targeted killing program. It claimed – for the first time in American history – the

constitutional authority to target its citizens. It continues to assert the
same specious arguments to prevent the release of Guantánamo detainees,
while pretending that it would prefer to do otherwise. It is clear that the
constitutional crisis created by executive response to the 9/11 attacks continued into the second decade of the twenty-first century, and that the executive would continue to govern in a manner that was inconsistent with
the rule of law, unless the other branches of government were prepared
to intervene. Unfortunately, the other branches of government did not,
and could not, intervene.

While many have argued that the Supreme Court's decisions addressing indefinite arbitrary detention at Guantánamo Bay were important rebukes to the executive, careful examination of these decisions revealed
that they produced only a rhetorical effect. Critically, they refused to address squarely the issue of whether the executive possessed a legitimate
power to expand its own powers. The court also failed to address the
most important case that came before it during that era. This is the case
of José Padilla. Padilla, an American citizen, was arrested within the
United States. He was held and tortured by the military after being classified an unlawful enemy combatant. Despite this set of actions being explicitly barred by statute, the court avoided deciding the case by invoking
the most technical reasons to decline jurisdiction, failing even to rebuke
the executive for these gross violations of *jus cogens* norms and its explicit
refusal to observe the laws.

This Supreme Court was only willing to craft narrow rulings when it
overturned even the most problematic administrative decisions. The court
also granted purely nominal relief to those who suffered violations of
their non-derogable rights, and it left the subsequent enforcement of its
decisions to the lower courts. However, when detainees and others began
to prevail on these claims at trial, the intermediate-level federal appellate
courts intervened, overturning rulings against the executive in connection with arbitrary detention, torture, and warrantless surveillance.

These courts created elaborate doctrines that allow the executive to
avoid facing decisions on the merits when it is charged with even the
most serious allegations of wrongdoing. These doctrines comprise a set of
jurisdictional and evidentiary rules – foremost among them the political
questions doctrine and the state secrets privilege – that have made the

access to the courthouse that the Supreme Court mandated in its narrow decisions utterly meaningless, as numerous statements of federal trial judges lamenting these doctrines have made clear. It is now impossible for these plaintiffs to obtain information during the discovery process about the abuses to which they were subjected. Appellate courts now routinely cite the failure to obtain this evidence in discovery to justify dismissal of these lawsuits.

As a result, it is impossible for defendants making the most serious allegations against the executive to receive justice. Additionally, the Supreme Court refuses to sit in judgment on appeals challenging the executive's violation of non-derogable norms. The judiciary can play no meaningful role in controlling the executive's violation of non-derogable rights, violations which continue unabated. The Supreme Court's statements in cases such as *Boumediene v. Bush* created a simulacrum of judicial oversight, one that conceals the disappearance of the rule of law.

The remarkably different approaches of the higher federal courts in 1974 and in the twenty-first century can be explained by the changing judicial appointment process. This process acquired an increasing importance resulting from the Supreme Court demonstrating its willingness to impede an overweening executive during Watergate.

Shortly before Watergate, the executive began to place jurists onto the benches of the nation's most influential courts because of its faith in their loyalty. This process has shaped the US Supreme Court, as it is now populated with judges with close and longstanding connections to the executive branch. These justices take similar stances on executive powers regardless of the party of the president who nominated them.

When Alito was appointed, the Senate had access to more information about the nominees' approaches to executive power than ever before. In Alito's case, this led to a Senate discussion of the application form Alito submitted for employment within the executive, in which he made clear his views on executive supremacy over the judiciary. His views were so extreme that Senators noted that they effectively repudiated the rule of law. However, despite this, Alito was confirmed as a Supreme Court justice. Additionally, the Senate confirmed numerous judges with very problematic views of executive power and ties to the executive branch to courts that are nearly as important, particularly the DC Circuit.

Congress supported the executive each time Supreme Court judgments would have otherwise required it to modify its practices, however slightly. In particular, Congress twice allowed the executive to revive the CSRTs at Guantánamo Bay, which the executive established and conducted on the basis of its theory of the executive's inherent authority. The re-establishment of these tribunals gave the detention facility renewed purpose and allowed for such dubious prosecutions as the process brought against Omar Khadr, a fifteen-year-old child soldier who allegedly threw a grenade after being attacked by American forces in Afghanistan.

Congress's rare legislative initiatives to stem the executive's violations of non-derogable rights were easily bypassed by the executive, at which point Congress simply ignored the pertinent signing statements. The most prominent of the examples discussed was the statement attached to the Detainee Treatment Act, which purported to ban torture. In it, the executive openly admitted that it would not change its practices, defending waterboarding as essential to American security. However, Congress made an ineffectual and wholly rhetorical response. This, unfortunately, served to persuade the public that torture was now banned, while it is still authorized. Congress also failed to address problems related to the statutory authorizations for the use of force in Afghanistan and Iraq, which were so broad that in 2013 the executive was able to assert that these also allowed them to conduct aggressive military operations in Pakistan, Yemen, and Somalia.

President Bush was not impeached by Congress, or sanctioned in any way by the legislature. The House Judiciary Committee provided both chambers of Congress with evidence of far more serious violations than those that led to Nixon's resignation, as detailed in the report of the majority staff to Representative John Conyers. As well, Congress possessed successive reports of the Special Senate Committee on Intelligence that investigated the executive's manipulation of pre-war intelligence. Despite these revelations, leaders of both parties colluded to block even the discussion of impeachment.

Congress, like the courts, has proven itself so willing to stand by while the executive usurped its critical functions. Ever-increasing amounts of money are required to run for national office; important sources of these funds are connected to lobbies associated with military and intelligence contracting. The rise of what President Dwight Eisenhower called the military-industrial complex affected American politics on a fundamental level, catalysing legislators' virtually reflexive support for the executive's attempts to promote aggressive war.

The existing US political-economic structure prevents the legislature from re-establishing the rule of law in the same manner that it did during the congressional resurgence of 1974–1980. Moreover, the elimination of restrictive campaign finance laws ensures the pre-eminence of the military-industrial complex in forging American foreign policy, which as a result will be consistently aggressive and supportive of violations of non-derogable rights.

America does not comply with the fundamental norms of the rule of law state, and there is no meaningful prospect of the rule of law being restored in the near future. It is important to be clear about the implications of this conclusion. Furthermore, it is also vital to understand what this does not entail. The United States remains a country where its citizens enjoy broad political and social rights, which are routinely adjudicated in its courts. However, in the context of what it calls the war on terror, the executive detains, tortures, and kills those it suspects of links to terrorism in secret, and does so without review. It continues to expand the scope of its own powers to do so, both geographically and conceptually, by authorizing itself to abduct suspects worldwide before subjecting them to arbitrary detention with no judicial review in Afghanistan or elsewhere, and by arguing that no other governmental branch can challenge its determination that the targeted killing of American citizens is constitutional.

A state with an executive that cannot be prevented from systematically violating non-derogable rights at will cannot be considered a functioning rule of law state. The fact that the president is nominally accountable to the electorate is immaterial, as there are numerous historical examples of elective dictatorships, none of which could ever be considered to be governed in accordance with the rule of law. Additionally, the power of the military-industrial complex over the electoral process makes the mandate of the electorate an increasingly minor constraint on the new imperial presidency.

One final objection offered to this conclusion: despite the fact that the executive possesses no limitations on its powers, it exercises these sparingly, and largely outside of its own borders. Even in the context of the war on terror, the executive branch of the US government recognizes that its citizens are the bearers of rights, derived from both its Constitution and international law. There is no debate on the question of whether citizens possess a broad set of substantive rights; the problem is the creation of constitutional theory that allows the executive to violate non-derogable rights with impunity. Even if it exercises these powers infrequently within the nation's borders at present, it is troubling, as it provides the executive with a set of unreviewable and secret powers to violate *jus cogens* norms, including those of its citizenry, during a future crisis. Rule of law cannot owe its existence to the good graces of an unaccountable executive: benevolent dictatorship is simply inimical to the normative core of the rule of law.

Furthermore, substantial attacks on the United States have always created a climate in which there is considerable pressure on the executive to engage in mass violations of non-derogable norms. The attack on Pearl Harbor led to the involuntary detention of Japanese Americans, but this did not persist long after the war ended. Conversely, the 9/11 attacks created a parallel regime of detention and torture, along with a system of extrajudicial execution that remains firmly in place.

America's failure to comply with the fundamental obligations of the rule of law has created a dangerous state of affairs, in which non-derogable norms are at serious risk of being violated at will. While these violations are infrequent within its own borders at present, the prospect of what might occur in the event of another seriously unsettling act of violence is deeply troubling. Before this occurs, it is vital for those interested in human rights to face up to the demise of the rule of law.

Afterword

"[E]verybody is feeling that security is going to rule ... and so we're going to have to do certain things that were frankly unthinkable a year ago";[1] "When you get these terrorists, you have to take out their families";[2] "They want to kill our country. They want to knock out our cities. And don't tell me it doesn't work – torture works ... we should go much stronger than waterboarding";[3] "And by the way, with Iran, when they circle our beautiful destroyers with their little boats ... they will be shot out of the water."[4]

– Donald Trump, campaigning for the presidency of the United States

Friday, 20 January 2017, marks a new era of American history: when the permanent state of emergency evolved into something entirely new. Until then, it could be argued that the United States was still dismantling its rule of law, owing to the ambiguous significance of an executive which possessed a vast panoply of unconstitutional powers that were rarely used within its borders. Over sixteen years, the stage was set for a strongman who was prepared to turn the key and accelerate the imperial presidency. Donald Trump appeared on that stage and seized the opportunity. The future of the United States will not be the history of the continued demise of the rule of law. It will be the story of a new regime's construction around the central pillar of elective dictatorship.

President Trump's inauguration brought to power a populist who promised to take charge of the nation's safety. Central to his platform was the promise to take extreme measures to protect the nation from a shadowy enemy, one with a fifth column inside the United States prepared to strike. Trump has shown no inclination to learn from history, but instead looks with favour on the worst crises of the rule of law, including the mass internment of citizens of suspect ethnicity and religion. He promised to surpass the most serious violations of non-derogable rights that the world witnessed during the war on terror, for which he was applauded.

Donald Trump came to power at a time in which his party also controls both branches of the legislature. This heralds the crossing of another threshold between an imperial presidency and an elective dictatorship. While President Obama had free rein to implement an unconstitutionally broad set of executive powers in foreign affairs and intelligence matters, when he attempted to govern by executive orders within the United States the legislature rebelled, blocking or stalling initiatives related to health care and immigration. This is unlikely to be the case under Trump.

The populist flood that brought Trump to power extinguished moderate Republicanism. The dynamic that began with the Tea Party movement in 2009 has been one in which waves of outsider candidates, who had campaigned on anti-establishment platforms, displace earlier sets of legislators. This is particularly pronounced in the House of Representatives, as its members serve two-year terms. As soon as legislators move to the capital to represent their constituents, they are open to the charge of having become "sellouts" or "Beltway insiders" from Washington.

Successive iterations of this cycle produced a level of anti-establishment discourse within the Republican Party that made Trump's candidacy possible (or, conversely, doomed the campaign of Jeb Bush, formerly thought invincible). Accordingly, it is clear that Trump is in tune with the contemporary spirit of the party faithful. The Republican old guard has been routed: while George W. Bush revealed publicly that he did not vote for Trump, the "Never Trump" caucus proved marginal when the votes were counted: Gary Johnson (the right-wing alternative running on the Libertarian Party ticket) received only 3 per cent of the vote, a figure that was too low even to tip the election to the Democratic Party.

This dynamic gives Trump leverage within the legislature. If he is unable to obtain legislation from the Republican-controlled Congress, he could bring pressure to bear on those legislators who refuse to co-operate with his agenda. Some indication of how this would unfold is provided by the dispute between Trump and House majority leader Paul Ryan in 2016. Trump refused to endorse Ryan in his contest in his district's primary election until August.

Presidential intervention into these contests could prove decisive for legislators of both branches of Congress. It is notable that Senate majority leader Mitch McConnell fought a difficult primary election to retain his own seat in 2014; a previously unknown challenger affiliated with the Tea Party won 35 per cent of the votes – something that would have been virtually unthinkable before 2008, when even rank-and-file Republican senators rarely faced serious challenges in the party primaries.

As Trump has the whip hand over these Republican legislators, it is difficult to imagine them blocking his policies, whether domestic or foreign. Should they attempt to do so, it is likely that he would resort to issuing executive orders and decrying their obstruction of the popular will. Given his position of strength, this would likely prove a winning strategy, even against Senate filibusters – however dangerous it might be to what remains of the separation of powers. The most important political development of the new regime is likely to be the ever-increasing concentration of political power within the presidency.

As troubling as this control over both legislative and executive power might be, it is far more disturbing to think of how Trump might make use of emergency powers. During the campaign, many observers called attention to concerns about entrusting President Trump with the "nuclear football." Very few expressed unease about the handover of the "playbook" for drone strikes, despite this conferring more practical unconstitutional power to the president. Trump has inherited a well-oiled machine for the execution of extrajudicial death warrants, at a time when US involvement in a number of conflicts is ratcheting upwards. In addition to Afghanistan, Iraq, Syria, and Somalia, military intervention into Yemen is escalating at an alarming pace.

The projection of military power inevitably leads to blowback. When the reaction comes from a state party, this is called war; when the reaction comes from a non-state actor, it is usually described as terrorism. President Trump will be called upon to react to acts of war or major terrorist attacks. Before the dismantling of the rule of law in the United States, there were effective limits on the executive's ability to violate non-derogable rights. Now that there is a president who would likely be inclined to authorize widespread violations of these rights within the nation's borders (including indefinite arbitrary detention and torture) there are no such limits, and no branch of government remaining that would be inclined to erect them.

In her concession speech, Hillary Clinton said that "[o]ur constitutional democracy ... enshrines the rule of law ... We respect and cherish [this value], too, and we must defend [it]." In many ways, this is a laudable statement. It raises two issues, however. The rule of law is not a merely a "value." It is a set of specific constitutional rights, an achievement that even radical critics acknowledged to be "an unqualified human good." The reduction of the objective standard for judging the government's conduct to an abstract aspirational ideal is part of what allowed America to degenerate into an elective dictatorship. When the rule of law is stripped of determinate content, the executive invariably asserts new powers, including the power to judge, in its sole discretion, whether non-derogable rights should be respected.

Officials in the Bush and Obama administrations adopted and maintained constitutional theories about executive power that were contrary to the rule of law. As secretary of state, Hillary Clinton argued that the executive had the power to unleash devastating attacks on foreign countries, and that no other branch of government could stop it, contrary to the Constitution's Declare War Clause and the War Powers Resolution. The immediate result was the transformation of Libya into a failed state and an important safe haven for ISIS. Another less visible effect was its contribution to the destruction of the American rule of law. As this standard of governmental responsibility must be embedded in the constitutional order of the state in order to function, it not something one can defend once it has been lost. Those who dismantled it have sown the wind, and they shall reap the whirlwind.

Notes

Notes, including judicial opinions and legislation, are formatted following the *Chicago Manual of Style* 16th ed. Access dates are provided for online sources, so that any dead links or 404 errors can be located using the Internet Archive, at www.archive.org.

INTRODUCTION

1 Philip Alston, "Report of the Special Rapporteur on Extrajudicial, Summary or Arbitrary Executions, Philip Alston," United Nations Human Rights Council, 28 May 2010, accessed 27 October 2016, http://www2.ohchr.org/english/bodies/hrcouncil/docs/14session/A.HRC.14.24.Add6.pdf A/HRC/14/24/Add.6.

2 Human Rights Watch, "No Direction Home: Returns from Guantanamo to Yemen," *Human Rights Watch*, 28 March 2009, accessed 27 October 2016, https://www.hrw.org/report/2009/03/28/no-direction-home/returns-guantanamo-yemen.

3 Human Rights Watch, "Getting Away with Torture: The Bush Administration and the Mistreatment of Detainees," *Human Rights Watch*, 12 July 2011, accessed 27 October 2016, https://www.hrw.org/report/2011/07/12/getting-away-torture/bush-administration-and-mistreatment-detainees.

4 Congressional Research Service, "National Defense Authorization Act," *Congressional Research Report*, 2012, 18–23.

5 Alston, "Report of the Special Rapporteur," 7.

6 Ibid. Quoted in New America Foundation, "Analysis of US Drone Strikes in Pakistan, 2004–2010," accessed 26 May 2014, http://counterterrorism.newamerica.net/drones#2010chart.

7 Alston, "Report of the Special Rapporteur," 8.

8 Mark Hosenball, "Secret Panel Can Put Americans on a Kill List," *Reuters*, 5 October 2011, accessed 26 May 2014, http://www.reuters.com/article/2011/10/05/us-cia-killlist-idUSTRE79475C20111005.

9 Amnesty International, "Human Rights Scandal," *Amnesty International Commission on Human Rights*, 2004, accessed 26 May 2014, web. archive.org/web/20060712192510/http://web.amnesty.org/library/Index/ENGIOR410242004?openandof=ENG-USA.

10 Ibid.

11 Boumediene v. Bush, 553 U.S. 723, 779 (2008).

12 Kim Lane Schepple, "The New Judicial Deference," *Boston University Law Review* 89 (2012): 141–2 (internal quotations removed).

13 Latif v. Obama, 666 F.3d 746 (D.C. Cir. 2011).

14 Erwin Chermerinsky, "Losing Interest," *National Law Journal*, 25 June 2012, accessed 30 May 2014, http://www.nationallawjournal.com/id=1202560493349/Losing-interest?slreturn=20140430212937.

15 Human Rights Watch, "Getting Away with Torture," 70.

16 Ibid., 54.

17 Mark Mazzetti and Charlie Savage, "No Criminal Charges Sought over CIA Tapes," *New York Times*, 10 November 2012, accessed 27 October 2016, http://www.nytimes.com/2010/11/10/world/10tapes.html.

18 Al-Zahrani v. Rodriguez, 669 F.3d 315 (D.C. Cir. 2012).

19 Military Commissions Act 2006, Pub. L. No.109-366 § 7(e)(2).

20 Peter Masciola, "Bullets in Furtherance of Meeting of 4 February 2009," United States Department of Defense, accessed 26 May 2014, http://www.defenselink.mil/pubs/App11.pdf.; Charlie Savage, "Guantánamo Conditions Slip, Military Lawyers Say," *New York Times*, 24 February 2012, accessed 27 October 2016, http://www.nytimes.com/2012/02/25/us/guantanamo-conditions-have-fallen-military-lawyers-say.html.

21 Amy Davidson, "Wikileaks: The Uses of Guantánamo," *New Yorker*, 25 April 2011, accessed 27 October 2016, http://www.newyorker.com/news/amy-davidson/wikileaks-the-uses-of-guantnamo.

22 John Yoo and Robert Delahunty, "Authority for Use of Military Force to Combat Terrorist Activities within the United States," United States Department of Justice, Washington Office of Legal Counsel, 23 October 2001; Patrick Philbin, "Legality of the Use of Military Commissions to Try Terrorists," *United States Department of Justice, Washington Office of Legal Counsel*, 6 November 2001.

23 "Mr. Padilla's Reply to the Government's Response to the Motion to Dismiss for Outrageous Government Conduct," *United States v. Padilla*, Case No. 04-60001-Cr-COOKE/BROWN S.D. Fl. (Miami, 4 October 2006), 6.

24 Jenny Martinez, "Process and Substance in the 'War on Terror,'" *Columbia Law Review* 1013 (2008): 1039.

25 Congressional Research Service, "National Defense Authorization Act," 16.

26 Ibid.

27 American Law Institute, *Restatement of the Law Third, Restatement of the Foreign Relations Law of the United States* (St Paul, MN: American Law Institute Publishers, 1987), section 702.

28 *Authorization for the Use of Military Force 2001*, Public Law 107-40115.

29 Yoo and Delahunty, "Authority for Use of Military Force"; Philbin, "Legality of the Use of Military Commissions."

30 John Yoo, "Memorandum for the Attorney-General from John C. Yoo," United States Department of Justice, Washington Office of Legal Counsel, 2 November 2001, accessed 26 May 2014, http://www.aclu.org/files/assets/NSA_Wiretapping_OLC_Memo_Nov_2_2001_Yoo.pdf.

31 John Yoo, "Memorandum Opinion for the Deputy Counsel to the President: The President's Constitutional Authority to Conduct Military Operations and Nations Supporting Them," United States Department of Justice, Washington Office of Legal Counsel, 25 September 2001, accessed 30 May 2014, http://dspace.wrlc.org/doc/bitstream/2041/70942/00110_010925display.pdf.

32 Jo Becker and Scott Shane, "Secret 'Kill List' Proves a Test of Obama's Principles and Will," *New York Times*, 29 May 2012, accessed 27 October 2016, http://www.nytimes.com/2012/05/29/world/obamas-leadership-in-war-on-al-qaeda.html.

33 Bruce Ackerman, *The Decline and Fall of the American Republic* (Boston: Harvard University Press, 2010), 119–23.

34 United States Senate Select Committee on Intelligence, "Final Report of the Select Committee to Study Governmental Operations with Respect to Intelligence Activities," United States Senate Select Committee on Intelligence, 1976.

35 United States v. Nixon, 418 U.S. 683 (1974).

36 Hughes-Ryan Act 1974, Pub. L. No. 93-559 § 32; War Powers Resolution 1974, Pub. L. 93-148.

37 Authorization for the Use of Military Force 2001, Pub. L. 107-40115.

38 Hamdi v. Rumsfeld, 542 U.S. 507 (2004).

39 Rumsfeld v. Padilla, 542 U.S. 426 (2004).

40 Boumediene v. Bush, 553 U.S. 723 (2008).

41 Latif v. Obama, 677 F. 3d 1175 (D.C. Cir. 2012).

42 Kiyemba v. Obama, 561 F. 3d 509 (D.C. Cir. 2009).

43 Al-Zahrani v. Rodriguez, 669 F. 3d 315 (D.C. Cir. 2012).

44 Detainee Treatment Act 2005, 119 Stat. 2739 (2005).

45 Military Commissions Act 2006, amending U.S.C., title 18, § 2241(e).

CHAPTER ONE

1 Brian Z. Tamanaha, *On the Rule of Law: History, Politics, Theory* (Cambridge: Cambridge University Press, 2004), 15.

2 Judith N. Shklar, "Political Theory and the Rule of Law," in *The Rule of Law: Ideal or Ideology*, eds. Allan C. Hutcheson and Patrick Monahan (Toronto: Carswell, 1987), 1.

3 Kenneth Pennington, *The Prince and the Law, 1200–1600* (Berkeley: University of California Press, 1993).

4 Harold Berman, *Law and Revolution: The Formation of the Western Legal Tradition* (Cambridge, MA: Harvard University Press, 2009).

5 Tamanaha, *On the Rule of Law*, 15–27.

6 Anthony Mathews, *Law, Order and Liberty in South Africa* (Berkeley: University of California Press, 1972), 6.

7 Magna Carta (1297).

8 Julian H. Franklin, *Jean Bodin and the Rise of Absolutist Theory* (Cambridge: Cambridge University Press, 2009).

9 Thomas Sorrell, *The Cambridge Companion to Hobbes* (Cambridge: University Press, 1996).

10 George Barnett Smith, *History of the English Parliament, Volume Two* (London: Ward, Lock, Bowden, and Company, 1892).

11 Thomas Babbington Macauley, *The History of England from the Ascension of James II* (London: Longmans, Green, and Company, 1889).

12 Samuel Rowson Gardiner, *History of the Great Civil War, 1642–1649* (London: Longmans, Green, and Company, 1888).

13 Herbert Butterfield, *The Whig Interpretation of History* (New York: W.W. Norton, 1965).

14 Henry Hallam, *The Constitutional History of England* (London: Longmans, Green, and Company, 1827), 441.

15 Edmund Robertson, "Hallam, Henry," in *Encyclopaedia Britannica*, 11th ed., ed. Hugh Chisholm, 1911, 852.

16 "Declaration of the Prince of Orange, October 10, 1688," reprinted in *A Kingdom without a King: The Journal of the Provisional Government in the Revolution of 1688*, ed. Robert Beddard (Oxford: Phaidon, 1988), 145–9.

17 Albert Venn Dicey, *Introduction to the Study of the Law of the Constitution* (London: Macmillan, 1915), 120–1.

18 Albert Venn Dicey, "General Characteristics of Existing English Constitutionalism," in *General Characteristics of English Constitutionalism: Six Unpublished Lectures*, ed. Peter Raina (Oxford: Peter Lang, 2009), 65.

19 Martin Loughlin, *Public Law and Political Theory* (Oxford: Clarendon Press, 1992), 17.

20 John Phillip Reid, *Constitutional History of the American Revolution: The Authority of Law* (Madison: University of Wisconsin Press, 1993).

21 Stephane Beaulac, "The Rule of Law in International Law Today," in *Relocating the Rule of Law*, eds. Gianluggi Palombella and Neil Walker (Portland, OR: Hart Publishing, 2009), 197–224.

22 H. Patrick Glenn, "Sustainable Diversity in Law," in *Legal Pluralism and Development: Scholars and Practitioners in Dialogue*, ed. Brian Z. Tamanaha et al. (Cambridge: Cambridge University Press, 2012), 98.

23 Universal Declaration of Human Rights, UNGA Res 217 A(III), (1948).

24 UNGA Report of the Secretary-General, Strengthening the Rule of Law 49/519 (1994), paras 5(a)–(c), 5(k).

25 Ibid.

26 Ryan Patrick Alford, "Rule of Law at the Crossroads," *Utah Law Review* 1203 (2011): 1244–50.

27 William Blackstone, *Commentaries on the Laws of England: Volume One* (Charleston, SC: Nabu Press, 2010), 146–7.

28 Act Abolishing the Star Chamber 1641.

29 Ryan Patrick Alford, "The Star Chamber and the Regulation of the Legal Profession, 1570–1640," *American Journal of Legal History* 51, no. 690 (2011): 723–6; David Jardine, *A Reading on the Use of Torture in the Criminal Law of England* (London: Baldwin and Cradock, 1837).

30 Habeas Corpus Act 1679; Habeas Corpus Act 1640.

31 Habeas Corpus Act 1679.

32 Slave Trade Act 1807, Debtor's Act 1869, Act of Parliament (Commencement) Act 1793, Married Women's Property Act 1893, Roman Catholic Relief Act 1829, Jews Relief Act 1858, Universities Tests Act 1871.

33 General Comment 29 to the ICCPR para. 16.

34 Steven L. Winter, *A Clearing in the Forest: Law, Life, and Mind* (Chicago: University of Chicago Press, 2001), 186–222.

35 Sanne Taekema, *The Concept of Ideals in Legal Theory* (The Hague: Kluwer Law International, 2003), 197–206.

36 Frank I. Michelman, "Constitutionally Binding Social and Economic Rights as a Compelling Idea," in *Social and Economic Rights in Theory and Practice*, ed. Helena Alviar Garcia, Karl Kare, and Lucy A. Williams (New York: Routledge, 2015).

37 Lon L. Fuller, "Positivism and Fidelity to Law: A Reply to Professor Hart," *Harvard Law Review* 71, no. 593: 630–72.

38 Ibid.

39 Friedrich Hayek, *The Road to Serfdom* (Chicago: University of Chicago Press, 1944), 54.

40 Jeremy Waldron, "Positivism and Legality: Hart's Equivocal Response to Fuller," *New York University Law Review* 83 (2008): 1135.

41 H.L.A. Hart, "Problems of Philosophy in Law," in *The Encyclopedia of Philosophy*, vol. 5, ed. Paul Edwards (Prentice Hall, 1967), 264.

42 Waldron, "Positivism and Legality," 1146.

43 H.L.A. Hart, *Law, Liberty, and Morality* (Stanford: Stanford University Press, 1963), 12.

44 Jeremy Waldron, "Is the Rule of Law an Essentially Contested Concept?," *Law and Philosophy* (2002): 137.

45 Tamanaha, *On the Rule of Law*, 4.

46 Michael Neumann, *The Rule of Law: Politicizing Ethics* (Burlington, VT: Ashgate, 2002), 3–6.

47 T.R.S. Allan, "Legislative Supremacy and the Rule of Law: Democracy and Constitutionalism," *Cambridge Law Journal* 44 (1985): 111.

48 T.R.S. Allan, *Law, Liberty, and Justice: The Legal Foundations of British Constitutionalism* (Oxford: Oxford University Press, 1993).

49 Arthur Goodhart, "The Rule of Law and Absolute Sovereignty," *University of Pennsylvania Law Review* 106 (1958): 943, 955.

50 Oren Gross, "Chaos and Rules: Should Responses to Violent Crises Always Be Constitutional?," *Yale Law Journal* 112 (2003): 1011; Michael Stokes Paulsen, "The Constitution of Necessity," *Notre Dame Law Review* 79 (2004): 1257.

51 Ryan Patrick Alford, "Is an Inviolable Constitution a Suicide Pact?," *Saint Louis University Law Review* 58 (2014): 355, 359.

52 David Dyzenhaus, "Humpty Dumpty Rules or the Rule of Law: Legal Theory and the Adjudication of National Security," *Australian Journal of Legal Philosophy* 28, no. 1(2003): 39.

53 Hans Kletcatsky, "Reflections on the Rule of Law and in Particular on the Legality of Administrative Action," *Journal of the International Commission of Jurists* 4 (1963): 209.

54 Howard Tolley, *The International Commission of Jurists: Global Advocates for Human Rights* (Philadelphia: University of Pennsylvania Press, 1994), 69.

55 Ibid., 74–7.

56 Joseph Raz, "The Rule of Law and Its Virtue," *Law Quarterly Review* 195 (1977): 211. Raz argues the rule of law only extends to guarantees of procedural fairness, and takes issue with the claim that a rule of law state must protect its citizens against violations of *jus cogens* norms – a philosophical cavil that has no traction in practical jurisprudence.

57 International Commission of Jurists, "Executive Action and the Rule of Law: A Report on the Proceedings of the International Congress of Jurists, Rio de Janeiro, Brazil, Reprinting the Conclusions of the New Delhi Conference, the Conclusions of the Lagos Conference and the Conclusions of the Rio Congress, Along with the Proceedings of the Rio Congress," *International Commission of Jurists*, 1962, 13.

58 Ibid., 111.
59 Ibid., 27.
60 Ibid., 17.
61 Ibid., 27.
62 Ibid.
63 Anthony S. Mathews, *Freedom, State Security and the Rule of Law: Dilemmas of the Apartheid Society* (Berkeley: University of California Press, 1986), 25.
64 Ibid.
65 Jurists, "Executive Action and the Rule of Law," 3.
66 Ibid., 12.
67 Ibid., 23.
68 Ibid., 17 (emphasis added).
69 See Anne-Marie Slaughter, Alec Stone Sweet, and Joseph H.H. Weiler, *The European Courts and National Courts: Doctrine and Jurisprudence* (Oxford: Hart Publishing, 1998), 92–103.
70 Jurists, "Executive Action and the Rule of Law," 27.
71 Ibid., 107–8.
72 Ibid., 3.
73 Mathews, *Freedom, State Security and the Rule of Law*, 265.
74 International Commission of Jurists, "Executive Action and the Rule of Law," 8.
75 M.J.C. Vile, *Constitutionalism and the Separation of Powers* (Indianapolis, IN: Liberty Fund, 1998), 36–43.
76 John Fortescue, *The Governance of England: Otherwise Called the Difference between an Absolute and a Limited Monarchy*, first published 1714 (Clark, NJ: Lawbook Exchange, 2010), 109–13.
77 J.W. Gough, *Fundamental Law in English History* (Oxford: Clarendon Press, 1955), 66–79.
78 M.J.C. Vile, *Constitutionalism and the Separation of Powers* (Indianapolis, IN: Liberty Fund, 1998), 36–43.
79 Ibid., 133.
80 Ibid., 110–15.
81 U.S. Const. art. 1.
82 U.S. Const. art. 2 § 4.
83 U.S. Const. art. 3 § 1 and 2.
84 Ralph Ketcham, *James Madison: A Biography* (Charlottesville: University of Virginia Press, 1971), 229.
85 James Madison, "Federalist No. 10," in *The Federalist Papers*, ed. Clinton Rossiter (New York: Penguin Putnam, 1991), 47.
86 Madison, "Federalist No. 47," in ibid., 271.
87 Alexander Hamilton, "Federalist No. 78," in ibid., 436.

CHAPTER TWO

1   Arthur Schlesinger, Jr, *The Imperial Presidency* (Boston: Houghton Mifflin Company, 2004), x–xv.
2   Gene Healey, *The Cult of the Presidency: America's Dangerous Devotion to Executive Power* (Washington: Cato Institute, 2008), 46.
3   Ibid., 38–45.
4   Alexander Hamilton, "Federalist No. 8," in *The Federalist Papers*, eds. Charles R. Kesler and Clinton Rossiter (New York: Mentor, 1999), 36.
5   James Madison, "Federalist No. 10," in *The Federalist Papers*, eds. Charles R. Kesler and Clinton Rossiter (New York: Mentor, 1999), 45–52.
6   Healey, *The Cult of the Presidency*, 28–33.
7   Hamilton, "Federalist No. 8," 36.
8   Neutrality Act 1794, ch. 50, 1 Stat. 38 (1794); Neutrality Act 1817, 3 Stat. 370, § 1 (1817); Jules Lobel, "Covert War and the Constitution," *Journal of National Security Law and Policy* 5 (2012): 393, 398–9.
9   Hamilton, "Federalist No. 8," 35.
10 Ibid., 419.
11 James Madison, "Letters of Helvidius, Nos. 1–4," in *Letters and Other Writings of James Madison Volume Two* (Philadelphia: J.B. Lippincott and Company, 1865), 67.
12 Madison, "Letter to Thomas Jefferson of May 13, 1798," in *Letters and Other Writings Vol. Two*, 141.
13 Alexis de Tocqueville, *Democracy in America*, vol. 1 (New York: George Adlard, 1839), 130.
14 Schlesinger, *The Imperial Presidency*, 100–87.
15 Thomas Jefferson, *The Writings of Thomas Jefferson*, vol. 7, ed. H.A. Washington (Washington: Taylor and Maury, 1854), 178.
16 Leonard W. Levy, *Jefferson and Civil Liberties: The Darker Side* (Chicago: Elephant, 1989), 71–2; Gary Wills, "The Strange Case of Jefferson's Subpoena," *New York Review of Books* 2 May 1974, accessed 27 October 2016, http://www.nybooks.com/articles/1974/05/02/the-strange-case-of-jeffersons-subpoena/.
17 Marbury v. Madison, 5 U.S. 137 (1803).
18 Burr v. United States, 25 F. Cas 30 (C.D. Va. Circ. 1807).
19 Lawrence M. Friedman, *A History of American Law*, 3rd ed. (New York: Simon and Schuster, 2005), 86.
20 Jonathan Hafetz, "A Different View of the Law: Habeas Corpus during the Lincoln and Bush Presidencies," *Chapman Law Review* 12 (2008): 439, 444–6.
21 Ex Parte Milligan 71 U.S. 2 (1866).

22 Schlesinger, *The Imperial Presidency*, 66.

23 Tenure of Office Act 1867, 14 Stat. 430, § 154.

24 Ibid., 71–5.

25 Ibid., 61.

26 Schlesinger, *The Imperial Presidency*, x.

27 Eric A. Nordlinger, *Isolationism Reconfigured: American Foreign Policy for a New Century* (Princeton: Princeton University Press, 1995), 12.

28 Ronald E. Powaski, *Toward an Entangling Alliance: American Isolationism and Europe 1901–1950* (New York: Greenwood Press, 1991), 110.

29 Healey, *The Cult of the Presidency*, 89–104.

30 Schlesinger, *The Imperial Presidency*, 176.

31 Christine Ann Lobasso, "Elevation of the Individual: International Legal Issues That Flow from the American Internment of the West Coast Japanese during World War II," *Touro International Law Review* 8 (1998): 45.

32 Schlesinger, *The Imperial Presidency*, 115.

33 Congressional Research Service, "National Emergency Powers," *Congressional Research Service*, 2007, 1.

34 Franklin D. Roosevelt, "Remarks to Congress of 27 September 1942." Quoted in Schlesinger, *The Imperial Presidency*, 115.

35 Ibid.

36 William H. Rehnquist, *All the Laws but One: Civil Liberties in Wartime* (New York: Knopf, 1988), 136–8, 184–202.

37 Exec. Order No. 9066, 7 Fed. Reg. 1407 (February 25, 1942).

38 Neal Katyal, "Confession of Error: The Solicitor-General's Mistakes during the Japanese-American Internment Cases," *United States Department of Justice, Justice Blogs*, 20 May 2011, accessed 26 May 2014, https://www.justice.gov/opa/blog/confession-error-solicitor-generals-mistakes-during-japanese-american-internment-cases.

39 Schlesinger, *The Imperial Presidency*, 115.

40 Korematsu v. United States, 584 F. Supp 1406 (N.D. Cal. 1984).

41 Korematsu v. United States, 323 U.S. 245 (1944) (Jackson J).

42 Ex Parte Quirin 317 U.S. 1 (1942).

43 Glenn Sulmasy, "*Ex Parte Quirin* and Military Commissions under the Obama Administration," *University of Toledo Law Review* 41 (2010): 767, 773.

44 Jack Goldsmith, "Justice Jackson's Unpublished Opinion in *Ex Parte Quirin*," *Green Bag Law Journal* 3, 2nd series, (2006): 223, 226.

45 Stuart Scheingold, *The Law in Political Integration: The Evolution and Integrative Implications of the Regional Legal Processes in the European Community* (Cambridge, MA: Harvard University, 1971), 21. Scheingold was referring in particular to the European Court of Justice.

46 Goldsmith, "Justice Jackson's Unpublished Opinion," 227.

47 Ex Parte Quirin, 30–1.

48 Roper Center for Public Opinion Archives, "Job Performance Ratings for President Truman," *Roper Center for Public Opinion*, accessed 26 May 2014, http://webapps.ropercenter.uconn.edu/CFIDE/roper/presiden tial/webroot/presidential_rating_detail.cfm?allRate=True&president Name=Truman#.UJWMCoaTZpg.

49 Schlesinger, *The Imperial Presidency*, xv.

50 Healey, *The Cult of the Presidency*, 93–4.

51 Schlesinger, *The Imperial Presidency*, 167.

52 Proclamation No. 2914, 15 Fed. Reg. 9029 (December, 19 1950)

53 See U.S.C., title 18, § 1601.

54 Jill Elaine Hasday, "Civil War as Paradigm: Re-establishing the Rule of Law at the End of the Cold War," *Kansas Journal of Law and Public Policy* 5 (1996): 137.

55 Healey, *The Cult of the Presidency*, 89–91.

56 Schlesinger, *The Imperial Presidency*, 133.

57 Ibid., 135.

58 U.S. Const. art.1, § 8, cl. 11.

59 Ibid., 178.

60 James L. Sundquist, *The Decline and Resurgence of Congress* (Washington: Brookings Institution, 1981), 239–41.

61 Youngstown Sheet & Tube Co v. Sawyer, 343 U.S. 579 (1952).

62 Ken Gormley, "Foreword: Truman and the Steel Seizure Case: A Symposium," *Duquesne Law Review* 41 (2002): 667–78.

63 Edward S. Corwin, "The Steel Seizure Case: A Judicial Brick without Straw," *Columbia Law Review* 53 (1953): 53, 66.

64 Schlesinger, *The Imperial Presidency*, 143–7.

65 Zemel v. Rusk, 381 U.S. 1 (1965).

66 Schlesinger, *The Imperial Presidency*, 167.

67 Ibid.

68 Ibid., 151–87.

69 Joint Anti-Fascist Refugee Committee v. McGrath, 341 U.S. 123 (1951).

70 Peters v. Hobby, 349 U.S. 331 (1955).

71 This analysis draws upon neo-functionalist theories of judicial decision making (which are themselves derived from neorealism in political science); these theories "explicitly brought political interests into the judicial calculus." Karen J. Alter, *Establishing the Supremacy of European Law: The Making of an International Rule of Law in Europe* (Oxford: Oxford University Press, 2001), 40–5.

72 David Gray Adler, "*The Steel Seizure Case* and Inherent Presidential Power," *Constitutional Commentary* 19 (2002): 155, 160.

73   Southeast Asia Resolution 1964, Pub. L. 88–308.

74   See Mark Lisheron, "In Tapes, LBJ Accuses Nixon of Treason," *Austin American-Statesman*, 5 December 2008, accessed 26 May 2014, https://web.archive.org/web/20081208104725/http://www.statesman.com/news/content/news/stories/local/12/05/1205lbjtapes.html.

75   Andrew Rudalevige, *The New Imperial Presidency: Renewing Presidential Power after Watergate* (Ann Arbor: University of Michigan Press, 2005), 80.

76   Peter M. Shane, *Madison's Nightmare: How Executive Power Threatens American Democracy* (Chicago: University of Chicago Press, 2008), 67.

77   Schlesinger, *The Imperial Presidency*, 187.

78   Ibid.

79   Sundquist, *The Decline and Resurgence of Congress*, 250, quoting Senator Jacob Javits's remarks as recorded in the Congressional Record of 1 May 1970.

80   Rudalevige, *The New Imperial Presidency*, 81.

81   Schlesinger, *The Imperial Presidency*, 187.

82   Ibid., 191.

83   Ibid., 203.

84   Youngstown Sheet & Tube Co v. Sawyer, 343 U.S. 579, 637–8 (1952) (Jackson, J. concurring).

85   Healey, *The Cult of the Presidency*, 7–9.

86   Schlesinger, *The Imperial Presidency*, 302.

87   War Powers Resolution 1973, Publ. L. 93–148.

88   Schlesinger, *The Imperial Presidency*, 434.

89   Rudalevige, *The New Imperial Presidency*, 83.

90   Sundquist, *The Decline and Resurgence of Congress*, 256.

91   U.S. Const. art. 1, § 8, cl. 1.

92   U.S. Const. art. 1, § 7, cl. 2–3.

93   Sundquist, *The Decline and Resurgence of Congress*, 203.

94   Rudalevige, *The New Imperial Presidency*, 89.

95   Joseph T. Sneed, "Memorandum of Deputy Attorney General Joseph T. Sneed to the Senate Committee on Separation of Powers: Presidential Authority to Impound Appropriated Funds," United States Department of Defense, Washington Office of Legal Counsel, 6 February 1973, 10–11.

96   Sundquist, *The Decline and Resurgence of Congress*, 208, quoting testimony of Deputy Attorney General Joseph T. Sneed of 7 February 1973 before the Senate Governmental Operations and Judiciary Committee.

97   Local 2677 v. Phillips, 358 F. Supp 60 (District of D.C. 1973).

98   Wright v. United States, 302 U.S. 583 (1938).

99   Schlesinger, *The Imperial Presidency*, 244.

100 Ibid.

101 Ibid., 246.

102 Seymour M. Lipset, "Polls and Protests," *Foreign Affairs* 49 (1971): 548, 550–3.

103 Central Intelligence Agency, "CIA Notes on Meeting with the President on Chile," National Security Archive, 15 September 1970, accessed 26 May 2014, http://www2.gwu.edu/~nsarchiv/NSAEBB/NSAEBB8/ch26-01.htm.

104 Central Intelligence Agency, "CIA Operating Guidance Cable on Coup Plotting," National Security Archive, 16 October 1970, accessed 26 May 2014, http://www2.gwu.edu/~nsarchiv/NSAEBB/NSAEBB8/docs/doco 5.pdf.

105 Schlesinger, *The Imperial Presidency*, 257.

106 Ibid.

107 Ibid. (emphasis added).

108 United States v. United States District Court, 407 U.S. 297 (1972).

109 Omnibus Crime Control and Safe Streets Act 1968, Pub. L. 90–351.

110 Meiklejohn Civil Liberties Institute, *Landmark Cases Left Out of Your Textbooks: Herein Restored by the Original Lawyers and Litigants and by Meiklejohn Legal Interns* (Berkeley, CA: Meiklejohn Civil Liberties Institute, 2006), 46.

111 United States v. Sinclair 321 F. Supp. 1074 (E.D. Mich. 1971).

112 United States v. United States District Court, 407 U.S. 325 (1972) (Douglas J).

113 Ibid., 315 (J. Powell quoting Senator Gary Hart).

114 United States Senate, "Senate Committee to Study Governmental Operations with Respect to Intelligence Activities, Intelligence Activities and the Rights of Americans," S. Rep. No. 94-755, book 2, 7 (1976).

115 Tracey Macklin, "The Bush Administration's Terrorist Surveillance Program and the Fourth Amendment's Warrant Requirement: Lessons from Justice Powell and the Keith Case," *University of California Davis Law Review* 41 (2008): 1259, 1289.

116 Ibid., 1264.

117 Ibid., 1263.

118 Rudalevige, *The New Imperial Presidency*, 93.

119 United States v. Nixon 418 U.S. 683 (1974).

120 Shane, *Madison's Nightmare*, 123.

121 Jud. Comm. H.R., Articles of Impeachment of Richard Nixon, H.R. Rep. No. 1305, 93rd Cong., 2d Sess., § 2 (1974).

122 Ibid., § 3.

123 Shane, *Madison's Nightmare*, 63.

124 Ibid.
125 Rudalevige, *The New Imperial Presidency*, 102, quoting the remarks of Representative Gillis Long on the floor of Congress.
126 Rudalevige, *The New Imperial Presidency*, 100.
127 Train v. New York, 420 U.S. 35 (1975).
128 Campaign Clean Water Inc. v. Train, 489 F2d 498 (4th Cir. App. 1975).
129 Congressional Budget Act and Impoundment Act 1974, Pub. L. No. 93-344.
130 Louis Fisher, *Congressional Abdication on War and Spending* (College Station: Texas A&M Press, 2000), 119, quoting Senator Sam Ervin's speeches from the floor.
131 Congressional Budget Act and Impoundment Act 1974, Pub. L. No. 93-344.
132 Rudalevige, *The New Imperial Presidency*, 128–30; U.S. Const. art.1, § 8, cl. 1; United States v. Butler, 297 U.S. 1 (1936).
133 Rudalevige, *The New Imperial Presidency*, 130, quoting the remarks of Senate Budgetary Chair Brock Adams.
134 Sundquist, *The Decline and Resurgence of Congress*, quoting Committee Reform Amendments 1974, House Report 93-916.
135 Privacy Act 1974, Publ. L. No. 93-579.
136 Freedom of Information Act 1966, Pub. L. No. 89-554.
137 Rudalevige, *The New Imperial Presidency*, 106–8.
138 Internal Security Act 1950, 64 Stat. 993.
139 Masumi Izumi, "Prohibiting 'American Concentration Camps': Repeal of the Emergency Detention Act and the Public Historical Memory," *Pacific Historical Review* 74 (2005): 165, 170–8.
140 Christian Smith, *Resisting Reagan: The U.S. Central America Peace Movement* (Chicago: University of Chicago Press, 1996), 310.
141 Non-Detention Act 1971, Pub. L. No. 92-128.
142 National Emergencies Act 1974, Pub. L. No. 94-412.
143 Congressional Research Service, "Martial Law and National Emergency," 2005, 1 (see also the Senate Committee on Government Operations and the Special Committee on National Emergencies and Delegated Emergency Powers, "The National Emergencies Act").
144 International Emergency Economic Powers Act 1977, Pub. L. No. 95-223.
145 Rudalevige, *The New Imperial Presidency*, 114.
146 Frederick Schwarz and Aziz Huq, *Unchecked and Unbalanced: Presidential Power in a Time of Terror* (New York: W.W. Norton, 2007), 50–3.
147 Ibid., 120.
148 Church Committee Report, book 2, 137, 265.
149 Schwarz and Huq, *Unchecked and Unbalanced*, 44.

150 Kathryn S. Olmstead, *Challenging the Secret Government: The Post-Watergate Investigations of the* CIA *and* FBI (Chapel Hill: University of North Carolina Press, 1996), 88, 96.

151 Church Committee Report, section 18, 1.

152 Church Committee Report, book 2, v.

153 Schwarz and Huq, *Unchecked and Unbalanced*, 51.

154 Foreign Intelligence Surveillance Act 1978, Pub. L. No. 95-511.

155 J. Anthony Lukas, *Nightmare: The Underside of the Nixon Years* (Athens: Ohio University Press, 1999), 541, quoting Representative William Cohen.

156 Frank Smist, Jr, *Congress Oversees the United States Intelligence Community, 1947–1989* (Knoxville: University of Texas Press, 1990), 81, quoting interview of Senator Frank Church by Frank Smist, Jr, 23 April 1983.

157 Sundquist, *The Decline and Resurgence of Congress*, 331.

158 Harvey G. Zeidenstein, "The Reassertion of Congressional Power: New Curbs on the President," *Political Science Quarterly* 93 (1978): 393, 409.

159 Rudalevige, *The New Imperial Presidency*, 196–203.

160 Ibid., 212, 511.

CHAPTER THREE

1   Brian R. Dirck, *Waging War on Trial* (Santa Barbara: ABC-CLIO, 2003), 71–4.

2   James Mann, *Rise of the Vulcans: The History of Bush's War Cabinet* (New York: Viking, 2004), 10, 12, 100.

3   Ibid., 90–4.

4   International Commission of Jurists, "The Rule of Law in a Free Society: A Report," Report presented at the International Congress of Jurists, New Delhi, India, 10 January 1959, 217–18.

5   Charlie Savage, *Takeover: The Return of the Imperial Presidency and the Subversion of American Democracy* (New York: Little Brown, 2007), 34–7.

6   Ibid., 26.

7   Charlie Savage, "Takeover: Return of the Imperial Presidency," *Washburn Law Journal* 48 (2009): 299, 306.

8   Savage, *Takeover*, 26.

9   Ibid., 26–37.

10 Ibid., 50.

11 *Report of the Congressional Committees Investigating the Iran-Contra Affair* (New York: Random House, 1988). Quoted in Theodore Draper, *A Very Thin Line* (New York: Hill and Wang, 1991), 17–24.

12 Ibid., 375–462 (minority report).

13 See chapter 2 in this work.

14 Church Committee Report, book 4, 166.

15 Ryan Patrick Alford, "Is an Inviolable Constitution a Suicide Pact?,"
    Saint Louis University Law Journal 58 (2014): 355.

16 Remarks of Richard Cheney for the minority, in Report of the Congres-
    sional Committees. Quoted in Draper, *A Very Thin Line*, 360.

17 Richard Cheney, "Covert Operations: Who's in Charge?," *Wall Street
    Journal*, 8 May 1988, A30.

18 Frederick Schwarz and Aziz Huq, *Unchecked and Unbalanced: Presiden-
    tial Power in a Time of Terror* (New York: W.W. Norton, 2007), 160–1.

19 Youngstown Sheet & Tube Co. v. Sawyer, 343 U.S. 579 (1952).

20 See chapter 1 in this work.

21 Savage, *Takeover*, 56.

22 Ibid., 61.

23 Minority Report of the Iran-Contra Committee, in Report of the Con-
    gressional Committees. Quoted in Draper, *A Very Thin Line*, 160.

24 Savage, *Takeover*, 60.

25 Schwarz and Huq, *Unchecked and Unbalanced*, 160.

26 Savage, *Takeover*, 61.

27 Richard Cheney, "Congressional Overreaching in Foreign Policy," n.d.,
    accessed 30 May 2014, http://s3.documentcloud.org/documents/339579/
    congressional-overreaching-cheney.pdf.

28 Project for the New American Century, "Rebuilding America's Defenses:
    Strategies, Forces, and Resources for the New Century," September
    2000, accessed 30 May 2014, http://www.webcitation.org/5e3est5lT.

29 Ebrahim Afsah, "Creed, Cabal or Conspiracy: The Origins of the Cur
    rent Neo Conservative Revolution in US Strategic Thinking," *German
    Law Journal* (2003): 901, 903.

30 John Ehrenberg et al., eds., *The Iraq Papers* (Oxford: Oxford University
    Press, 2010), 21, reprinting the PNAC "Statement of Principles" of 3
    June 1997.

31 Ibid., 51.

32 Rudalevige, *The New Imperial Presidency*, 211.

33 Ibid.

34 Bush v. Gore 531 U.S. 98 (2004).

35 Rules of the Senate of the United States No. 22.

36 Rudalevige, *The New Imperial Presidency*, 213. On a personal note, the
    author (who was teaching in the United States on 9/11) recalls that many
    of his students were too frightened to return to classrooms for more than
    a week after the attacks, and were outraged at the suggestion that classes
    should recommence. Any suggestion of a return to normality at that time
    was treated as sacrilege.

37   Stephen Webb, *American Providence: A Nation with a Mission* (New York: Continuum, 2004), 20–7.

38   Barbara Kirshenblatt-Gimblett, "Kodak Moments, Flashbulb Memories: Reflections on 9/11," *The Drama Review* 47 (2008): 11, 12.

39   United States Department of Justice, *Amerithrax Investigative Summary*, 19 February 2010, accessed 30 May 2014, http://www.justice.gov/amerithrax/docs/a-post-letter.pdf.

40   President Bush, Address to Congress, 20 September 2001.

41   Rudalevige, *The New Imperial Presidency*, 215. Quoting Representative Maxine Waters.

42   Savage, *Takeover*, 76.

43   Ahmed Rashid, *Descent into Chaos: The U.S. and the Disaster in Pakistan, Afghanistan, and Central Asia* (New York: Viking, 2008), 64.

44   Richard A. Clarke, *Against All Enemies: Inside America's War on Terror* (New York: Free Press, 2004), 30.

45   See chapter 2 in this work.

46   Michael Genovese, "Impeachment of Richard Nixon," in *The Encyclopedia of the American Presidency* (New York: Facts on File, 2010), 267.

47   Arthur Schlesinger, *The Imperial Presidency* (Boston: Houghton Mifflin Company, 2004), 187.

48   Rudalevige, *The New Imperial Presidency*, 215.

49   107 Cong. Rec. 1st sess. S9949-S9551 (Oct. 1, 2001); see also Congressional Research Service, "Authorization for Use of Military Force in Response to the 9/11 Attacks: Legislative History," 16 January 2007.

50   Rudalevige, *The New Imperial Presidency*, 216.

51   Congressional Research Service, "Authorization for Use of Military Force," 2.

52   Ibid.

53   *United States v Goering*, *American Journal of International Law* 41 (1946): 186.

54   "The National Security Strategy of the United States of America," 22 September 2002, accessed 14 May 2014, mssarchive.us/NSSR/2002.pdf.

55   Congressional Research Service, "Authorization for Use of Military Force," 3.

56   Authorization for the Use of Military Force 2001, Pub. L. No. 1070-40.

57   Gene Healey, *Cult of the Presidency: America's Dangerous Devotion to Executive Power* (Washington: Cato Institute, 2008), 153.

58   Posse Comitatus Act 1878, 20 Stat. 152 (1878).

59   Matthew Hammond, "The Posse Comitatus Act: A Principle in Need of Renewal," *Washington University Law Quarterly* 75 (1997): 953, 956–61.

60   Healey, *Cult of the Presidency*, 153–4.

61 Thomas Daschle, "Power We Didn't Grant," *Washington Post*, 23 December 2005.

62 Staff of the Majority of the Members of the House of Representatives Judiciary Committee, *The Constitution in Crisis: The High Crimes of the Bush Administration and Blueprint for Impeachment* (New York: Skyhorse, 2007), 130–1.

63 Congressional Research Service, "Declarations of War and Authorizations for the Use of Military Force: Historical Background and Legal Implications," 2011, 14.

64 Authorization for the Use of Military Force, Pub. L. No. 1070-40 (18 September 2001), at section 2(a) ("the President is authorized to use ... force against those nations ... he determines ... aided the terrorist attacks ... or harbored such persons").

65 Peter M. Shane, *Madison's Nightmare: How Executive Power Threatens American Democracy* (Chicago: University of Chicago Press, 2008), 93.

66 Gary Minda, "Congressional Authorization and Deauthorization of War: Lessons from the Vietnam War," *Wayne Law Review* 53 (2007): 943, 953–4.

67 House of Representatives Judiciary Committee, *The Constitution in Crisis*, 185–90.

68 See chapter 2 in this work.

69 Southeast Asia Resolution 1964, Pub. L. No. 88-408.

70 Healey, *The Cult of the Presidency*, 154.

71 Rachel Ward Saltzman, "Executive Power and the Office of Legal Counsel," *Yale Law and Policy Review* 28 (2009): 449–62.

72 American Bar Association Task Force on Presidential Signing Statements and the Separation of Powers Doctrine, "Report," 8 August 2006, accessed 30 May, 2014, 14–28, http://www.americanbar.org/content/dam/aba/migrated/leadership/2006/annual/dailyjournal/20060823144113.authcheckdam.pdf.

73 Charlie Savage, "Last Word: The Constitutional Implications of Presidential Signing Statements," *William and Mary Bill of Rights Journal* 16 (2007): 1, 18–19.

74 Walter Dellinger, "Memorandum to the Counsel to the President, The Legal Significance of Presidential Signing Statements," United States Department of Justice, Washington Office of Legal Counsel, 3 November 1993, accessed 30 May 2014, https://web.archive.org/web/20140113185128/http://www.justice.gov/olc/signing.htm.

75 American Bar Association, "Report of the Committee on Separation of Powers Adopted by the House of Delegates," 8 August 2006.

76 Charlie Savage, "Obama Looks to Limit Impact of Tactic Bush Used to Sidestep New Laws," *New York Times*, 9 March 2009, accessed

27 October 2016, http://www.nytimes.com/2009/03/10/us/politics/
      10signing.html?_r=0.

77   Faith Joseph Jackson, "The Constitutionality of Presidential Signing
      Statements," *Journal of Legislation* 35 (2009): 1, 9.

78   Eli Lake, "Obama Embraces Signing Statements after Knocking Bush for
      Using Them," *The Daily Beast*, 4 January 2012, accessed 30 May 2014,
      http://www.thedailybeast.com/articles/2012/01/04/obama-embraces-
      signing-statements-after-knocking-bush-for-using-them.html.

79   Marc N. Garber and Kurt A. Wimmer, "Presidential Signing Statements
      as Interpretations of Legislative Intent: An Executive Aggrandizement of
      Power," *Harvard Journal on Legislation* 24 (1987): 349, 372.

80   INS v. Chadha, 462 U.S. 919, 965 (1983).

81   William D. Popkin, "Judicial Use of Presidential Legislative History: A
      Critique," *Indiana Law Journal* 66 (1991): 699, 702–4.

82   "Statement of the President of 18 September 2001 on signing the Autho-
      rization for the Use of Military Force," in *Public Papers of the President
      of the United States, George W. Bush*, 2001, book 2, (Washington: US
      Government Printing Office, 2003), 1124–5 (emphasis added).

83   Department of State, "Designation of al-Shabaab as a Foreign Terrorist
      Organization," 73 Fed. Reg. 31, Public Notice 6136, February 26, 2008.

84   Ken Menkhaus, *Somalia: State Collapse and the Threat of Terrorism*
      (London: Routledge, 2004), 65; Scott Baldauf, "What Is Somalia's al-
      Shabaab?," *Christian Science Monitor*, 26 October 2011, accessed 27
      October 2016,
      http://www.csmonitor.com/World/Africa/2011/1026/What-is-Somalia-s-
      Al-Shabab/Is-Al-Shabab-really-affiliated-with-Al-Qaeda.

85   Eric Posner, "The War on Terror Will Ever Be with Us," *Slate*, 11
      December 2012, accessed 30 May 2014, http://www.slate.com/articles/
      news_and_politics/view_from_chicago/2012/12/jeh_johnson_is_wrong_
      the_fight_with_al_qaida_continues.htm.

86   Mary Ellen O'Connell, "When Is a War Not a War? The Myth of the
      Global War on Terror," ILSA *Journal of Comparative Law* 22 (2005): 1.

87   See James Madison, *The Writings of James Madison*, vol. 6 (New York:
      G.P. Putnam and Sons, 1906), 148.

88   Bradley Lipton, "A Call for Institutional Reform of the Office of Legal
      Counsel," *Harvard Law and Policy Review* 4 (2010): 241, 249.

89   Christopher May, *Presidential Defiance of "Unconstitutional" Laws: Re-
      viving the Royal Prerogative* (Westport, CT: Greenwood, 1998), 131–49.

90   See Ross L. Weiner, "The Office of Legal Counsel and Torture: The Law
      as Both a Sword and a Shield," *George Washington Law Review* 77
      (2009): 524.

91   Lipton, "A Call for Institutional Reform," 250.

92 Ibid., 254–5.

93 See Dawn E. Johnsen, "Faithfully Executing the Laws: Internal Legal Constraints on Executive Power," UCLA *Law Review* 54 (2007): 1559.

94 Jack Goldsmith, *The Terror Presidency: Law and Judgment inside the Bush Administration* (New York: W.W. Norton, 2007), 144.

95 John Yoo, "Memorandum Opinion for the Deputy Counsel to the President: The President's Constitutional Authority to Conduct Military Operations and Nations Supporting Them," Washington Office of Legal Counsel, 25 September 2001, accessed 30 May 2014, http://dspace.wrlc.org/doc/bitstream/2041/70942/00110_010925display.pdf.

96 Rudalevige, *The New Imperial Presidency*, 219.

97 Ibid.

98 Sel. Sen. Comm. on Intelligence, "Report of the Select Committee on Intelligence on Postwar Findings about Iraq's WMD Programs and Links to Terrorism and How They Compare with Prewar Assessments," 8 September 2006, accessed 30 May 2014, http://intelligence.senate.gov/phaseiiaccuracy.pdf.

99 People's Mojahedin Organization of Iran v. United States Department of State, 182 F3d 17, 21 (D.C. Cir. 2004). It should also be noted that the Department of State subsequently delisted the MEK, "revok[ing] its designation as a Foreign Terrorist Organization." "Delisting of the Mujahedin-e Khalq," United States Department of State, accessed 30 May 2014, http://www.state.gov/r/pa/prs/ps/2012/09/198443.htm.

100 Lauren Johnston, "Iraqi Drones Not for WMD," CBC *News*, 28 August 2009, http://www.cbsnews.com/news/iraqi-drones-not-for-wmd/.

101 Scott Peterson, "The Case of the Deadly Drone," *Christian Science Monitor*, 13 March 2003, accessed 27 October 2016, http://www.csmonitor.com/2003/0313/p06s01-woiq.html.

102 Yoo, "Memorandum Opinion for the Deputy Counsel."

103 Savage, *Takeover*, 134–8.

104 *Journals of the Continental Congress*, Articles of War, 30 June 1775, accessed May 30, 2014, http://avalon.law.yale.edu/18th_century/contcong _06-30-75.asp.

105 Uniform Code of Military Justice, art. 18, U.S.C., title 10, § 818.

106 Savage, *Takeover*, 137–9.

107 Ibid., 134.

108 David Glazier, "A Self-Inflicted Wound: A Half-Dozen Years of Turmoil over the Guantánamo Military Commissions," *Lewis & Clark Law Review* 121 (2008): 148.

109 Savage, *Takeover*, 138.

110 Glazier, "A Self-Inflicted Wound," 147.

111 Savage, *Takeover*, 136.

112 Patrick Philbin, "Legality of the Use of Military Commissions to Try Terrorists," United States Department of Justice, Washington Office of Legal Counsel, 6 November 2001, accessed 30 May 2014, http://www.gwu.edu/~nsarchiv/torturingdemocracy/documents/20011106.pdf.

113 Rachel Saltzman, "Executive Policy and the Office of Legal Counsel," *Yale Law and Policy Review* 28 (2010): 439, 445.

114 Neal K. Katyal and Laurence H. Tribe, "Waging War, Deciding Guilt: Trying the Military Tribunals," *Yale Law Journal* 111 (2002): 1261.

115 Exec. Military Order. Detention, Treatment, and Trial of Certain Non-Citizens in the War Against Terrorism, 66 No. 222 Fed. Reg. 57,833 (13 November 2001).

116 Katyal and Tribe, "Waging War, Deciding Guilt," 1261.

117 Protocol Additional to the Geneva Conventions of 12 August 1949, and Relating to the Protections of Victims of International Armed Conflict, adopted 8 June 1977, art. 75, 1125 U.N.T.S. 3. While the United States did not ratify Protocol I, it has the status of customary international law and is therefore binding upon it. See Michael Matheson, "The United States Position on the Relation of Customary International Law to the 1977 Protocols Additional to the 1949 Geneva Convention," *American University Journal of International Law and Policy* 2 (1987): 427–8.

118 John Yoo and Robert Delahunty, "Draft Memorandum for William J. Haynes II: Application of Treaties and Laws to al Qaeda and Taliban Detainees," Washington, Office of Legal Counsel, 9 January 2002, accessed 30 May 2014, http://www.torturingdemocracy.org/documents/20020109.pdf.

119 Jay S. Bybee, "Memorandum to White House Counsel Alberto Gonzales and Department of Defense General Counsel William J. Haynes II: Application of Treaties and Laws to Al Qaeda and Taliban Detainees," Washington, Office of Legal Counsel, 22 January 2002, accessed 30 May 2014, http://www.torturingdemocracy.org/documents/20020122.pdf.

120 Barack Obama, "Remarks by the President on National Security," 21 May 2009, accessed 30 May 2014, http://www.whitehouse.gov/the-press-office/remarks-president-national-security-5-21-09.

121 Department of Justice and Department of Defense Press Release, "Departments of Justice and Defense Announce Forum Decisions for Ten Guantanamo Detainees," press release, 19 November 2009, accessed 30 May 2014, http://www.justice.gov/opa/pr/2009/November/09-ag-1224.html.

122 Kiyemba v. Obama, 605 F3d 1046 (D.C. Cir. 2010).

123 CBS News, "Obama Makes Plans to Close Guantanamo," 11 February 2009, accessed 30 May 2014, http://www.cbsnews.com/stories/2008/11/14/eveningnews/main4606261.shtml.

124 Exec. Order No. 13,492, "Review and Disposition of Individuals De-
     tained at the Guantánamo Bay Naval Base and Closure of Detention
     Facilities," 74 Fed. Reg. 4897, 22 January 2009.

125 Charlie Savage, "Plan to Move Guantanamo Detainees Faces New
     Delay," *New York Times*, 9 December 2009, accessed 30 May 2014,
     http://www.nytimes.com/2009/12/23/us/politics/23gitmo.html.

126 Ibid.

127 Charlie Savage, "Bill to Ease Transfers of Guantánamo Detainees Moves
     through Senate," *New York Times*, 24 June 2013, accessed 30 May
     2014, http://www.nytimes.com/2013/06/25/us/bill-allowing-guantanamo
     -detainees-to-be-moved-advances.html.

128 Ike Skelton National Defense Authorization Act for Fiscal Year 2011,
     Pub. L. No. 111-383.

129 Exec. Order No. 13,567, "Periodic Review of Individuals Detained at
     Guantánamo Bay Naval Station Pursuant to the Authorization for Use of
     Military Force," 7 March 2011, accessed 30 May 2014, https://www.fas.
     org/irp/offdocs/eo/eo-13567.htm.

130 Decision on Request for Precautionary Measures (Detainees at Guan-
     tanamo Bay, Cuba) 41 ILM 532 (2002) (Inter-American Court of
     Human Rights).

131 Katyal and Tribe, "Waging War, Deciding Guilt," 1266.

132 Reid v. Covert, 354 U.S. 1, 11 (1957).

133 Philbin, "Legality of the Use of Military Commissions," 111.

134 Johan Steyn, "Guantanamo Bay: The Legal Black Hole," *International
     and Comparative Law Quarterly* 53 (2004): 1.

135 Patrick Philbin, "Memorandum for Alberto R. Gonzales, Counsel to the
     President: Legality of the Use of Military Commissions to Try Terror-
     ists," Washington Office of Legal Counsel, 6 November 2001, accessed
     30 May 2014, http://www2.gwu.edu/~nsarchiv/torturingdemocracy/
     documents/20011106.pdf.

136 Ibid.

137 See for example Zadvydas v Davis, 533 U.S. 678, 692–3 (2004).

138 "Senate Majority Staff Report," *Report of the Congressional Commit-
     tees*, 105, quoting editorial staff of the *New York Times*, "Tortured
     Justice," *New York Times*, 8 December 2008.

139 Steyn, "Guantanamo Bay: The Legal Black Hole," 1.

140 Rudalevige, *The New Imperial Presidency*, 226.

141 Alberto Gonzales, "Memorandum to President Bush: Decision Re Appli-
     cation of the Geneva Convention on Prisoners of War to the Conflict
     with al Qaeda and the Taliban," 25 January 2002, accessed 30 May
     2014, http://www.torturingdemocracy.org/documents/20020125.pdf.

142 U.S.C., title 18, § 2340A.

143 United Nations Convention on Torture and Other Cruel, Inhuman or Degrading Treatment or Punishment, 1465 U.N.T.S. 85 (10 December 1984).

144 Yoo, "Draft Memorandum for William J. Haynes II."

145 Jay Bybee, "Memorandum for Alberto R. Gonzales, Counsel to the President, Re: Standards for Conduct of Interrogation," 1 August 2002, accessed 30 May 2014, http://fl1.findlaw.com/news.findlaw.com/nytimes /docs/doj/bybee80102mem.pdf.

146 Rudalevige, *The New Imperial Presidency*, 229.

147 Bybee, "Memorandum for Alberto R. Gonzales," 3.

148 See Evan Wallach, "Drop by Drop: Forgetting the History of Water Torture in U.S. Courts," *Columbia Journal of Transnational Law* 45 (2007): 468, 484–9, discussing United States v. Nakamura (International Military Tribunal for the Far East 1947).

149 United States v. Lee, 744 F2d 1124 (5th Cir. 1984).

150 Wallach, "Drop by Drop," 468.

151 Stanley Moskowitz, "Memorandum for the Record: Interrogations," Congressional Research Service, 30 November 2004.

152 See Havlish v. Bin Laden, 2011 U.S. Dist LEXIS 155899 (S.D.N.Y. 2011), Findings of Fact and Conclusions of Law at para. 94.

153 Richard Bonney, *False Prophets: The "Clash of Civilizations" and the Global War on Terror* (Oxford: Peter Lang, 2008), 265.

154 Stephen Bradbury, "Re: Application of United States Obligations under Article 16 of the Convention against Torture to Certain Techniques That May Be Used in the Interrogation of High Value al Qaeda Detainees," Washington Office of Legal Counsel, 30 May 2005, 29, accessed 30 May 2014, http://web.archive.org/web/20100215233105/http://luxmedia. vo.llnwd.net/o10/clients/aclu/olc_05302005_bradbury.pdf.

155 Timothy Noah, "Water-Bored: Al-Qaida's Plot to Bomb the Liberty Tower Was Not Worth Torturing Anyone Over," *Slate*, 29 April 2009, accessed 30 May 2014, http://www.slate.com/articles/news_and_ politics/chatterbox/2009/04/waterboredhtml.

156 Ali Frick, "Why Bush's 'Enhanced Interrogation' Program Failed," *Think Progress*, accessed 30 May 2014, http://thinkprogress.org/report/why-enhanced-interrogation-failed/?mobile=nc#Ic.; see also the comments of former CIA director Mike Hayden: "I'm willing to concede the point that no one gave us valuable or actionable intelligence while they were, for example, being waterboarded," http://www.weku.fm/post/did harsh interrogation tactics lead bin laden.

157 Philippe Sands, *The Torture Team: Rumsfeld's Memo and the Betrayal of American Values* (New York: Palgrave McMillan, 2008), 116–20.

158 Jeffrey Kassin, "United States Moral Authority Undermined: The For-

eign Affairs Costs of Abusive Detentions," *Cardozo Public Law Policy and Ethics Journal* 4 (2006): 450.

159 David Glazier, "Playing by the Rules: Combating al-Qaeda within the Rule of Law," *William and Mary Law Review* 51 (2010): 1030.

160 Senate Armed Services Committee, "Inquiry of the Treatment of Detainees in U.S. Custody: Report of the Committee on Armed Services of the United States Senate," 110th Cong., 2nd Sess., 20 November 2008.

161 Mark Benjamin, "Torture Planning Began in 2001, Senate Report Reveals," *Salon Magazine*, 22 April 2009, accessed 30 May 2014, http://www.salon.com/2009/04/22/benjamin.; see also Sands, *The Torture Team*, 63, 81, 118.

162 Senate Armed Services Committee, "Inquiry of the Treatment of Detainees," 41.

163 Jonathan S. Landay, "Report: Abusive Tactics Used to Seek Iraq-al Qaida Link," *McClatchy Newspapers*, 21 April 2009, accessed 30 May 2014, http://www.mcclatchydc.com/2009/04/21/66622/report-abusive-tactics-used-to.html.

164 Lawrence Wilkerson, "The Truth about Dick Cheney," *The Washington Note*, 13 May 2009, accessed 30 May 2014, http://www.thewashington note.com/archives/2009/05/the_truth_about/.

165 Colin Powell, "Speech to the Plenary Session of the United Nations Security Council," 5 February 2003, accessed 30 May 2014, http://web. archive.org/web/20070109235502/http://www.state.gov/secretary/former/powell/remarks/2003/17300.htm.

166 Brian Ross and Richard Esposito, "CIA's Harsh Interrogation Techniques Described," *ABC News*, 18 November 2005, accessed 30 May 2014, http://abcnews.go.com/WNT/Investigation/story?id=132866.

167 UN General Assembly, "Convention Relating to the Status of Refugees," 28 July 1951, UNTS, vol. 189, art. 33, 137.

168 Human Rights Watch, "Delivered into Enemy Hands: U.S.-led Abuse and Rendition of Opponents to Gaddafi's Libya," *Human Rights Watch*, 6 September 2012, accessed 30 May 2014, http://www.hrw.org/sites/default/files/reports/libya0912webwcover_1.pdf.

169 Ibid.

170 Wilkerson, "The Truth about Dick Cheney."

171 Peter Finn, "Detainee Who Gave False Iraq Data Dies in Prison in Libya," *Washington Post*, 12 May 2009, accessed 30 May 2014, http://www.washingtonpost.com/wpdyn/content/article/2009/05/11/AR2009051103412.html.

172 Barton Gellman, *Angler: The Cheney Vice-Presidency* (New York: Penguin Press, 2008), 141, quoting Senator Frank Church, *Meet the Press*, NBC, 29 October 1975.

173 Philip Taubman, "Sons of the Black Chamber," *New York Times*, 19
     September 1982, accessed 30 May 2014, http://www.nytimes.com/
     1982/09/19/books/sons-of-the-black-chamber.html?pagewant.
174 Gellman, *Angler*, 142.
175 Ibid.
176 Foreign Intelligence Surveillance Act 1978, Pub. L. No. 95-511.
177 Yoo and Delahunty, "Authority for Use of Military Force."
178 Gellman, *Angler*, 145–6.
179 David Luban, "Liberalism, Torture, and the Ticking Bomb," *Virginia
     Law Review* 91 (2005): 1425, 1444.
180 Trevor Morrison, "Constitutional Avoidance in the Executive Branch,"
     (2006) 106 *Columbia Law Review* 106 (2006): 1189, 1231, quoting
     Harold Koh.
181 David Glenn, "'Torture Memos' vs. Academic Freedom," *Chronicle of
     Higher Education*, 20 March 2009, quoting former assistant deputy
     Attorney General Jack Goldsmith.
182 David Barron, "Memorandum for the Attorney General Re: Withdrawal
     of Office of Legal Counsel Opinion," Washington Office of Legal Coun-
     sel, 11 June 2009, accessed 30 May 2014, http://www.justice.gov/olc/
     2009/memo-barron2009.pdf.
183 Office of Professional Responsibility, "Investigation into the Office of
     Legal Counsel's Memoranda concerning Issues Related to the Central
     Intelligence Agency's Use of 'Enhanced Interrogation Techniques' on
     Suspected Terrorists," 29 July 2009, 251, accessed 30 May 2014,
     https://www.aclu.org/files/pdfs/natsec/opr20100219/20090729_OPR_
     Final_Report_with_20100719_declassifications.pdf.
184 Ibid., 254.
185 Ibid., 257.
186 Joe Palazzo, "David Margolis – the Institutionalist," *Main Justice:
     Politics, Policy and the Law*, 19 April 2010, accessed 30 May 2014,
     http://www.mainjustice.com/2010/04/19/the-institutionalist/.
187 Ibid.
188 Scott Horton, "Prosecutorial Ethics Lite," *Harper's Magazine*, 12 Jan-
     uary 2008, http://harpers.org/blog/2008/01/prosecutorial-ethics-lite/.
189 David Luban, "David Margolis Is Wrong," *Slate*, 22 February 2010,
     accessed 30 May 2014, http://www.slate.com/articles/news_and_politics
     /jurisprudence/2010/02/david_margolis_is_wrong.html.
190 Dalia Lithwick, "Torture Bored," *Slate*, 22 February 2012, accessed 30
     May 2014, http://www.slate.com/articles/news_and_politics/jurispru
     dence/2010/02/torture_bored2.html.
191 Office of Professional Responsibility, Department of Justice "Investiga-
     tion into the Office of Legal Counsel," 64.

192 Ibid., 634.
193 Wayman v. Southard, 23 U.S. 1 [1825].

CHAPTER FOUR

1 Seth Harold Weinberger, *Restoring the Balance: War Powers in an Age of Terror* (Santa Barbara: ABC-CLIO, 2009), 115–16.
2 Anthony Gregory, *The Power of Habeas Corpus in America: From the King's Prerogative to the War on Terror* (Cambridge: Cambridge University Press, 2013), 257–69.
3 Kiyemba v. Obama, 561 F.3d 509 (D.D.C. 2009).
4 Al-Maqaleh v. Gates, 605 F.3d 84 (D.D.C. 2010).
5 Hamdi v. Rumsfeld 542 U.S. 507 (2004).
6 Kim Lane Schepple, "The New Judicial Deference," *Boston University Law Review* 92 (2012): 89, 112.
7 Hamdi v. Rumsfeld, 243 F. Supp. 2d 531 (D.D.C. 2002).
8 Ibid. See also e.g. Padilla v. Rumsfeld, 352 F.3d 695 (2d Cir. 2003), 724; ACLU v. NSA, 436 F. Supp. 2d 754 (D.D.C. 2007); Ali Ahmed v. Obama, 657 F. Supp. 2d 51 (D.D.C. 2009); Amnesty International v. Clapper 667 F.3d 163 (D.C. Cir. 2011) (all cases discussed below).
9 Hamdi v. Rumsfeld, 316 F. 3d 450, 459 (D.C. Cir. 2003).
10 Hamdi v. Rumsfeld, 542 U.S. 507, 535–6 (2004).
11 Schepple, "The New Judicial Deference," 118.
12 Ibid., 119.
13 Ex Parte Milligan, 72 U.S. 2 (1866).
14 Rasul v. Bush, 542 U.S. 466 (2004).
15 Patrick Philbin and John Yoo, "Memorandum to William J. Haynes, General Counsel, Department of Defense: Possible Habeas Jurisdiction over Aliens Held at Guantanamo Bay, Cuba," Washington Office of Legal Counsel, 28 December 2001, accessed 30 May 2014, http://www.torturingdemocracy.org/documents/20011228.pdf.
16 Johan Steyn, "Guantanamo Bay: The Legal Black Hole," *International and Comparative Law Quarterly* 53 (2004): 1.
17 Johnson v. Eisentrager, 339 U.S. 763 (1950).
18 Ibid., 777; see also United Nations War Crimes Commission, *Trials of War Criminals*, vol. XIV (United Nations War Crimes Commission, 1949).
19 *Rasul*, 476.
20 Ibid., 483.
21 Schepple, "The New Judicial Deference," 128.
22 *Rasul*, 485.
23 Ibid., 120.
24 See, e.g., Stephen Henderson, "Detainees Win Access to Courts; Supreme

Court Rulings Deliver a Legal Blow to the Administration's Antiterrorism Policy," *Philadelphia Inquirer*, 29 June 2004.

25 Padilla v. Rumsfeld, 352 F. 3d 695, 724 (D.C. Cir. 2003).

26 Schepple, "The New Judicial Deference," 115.

27 Jenny Martinez, "Process and Substance in the 'War on Terror,'" *Columbia Law Review 108* (2008): 1013, 1039.

28 Schepple, "The New Judicial Deference," 116.

29 Rumsfeld v. Padilla, 542 U.S. 426, 465 (2004) (Stevens, J., joined by Breyer, Ginsberg, Souter, JJ., dissenting).

30 Hamdi v. Rumsfeld, 542 U.S. 508, 554 (2004) (Scalia, J., joined by Stevens, J., dissenting).

31 Non-Detention Act 1971, Pub. L. No. 92-128.

32 Congressional Research Service, "Detention of American Citizens as Enemy Combatants," Congressional Research Service, 15 March 2004, 2.

33 Ibid., 5.

34 Human Rights First, "José Padilla, U.S. Citizen," *In the Courts*, http://web.archive.org/web/20100217085312/http://www.humanrightsfirst.org/us_law/inthecourts/supreme_court_padilla.aspx.

35 Schlepple, "The New Judicial Deference," 121.

36 Hanft v. Padilla, 546 U.S. 1084 (2006).

37 Hamdan v. Rumsfeld, [] 548 US 577 (2006).

38 Uniform Code of Military Justice, U.S.C. title 10 ch. 47.

39 Rasul v. Bush 542 U.S. 466, 612 (2004) (Stevens, J.) (plurality opinion).

40 This was also implicitly supported by the logic of Boumediene v. Bush, 553 U.S. 723, 794–95 (2008).

41 Schepple, "The New Judicial Deference," 135.

42 Linda Greenhouse, "Justices, 5–3, Broadly Reject Bush Plan to Try Detainees," *New York Times*, 29 June 2006, accessed 30 May 2014, http://www.nytimes.com/2006/06/30/washington/30hamdan.html?pagewanted=all&_r=0.

43 Boumediene v. Bush, 553 U.S. 723 (2008).

44 Schlepple, "The New Judicial Deference," 140.

45 Lord Woolf, Jeffrey Jowell, and Andy Le Sueur, eds., "Procedural Fairness: Introduction, History and Comparative Perspectives," *De Smith, Judicial Review*, 6th ed. (London: Sweet and Maxwell, 2007), 317–57.

46 Schepple, "The New Judicial Deference," 141–2.

47 *Boumediene*, 976–98.

48 Jess Braven, *The Terror Courts: Rough Justice at Guantanamo Bay* (New Haven: Yale University Press, 2013), 27–8.

49 Erwin Chemerinsky, "Losing Interest," *National Law Journal*, 25 June 2012, accessed 30 May 2014, http://www.nationallawjournal.com/id=1202560493349/Losing-interest?slreturn=20140430212937.

50 Center for Constitutional Rights, "*Kiyemba v. Obama*: Synopsis," accessed 30 May 2014, http://ccr.justice.org/Kiyemba-v-Obama.

51 Kiyemba v. Obama, No. 08-5424, 2 (D.C. Circuit) (Rogers, J., concurring), accessed 30 May 2014, http://ccrjustice.org/files/2009-02-18%20 Kiyemba%20opinion.pdf.

52 Ibid.

53 "Order," Kiyemba v. Obama, No. 08-5424, 20 October 2008, accessed 30 May 2014, http://ccrjustice.org/files/stay%20order.pdf.

54 "Statement of Breyer, J., joined by Kennedy, Ginsburg, and Sotomayor, JJ.," *Lawfare Blog*, 18 April 2011, accessed 30 May 2014, www.law fareblog/2011/04/supreme-court-denies-cert-in-kiyemba.

55 Latif v. Obama, 677 F.3d 1175 (D.C. Cir. 2012).

56 Ali Ahmed v. Obama 657 F. Supp.2d 51, 57 (D.D.C. 2009); see also Andy Worthington, "Judge Condemns 'Mosaic' of Guantánamo Intelligence, and Unreliable Witnesses," 14 May 2009, accessed 30 May 2014, http://www.andyworthington.co.uk/2009/05/14/judge-condemns-mosaic-of-guantanamo-intelligence-and-unreliable-witnesses/.

57 Ibid., 58.

58 Jasmeet K. Ahuja and Andrew Tutt, "Evidentiary Rules Governing Guantánamo Habeas Petitions: Their Effects and Consequences," *Yale Law and Policy Review* 31 (2012): 185, 198–9.

59 Chemerinsky, "Losing Interest."

60 Birgitta Jónsdóttir, "Evidence of a US Judicial Vendetta against Wiki Leaks Activists Mounts," *The Guardian*, 3 July 2012, accessed 30 May 2014, http://www.guardian.co.uk/commentisfree/2012/jul/03/evidence-us-judicial-vendetta-wikileaks-activists-mounts.

61 Scott Shane and Benjamin Weiser, "Judging Detainees Risk, Often with Flawed Evidence," *New York Times*, 24 April 2011, accessed 30 May 2014, http://www.nytimes.com/2011/04/25/world/guantanamo-files-flawed-evidence-for-assessing-risk.html?pagewanted=all.

62 "Memorandum of Human Rights Watch Submitted to the Foreign Affairs Committee of the Parliament of the United Kingdom," 30 April 2008, 2. ("[M]ilitary commissions set up to try terrorism suspects at Guantanamo explicitly authorize the use of evidence obtained in cruel, inhuman, and degrading interrogations.")

63 Ibid.

64 "JTF-GTMO Matrix of Threat Indicators for Enemy Combatants," *New York Times*, 24 April 2011, accessed 30 May 2014, http://www.nytimes.com/interactive/2011/04/24/world/guantanamo-guide-to-assessing-prisoners.html.

65 Shane and Weiser, "Judging Detainees Risk."

66 "JTF-GTMO Matrix," n9.

67 Denise Winterman, "Casio F-91W: The Strangely Ubiquitous Watch," *BBC News Magazine*, 26 April 2011, accessed 30 May 2014, http://www.bbc.co.uk/news/magazine-13194733.

68 Associated Press, "Common Casio Watch Becomes Evidence at Guantanamo," 9 March 2006, accessed 31 May 2014, http://www.sddt.com/Search/article.cfm?SourceCode=200603091aq#.UQQqZIbLHIU.

69 Shane and Weiser, "Judging Detainees Risk."

70 Ibid.

71 Latif v. Obama, 677 F.3d 1175, 1215 (D.C. Cir. 2012) (Tatel J dissenting).

72 Hanna F. Madbak, "U.S. Supreme Court Denies Guantánamo Detainee Cert. Petitions Concerning Habeas Review," *New York State Bar Association Blog*, 7 May 2011, accessed 31 May 2014, nysbar.com/blogs/ExecutiveDetention/2011/05/.

73 Chemerinsky, "Losing Interest."

74 Julian E. Barnes, "Will U.S. Send More Detainees to Guantanamo?," *Wall Street Journal*, 13 July 2011, accessed 31 May 2014, http://blogs.wsj.com/washwire/2011/07/13/will-u-s-send-more-detainees-to-guantanamo/.

75 "Bush Admits to CIA Secret Prisons," *BBC News*, 7 September 2006, accessed 31 May 2014, http://news.bbc.co.uk/2/hi/americas/5321606.stm.

76 Spencer Ackerman, "U.S. May Indefinitely Detain Secret Prisoners Held in Afghanistan," *The Guardian*, 30 May 2014, accessed 30 November 2014, http://www.theguardian.com/world/2014/may/30/afghanistan-troops-withdrawal-bagram-detainees.

77 Adam Goldman and Kathy Gannon, "Death Shed Light on CIA 'Salt Pit' Near Kabul," *NBC News*, 28 March 2010, http://www.nbcnews.com/id/36071994/ns/us_news-security/#.

78 Al-Maqaleh v. Gates, 604 F. Supp. 205 (D.D.C. 2009).

79 Ibid., 230.

80 Ibid., 235.

81 Al-Maqaleh v. Gates, 605 F.3d 84 (D.C. Cir. 2010).

82 Ibid., 95.

83 Ibid., 95–9.

84 Graham Bowley, "United States Puts Transfer of Detainees to Afghans on Hold," *New York Times*, 9 September 2012, accessed 31 May 2014, http://www.nytimes.com/2012/09/10/world/asia/us-puts-afghan-transfers-at-parwan-prison-on-hold.html?_r=0.

85 Stephen Vladeck, "Al-Maqaleh II: Formalizing Boumediene's Functional Approach to Habeas Jurisdiction," *Lawfare Blog*, 30 October 2012, accessed 31 May 2014, http://www.lawfareblog.com/2012/10/more-on-maqaleh-ii/.

86 Quil Lawrence, "Afghans Worry Bagram Could Turn into Guantanamo,"

Morning Edition, NPR, 4 June 2012, accessed 31 May 2014, http://www.npr.org/2012/06/04/154268385/afghans-worry-bagram-could-turn-into-guantanamo.

87 Bowley, "United States Transfer of Detainees."
88 Rod Nordland, "Detainees Are Handed Over to Afghans, but Not Out of Americans' Reach," *New York Times*, 30 May 2012, http://www.nytimes.com/2012/05/31/world/asia/in-afghanistan-as-bagram-detainees-are-transferred-united-states-keeps-its-grip.html?pagewanted=all.
89 Benjamin Wittes, "Comments on *Maqaleh* and *Hamidullah*," *Lawfare Blog*, 19 October 2012, accessed 31 May 2014, http://www.lawfareblog.com/2012/10/comments-on-maqaleh-and-hamidullah/.
90 Patrick O'Neill, "U.S. Press Blackout at Guantánamo Pierced, Brutal Treatment Exposed," *The Militant*, 1 April 2002, accessed 30 November 2014, http://www.themilitant.com/2002/6613/661302.html.
91 Stephen Vladeck, "The New National Security Canon," *American University Law Review* 61 (2012): 1295, 1329.
92 Padilla v. Yoo, 670 F.3d 540, 548 (9th Cir. 2009).
93 Ibid., 548.
94 Vladeck, "The New National Security Canon," 1317.
95 Religious Freedom Restoration Act 1993, Pub. L. No. 103-141, 107 Stat. 1488 (16 November 1993).
96 Rasul v. Myers, No. 06-5209 (24 April 2009) (D.C. Cir.), accessed 31 May 2014, http://www.cadc.uscourts.gov/internet/opinions.nsf/1C572595EB3EF7248525780000761C90/$file/06-5209-1177375.pdf.
97 Ibid.
98 Al-Zahrani v. Rodriguez, 669 F.3d 315 (D.C. Cir. 2012).
99 Pete Yost, "Questions Raised over Deaths of 3 Guantanamo Detainees Raised by Magazine Article," Canadian Press, 2010, accessed 31 May 2014, https://web.archive.org/web/20100121041245/http://www.google.com/hostednews/canadianpress/article/ALeqM5h97BGvSdx97hHzNDkUiDzI8JsB7A.
100 Mark Denbeaux et al., *Death in Camp Delta*, Seton Hall University School of Law Center for Policy and Research, ii, accessed 31 May 2014, http://law.shu.edu/ProgramsCenters/PublicIntGovServ/policyresearch/upload/gtmo_death_camp_delta.pdf.
101 Scott Horton, "The Guantánamo 'Suicides': A Camp Delta Sergeant Blows the Whistle," *Harper's Magazine*, March 2010, accessed 31 May 2014, http://harpers.org/archive/2010/03/the-guantanamo-suicides/?single=1.
102 Boumediene v. Bush, 553 U.S. 771, 755 (2008).
103 Minneci v. Pollard, 32 SCt 617 (2012).
104 *Rasul*.

105 El-Masri v. United States, 479 F.3d 296 (D.C. Cir. 2007).
106 El-Masri v. The Former Yugoslav Republic of Macedonia, No. 39630/09
     (European Court of Human Rights 2012) 13 December 2012, 63.
107 Ibid.
108 Elizabeth Wilson, "'Damages or Nothing': The Post-Boumediene Consti-
     tution and Compensation for Human Rights Violations after 9/11,"
     Seton Hall Law Review 41 (2001): 1491, 1512–13.
109 Charlie Savage, "Guantánamo Conditions Slip, Military Lawyers Say,"
     New York Times, 24 February 2012; see also Peter Masciola, "Memo-
     randum of Col. Peter Masciola, Bullets in Furtherance of Meeting of 4
     February 2009," accessed 31 May 2014, http://www.defenselink.mil/
     pubs/App11.pdf.
110 Respondent's Motion to Refer the Counsel-Access Issue for Decision
     by a Single District Judge and to Hold in Abeyance Former Petitioners
     Esmail's and Uthman's Motions for Order Concerning the Protective
     Order, Abdah v. Obama, No. 04-Civ-1254 (D.D.C. 2012), accessed
     31 May 2014, http://images.politico.com/global/2012/07/gitmocounsel
     motn.pdf.
111 Marc Ambinder, "Inside the Secret Interrogation Facility at Bagram,"
     The Atlantic, 14 May 2010, accessed 31 May 2014, http://www.the
     atlantic.com/politics/archive/10/05/inside-the-secret-interrogation-
     facility-at-bagram/56678/#.
112 Open Society Foundations Regional Policy Initiative on Afghanistan
     and Pakistan, "Confinement Conditions at a U.S. Screening Facility on
     Bagram Air Base," 14 October 2010, http://www.opensocietyfoundations.
     org/sites/default/files/confinement-conditions-20101014.pdf.
113 Jeffrey S. Kaye, "How the U.S. Army's Field Manual Codified Torture –
     and Still Does," *AlterNet*, 6 January 2009, accessed 31 May 2014,
     http://www.alternet.org/story/117807/how_the_u.s._army%27s_field
     _manual_codified_torture_—_and_still_does.
114 Headquarters, Department of the Army, "Human Intelligence Collector
     Operations (FM 2-22.3 (amending FM 34-52))," September 2006, ac-
     cessed 31 May 2014, https://www.fas.org/irp/doddir/army/fm2-22-3.pdf.
115 Exec. Order No. 13,491, "Ensuring Lawful Interrogations," 22 January
     2009, accessed 31 May 2014, http://www.whitehouse.gov/the_press_
     office/EnsuringLawfulInterrogations.
116 Amnesty International, *The Army Field Manual: Sanctioning Cruelty?*
     19 March 2009, accessed 31 May 2014, http://www.amnesty.org.au/
     hrs/comments/20575/.
117 Exec. Order No. 13,491, § 5(e).
118 Ambinder, "Inside the Secret Interrogation Facility."
119 Ibid.

120 Human Rights Watch, "Letter from Interrogators and Intelligence Offi-cials," 16 November 2010, accessed 31 May 2014, http://www.human rightsfirst.org/our-work/law-and-security/torture-and-accountability/appendix-m-of-the-army-field-manual/letter-from-interrogators-and-intelligence-officials/.

121 Scott Shane, "Interrogations' Effectiveness May Prove Elusive," *New York Times*, 22 April 2009, accessed 27 October 2016, http://www.ny times.com/2009/04/23/us/politics/23detain.html.

122 "Tracking America's Drone War," *Washington Post*, accessed 31 May 2014, http://apps.washingtonpost.com/foreign/drones/; see also Chris Woods and Alice K. Ross, "Revealed: US and Britain Launched 1,200 Drone Strikes in Recent Wars," *Bureau of Investigative Journalism*, 12 December 2012, http://www.thebureauinvestigates.com/2012/12/04/revealed-us-and-britain-launched-1200-drone-strikes-in-recent-wars/.

123 Scott Shane, "U.S. Approves Targeted Killing of American Cleric," *New York Times*, 6 April 2010, accessed 31 May 2014, http://www.nytimes.com/2010/04/07/world/middleeast/07yemen.html.

124 Complaint for Declaratory and Injunctive Relief at Prayer for Relief, Al-Aulaqi v. Obama, 2010 WL 3478666 (D.D.C. 2010).

125 Ibid.

126 Ibid., para. 11.

127 Ibid.

128 Opposition to Plaintiff's Motion for Preliminary Injunction and Memo-randum in Support of Defendant's Motion to Dismiss at para. 19-35, Al-Aulaqi v. Obama, 2010 WL 3478666 (D.D.C. 2010).

129 Al-Aulaqi v. Obama, 727 F.Supp.2d 1 (D.D.C. 2010).

130 Ibid., 18. The court's spelling of Anwar Al-Awlaki's name has been adjusted to correspond with the way it has been transliterated within this chapter.

131 Ibid., 17.

132 El-Shifa v. United States, 378 F.3d 1346 (D.C. Cir. 2004).

133 Shane, "U.S. Approves Targeted Killing."

134 Ibid., 70 (emphasis added).

135 Ibid., 75.

136 Ibid., 77 (internal quotation marks removed; emphasis added).

137 Ibid., 72, 77.

138 Rosenberg v. United States, 346 U.S. 273, 294 (1953) (Clark, J, concur-ring for six Justices).

139 Exec. Order No. 13,526, "Classified National Security Information," § 1.1(a)(4), 29 December 2009, accessed 27 October 2016, http://www.whitehouse.gov/the-press-office/executive-order-classified-national-security-information.

140   New York Times v. Department of Justice, 11 Civ. 9336 (CM) (S.D.N.Y. 2012).

141   American Civil Liberties Union, "Department of Justice 'Request Under Freedom of Information Act, Nathan Wessler,'" 19 October 2011, accessed 31 May 2014, 3, http://www.aclu.org/files/assets/awlaki_foia _final_2011_10_19.pdf.

142   Ibid., quoting Charlie Savage, "Secret U.S. Memo Made Legal Case to Kill a Citizen," *New York Times*, 9 October 2011, http://www.nytimes. com/2011/10/09/world/middleeast/secret-us-memo-made-legal-case-to-kill-a-citizen.html?pagewanted=all.

143   Ryan Patrick Alford, "The Rule of Law at the Crossroads: Consequences of Targeted Killing of Citizens," *Utah Law Review* (2011): 1203, 1271–2.

144   Mathews v. Eldridge, 424 U.S. 319 (1976).

145   It should be noted that the defendants in Star Chamber proceedings had, in fact, significantly more procedural due process. Ryan Patrick Alford, "The Star Chamber and the Regulation of the Legal Profession, 1570– 1640," *American Journal of Legal History* 51 (2011): 653.

146   Savage, "Secret U.S. Memo Made Legal Case."

147   *Al-Aulaqi.*

148   Memorandum of Law in Support of Defendant's Motion for Summary Judgment, New York Times v. Department of Justice, 11 Civ. 9336 (CM) (S.D.N.Y. 2012).

149   Memorandum of Law in Support of Plaintiff's Cross-Motion for Partial Summary Judgment and in Opposition to Defendant's Motion for Summary Judgment, p. 13, New York Times v. Department of Justice, 11 Civ. 9336 (CM) (S.D.N. 2012).

150   Ibid., 13.

151   New York Times v. Department of Justice, 11 Civ. 9336, 4-5 (CM) (S.D.N.Y. 2013) (emphasis added).

152   Ibid., 38.

153   Ibid., 60.

154   Ibid., 18–19.

155   Ibid., 19.

156   Ibid.

157   Lewis Carroll, *Through the Looking Glass* (London: Collins Clear-Type Press, 1934), 205.

158   House Committee on the Judiciary Majority Staff Report to Chairman John C. Conyers, Jr. "Reining in the Imperial Presidency: Lessons and Recommendations Relating to the Presidency of George W. Bush," Government Printing Office, 2009, 147.

159 Declarations of Mark Klein and Scott Marcus, Amnesty v. Blair, 08 Civ. 6259 (S.D.N.Y. 2008).

160 Philip Shenon, "Secret Court Says F.B.I. Aides Misled Judges in 75 Cases," *New York Times*, 20 November 2001, http://www.nytimes.com/ 2002/08/23/us/secret-court-says-fbi-aides-misled-judges-in-75-cases.html.

161 "Letter from Laurence Tribe to the Hon. John Conyers, Jr.," US House of Representatives, 6 January 2006.

162 George W. Bush, "Address to a Joint Session of Congress and the American People," press release, 20 September 2001, accessed 31 May 2014, http://georgewbush-whitehouse.archives.gov/news/releases/2001/09/ 20010920-8.html.

163 Lisa Myers, Douglas Pasternak, and Rich Gardella, "Is the Pentagon Spying on Americans," NBC *News*, 14 December 2005, accessed 31 May 2014, http://www.nbcnews.com/id/10454316/ns/nbc_nightly_news_with _brian_williams-nbc_news_investigates/t/pentagon-spying-americans/ #.WAlY_-ArJaQ.

164 Frederick Schwarz and Aziz Huq, *Unchecked and Unbalanced: Presidential Power in a Time of Terror* (New York: New Press, 2007), 134.

165 Ibid., 135.

166 Charlie Savage, *Takeover: The Return of the Imperial Presidency and the Subversion of American Democracy* (New York: Little, Brown, 2007), 115.

167 Schwartz and Huq, *Unchecked and Unbalanced*, 159, 135 (emphasis in original).

168 Complaint in ACLU v. NSA, 06 Civ. 10204 (D.D.C. 2006), accessed 31 May 2014, http://www.aclu.org/images/nsaspying/asset_upload_file137_ 23491.pdf.

169 Ibid., 15–16.

170 Ibid., 18.

171 Ibid., 44–6.

172 Ibid., 59.

173 ACLU v. NSA, 436 F.Supp.2d 754 (D.D.C. 2007).

174 Ibid., 771.

175 Ibid., 778.

176 Ibid., 781.

177 ACLU v. NSA, 493 F.3d 644 (D.C. Cir. 2007).

178 Ibid., 653.

179 Amnesty International v. McConnell, 646 F.Supp.2d 633 (D.C. Cir. 2009).

180 American Civil Liberties Union, "Memorandum of the General Counsel, Federal Bureau of Investigation," 1 October 2010, accessed 31 May

2014, http://www.aclu.org/files/pdfs/natsec/faafoia20101129/FAAF
        BI0072.pdf.

181   James Risen and Eric Lichtblau, "Court Affirms Wiretapping without
        Warrants," *New York Times*, 16 January 2009, accessed 31 May 2014,
        http://www.nytimes.com/2009/01/16/washington/16fisa.html?_r=2
        &hp&.

182   Ellen Nakashima and Dan Eggen, "Former CEO Says U.S. Punished
        Phone Firm," *Washington Post*, 13 October 2007, accessed 31 May
        2014, http://www.washingtonpost.com/wp-dyn/content/article/2007/
        10/12/AR2007101202485_pf.html.

183   In Re: Directives [redacted text] * Pursuant to Section 105B of the For-
        eign Intelligence Surveillance Act, FISCR No. 08-01 (Foreign Intelligence
        Surveillance Court 2009), accessed 31 May 2014, http://www.fas.org/
        irp/agency/doj/fisa/fiscro82208.pdf.

184   Bruce Ackerman and Oona Hathaway, "Limited War and the Constitu-
        tion: Iraq and the Crisis of Presidential Legality," *Michigan Law Review*
        109 (2011): 453.

185   John Yoo, *The Powers of War and Peace* (Chicago: University of
        Chicago, 2005), 97–100.

186   Brian J. Lithwack, "Putting Constitutional Teeth into a Paper Tiger:
        How to Fix the War Powers Resolution," *National Security Law Brief*
        2 (2011): 2, 4.

187   Ibid., 13.

188   Theodore Olson, "Memorandum Opinion for the Attorney General:
        Presidential Power to Use Armed Forces Abroad without Statutory Au-
        thorization," Washington Office of Legal Counsel, 12 February 1980,
        accessed 31 May 2014, http://www.yale.edu/lawweb/jbalkin/cases/4a
        OpOffLegalCounsel185.pdf.

189   Lithwack, "Putting Constitutional Teeth into a Paper Tiger," 5.

190   War Powers Resolution 1973, Pub. L. No. 93-148.

191   Kucinich v. Obama, 821 F. Supp. 2d 110 (D.D.C. 2011).

192   Ibid., 113.

193   Kucinich v. Bush, 236 F. Supp. 2d 1, 23-24 (D.D.C. 2002), citing
        Chenoweth v. Clinton, 181 F.3d 112, 116 (D.C. Circuit 1999).

194   El-Shifa v. United States, 607 F.3d 836, 857 (D.C. Cir. 2011).

195   Kucinich v. Obama, 821 F. Supp. 2d 110, 124 n 9 (D.D.C. 2011).

196   Johnson v. Eisentrager, 339 U.S. 763, 789 (1950).

197   Kucinich v. Obama, 821 F. Supp. 2d 110, 116 n 4 (D.D.C. 2011).

198   Crockett v. Reagan, 720 F.2d 1355 (D.C. Cir. 1982).

199   See e.g., Lowry v. Reagan, 676 F. Supp. 333 (D.D.C. 1987); Sanchez-
        Espinoza v. Reagan, 568 F. Supp. 596 (D.D.C. 1983).

200   Order Denying the Writ of Certiorari in Latif v. Obama, Al-Bihani v.

Obama, Uthman v. Obama, Almerfedi v. Obama, Al-Kandari v. Obama, Al-Madhwani v. Obama, Al-Alwi v. Obama, 132 S. Ct. 2741 (2012).

201 Kiyemba v. Obama, 131 S. Ct. 1631 (2011).

202 Lebron v. Rumsfeld, 132 S. Ct. 2751 (2012).

203 Rasul v. Myers, 130 S. Ct. 1013 (2009).

204 "Statement of Lawyers Who Represented Adnan Farhan Latif," *Lawfare Blog*, 11 September 2012, accessed 31 May 2014, http://www.lawfare blog.com/2012/09/statement-of-latif-legal-team/.

205 Ben Fox, "Guantanamo Bay Prisoner Dies in Detention," Associated Press, 9 September 2012, accessed 31 May 2014, http://www.huffington post.com/2012/09/10/guantanamo-bay-prisoner-dies_n_1871100.html.

206 El-Shifa v. United States, 131 S. Ct. 997 (2011).

207 See, e.g., Chenoweth v. Clinton, 120 S. Ct. 1286 (2000).

208 Clapper v. Amnesty International, 132 S. Ct. 2431 (2012).

209 Amnesty International v. Clapper, 667 F.3d 163 (2d Cir. 2011).

210 Amnesty International v. McConnell, 646 F. Supp. 2d 633 (2009).

211 ACLU v. NSA, 493 F.3d 644 (6th Cir. 2007).

212 ACLU v. NSA, 128 S. Ct. 1324 (2008).

CHAPTER FIVE

1 See chapter 1 in this work.

2 U.S. Const. art. 3, § 2, cl. 2.

3 David J. Russo, *American History from a Global Perspective: An Interpretation* (Westport, CT: Greenwood Praeger, 2000), 58.

4 Matthew D. Marcotte, "Advice and Consent: A Historical Argument for Substantive Senatorial Involvement in Judicial Nominations," *New York University Journal of Legislation and Public Policy* 5 (2001): 519, 528.

5 Alexander Hamilton, in *The Records of the Convention of 1787*, ed. Max Farrand (Max Farrand 1937), 233.

6 Adam J. White, "Toward the Framers' Understanding of 'Advise and Consent': A Historical and Textual Inquiry," *Harvard Journal of Law and Public Policy* 29 (2001): 103, 113.

7 Marcotte, "Advice and Consent," 532.

8 International Commission of Jurists, "A Report of the Proceedings of the African Conference on the Rule of Law," *International Commission of Jurists*, 1961, 21.

9 Marcotte, "Advice and Consent," 533.

10 Ibid., 534. Quoting Luther Martin, "Address before the Maryland House of Representatives," 29 November 1787, reprinted in Farrand, *The Records of the Convention*, vol. 3, 158.

11 George Mason, in *Papers of George Mason*, vol. 3, ed. Robert Rutland (Chapel Hill: University of North Carolina Press, 1970), 928.

12 United States Senate, "Senate Committee Hearings on the Judicial Nomination Process," *Drake Law Review* 50 (2001): 548n30.

13 White, "Toward the Framers' Understanding," 127.

14 Marcotte, "Advice and Consent," 536.

15 Treaty of Amity, Commerce, and Navigation 1794 (Jay Treaty), 1 Stat. 116.

16 George C. Herring, *From Colony to Superpower: U.S. Foreign Relations Since 1776* (Oxford: Oxford University Press, 2008), 79.

17 James Haw, *John and Edward Rutledge of South Carolina* (Athens: University of Georgia Press, 1997), 248–51.

18 John Hollitz, *Contending Voices: Biographical Explorations of the American Past*, vol. 1 (Boston: Cengage Learning, 2010), 83.

19 Ibid.

20 John Anthony Maltese, *The Selling of Supreme Court Nominees* (Baltimore, MD: Johns Hopkins University Press, 1998), 34.

21 Joseph R. Biden, "The Constitution, the Senate, and the Court," *Wake Forest Law Review* 24 (2001): 951, 953.

22 See chapter 2 in this work.

23 Ibid.

24 See Marian C. McKenna, *Franklin Roosevelt and the Great Constitutional War* (New York: Fordham University Press, 2002), 520–1.

25 Franklin Delano Roosevelt, *The Fireside Chats of Franklin Delano Roosevelt* (St Petersburg, FL: Red and Black Publishers, 2008), 45.

26 Sen. Com. on the Judiciary, "Reorganization of the Federal Judiciary," 75th Cong., 1st Sess. 1937, *Senate Reports*, 711, 10, 23.

27 Ex Parte Quirin, 317 U.S. 1 (1942).

28 See chapter 2 in this work.

29 John W. Dean, *Broken Government: How Republican Rule Destroyed the Legislative, Executive, and Judicial Branches* (New York: Viking, 2007), ch. 3.

30 Sheldon Goldman, *Picking Federal Judges: Lower Court Selection from Roosevelt through Reagan* (New Haven, CT: Yale University Press, 1997), 30.

31 Ibid.

32 See chapter 2 in this work.

33 Goldman, *Picking Federal Judges*, 172.

34 Ibid.

35 Neil McFeely, *Appointment of Judges: The Johnson Presidency* (Austin: University of Texas, 1987), 15.

36 Ibid., 84.

37 Charles Ashman, *The Finest Judges Money Can Buy* (Los Angeles: Nash Publishing, 1973), 212.

38 Artemus Ward, "An Extraconstitutional Arrangement: Lyndon Johnson and the Fall of the Warren Court," in *White House Studies Compendium*, vol. 2, ed. Robert Watson (New York: Nova Science, 2007), 99–101.

39 Ashman, *The Finest Judges*, 213.

40 Ward, "An Extraconstitutional Arrangement," 104–5.

41 Joseph Califano, *The Triumph and Tragedy of Lyndon Johnson* (New York: Simon and Schuster, 2003), 316–17.

42 Thomas R. Hensley, Kathleen Hale, and Carl Snook, *The Rehnquist Court: Justices, Rulings, and Legacy* (Santa Barbara, CA: ABC-CLIO, 2006), 50.

43 Dean, *Broken Government*, ch. 3.

44 George J. Vieth, *Black April: The Fall of South Vietnam, 1973–75* (New York: Encounter Books, 2012), 23–5.

45 Dean, *Broken Government*.

46 Ashman, *The Finest Judges*, 198.

47 Joseph Calluori, "The Supreme Court under Siege: The Battle over Nixon's Nominees," in *Richard M. Nixon: Politician, President, Administrator*, eds. Leon Freidman and William Levantrosser (New York: Greenwood, 1991), 362–4.

48 Ibid., 215.

49 Goldman, *Picking Federal Judges*, 199.

50 Linda Greenhouse, *Becoming Justice Blackmun: Harry Blackmun's Supreme Court Journey* (New York: Times Books, 2007), 28.

51 "The Nation: Nixon's Not So Supreme Court," *Time*, 25 October 1971.

52 See David Alistair Yalof, *Pursuit of Justices: Presidential Politics and the Selection of Supreme Court Justices* (Chicago: University of Chicago Press, 2001), 115–25.

53 See "Attorney General Mitchell Terminates Association's Advance Screening of Supreme Court Nominees," *ABA Journal*, December 1971, 1175.

54 Robert Henry, "The Players and the Play," in *The Burger Court: Counter-Revolution or Confirmation?*, ed. Bernard Schwartz (New York: Oxford University Press, 1998), 23.

55 Arthur H. Garrison, *Supreme Court Jurisprudence in Times of National Crisis, Terrorism, and War: A Historical Perspective* (Lanham, MD: Lexington, 2011), 381.

56 Jeffrey Toobin, *The Nine: Inside the Secret World of the Supreme Court* (New York: Doubleday, 2007), 6.

57 Mark Tushnet, *A Court Divided: The Rehnquist Court and the Future of Constitutional Law* (New York: W.W. Norton, 2005), 25.

58 Brown v. Board of Education, 347 U.S. 483 (1954).

59 Plessy v. Ferguson, 163 U.S. 537 (1896).

60 Richard Kluger, *Simple Justice* (New York: Knopf, 1975), 606–9.

61 132 Cong. Rec. Statement of Elise Douglas, (Government Printing Office 1986) part 10, 23548.

62 Terry v. Adams, 345 U.S. 461 (1953).

63 Tinsley Yarbrough, *The Rehnquist Court and the Constitution* (Oxford: Oxford University Press, 2000), 2–3.

64 Ori Nir, "Groups Hail Rehnquist, but Dershowitz Offers Dissent," *Jewish Daily Forward*, 9 September 2005.

65 Tony Mauro, "Rehnquist FBI File Sheds New Light on Drug Dependence, Confirmation Battles," *Legal Times*, 4 January 2007.

66 Peter D. Bryson, *Comprehensive Reviews in Toxicology: For Emergency Clinicians* (Washington: Taylor and Francis, 1996).

67 Mauro, "Rehnquist FBI File."

68 See, e.g., "Response of Paul P. Colborne to Freedom of Information Act Request Dated April 24, 2012," Department of Justice, 7 June 2012, accessed 31 May 2014, http://www.governmentattic.org/6docs/DOJ_LegalCounselOpinions_1998-2012.pdf.

69 Arthur H. Garrison, *Supreme Court Jurisprudence in Times of National Crisis, Terrorism and War* (New York: Lexington Books, 2003), 280–5.

70 Arthur Schlesinger Jr, *The Imperial Presidency* (Boston: Houghton Mifflin, 2004), 190.

71 Ibid.

72 Ibid., 257.

73 See chapter 4 in this work.

74 See chapter 2 in this work.

75 United States v. U.S. District Court, 407 U.S. 297 (1972).

76 See, e.g., United States v. U.S. District Court, 407 U.S. 297 (1972); United States v. Nixon [] 418 U.S. 683 (1974).

77 See chapter 2 in this work.

78 Ibid.

79 The formal name was the Senate Select Committee on Presidential Campaign Activities.

80 Bob Woodward and Carl Bernstein, *Watergate: The Final Days* (New York: Simon and Schuster, 2005), 54–9.

81 Ibid., 60–6.

82 Ibid., 70–1.

83 Robert H. Bork, *Saving Justice: Watergate, the Saturday Night Massacre, and Other Adventures of a Solicitor General* (New York: Encounter Books, 2013).

84 United States v. Nixon, 418 U.S. 683 (1974).

85 United States v. U.S. District Court, 407 U.S. 297 (1972).

86 See chapter 3 in this work.

87 United States Senate, *William H. Rehnquist, Chief Justice of the United States: Memorial Tributes* (Government Printing Office 2007), 80.

88 See Michael Schaller, "Reagan and the Cold War," in *Deconstructing Reagan: Conservative Mythology and America's Fortieth President*, eds. Kyle Longley, Jeremy D. Meyer, and Michael Schaller (Armonk, NY: M.E. Sharpe, 2007), 40.

89 See chapter 2 in this work.

90 David Shapiro "William Hubbs Rehnquist," in *The Justices of the United States Supreme Court: Their Lives and Major Opinions*, vol. 5, ed. Leon Friedman (New York: Chelsea House, 1978), 111.

91 See John A. Jenkins, *The Partisan* (New York: Public Affairs, 2012), 131–76.

92 Ibid.

93 See David L. Hudson, *The Rehnquist Court: Understanding Its Impact and Legacy* (Westport, CT: Greenwood, 2007), 15–22.

94 See generally Edward Lazarus, *Closed Chambers* (New York: Penguin, 1999).

95 Bob Woodward and Scott Armstrong, *The Brethren: Inside the Supreme Court* (New York: Simon and Schuster, 2005), 407–8; Shapiro, "William Hubbs Rehnquist," 121.

96 Thomas R. Hensley, Kathleen Hale, Carl Snook, *The Rehnquist Court: Justices, Rulings, and Legacy* (Santa Barbara, CA: ABC-CLIO, 2006), 61.

97 Yarborough, *The Rehnquist Court and the Constitution*, 1–11.

98 Alan Cooperman, "Sedative Withdrawal Made Rehnquist Delusional in '81," *Washington Post*, 5 January 2007, accessed 31 May 2014, http://www.highbeam.com/doc/1P2-5769375.html.

99 Later, as a judge, "Scalia displayed particular deference to goals of the military and intelligence agencies, and consistently made separation-of-powers arguments to oppose judicial involvement, relying on the political questions doctrine and restrictive theories of standing" (as discussed in the last chapter). Stephen J. Adler, "Court Nominee Is Savvy and Aggressive," *The American Lawyer*, 21 June 1986, A10.

100 James Brian Staab, *The Political Thought of Justice Antonin Scalia: A Hamiltonian on the Supreme Court* (Lanham, MD: Rowman and Littlefield, 2006), 18, 24.

101 Senate Judiciary Committee, "Report of the Committee on the Judiciary, United States Senate, Nomination of Robert H. Bork to be an Associate Justice of the United States Supreme Court," Government Printing Office, 1987.

102 Toobin, *The Nine*, 26–7.

103 Anthony Lewis, "Bork Embraces Executive Power," *Miami News*, 28 August 1987.

104 Kenneth B. Noble, "New Views Emerge of Bork's Role in Watergate Dismissals," *New York Times*, 26 July 1987.

105 See Joan Biskupic, *American Original: The Life and Constitution of Supreme Court Justice Antonin Scalia* (London: MacMillan, 2009), 42–7.

106 Hensley, Hale, and Snook, *The Rehnquist Court*, 59, 61.

107 Cheney v. United States District Court for the District of Columbia, 541 U.S. 915 (2004).

108 Federal Advisory Committee Act 1972, Pub. L. No. 92–463.

109 Motion to Recuse, Cheney v. United States District Court, WL 3741418 (D.D.C. 2004), 7.

110 David G. Savage and Richard A. Serrano, "Scalia Was Cheney Hunt Trip Guest; Ethics Concern Grows," *Los Angeles Times*, 5 February 2004, accessed 31 May 2014, http://articles.latimes.com/2004/feb/05/nation/na-ducks5.

111 Toobin, *The Nine*, 276.

112 Ibid.

113 Cheney v. United States District Court for the District of Columbia, 541 U.S. 915, 925–6 (2004).

114 Ibid.

115 Wickard v. Filburn, 317 U.S. 111 (1942).

116 See, e.g., Gonzales v. Raich, 545 U.S. 1 (2005).

117 Ex Parte Milligan, 71 U.S. 2 (1866).

118 Jonathan Hafetz, *Habeas Corpus after 9/11: Confronting America's New Global Detention System* (New York: New York University Press, 2011), 100.

119 Toobin, *The Nine*, 253.

120 Ibid., 203.

121 See chapter 2 in this work.

122 Martin Metzner et al., *The Miami Herald Report: Democracy Held Hostage* (New York: St Martin's Press, 2001), 173.

123 Bush v. Gore, 531 U.S. 98 (2000).

124 Toobin, *The Nine*, 174.

125 Ibid.

126 Kevin Merida and Michael Fletcher, *Supreme Discomfort: The Divided Soul of Clarence Thomas* (New York: Doubleday, 2007), 326.

127 Ryan Malphurs, *Rhetoric and Discourse in Supreme Court Oral Arguments* (New York: Routledge, 2013), 186.

128 Evan Thomas and Michael Isikoff, "The Truth behind the Pillars," *Newsweek*, 25 December 2000/1 January 2001, 46.

129 Denis Steven Rutkus et al., *Supreme Court Nominations* (Alexandria, VA: TheCapitol.Net 2005), 18.

130 Toobin, *The Nine*, 327–9.

131 Dissent of Justice Stevens to Order Granting Stay and Petition for Certiorari, Bush v. Gore, 531 U.S. 1046, 1047 (2000).

132 National Socialist Party of America v. Skokie, 434 U.S. 1327, 1328 (1977).

133 Dissent of Justice Stevens to Order Granting Stay and Petition for Certiorari, Bush v. Gore, [] 531 U.S. 1046, 1046-1047 (2000).

134 Ibid.

135 Toobin, *The Nine*, 163–4.

136 Dissent of Justice Stevens to Order Granting Stay and Petition for Certiorari, Bush v. Gore. 531 U.S. 1046, 1046–7 (2000).

137 Toobin, *The Nine*.

138 See, e.g., Alan Dershowitz, *Supreme Injustice: How the High Court Hijacked Election 2000* (Oxford: Oxford University Press, 2001).

139 *Bush*, 531 U.S. 98, 109 (2000).

140 *Bush*, 531 U.S. 98, 128-129 (2000) (Stevens, J. dissenting).

141 Toobin, *The Nine*, 176.

142 See Christopher P. Banks, David B. Cohen, John C. Green, eds., *The Final Arbiter: The Consequences of Bush v. Gore for Law and Politics* (Albany: State University of New York Press, 2005).

143 Ibid.

144 United States v. Nixon, 418 U.S. 683 (1974); *Bush*, 531 U.S. 98 (2000).

145 Cynthia Arnson, *Crossroads: Congress, the President, and Central America, 1976–1993* (University Park: Pennsylvania State University Press, 1993), 297.

146 Ibid., 299.

147 Toobin, *The Nine*, 236.

148 Ibid., 260.

149 Ibid., 277.

150 Ibid., 260.

151 See also Albert Gore, *The Assault on Reason* (New York: Penguin, 2007), 228.

152 See Todd C. Peppers and Artemus Ward, eds., *In Chambers: Stories of Supreme Court Law Clerks and Their Justices* (Charlottesville: University of Virginia Press, 2012), 99–107.

153 Rehnquist died three weeks before Roberts was formally appointed by the president, but his passing was too late for any of his files to be archived and catalogued before that time.

154 Geoff Colvin, "On History's Stage: Chief Justice John Roberts Jr.," *Fortune*, 3 January 2011, accessed 31 May 2014, http://www.samachar.com /On-historys-stage-Chief-Justice-John-Roberts-Jr-lbdxS5jjfia.html.

155 Toobin, *The Nine*, 263.

156 Ibid.

157 Ibid.

158 Colvin, "On History's Stage."

159 Toobin, *The Nine*, 264.

160 Cong. Rec., Senate, vol. 151, part 16, 21205.

161 Hamdan v. Rumsfeld, 415 F.3d 33 (D.C. Cir. 2005).

162 Hamdi v. Rumsfeld, 542 U.S. 507 (2004).

163 Hamdan v. Rumsfeld, 415 F.3d 33 (D.C. Cir. 2005). Hamdan's convictions were ultimately overturned in 2012.

164 Ibid.

165 Toobin, *The Nine*, 277.

166 Cong. Sen. Reports, No. 15017, *Government Printing Office*, 2007.

167 Toobin, *The Nine*, 278.

168 Douglas Daniel, "White House Won't Give Out All Roberts Memos," *Truth Out*, 24 July 2005, accessed 31 May 2014, http://www.truth-out.org/archive/component/k2/item/56052:white-house-wont-show-all-roberts-papers.

169 Toobin, *The Nine*, 311.

170 Lawrence E. Walsh, *Firewall: The Iran-Contra Conspiracy and Cover-Up* (New York: W.W. Norton, 2007), 371–86.

171 *Almanac of the Federal Judiciary Volume Five* (New York: Aspen, 2001), 5.

172 Toobin, *The Nine*, 311.

173 Samuel Alito, Jr, "Personal Qualifications Statement," *FindLaw*, 15 November 1985, accessed 31 May 2014, http://news.findlaw.com/hdocs/docs/alito/111585stmnt.html.

174 Roe v. Wade, 410 U.S. 113 (1973).

175 Alito, "Personal Qualifications Statement."

176 Toobin, *The Nine*, 315.

177 Alito, "Personal Qualifications Statement."

178 Ibid. (emphasis added).

179 Ibid.

180 Toobin, *The Nine*, 366.

181 Rutkus, *Supreme Court Nominations*, 45–6.

182 Ibid.

183 "United States Government Manual 2011," Government Printing Office, 2011, 17.

184 "United States House of Representatives Telephone Directory," Government Printing Office, 2007, 318.

185 Charles Hurt, "Biden Says Filibuster on Alito Unlikely; Up-or-Down Vote Expected," *Washington Times*, 7 November 2005, accessed 31 May 2014, http://www.highbeam.com/doc/1G1-138405459.html.

186 Charles Babbington, "Kerry Defends Senate Filibuster on Alito as 'A

Vote on History,'" *Washington Post*, 28 January 2006, accessed 31 May 2014, http://www.washingtonpost.com/wp-dyn/content/article/2006/01/27/AR2006012701405.html.

187 Kevin Schultz, *America Unbound: A U.S. History Primer* (Boston: Wadsworth, 2010), 454.

188 Susan Welch, et al., *Understanding American Government* (Boston: Wadsworth, 2008), 448.

189 O'Connor was a graduate of Stanford Law School, serving on the Arizona Court of Appeals at the time. Henry Julian Abraham, *Justices, Presidents, and Senators: A History of the U.S. Supreme Court* (Lanham, MD: Rowman and Littlefield, 2008), 266.

190 Sotomayor had attended Princeton and Yale Law School, and had eighteen years of service in the federal judiciary, including ten on the Second Circuit. See Meg Greene, *Sonia Sotomayor* (Santa Barbara, CA: ABC-CLIO, 2012), 139–47.

191 Hudson, *The Rehnquist Court: Understanding Its Impact and Legacy*, 40–2.

192 Stevens's lack of deference has been a longstanding feature of his approach to constitutional interpretation and jurisprudence; see generally, e.g., Thomas M. Franck, *Political Questions, Judicial Answers: Does the Rule of Law Apply to Foreign Affairs?* (Princeton, NJ: Princeton University Press, 1992).

193 Susan Navarro Smelcer, *From Solicitor General to Supreme Court Nominee* (Washington: Diane Publishing, 2010), 14.

194 Barry Leonard, *Investigation of Allegations into Politicized Hiring in the Department of Justice* (Washington: Diane Publishing, 2010), 3.

195 See Michael J. Gerhardt, *The Federal Appointments Process: A Constitutional and Historical Analysis* (Durham, NC: Duke University Press, 2003), 392.

196 Nina Totenberg, "Seen as a Rising Star, Kagan Has a Limited Paper Trail," NPR, 9 May 2010, accessed 31 May 2014, http://www.npr.org/templates/story/story.php?storyId=126611113.

197 Ibid.

198 Glenn Greenwald, "The Case against Elena Kagan," *Salon*, 13 April 2010, accessed 31 May 2014, http://www.salon.com/2010/04/13/kagan_3/.

199 Ibid.

200 Neil K. Katyal, "Internal Separation of Powers: Checking Today's Most Dangerous Branch from Within," *Yale Law Journal* 115 (2006): 2314, 2343–5.

201 Sasha Isenberg, "Obama Taps Harvard Law School Dean as Solicitor General," *Boston Globe*, 6 January 2009; see also Eric Lichtblau,

"Potential Justice's Appeal May Be Too Bipartisan," *New York Times*,
16 May 2009, accessed 31 May 2014, http://www.nytimes.com/2009/
05/17/us/17kagan.html?_r=0.

202 Greenwald, "The Case against Elena Kagan."

203 Lichtblau, "Potential Justice's Appeal."

204 "Possible Candidates," *New York Times*, 9 April 2010, accessed 31 May
2014, http://www.nytimes.com/interactive/2010/04/09/us/politics/201
00409-stevens-candidates.html.

205 Ed Whelan, "Will the Left Oppose Elena Kagan?," *National Review*,
10 March 2010, accessed 31 May 2014, http://www.nationalreview.
com/bench-memos/49237/will-left-oppose-elena-kagan/ed-whelan.

206 See chapter 4 in this work.

207 Order Denying the Writ of Certiorari in Latif v. Obama, Al-Bihani v.
Obama, Uthman v. Obama, Almerfedi v. Obama, Al-Kandari v, Obama,
Al-Madhwani v. Obama, Al-Alwi v, Obama, 132 S. Ct. 2741 (2012).

208 Richard Malphurs, *Rhetoric and Discourse in Supreme Court Oral
Arguments* (New York: Routledge, 2013), 186.

209 Toobin, *The Nine*, 327–9.

210 H. Jefferson Powell, *Constitutional Conscience: The Moral Dimension of
Judicial Decision* (Chicago: University of Chicago Press, 2008), 16.

211 Lyle Denniston, "Is the 'Rule of Four' Firmly Intact?," panel discussion,
Yale Law School, 18 September 2009, accessed 31 May 2014, http://
www.law.yale.edu/documents/pdf/Clinics/Lyle_Denniston.pdf.

212 See chapter 4 in this work.

213 Christopher P. Banks, *Judicial Politics in the D.C. Circuit Court* (Baltimore, MD: Johns Hopkins University Press, 1999), 4.

214 Ashman, *The Finest Judges*, 233.

215 Banks, *Judicial Politics*, 106.

216 El Shifa v. United States, 131 S. Ct. 997 (2011), writ of certiorari denied.

217 Banks, *Judicial Politics*, 108.

218 Ibid.

219 Ibid., 108–10.

220 Melanie Wachtell and David Thompson, "An Empirical Analysis of
Supreme Court Certiorari Petition Procedures," *George Mason University Law Review* 16 (2009): 237, 241.

221 Banks, *Judicial Politics*, 114.

222 Ibid., 116.

223 Ibid., 53.

224 "Biographical Entry: Judge Laurence H. Silberman," United States Court
of Appeals for the District of Columbia Circuit, http://www.cadc.us-
courts.gov/internet/home.nsf/content/VL+-+Judges+-+LHS.

225 Jeffrey Brandon Morris and Chris Rohmann, *Calmly to Poise the Scales of Justice: A History of the Courts of the District of Columbia Circuit* (Durham, NC: Carolina Academic Press, 2001), 323.

226 See G.R. Urban, *Radio Free Europe and the Pursuit of Democracy* (New Haven, CT: Yale University Press, 1997), 46–51.

227 See David P. Barash and Charles P. Webel, "Material-Support Law Called Anti-Terror Warning of Choice," in *Issues in Peace and Conflict Studies* (London: SAGE, 2002), 384.

228 Stephen Vladeck, "The D.C. Circuit after Boumediene," *Seton Hall Law Review* 41 (2011): 1451.

229 Bush v. Gherebi, 542 U.S. 952 (2004).

230 Ibid.

231 See Rumsfeld v. Padilla, 351 F.3d 695 (D.C. Cir. 2004).

232 Boumediene v. Bush, 553 U.S. 723 (2008).

233 See "A Right without a Remedy," *New York Times*, 28 February 2011, http://www.nytimes.com/2011/03/01/opinion/01tue1.html.

CHAPTER SIX

1 Karen Greenberg, *The Least Worst Place: The First 100 Days of Guantanamo* (Oxford: Oxford University Press, 2006), 23–6.

2 Ibid., 38.

3 Ibid.

4 Cong. Rec. Senate (24 January 2002) 192.

5 Haitian Centers Council v. Sale, 823 F. Supp. 1028 (D.C.D.C. 1993).

6 Greenberg, *The Least Worst Place*, 177–80.

7 See generally William C. Banks and Peter Raven-Hansen, *National Security Law and the Power of the Purse* (Oxford: Oxford University Press, 1994).

8 Hamdi v. Rumsfeld, 542 U.S. 507 (2006).

9 Hamdan v. Rumsfeld, 548 U.S. 557 (2006).

10 See chapter 1 in this work.

11 Donald Rumsfeld's comments quoted in Ken Ballen and Peter Berger, "The Worst of the Worst?," *Foreign Policy*, 20 October 2008, www .foreignpolicy.com/articles/2008/10/19/the_worst_of_the_worst.

12 Chairman of the Joint Chiefs of Staff General Richard B. Meyers's comments quoted in Elspeth van Veeren, "Clean War, Invisible War, Liberal War: The Clean and Dirty Politics of Guantanamo," in *Liberal Democracies at War: Conflict and Representation*, ed. Alexander Knapp and Hilary Footitt (New York: Bloomsbury, 2013), 94.

13 See generally Andy Worthington, *The Guantánamo Files* (London: Pluto Press, 2007).

14 Hamdan v. Rumsfeld, 548 U.S. 557 (2006).

15 See chapter 3.

16 Geneva Convention Relative to the Treatment of Prisoners of War, article 4, 75 U.N.T.S. 135 (entered into force 21 October 1950).

17 In doing so, they followed the lead provided by the executive branch, see Exec. Order No. 13,440, "Interpretation of the Geneva Conventions Common Article 3 as Applied to a Program of Detention and Interrogation Operated by the Central Intelligence Agency," 20 July 2007, accessed 1 June 2014, https://www.fas.org/irp/offdocs/eo/eo-13440.htm; see also Allison Danner, "Defining Unlawful Enemy Combatants: A Centripetal Story," *Texas International Law Journal* 43 (2007): 1.

18 Michelle Sheppard, *Guantanamo's Child* (Mississauga, ON: John Wiley and Sons, 2008), 1–3.

19 U.S.C., title 10, §948c (d).

20 Hamdi v. Rumsfeld, 542 U.S. 507 (2006).

21 Marjorie Cohn, "Five 'High-Value' Guantanamo Detainees Improperly Presumed Guilty," *Truth Out*, 3 July 2013, http://www.truth-out.org/news/item/17367-five-high-value-guantanamo-detainees-improperly-presumed-guilty.

22 The Supreme Court has held that the denial of a security clearance is non-justiciable. Department of the Navy v. Egan, 484 U.S. 518 (1988).

23 U.S.C., title 10, §948b (g).

24 U.S.C., title 10, §948b (d)(1)(B).

25 U.S.C., title 10, §948d (d).

26 U.S.C., title 10, §950j (b).

27 Alberto Gonzales, "Memorandum to the President, 'Decision Re: Application of the Geneva Convention on Prisoners of War to the Conflict with Al-Qaeda and the Taliban,'" Washington Office of the White House Counsel, 25 January 2002, http://news.findlaw.com/hdocs/docs/torture/gnzls12502mem2gwb.html.

28 Military Commissions Act 2006, Pub. L. No. 109-366.

29 Ibid., section 6(a)(3)(A).

30 U.S. Const. art. 6, cl. 2.

31 See Carlos Manuel Vasquez, "Treaties as Supreme Law of the Land: Judicial Interpretation of Treaties," *Harvard Law Review* 122 (2008): 599.

32 "Byrd Amendment," accessed 1 June 2014, http://thomas.loc.gov/cgi-bin/query/R?r109:FLD001:S60420.

33 "Senate Amendment 5088 to Bill 3930," accessed 1 June 2014, http://thomas.loc.gov/cgi-bin/query/D?r109:1:./temp/~r109usu1dE.

34 "Voting Tally for Senate Amendment 5088 to Bill 3930," accessed 1 June 2014, http://www.senate.gov/legislative/LIS/roll_call_lists/roll_call_vote_cfm.cfm?congress=109&session=2&vote=00258.

35 Chris Den Hartog and Nathan W. Monroe, *Agenda Setting in the U.S.*

Senate: Costly Consideration and Majority Party (Cambridge: Cambridge University Press, 2011), 105.

36 David Friedman, "The Democratic Party and the Future of American Politics," *New Politics* 11 (2007): http://newpol.org/content/democratic-party-and-future-american-politics.

37 Boumediene v. Bush, 553 U.S. 723 (2008).

38 Ibid., 726.

39 Military Commissions Act 2006, Pub. L. 109–366.

40 See e.g. Deborah Pearlstein, "Military Commissions, Round 3," *Opinio Juris*, 23 October 2009, accessed 1 June 2014, http://opiniojuris.org/2009/10/23/military-commissions-round-3/.

41 Congressional Research Service, "Enemy Combatant Detainees: 'Habeas Corpus' Challenges in Federal Court," 2011, accessed 1 June 2014, 21, http://books.google.ca/books?id=UI4pHjIOEQAC&pg=PA22&dq=mca+2009+more+rights+procedural&hl=en&sa=X&ei=YHg_UoyVHM PuiQLprYCwCQ&ved=0CEcQ6AEwBA#v=onepage&q=mca%202009%20more%20rights%20procedural&f=false.

42 This is because the Supreme Court's decision in *Boumediene v. Bush* made further trials under the MCA 2006 impossible. See Boumediene v. Bush, 553 U.S. 723 (2008).

43 See Glenn Greenwald, "Interview with Senator Chris Dodd," *Salon*, 5 August 2007, accessed 1 June 2014, http://www.salon.com/2007/08/05/dodd_interview/.

44 Roza Pati, *Due Process and International Terrorism* (Boston: Martinus Nijhoff, 2009), 414–24.

45 American Civil Liberties Union, "Al-Qosi Plea Is First Conviction in Broken Military Commissions under Obama," press release, 7 July 2010, https://www.aclu.org/human-rights-national-security/al-qosi-plea-first-conviction-broken-military-commissions-under-obama.

46 Thomas McDonnell, *The United States, International Law and the Struggle against Terrorism* (New York: Routledge, 2010), 69.

47 Detainee Treatment Act 2005, Pub. L. 109–48.

48 See Jules Pfiffner, *Power Play: The Bush Presidency and the Constitution* (Washington: Brookings Institution Press, 2008), 159–60.

49 Alfred W. McCoy, "Invisible in Plain Sight: CIA Torture Techniques Go Mainstream," *Amnesty International Magazine*, March 2006, accessed 1 June 2014, https://web.archive.org/web/20080828174831/http://www.amnestyusa.org/magazine/invisible_in_plain_sight.html.

50 See, e.g., Associated Press, "Vatican Calls Prison Abuse a Bigger Blow to U.S. Than Sept. 11," *USA Today*, 12 May 2004, accessed 1 June 2014, http://usatoday30.usatoday.com/news/world/iraq/2004-05-12-vatican-iraqi-abuse_x.htm.

51 Antonio Taguba, "Article 15-6 Investigation of the 800th Military Police

Brigade," *FindLaw*, 30 July 2004, http://news.findlaw.com/hdocs/docs/
iraq/tagubarpt.html.

52 See generally Philippe Sands, *The Torture Team* (New York: Penguin,
2008). Donald Rumsfeld had pushed for more lenient standards for
"stress positions," writing "I can stand for 8–10 hours a day. Why are
detainees limited to 4 hours?"

53 Alfred W. McCoy, *Torture and Impunity: The U.S. Doctrine of Coercive
Interrogation* (Madison: University of Wisconsin Press, 2012), 414–24.

54 Douglas V. Porpora, "Abu Ghraib and Torture: Whither Dostoyevsky?,"
in *Post-Ethical Society: The Iraq War, Abu Ghraib, and the Moral Failure
of the Secular Society*, eds. Porpora et al. (Chicago: University of
Chicago Press, 2013), 125.

55 Headquarters, Department of the Army, "Human Intelligence Collector
Operations (FM 2-22.3)," *Department of the Army*, 2006, accessed 1
June 2014, https://www.fas.org/irp/doddir/army/fm2-22-3.pdf.

56 The executive branch purports to retain the power to revise the Army
Field Manuals and "additional guidance" on the applicability of torture
bans to intelligence agencies. See Joseph Margulies, *Guantanamo and the
Abuse of Presidential Power* (New York: Simon and Shuster, 2006),
245–7; see also Center for Constitutional Rights, "CCR Praises Obama
Orders, Cautions against Escape Hatch for Torture," 22 January 2009,
http://www.ccrjustice.org/newsroom/press-releases/ccr-praises-obama-
orders%2C-cautions-against-escape-hatch-torture.

57 See Headquarters, Department of the Army, "Appendix M: Restricted
Interrogation Technique – Separation," *Department of the Army*, 2006,
accessed 1 June 2014, https://rdl.train.army.mil/catalog/view/100.ATSC/
10492372-71C5-4DA5-8E6E-649C85E1A280-1300688170771/2-22.3/
appm.htm.; this document explicitly authorizes the "Fear Up" technique,
and had previously been understood to authorize such techniques as ter-
rorizing detainees with attack dogs, as pictured in photographs released
from Iraq (see photograph of detainee Mohammad Bollendia being
threatened by Sergeant Santos Cardona and his attack dog, at: http://rex
curry.net/dog-torture-terrorism-abu-ghraib1b.jpg). The *Washington Post*
revealed that these techniques had been brought to Iraqi detention facilities from Guantánamo. Josh White, "Abu Ghraib Dog Tactics Came
from Guantanamo," *Washington Post*, 27 July 2005, accessed 1 June
2014, http://www.washingtonpost.com/wp-dyn/content/article/2005/
07/26/AR2005072601792.html.

58 U.S.C, title 18, § 2340A.

59 Congressional Research Service "The U.N. Convention against Torture:
Overview of Implementation," 2009.

60 Phillip Alston and Ryan Goodman, *International Human Rights* (Oxford: Oxford University Press, 2013), 271.

61 Pub. L. No.109-163, div. A, title 14.

62 Sen. Amendment 2516, 109th Cong., lst Sess. (Sen.) § 104 (2006).

63 George W. Bush, "President's Statement on Signing of H.R. 2863, the Department of Defense, Emergency Supplemental Appropriations to Address Hurricanes in the Gulf of Mexico, and Pandemic Influenza Act 2006," news release, White House, accessed 1 June 2014, http://georgewbush-whitehouse.archives.gov/news/releases/2005/12/print/20051230-8.html.

64 Hamdi v. Rumsfeld, 542 U.S. 507 (2006).

65 Barton Gellman and Jo Becker, "Pushing the Envelope on Presidential Power," *Washington Post*, 25 June 2007, accessed 1 June 2014, http://blog.washingtonpost.com/cheney/chapters/pushing_the_envelope_on_presi/.

66 Detainee Treatment Act 2005, § 1005(e)(1)(B).

67 See generally Arthur Schlesinger, Jr, *The Imperial Presidency* (Boston: Houghton Mifflin, 2004).

68 U.S. Const. art. 1, § 8, cl. 11.

69 See e.g. John Yoo, "Memorandum Opinion for the Deputy Counsel to the President: The President's Constitutional Authority to Conduct Military Operations and Nations Supporting Them," Washington Office of Legal Counsel, 25 September 2001, accessed 30 May 2014, http://dspace.wrlc.org/doc/bitstream/2041/70942/00110_010925display.pdf.

70 George W. Bush, "President's Remarks at the United Nations General Assembly," news release, White House, 12 September 2002, accessed 1 June 2014, http://georgewbush whitehouse archives.gov/news/releases/2002/09/print/20020912-1.html.

71 *Daily Mail*, "Bush Wins Congress Backing over War on Iraq," 16 October 2002, accessed 1 June 2014, http://www.dailymail.co.uk/news/article-142230/Bush-wins-Congress-backing-war-Iraq.html.

72 Boothie Cosgrove-Mather, "Poll: Talk First, Fight Later," CBS News, 23 January 2003, http://www.cbsnews.com/stories/2003/01/23/opinion/polls/main537739.shtml.

73 David Cortright, "The World Says No: The Global Movement against War in Iraq," in *The Iraq Crisis and World Order: Structural, Institutional and Normative Challenges*, eds. Thakur Ramesh and Waheguru Pal Singh Sidhu (Tokyo: United Nations Press, 2006), 75–91.

74 Sue Chan, "Massive Anti-War Outpouring," CBS News, 15 February 2003, accessed 1 June 2014, http://www.cbsnews.com/stories/2003/02/16/iraq/main540782.shtml.

75 New York Civil Liberties Union, *Arresting Protest*, April 2003, accessed
   1 June 2014, https://www.aclu.org/sites/default/files/FilesPDFs/nyclu_
   arresting_protest1.pdf.

76 Mark Thompson and Michael Duffy, "Donald Rumsfeld: Pentagon
   Warlord," *Time*, 19 January 2003, accessed 1 June 2014, http://nufon.
   tripod.com/0061.htm.

77 "Blix Casts Doubt on WMDs," *The Guardian*, 19 May 2003, accessed
   1 June 2014, https://web.archive.org/web/20130827033434/http://www.
   theguardian.com/world/2003/may/23/iraq1.

78 Carlo Bonini and Giuseppe D'Avanza, "Doppiogiochisti e dilettanti tutti
   gli italiani del Nigergate," *La Repubblica*, 24 October 2005, accessed
   1 June 2014, http://www.repubblica.it/2005/j/sezioni/esteri/iraq69/
   sismicia/sismicia.html.

79 Luke Harding, "Germans Accuse US over Iraq Weapons Claim," *The
   Guardian*, 2 April 2004, accessed 1 June 2014, http://www.theguardian.
   com/world/2004/apr/02/iraq.germany.

80 Ibid.

81 Department of State, "PowerPoint Presentation Accompanying the Secretary's Speech at the UN," accessed 1 June 2014, http://www.state.
   gov/documents/organization/17434.pdf.

82 Arthur Borden, *A Better Country: Why America Was Right to Confront
   Iraq* (Lanham, MD: Hamilton Books, 2008), 45–6.

83 Carl W. Ford, "Memorandum to the Secretary: Niger/Iraq Uranium
   Story and Joe Wilson," Department of State, 7 July 2003, http://www.
   state.gov/documents/organization/122494.pdf.

84 Joby Warrick, "Warnings on WMD 'Fabricator' Were Ignored, Ex-CIA
   Aide Says," *Washington Post*, 25 June 2006, accessed 1 June 2014,
   http://www.washingtonpost.com/wp-dyn/content/article/2006/06/24/
   AR2006062401081_pf.html.

85 Richard W. Stevenson, "Remember 'Weapons of Mass Destruction?'
   For Bush, They Are a Nonissue," *New York Times*, 8 December 2003,
   accessed 1 June 2014, http://www.nytimes.com/2003/12/18/politics/
   18PREX.html.

86 Library of Congress, "Bill Summary & Status, 107th Congress (2001–
   2002), House Joint Resolution 114," accessed 1 June 2014, http://
   thomas.loc.gov/cgi-bin/bdquery/z?d107:H.J.Res114.

87 Library of Congress, "Bill Summary & Status, 107th Congress (2001–
   2002) House Joint Resolution 114, Cosponsors," accessed 1 June 2014,
   http://thomas.loc.gov/cgi-bin/bdquery/z?d107:HJ00114:@@@P.

88 Library of Congress, "Bill Summary & Status, 107th Congress (2001–
   2002) Senate Joint Resolution 45," accessed 1 June 2014, http://thomas.
   loc.gov/cgi-bin/bdquery/z?d107:SJ00045:@@@P.

89 Ibid.

90 Donald E. Nuechterlein, *Defiant Superpower: The New American Hegemony* (Washington: Potomac Books, 2005), ch. 3.

91 Clerk of the House of Representatives, "On Agreeing to the Spratt of South Carolina Substitute Amendment, 107th Congress, U.S. House of Representatives," 10 October 2002; Clerk of the House of Representatives, "On Agreeing to the Amendment (Levin Amdt. No. 4862), 107th Congress, U.S. Senate," 10 October 2002.

92 Winslow T. Wheeler, *The Wastrels of Defense: How Congress Sabotages U.S. Security* (Annapolis, MD: Naval Institute Press, 2004), 220.

93 Michele L. Swers, *Women in the Club: Gender and Policy Making in the Senate* (Chicago: University of Chicago Press, 2013), 213.

94 The book will not address the argument that the requirements of the Declare War Clause are not met by a statute that is not styled as a declaration of war.

95 William Boardman, "America's 'Permanent War': The 'Authorization to Use Military Force' Forever?," *Global Research*, 26 May 2013, http://www.globalresearch.ca/americas-permanent-war-the-authorization-to-use-military-force-forever/5336452.

96 See Neal Devins and Louis Fisher, *The Democratic Constitution* (Oxford: Oxford University Press, 2004), 122–6.

97 Mary Cardaras, *Fear, Power, and Politics: The Recipe for War in Iraq after 9/11* (Lanham, MD: Lexington Books, 2013), 218.

98 Seth Harold Weinberger, *Restoring the Balance: War Powers in an Age of Terror* (Santa Barbara, CA: ABC-CLIO, 2009), 17–22.

99 For example, David Cameron called for a no-fly zone on 28 February 2011, less than two weeks after the very first protests in Benghazi against the regime. "As It Happens: Libyan Uprising February 25," *Times* (London), 25 March 2011, accessed 1 June 2014, http://www.thetimes.co.uk/tto/news/world/middleeast/article2926163.ece.

100 Ibid.

101 Jonathan Marcus, "Libya: French Plane Fires on Military Vehicle," *BBC News*, 19 March 2011, http://www.bbc.co.uk/news/world-africa-12795971.

102 Thomas Harding, "Col Gaddafi Killed: Convoy Bombed by Drone Flown by Pilot in Las Vegas," *Telegraph*, 21 October 2011, accessed 1 June 1 2014, http://www.telegraph.co.uk/news/worldnews/africaandindianocean/libya/8839964/Col-Gaddafi-killed-convoy-bombed-by-drone-flown-by-pilot-in-Las-Vegas.html.

103 War Powers Resolution 1973, No. 93–148.

104 See, e.g. Glenn Greenwald, "Tells Congress (Again) – We Won't Abide by Your 'Laws,'" *Unclaimed Territory*, 26 March 2006, http://glenn

greenwald.blogspot.ca/2006/03/administration-tells-congress-again-we.html.

105 U.S.C., title 50 § 1544(b).

106 Jennifer Steinhauer, "Boehner Warns Obama on Libya Operations," *The Caucus* (blog), *New York Times*, 14 June 2011, http://thecaucus.blogs.nytimes.com/2011/06/14/boehner-warns-obama-on-libya-operations/?_r=0.

107 Bruce Ackerman, "Legal Acrobatics, Illegal War," *New York Times*, 21 June 2001, A27.

108 Michael Isikoff, "On Libya, President Obama Evaded Rules on Legal Disputes, Scholars Say," MSNBC, 21 June 2011, accessed 1 June 2014, http://www.msnbc.msn.com/id/43474045/ns/politicswhite_house/t/libya-president-obama-evaded-rules-legal-disputes-scholars-say/.

109 Ibid.

110 Philip Elliot, "Obama Trying to Sway War-Weary Public on Syria," *Lubbock Avalanche-Journal*, 9 September 2013, accessed 1 July 2014, http://lubbockonline.com/filed-online/2013-09-09/obama-trying-sway-war-weary-public-syria#.UvwToYa4Ono.

111 Charles B. Cushman, *An Introduction to the U.S. Congress* (Armonk, NY: M.E. Sharpe, 2006), 61–8.

112 Susan Crabtree, "Clinton to Congress: Obama Would Ignore Your War Resolutions," *Talking Points Memo*, 20 March 2011, accessed 1 June 2014, http://talkingpointsmemo.com/dc/clinton-to-congress-obama-would-ignore-your-war-resolutions.

113 Ibid.; see also Robert J. Delahunty, "War Powers Irresolution: The Obama Administration and the Libyan Intervention," http://papers.ssrn.com/sol3/papers.cfm?abstract_id=1856764.

114 Campbell v. Clinton, 203 F.3d 19 (D.C. Cir. 2000).

115 See generally Mark L. Haas and David W. Lesch, *The Arab Spring: Change and Resistance in the Middle East* (Boulder, CO: Westview Press, 2012).

116 John R. Bolton, "Beyond the Axis of Evil: Additional Threats from Weapons of Mass Destruction," *The Heritage Foundation*, 6 May 2012, accessed 1 June 2014, http://www.heritage.org/research/lecture/beyond-the-axis-of-evil.

117 Tanya Reinhart, *Israel/Palestine: How to End the War of 1948* (New York: Seven Stories Press, 2002), 74–7.

118 "Syria Providing 'Wider Array' of Missiles to Hezbollah: US," *Agence France Presse*, 23 April 2010, http://www.google.com/hostednews/afp/article/ALeqM5gS-2z3_h12KyrCYwnFyVNwCmYO-A.

119 Craig Whitlock, "U.S. Secretly Backed Syrian Opposition Groups, Cables Released by WikiLeaks Show," *Washington Post*, 18 April 2011, http://www.washingtonpost.com/world/us-secretly-backed-syrian-oppo

sition-groups-cables-released-by-wikileaks-show/2011/04/14/AFip9hwD
_story.html.

120 Michael R. Gordon and Mark Landler, "Backstage Glimpses of Clinton
     as Dogged Diplomat, Win or Lose," *New York Times*, 2 February 2013,
     accessed 1 June 2014, http://www.nytimes.com/2013/02/03/us/politics/
     in-behind-scene-blows-and-triumphs-sense-of-clinton-future.html?page
     wanted=all&_r=1&.

121 Mike Mazzetti, Michael R. Gordon, and Mark Landler, "U.S. Is Said to
     Plan to Send Weapons to Syrian Rebels," *New York Times*, 13 June
     2013, accessed 1 June 2014, http://www.nytimes.com/2013/06/14/
     world/middleeast/syria-chemical-weapons.html?pagewante,d=all&_r=0.

122 David S. Cloud and Raja Abdulrahim, "U.S. Has Secretly Provided Arms
     Training to Syria Rebels Since 2012," *Los Angeles Times*, 21 June 2013,
     accessed 1 July 2014, http://articles.latimes.com/2013/jun/21/world/
     la-fg-cia-syria-20130622.

123 Ibid.

124 Ibid.

125 Hannah Allam, James Rosen, and Jonathan Landay, "U.S. Appears to
     Weigh Military Response to Alleged Syrian Use of Chemical Weapons,"
     McClatchey Wire Service, 25 August 2013, http://www.mcclatchydc.
     com/2013/08/25/200333/us-appears-to-weigh-military-response.html.

126 The formal name was the Select Committee on Intelligence on the U.S.
     Intelligence Community's Prewar Intelligence Assessments on Iraq.

127 Austin Sarat and Nasser Hussein, *When Governments Break the Law:
     The Rule of Law and the Prosecution of the Bush Administration* (New
     York: New York University Press, 2009), 7–9.

128 Albert L. Weeks, *The Choice of War: The Iraq War and the Just War
     Tradition* (Santa Barbara, CA: ABC-CLIO, 2009), 68.

129 Authorization for Use of Military Force against Iraq Resolution 2002,
     Pub. L. No. 107–243, whereas clauses, preamble.

130 James Risen, *State of War: The Secret History of the CIA and the Bush
     Administration* (New York: Free Press, 2006), 218–20.

131 Anthony Summers and Robbyn Swan, *The Eleventh Day: The Full Story
     of 9/11* (New York: Ballantyne, 2012), 571.

132 Select Senate Committee on Intelligence, "Report on the U.S. Intelli-
     gence Community's Prewar Intelligence Assessments on Iraq," 9 July
     2004, http://www.gpo.gov/fdsys/pkg/CRPT-108srpt301/pdf/CRPT-
     108srpt301.pdf.

133 Ibid., 15.

134 Ibid., 449–64.

135 Ibid., 449 ("Additional Views of Senators Durbin and Levin").

136 Michael Heazle, *Uncertainty in Policy Making: Values and Evidence in
     Complex Decisions* (Washington: Earthscan, 2010), 122.

137 Minority of the Senate Select Committee on Intelligence, "Whether Statements by U.S. Government Officials Were Substantiated by Intelligence Reports," in *Additional and Minority Views, SIIC Phase II Report*, 5 June 2009, accessed 1 June 2014, http://www.intelligence.senate.gov/080605/phase2b.pdf.

138 Senate Select Committee on Intelligence, "Select Committee on Intelligence on the U.S. Intelligence Community's Prewar Intelligence Assessments on Iraq Press Release of Intelligence Committee Senate Intelligence Committee Unveils Final Phase II Reports on Prewar Iraq Intelligence," press release, 5 June 2008, accessed 1 June 2014, http://www.intelligence.senate.gov/press/record.cfm?id=298775.

139 Suzanne Struglinski and Lisa Freidman, eds., *Almanac of the Unelected: Staff of the United States Congress* (Lanham, MD: Bernan Press, 2010), 10.

140 House Committee on the Judiciary Majority, "Staff Report to John C. Conyers Jr., Reining In the Imperial Presidency: Lessons and Recommendations Related to the Presidency of George W. Bush," 13 January 2009, accessed 1 June 2014, http://www.fas.org/irp/congress/2009_rpt/imperial-final.pdf.

141 David Schweigman, *The Authority of the Security Council under Chapter VII of the UN Charter* (The Hague: Kluwer Law International, 2001), 39–42.

142 Max Fisher, "Samantha Power's Case for Striking Syria," *Washington Post*, 7 September 2013, http://www.washingtonpost.com/blogs/worldviews/wp/2013/09/07/samantha-powers-case-for-striking-syria/.

143 David Bosco, "How President Obama Undermined His Legal Case for Syria Action," *Foreign Policy*, 26 August 2013, accessed 1 June 2014, http://bosco.foreignpolicy.com/posts/2013/08/26/how_president_obama_undermined_his_legal_case_for_syria_action.

144 Paul Lewis and Spencer Ackerman, "Obama's Syria Plans in Disarray after Britain Rejects Use of Force," *The Guardian*, 30 August 2013, accessed 1 June 2014, http://www.theguardian.com/world/2013/aug/30/obama-strike-syria-britain-vote.

145 Peter Flatters, "Syria Shows MPs Need Independent Analysis of Intelligence," *Politics.co.uk*, 2 September 2013, accessed 1 June 2014, http://www.politics.co.uk/comment-analysis/2013/09/02/comment-mps-must-be-trusted-with-more-intelligence-info.

146 Jon Day, "Memorandum from the Chairman of the Joint Intelligence Committee, Syria: Reported Chemical Weapons Use," 29 August 2003, accessed 1 June 2014, https://www.gov.uk/government/uploads/system/uploads/attachment_data/file/235094/Jp_115_JD_PM_Syria_Reported_Chemical_Weapon_Use_with_annex.pdf.

147 Damian McElroy, "UN Accuses Syrian Rebels of Chemical Weapons Use," *Telegraph*, 6 May 2013, accessed 1 June 2014, http://www.telegraph.co.uk/news/worldnews/middleeast/syria/10039672/UN-accuses-Syrian-rebels-of-chemical-weapons-use.html.

148 Pew Research Center, "Poll: Aug. 29–Sept. 1, 2013 N=1,000 adults nationwide. Margin of error ± 3.7"; ABC *News/Washington Post*, "Poll. Aug. 28–Sept. 1, 2013. N=1,012 adults nationwide. Margin of error ± 3.5," *Polling Report*, accessed 1 June 2014, http://www.pollingreport.com/syria.htm.

149 CNN Staff, "Text of Draft Legislation Submitted by Obama to Congress," *CNN*, 31 August 2013, accessed 1 June 2014, http://www.cnn.com/2013/08/31/us/obama-authorization-request-text/index.html?hpt=hp_t1.

150 Southeast Asia Resolution, Pub. L. No. 88–408.

151 Ibid.

152 Bruce Ackerman, "Bait and Switch," *Foreign Policy*, 3 September 2013, accessed 1 June 2014, www.foreignpolicy.com/articles/2013/09/03/bait_and_switch_obama_syria_congress?page=0,1.

153 See Select Senate Committee on Intelligence, "Report on the U.S. Intelligence Community's Prewar Intelligence Assessments on Iraq," 9 July 2004; "Report on Whether Public Statements Regarding Iraq by U.S. Government Officials Were Substantiated by Intelligence Information," 5 June 2008.

154 Zeina Karam and Kimberly Dozier, "Doubts Linger over Syria Gas Attack Evidence," *Detroit News*, 8 September 2013, http://www.detroitnews.com/article/20130908/NATION/309080015/Doubts-linger-over-Syria-gas-attack-evidence.

155 Patrick Wintour, "Sarin Gas Was Used in Syrian Chemical Weapons Attack, Says David Cameron," *The Guardian*, 7 September 2013, http://www.theguardian.com/world/2013/sep/05/sarin-syrian-chemical-weapons-cameron.

156 Garance Franke-Ruta, "American 'Boots on the Ground' in Syria? John Kerry's Facepalm Moment," *The Atlantic*, 3 September 2013, accessed 1 June 2014, http://www.theatlantic.com/politics/archive/2013/09/american-boots-on-the-ground-in-syria-john-kerrys-facepalm-moment/279312/.

157 Barbara Starr, "Military: Thousands of Troops Needed to Secure Syrian Chemical Sites," in *Security Clearance*, a blog on CNN, 22 February 2012, accessed 1 June 2014, http://security.blogs.cnn.com/2012/02/22/military-thousands-of-troops-needed-to-secure-syrian-chemical-sites/.

158 David Martosko, "Revealed: Pentagon Knew in 2012 That It Would Take 75,000 Ground Troops to Secure Syria's Chemical Weapons

Facilities," *Daily Mail*, 5 September 2013, accessed 1 June 2014, http://
www.dailymail.co.uk/news/article-2411885/Syrias-chemical-weapons-
Pentagon-knew-2012-75-000-ground-troops-secure-facilities.html#
ixzz2tAsg3ndw.

159   Reuters, "Hundreds of Syria Rebels Vow Loyalty to Al-Qaeda Groups,"
      Taipei Times, 21 September 2013, accessed 1 June 2014, http://www.
      taipeitimes.com/News/front/archives/2013/09/21/2003572649.

160   Josh Rogen, "Senate Breaks Own Rules in Rush to Vote on Syria War,"
      Daily Beast, 4 September 2013, accessed 1 June 2014, http://www.
      thedailybeast.com/articles/2013/09/04/senate-breaks-own-rules-in-rush-
      to-vote-on-syria-war.html.

161   Ackerman, "Bait and Switch."

162   Niels Lesniewski, "Text of Senate Draft Syria War Authorization,"
      Congressional Quarterly Roll Call, 3 September 2013, accessed 1 June
      2014, http://blogs.rollcall.com/wgdb/text-of-senate-draft-syria-war-
      authorization/.

163   Dave Espo and Julie Pace, "Obama Delays Syria Vote, Says Diplomacy
      May Work," *KSL.com*, 10 September 2013, accessed 1 June 2014,
      http://www.ksl.com/index.php?nid=235&sid=26795165&fm=most_
      popular.

164   U.S. Const., art. 2, § 4.

165   Bill Rhatican, ed., *White House under Fire* (Bloomington, IL: Author
      House, 2005), 399–400.

166   House of Representatives Committee on the Judiciary, "Impeachment of
      Richard M. Nixon, President of the United States: The Final Report of
      the Committee on the Judiciary, House of Representatives," *Government
      Printing Office*, 1974.

167   Matthew Rycroft, "Iraq: Prime Minister's Meeting, 23 July," *Times*
      (London), 23 July 2002, accessed 1 June 2014, http://web.archive.
      org/web/20110723222004/http://www.timesonline.co.uk/tol/news/uk/
      article387374.ece.

168   Ibid.

169   109th Cong., House Resolution 365 (Rep. John Conyers, Sponsor).

170   Charles Babington, "Democrats Won't Try to Impeach President," *Wash-
      ington Post*, 12 May 2006, accessed 1 June 2014, http://www.washing
      tonpost.com/wp-dyn/content/article/2006/05/11/AR2006051101950.
      html.

171   Nancy Zuckerbroad, "Pelosi Says Democrats Are Ready to Lead," *Fox
      News*, 8 November 2006, accessed 1 June 2014, http://www.foxnews.
      com/wires/2006Nov08/0,4670,Pelosi,00.html.

172   H.Res. 1258 (110th): Impeaching George W. Bush, President of the
      United States, of high crimes and misdemeanors.

173 David Swanson, *Daybreak: Undoing the Imperial Presidency and Forming a More Perfect Union* (New York: Seven Stories Press, 2009), 129.

174 House Committee on the Judiciary Majority Staff, "Reining In the Imperial Presidency."

175 Ibid., 12.

176 Douglas Kriner, "Can Enhanced Oversight Repair the 'Broken Branch,'" *Boston University Law Review* 89 (2009): 793.

177 Elizabeth Mendes and Joy Wilke, "Americans' Confidence in Congress Falls to Lowest on Record," *Gallup Politics*, 13 June 2013, accessed 1 June 2014, http://www.gallup.com/poll/163052/americans-confidence-congress-falls-lowest-record.aspx.

178 Doug Mataconis, "House and Senate Incumbent Re-election Rates Top 90%," *Outside the Beltway*, 13 December 2012, accessed 1 June 2014, http://www.outsidethebeltway.com/house-and-senate-incumbent-re-election-rates-top-90/.

179 Walter Karp, *Liberty under Siege* (New York: Franklin Square Press, 1993).

180 Ibid., 1–18.

181 Stephen Pelletiére, *Israel in the Second Iraq War: The Influence of Likud* (Santa Barbara, CA: Praeger Security International, 2010), 16.

182 Janice Wedel, *Shadow Elite* (New York: Basic Books, 2009), 191.

183 Karp, *Liberty under Siege*, 39.

184 Ibid., 15–16.

185 Robert Kaiser, "Money, Family Name Shaped Scaife Burdens of Wealth," *Washington Post*, 3 May 1999, A1.

186 Karp, *Liberty under Siege*, 20.

187 Ibid., 305.

188 Laurence Learner, *The Kennedy Men: 1901–1963* (New York: Harper Collins, 2001), 359.

189 Ted Sorenson, *Counselor: A Life at the Edge of History* (New York: Harper Collins, 2008).

190 Karp, *Liberty under Siege*, 305.

191 Robert D. Schulzinger, *A Time for War: The United States and Vietnam, 1941–1975* (Oxford: Oxford University Press, 1997), 100.

192 Karp, *Liberty under Siege*, 28.

193 Ibid.

194 Ibid., 29.

195 Ibid., 305.

196 Ibid., 260, 432.

197 Mike Gravel and Joe Lauria, *A Political Odyssey: The Rise of American Militarism and One Man's Fight to Stop It* (New York: Seven Stories Press, 2008), 126.

198   Karp, *Liberty under Siege*, 27.
199   Ibid.
200   Ibid., 41.
201   Brezhnev agreed to further concessions on SALT II.
202   Keith L. Shimko, *Images and Arms Control: Perceptions of the Soviet Union in the Reagan Administration* (Ann Arbor: University of Michigan Press, 1991), 177.
203   Quoted in Karp, *Liberty under Siege*, 59–60.
204   Ibid., 60.
205   Burton Hersh, *The Shadow President: Ted Kennedy in Opposition* (South Royalton, VT: Steerforth Press, 1997), 39–42.
206   James M. Scott, *Deciding to Intervene: The Reagan Doctrine and American Foreign Policy* (Durham, NC: Duke University Press, 1997), 17–39.
207   John Milburn, "Papers Shed Light on Eisenhower's Farewell Address," *USA Today*, 10 December 2010, accessed 1 June 2014, http://www.usa today.com/news/nation/2010-12-10-eisenhower-address_N.htm.
208   Dwight D. Eisenhower, "Military-Industrial Complex Speech," *Avalon Project*, 17 January 1961, http://avalon.law.yale.edu/20th_century/ eisenhower001.asp.
209   Hossein Askari, Amin Mohseni, and Shahrzad Daneshvar, *The Militarization of the Persian Gulf: An Economic Analysis* (Northampton, MA: Edward Elgar, 2009), 9.
210   Rolf Hackmann, *Globalization: Myth, Miracle, Mirage* (Lanham, MD: University Press of America, 2005), 202–3.
211   Alex Merck, *Sustainable Wealth: Achieve Financial Security in a Volatile World of Debt* (Hoboken, NJ: John Wiley and Sons, 2010), 96–102.
212   Federal Election Campaign Act 1971, Pub. L. No. 92–225.
213   Tillman Act of 1907, 34 Stat. 864.
214   Buckley v. Valeo, 424 U.S. 1 (1976).
215   James T. Bennett, *Stifling Political Competition* (New York: Springer, 2009), 69–75.
216   Kathleen Hall Jamieson, *Packaging the Presidency: A History and Criticism of Presidential Campaign Advertising* (Oxford: Oxford University Press, 1996), 378–445.
217   Ibid., 446–524.
218   Barbara Sinclair, *Party Wars: Polarization and the Politics of National Policy Making* (Norman, OK: University of Oklahoma Press, 2006), 140.
219   David Isenberg, "Budgeting for Empire: The Effect of Iraq and Afghanistan on Military Forces, Budgets, and Plans," *Independent Policy Report*, 30 January 2007, accessed 1 June 2014, http://www.indepen dent.org/pdf/policy_reports/2007-01-30-budgeting.pdf.

220 Leon V. Sigal, *The Changing Dynamics of U.S. Defense Spending* (West-port, CT: Praeger, 1999), 153–171.

221 Alexander DeVolpi et al., eds., *Nuclear Shadowboxing: Legacies and Challenges*, vol. 2 (Kalamazoo, MI: Fidlar Doubleday, 2005), 5–42.

222 "Snowden Reveals US Intelligence's Black Budget: $52.6 Billion on Secret Programs," *Russia Today*, 29 August 2013, accessed 1 June 2014, http://rt.com/usa/snowden-leak-black-budget-176/.

223 Citizens United v. Federal Elections Commission, 558 U.S. 310 (2010).

224 Office for Democratic Institutions and Human Rights, "Head of OSCE Election Body Concerned about U.S. Supreme Court Ruling on Election Spending," press release, 22 January 2010, https://web.archive.org/web/20130112213852/http://www.osce.org/odihr/elections/51838.

225 Alex Seitz-Wald, "Koch Brothers Break New Ground in Dark Money," *National Journal*, 13 September 2013, accessed 1 June 2014, http://www.nationaljournal.com/politics/koch-brothers-break-new-ground-in-dark-money-20130913.

226 David Kravets, "Lawmakers Who Upheld NSA Phone Spying Received Double the Defense Industry Cash," *Wired Magazine*, 26 July 2013, accessed 1 June 2014, http://www.wiredcom/threatlevel/2013/07/money-nsa-vote/.

227 Uniting and Strengthening America by Providing Appropriate Tools Required to Intercept and Obstruct Terrorism Act 2001, Pub. L. No. 107-56.

228 Ibid.

229 Glenn Kessler, "James Clapper's 'Least Untruthful' Statement to the Senate," *Washington Post*, 12 June 2013, http://www.washingtonpost.com/blogs/fact-checker/post/james-clappers-least-untruthful-statement-to-the-senate/2013/06/11/e50677a8-d2d8-11e2-a73e-826d299ff459_blog.html.

230 Ibid.

231 "Letter of Twenty-Six Senators to James Clapper," *The Guardian*, 27 June 2013, accessed 1 June 2014, http://www.theguardian.com/world/interactive/2013/jun/28/senators-letter-james-clapper.

232 Greg Henderson, "Obama to Leno: 'There Is No Spying on Americans,'" *NPR*, 13 August 2013, accessed 1 June 2014, http://m.npr.org/news/front/209692380.

233 Glenn Greenwald, "James Clapper, EU Play-Acting, and Political Priorities," *The Guardian*, 3 July 2013, http://www.theguardian.com/comment isfree/2013/jul/03/clapper-lying-snowden-eu-bolivia.

234 James Bamford, "They Know Much More Than You Think," *New York Review of Books*, 15 August 2013, accessed 27 October 2016,

http://www.nybooks.com/articles/2013/08/15/nsa-they-know-much-more
-you-think/.

235   Greenwald, "James Clapper, EU Play-Acting."

236   Jeremy Herb and Justin Sink, "Sen. Feinstein Calls Snowden's NSA Leaks
        an 'Act of Treason,'" *The Hill*, 10 June 2013, http://thehill.com/blogs/
        defcon-hill/policy-and-strategy/304573-sen-feinstein-snowdens-leaks-
        are-treason.

237   Catherine E. Shoichet, "Bolivia: Presidential Plane Forced to Land after
        False Rumors of Snowden Onboard," CNN, 3 July 2013, accessed 1 June
        2014, http://www.cnn.com/2013/07/02/world/americas/bolivia-presiden
        tial-plane.

238   Raju Chebium, "Feinstein to Review Surveillance Programs: But Critics
        Expect Little from Hearings," *Statesman Journal*, 24 August 2013,
        http://www.statesmanjournal.com/article/20130825/NEWS/3082500
        26/Feinstein-review-surveillance-programs.

239   Steve Coll, "The Spy Who Said Too Much: Why the Administration Tar-
        geted a C.I.A. Officer," *New Yorker*, 1 April 2013, accessed 1 June 2014,
        http://www.newyorker.com/reporting/2013/04/01/130401fa_fact_coll.

240   Ed Pilkington, "Bradley Manning's Treatment Was Cruel and Inhuman,
        UN Torture Chief Rules," *The Guardian*, 12 March 2012, accessed 1
        June 2014, http://www.theguardian.com/world/2012/mar/12/bradley-
        manning-cruel-inhuman-treatment-un.

241   "Video Shows 'US Attack' on Iraqis," *Al Jazeera English*, 5 April 2010,
        accessed 1 June 2014, http://www.aljazeera.com/news/americas/2010/
        04/201045123449200569.html.

242   Michael Hastings, "WikiLeaks Stratfor Emails: A Secret Indictment
        against Julian Assange?," *Rolling Stone*, 28 February 2013, accessed
        1 June 2014, http://www.rollingstone.com/politics/blogs/national-
        affairs/wikileaks-stratfor-emails-a-secret-indictment-against-assange-
        20120228.

243   Glenn Greenwald, "Glenn Greenwald: Detaining My Partner Was a
        Failed Attempt at Intimidation," *The Guardian*, 13 August 2013,
        accessed 1 June 2014, http://www.theguardian.com/commentisfree/
        2013/aug/18/david-miranda-detained-uk-nsa. David Miranda, who
        carried files between Greenwald and the journalist Laura Poitras, is also
        Greenwald's domestic partner.

244   David Carr, "War on Leaks Is Pitting Journalist vs. Journalist," *New
        York Times*, 25 August 2013, accessed 1 June 2014, http://www.nytimes.
        com/2013/08/26/business/media/war-on-leaks-is-pitting-journalist-vs-
        journalist.html?pagewanted=1.

AFTERWORD

1 Joel Connelly, "Carson Likens Syrian Refugees to Dogs; Trump Pledges 'Security Is Going to Rule,'" *Seattle Post-Intelligencer*, 19 November 2015, accessed 22 November 2016, http://blog.seattlepi.com/seattlepoli tics/2015/11/19/carson-likens-syrian-refugees-to-dogs-trump-pledges-security-is-going-to-rule/.

2 Joel Connelly, "Trump on Terrorists: 'You Have to Take Out Their Families,'" *Seattle Post-Intelligencer*, 2 December 2015, accessed 22 November 2015, http://blog.seattlepi.com/seattlepolitics/2015/12/02/trump-on-terrorists-you-have-to-take-out-their-families/.

3 Jenna Johnson, "Donald Trump on Waterboarding: 'Torture Works,'" *Washington Post*, 17 February 2016, accessed 21 November 2016, https://www.washingtonpost.com/news/post-politics/wp/2016/02/17/donald-trump-on-waterboarding-torture-works/.

4 Seema Mehta, "Trump: Iranians Who Harass U.S. Navy 'Will Be Shot Out of the Water,'" *Los Angeles Times*, 9 September 2016, accessed 21 November 2016, http://www.latimes.com/nation/politics/trailguide/la-na-trailguide-updates-trump-iranian-soldiers-who-harass-u-s-147347 2852-htmlstory.html.

Index